andy

Good luck with you

Alan Webb

1997

Managing Innovative Projects

Managing Innovative Projects

Alan Webb

Consultant, Member of The Institution of Electrical Engineers
and The Association of Project Managers

INTERNATIONAL THOMSON BUSINESS PRESS
I T P An International Thomson Publishing Company

London • Bonn • Boston • Johannesburg • Madrid • Melbourne • Mexico City • New York • Paris
Singapore • Tokyo • Toronto • Albany, NY • Belmont, CA • Cincinnati, OH • Detroit, MI

Managing Innovative Projects

Copyright © 1996 Alan Webb

First published 1996 by International Thomson Business Press

 A division of International Thomson Publishing Inc.
The ITP logo is a trademark under licence

British Library Cataloguing-in-Publication Data
A catalogue record for this book is available from the British Library

First edition published by Chapman & Hall 1994
Paperback edition published by ITBP 1996

Typeset in 9½/11½ Meridien by Excel Typesetters Company, Hong Kong
Printed in the UK by The Alden Press, Oxford

ISBN 1-86152-038-7

International Thomson Business Press
Berkshire House
168–173 High Holborn
London WC1V 7AA
UK

International Thomson Business Press
20 Park Plaza
14th Floor
Boston MA 02116
USA

Contents

Foreword

The publication of this book is very timely as there is increasing recognition of the importance of innovation to competitiveness and the wealth creation process.

In January 1993 the CBI and the DTI published the results of a major joint project to look into innovation practice in UK-based companies and identify the key ingredients for success. Sadly, the findings of this study suggested that only one in ten of the companies surveyed could be said to be truly innovative. However, three in ten showed good performance in many facets of the innovation process while five in ten showed some. Many of the shortcomings were due to inadequacies in the management of various aspects of the innovation process and a mismatch in the mix of these bearing in mind the companies' particular operations.

The report of this study forms the centerpiece of an ongoing awareness campaign by the CBI and DTI to encourage companies to look very closely at how their innovation processes can be improved, and to point to the many valuable tools which they can use to translate awareness into positive action. This book is such a tool and provides a comprehensive practical coverage of this vitally important subject. I am looking forward to a repeat of our study which will lift our one in ten to a much healthier proportion, and I hope this guide will take its place in contributing to such an improvement.

Mark H. J. Radcliffe
Confederation of British Industry

Preface

I have chosen the title *Managing Innovative Projects* as these three words sum up the purpose of the book exactly: 'managing' as it is written for practising managers, 'innovative' as it deals with the development of novel products and 'projects' as it explains the techniques that are generally referred to as 'project management' methods.

The creation of innovative products is among the most challenging of all managerial tasks as novelty implies a leap into the unknown; it is not for the faint-hearted, for there are shocks and surprises around every corner. Despite the challenging nature of the work, those who take on the task of managing innovation are often ill-equipped at the outset. For many it is a second career and something they were promoted into after a period of practising the discipline they learned in their youth. Our attitude towards management is still one that sees it as a skill that can be picked up casually as one progresses through an industrial career. Many skills can be learned from direct experience rather than formal education, and there can be no doubt that experienced people tend to make better decisions than inexperienced ones but – in today's world – experience acquired by chance is not enough. The past 40 years have seen a revolution in management techniques which has, for the most part, been made possible by the advent of computing. Information lies at the heart of the new techniques and all are aimed at one central objective: good decision-making. However, many of the techniques are not obvious or straightforward and casual contact will not be sufficient to bring understanding; in order to use them, they have to be learned. Today's Project Manager has the potential to be better informed than at any time before but he cannot exercise that potential until he knows two things: (a) what information it is possible to obtain, and (b) how to use it when he has it. This book sets out to inform the practising manager of the techniques that are available and, through example, give some guidance in their use.

In general, the projects that this book addresses are from the world of engineering; clearly this does not cover the whole spectrum of innovation, and for those who are looking specifically for advice on such matters as software development, I can only apologize if they are disappointed. Nevertheless, many of the methods and techniques are applicable to areas outside engineering as the principles of managerial control apply across the whole field of industrial activity.

For this book, a project will be confined to the development phase of a product. The production phase which normally follows development has not been considered as, in many organizations, this is viewed as a separate activity, managed by a separate division, and many Project Managers cease to have responsibility for the product once it enters production. I have further confined the discussion to those techniques that have come to be seen as 'project management methods' and this will account for some industrial aspects that some readers may consider absent. For example, 'total quality management' is a phrase that is heard everywhere, yet no mention is made here of this particular process and there are good reasons. First, the 'quality' aspects of a company's products are often only partly under the control of the Project Manager; he certainly has the power to influence part of the process through the structure, techniques, goals and budgets he allocates to the design process but beyond that the overall quality policy may be set at a level above him and in another division. Secondly, 'total quality management' has become something of an ill-defined, catch-all concept that consultants have latched onto as a justification for expensive studies of the client company's operations. What they may discover might be of benefit to the client but some of the recommendations have less to do with 'quality' in the conventional sense and more to do with management and operations, as the following quote from the *Sunday Times* of 18 October 1992 shows:

'In a TQM initiative, product development was identified as a problem.

'The reasons were two-fold. "Product development" was the responsibility of the engineering department, which managed projects to strict budgets. Products were developed with little or no input from manufacturing, leading to excessive manufacturing costs which, once designed in, could not be reduced. Second, the performance against cost rather than development milestones meant that engineering was slow to respond to projects that fell behind schedule.

'Identifying the issue was only the first step in improving the process. Management in engineering and manufacturing had to change long-held attitudes. They resolved the problem only when they worked together on finding a solution.'

In one sense, this can be seen as a 'total quality' problem; but in another sense, it can be considered as a failure of project management. In this respect, the entire book can be viewed as a contribution to the 'quality' of the approach to new product development.

It will be realized from a cursory glance at the chapters ahead that the development process has been divided into a series of discrete elements, each of which has specific methods designed to deal with the situations that arise and guide the manager towards the best solution. This compartmentalization is primarily for the convenience of the reader, for in practice many of the elements are performed in a parallel, interactive way where the results from one will have a direct bearing on the performance of another. Some of the techniques such as 'decision trees' derive simply from basic mathematics, while others have been developed as a specialized management method, for example, 'network analysis'. In the latter cases, a very brief history of the technique has been included as I feel that a greater insight into the method is gained if it is known what prompted the originators and what they hoped to achieve.

Where numerical methods are described, formulae have been quoted rather than derived as the original derivations are of academic interest only and, in many cases, the formulae are empirical and based solely on observation. What is more important is the use to which they are put and in each case a worked example has been provided to show the technique in operation. In this context, it should be noted that applications of the techniques which are headed 'Example' are fictitious. The data, however, is generally representative of a real situation but each example has been contrived to show the features of the method rather than to demonstrate reality. Those examples headed 'Case Study' or 'Case Example' are based on actual projects. In some cases, the information already exists in the public domain, but in others, where this is not so, the sources of these studies has been kept deliberately vague. In these instances, some journalistic licence has also been applied to simplify the issues involved and thus make the point more clearly, as well as making it impossible to identify the individuals or companies involved.

It would be difficult to leave the subject of project management techniques without some mention of the host of software packages that are making their way into every aspect of project work. Some contemporary management information techniques are only practical as a computerized method – where this is the case, representative software has been named. Brief descriptions are given of some of the products, but one must remember that software packages are constantly evolving and things may be said now that will be different by the time these words are read. It is therefore recommended that those interested in particular products should contact the vendors for the latest information; the contact addresses for all software mentioned is given at the end of the final chapter.

Managing innovative projects is not an easy task, but nothing that is really worth doing is easy at the start. This book is dedicated to those who do it in the hope that they will find it useful, instructive and a companion in their working lives.

Alan Webb

The reference to male Project Managers is used for convenience only and should not be taken to mean that all Project Managers are male

1

Introduction

- Innovation, the challenge for tomorrow
- The future for project management

Few will doubt that change is taking place within society at a faster rate than anything seen previously. The last century could be termed 'the age of coal', for coal provided a cheap and plentiful supply of energy; it opened up the world through railways and steamships and it brought energy into the home through electricity. Most of this century can be regarded as 'the age of oil'; it has made powered flight and personalized transport possible but also brought about mechanized warfare. Affordable and readily available energy to heat our homes, to transport us to and fro and power our machines has transformed and enriched the lives of ordinary people over the last two centuries in a way that would have been hard to imagine at the start of the Industrial Revolution. We now stand at the dawn of a new era, 'the age of information' (I might well have called it 'the age of electronics' but that might be too limiting as we see more radical processes invented). There is no doubt that we are the best-informed generation ever and there will be a continuing demand for more information. Cheap energy has freed mankind from the limits of his physique and the force of the elements; information should free the mind and the imagination.

Behind all these changes lie the processes of inventive discovery and innovation; they set mankind apart as a species, for they have allowed him to adapt the environment to suit himself, unlike the animals that rely on evolution to adapt to changes in their world.

Inevitably there is a price to be paid: invention creates new opportunities but these can just as easily be directed towards the processes of destruction as to enhancement. The environment has been improved for some – but by practices that damage it for others. Stability in the workplace has been replaced by uncertainty, and traditional industries have been replaced by new ones that have no use for the old skills. Indeed the future abounds with uncertainties and opportunities in equal measure: each new invention brings about change, but each change also creates a further opportunity for those who are able to respond to it.

1

Businesses must recognize this and continuously improve both the goods and services they offer. None can afford to be complacent and assume things will go on in the same old way, for the world is changing too quickly; innovation and adaptation must become endemic to the culture. Innovation, by its nature, implies a step into the unknown, and carries with it the risk that the result will not make a satisfactory return for the amount invested. However, failure to invest may ensure the eventual demise of the organization: to stand still is to go backwards as there will always be rivals who are prepared to invest in innovation to ensure a better future.

Innovative projects, the challenge of tomorrow

New product development is recognized by all industrial sectors as essential to business success but the pressure of competition is forcing companies to look both at their products and the way they undertake the development process. Contemporary products are no longer simple; in a growing number of instances, they are 'systems' that draw together products and processes from different disciplines and this has brought a new focus on the way that innovative development is handled. More companies are turning to the 'project'-based approach and it marks a departure from the traditional method by which companies have operated.

The term **project** has many definitions, but 'project' in an industrial sense has acquired a meaning of its own. To perform a 'project' is to go from an existing 'state A' to a different 'state B'. However, to be a 'project' in our sense, two other ideas need to be introduced: (a) that the result was expected, and (b) that 'state B' is something new. 'Project' thus contains four ideas: change, novelty, the future and a result. The result is important, for task to be a 'project' it must have a goal — something that is known at the start and the reason for the project. The concept of a project also implies a start and an end; the end occurs when the desired result has been achieved. It can of course be argued that every industrial action has a goal; if it has not, nobody would do it, and in one sense all industry can be viewed as a series of projects. However, the concepts of uniqueness and novelty (i.e. of something new, where nothing went before) further confines projects to one end of a spectrum of industrial activity that has well-known, repetitive and orderly processes at its other end.

Projects are located at the chaotic end of the spectrum where things are rarely repeated, the unexpected is to be expected and the only certainty is change. In such a situation, things have a tendency to disorder unless they are constantly directed towards the goal. Keeping things on course requires a leader, some one to plan, organize and control the task and to create order out of disorder. It is these properties that determine the concept of **project management**, for it can be defined as the task of directing novel and unique undertakings; one who practises in that role is a **Project Manager**. Projects stand at the exciting end of the spectrum, the work is challenging and varied and it is not surprising that many are attracted to project management and see it as a career enhancement.

Of course 'projects', as defined by a task that leads to a single and not-to-be-repeated result, have been undertaken since the earliest times but the concept of project management is a comparatively recent one. Thus, although projects have been pursued for a long time without the need for the separate discipline of project management, it does not follow that the role has been absent. The creation of the 'project' as a distinct activity within an organization is a response to the changes that have come about in current industrial undertakings, in particular:

- increasing technical demands;
- the inter-company and international nature of business.

The primary cause of these changes lies in the innovative process itself, for it has generated increasing levels of expectation in all aspects of life and, particularly, in our expectations of technology. This, in turn, has led to products with ever increasing technical demands. The fusion of different strands of technology has allowed the creation of products that have properties undreamed of but a few decades ago. In the last century the steam locomotive represented the highest level of transport technology, yet today we must look at the jet airliner. Most mechanical engineers, assuming they have the requisite manufacturing skills, could design and make a rudimentary steam engine that would generate enough power to haul a load; but few of those engineers could design a jet engine that would run, and of that number, far fewer could make an engine that generated any useful thrust. The jet engine is, however, only one of the systems that make up the complete aircraft; it is an amalgamation of mechanics, hydraulics, electronics, radar and computer hardware and software, bound together with such other disciplines as aerodynamics and control theory. Product sophistication is not the only factor in the increasing technical demands; in some cases, the requirements for a successful product may be beyond that achievable with current techniques and much of the project will revolve around developing new heights of sophistication in technology.

Contemporary projects are increasingly influenced by:

1. The growing complexity of products.
2. A tendency to specify products that are highly optimized for their role at the outset.
3. Competitive pressures which have brought cost to the forefront of product specification.

The advent of the computer has brought with it a range of analytical techniques that has allowed the designer to explore increasingly complex concepts for products and take those concepts to the limits of their performance. The result is that specifications for new products are highly optimized at the very start of the development process; there is, however, an inherent danger. In terms of functionality, products whose concepts are highly optimized are far less tolerant of minor deviations than those products of which less is expected. Should one small part of an optimized system fail to meet its specification, it can have an effect on the overall system which is disproportionately large. The result will be an over-run in project time and cost as considerable effort has to be put in to cure minor failures and it can lead to increased product cost as closer tolerance or higher-technology parts have to be created.

Competitive pressures, particularly from Third World producers, have forced the issues of quality and product cost to assume a greater significance than previously. Sir Sydney Camm, designer of the Hurricane fighter, once said that he never considered cost in the design of any aircraft until after the Second World War. At that time, quality and performance was paramount and price was secondary, but the postwar influx of Japanese goods showed that high quality could be obtained at low cost. With the increasing system complexity and optimization we have mentioned earlier, the challenge to engineers and managers is obvious.

The future for project management

Project management has evolved as a distinct discipline during the period since the Second World War. For some, the term 'project management' has become synonymous with the time–cost–quality triangle and the 'network analysis' method. Since then it has evolved more techniques of its own, together with a considerable amount of software specifically designed for project work. Through such bodies as the Association of Project Managers (UK) and The International Project Management Association, project management has acquired a professional standing that is internationally recognized. In the chapters that follow the more important techniques will be explained but it should be remembered that formalized techniques cover only some of the issues that are faced by Project Managers.

It is easy to think, with so much project management software available, that success in a project venture is just a matter of picking the right system and implementing it. In fact nothing could be further from the truth; despite the great amount of money that has been spent on developing and advertising computerized project management systems, they do not deal with many of the problems that daily confront the Project Manager. Of course computer systems play an important part but their role is largely confined to planning and monitoring the use of time and resources. Perhaps a use for computer technology that may be even more beneficial lies in the emerging field of knowledge-based systems, which may offer some help in evaluating at the outset the inherent risks and dangers in alternative project concepts. That could lead to a more balanced trade-off between risk, technology and expectation, which in time may be seen as the successor to time, cost and quality. Such systems could lead to projects that are viewed in a more realistic light at the outset and thus easier to manage.

Project management may have come of age but it has yet to define a framework, outside of the numerically based time–cost–performance triangle, that embraces the technological factors and their human responses; that, in turn, means a wider understanding among managers of all the issues that contribute to project success. One thing that has emerged very strongly from the project-based approach is the concept of the **project team**. Team working focuses attention on objectives, removes barriers to communication and releases creative energy through personal identification with the project goal. It may well be that project management will evolve in some industries towards 'product management', with projects being seen as a total process from the initial concept to the last item off the production line; each project being run in a more autonomous way with more scope for individuals.

One thing is very clear: project management in today's climate is an acquired skill; it does not come naturally and it needs to be taught and learned. The best hope for the future lies in industry recognizing this, ensuring that Project Managers are properly educated for the tasks that are required of them and that continued professional education is a natural part of their career progress.

2

Innovation and the creation of new products

- Innovate to survive
- The process of innovation
- Product life cycles
- Ideas for innovative products
- Strategies for innovative projects
- Funding innovative projects

Innovation as a way of survival

'Adapt or die' is as true in the business world as it is in the biological one. A failure to adapt to a changing environment has led to the extinction of countless species over the ages, the great reptiles being the prime examples. Not every class of animal achieved such a spectacular success, followed by such rapid demise, as the dinosaurs; some creatures developed such perfection in their adaptation to their environment that they have remained more or less unchanged since primeval times, for example, sharks. That may not be so surprising as the oceans exhibit far more stable conditions over a long period than the land masses; survival on land has always been more difficult than in the sea.

Similar comparisons can be drawn with industry; we all need food, it is among the most basic of our requirements and despite the ups and downs of the economic cycle, the demand for food remains constant. In general, we do not expect great innovation in food – there are new recipes, but new basic foodstuffs are rare and may take time to gain widespread acceptance. Meat substitutes, like the soya product KESP, have yet to make much impact on current eating habits. Many food products, such as breakfast cereals, have remained virtually unchanged for almost a century. Unless habits relating to what we call 'breakfast' change significantly, the familiar corn flakes will have an assured place on the table. Products of this type are like the sharks of the sea, perfectly adapted to their role and capable of continued existence with minimal change.

Even though innovation does exist within the food industry, it has tended to concentrate on the presentation and storage of food rather than new foodstuffs. Apart from the general difficulty of creating new food, four factors have combined to shape the direction in which food products have moved:

1. A growth in public awareness regarding food quality leading to both regulations and consumer demand for better-quality products.
2. A growth in awareness of cuisine outside the home country leading to a demand for greater food variety.
3. Increasing pressures on time available to people, particularly working women, for the preparation of food leading to a demand for convenience foods.
4. A growth in awareness of the relationship between diet and overall health leading to a demand for 'healthy' food products.

Industrial responses to these factors have come about in two ways:

1. Developments in presentation, packaging and storage of foods.
2. Improvements in kitchen technology.

Both these developments have combined to alter our eating and food preparation habits. Two significant technical developments have taken place over the past 25 years:

1. The home deep freezer.
2. The microwave oven.

The deep freezer allows improved life through:

- more free time: there are less individual shopping trips for an equivalent variety of food;
- improved quality: preserved food does not have to go through the canning or drying process;
- improved economy: by bulk purchasing.

The microwave oven directly addresses the convenience issue by making food very quick to prepare. The food manufacturers and processors have responded both to consumer demands and opportunities created by the technological innovations through the creation of:

- ready-prepared basic foods packaged for the freezer;
- complete meals ready to cook in containers suitable for microwave cooking;
- ready-prepared exotic or foreign dishes;
- low-fat, vegetarian or other 'healthy' food products.

The issue of convenience has also led to the creation of some foods in a new form, instant coffee being an example. Prior to the Second World War, coffee needed to be made either in a percolator from grounds or from a liquid concentrate, consequently

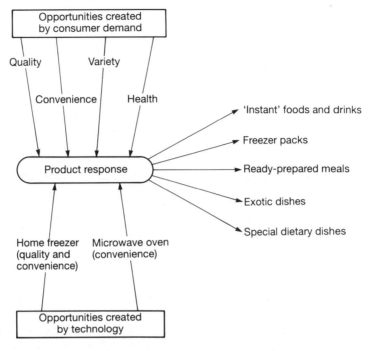

Figure 2.1 Product responses to opportunities in the food industry.

coffee drinking in the UK formed only a small percentage (≈5%) of the total market for hot drinks. However, in the 1950s two things changed: the arrival of coffee bars, which led to the habit of coffee drinking among young people, and the development of instant, granular coffee. These two factors have combined to increase the consumption of coffee to the extent that it is now the most popular hot drink. The health issue has of course not gone unnoticed by the coffee producers, who have responded by bringing out de-caffeinated coffee.

These examples from the food industry show that if a producing company wishes to maintain its share of the market, besides advertising and promotional activities it is necessary to adapt and innovate continuously. A failure to spot trends and tastes that demand new products is to ensure a declining place in a changing world. To stand still is, in effect, to go backwards as there will always be competitors who are committed to advancement through innovative new products. Change, whether it is in taste, fashion or technology, creates opportunities that are there to be identified and exploited. The position is summarized in Figure 2.1.

The process of innovation

Innovation in products can come about in two basic ways:

1. A discovery is made which leads to a new product. In this case, the market may not be perceived at the time the invention is made, or if a market is foreseen it may eventually turn out to be different from that originally envisaged.

2. A market need is foreseen and inventive, developmental work is done to create a product that will satisfy it.

The majority of innovative projects are of the second type. Pure inventive discovery cannot be relied upon to produce worthwhile results in a given timeframe; for such things to happen, either a series of fortunate coincidences must occur or some pure research must point out a potentially successful new application at a convenient point in time. For this reason, many companies rely on a strategy of both research and development, the former looking for something truly novel, the latter looking to refine and exploit existing technologies. When a discovery is made, it can give rise to a need that hitherto has not been seen as significant, possibly because it has previously been thought too difficult to satisfy; however, once the existence of the technology is known, it can make the need very pressing, for example, radar technology, as shown in Figure 2.2.

The need for an attacker to be as invisible as possible and the need for the defender to see what is coming have always been military objectives. However, the coupling of an observation that leads to the possibility of a need being satisfied in a way that is much more effective than anything known previously can start the process of innovative development. In a competitive situation such as weapons development, the emergence of one technology can be the stimulus to the development of a new technology to counter it; stealth aircraft have evolved directly as a result of the existence of radar. Stealth development came about from observations that showed marked differences in the radar returns from various aircraft which, in turn, led to a study of this phenomenon and thence to the rules by which aircraft could be designed to have minimal radar signatures. This example shows that each new invention or discovery alters the world in which we live to some extent: for many inventions the effects may be minimal, but for some the effect can be profound. This cycle of innovation is shown in Figure 2.3.

The marriage of an invention or a discovery with a need creates an opportunity for

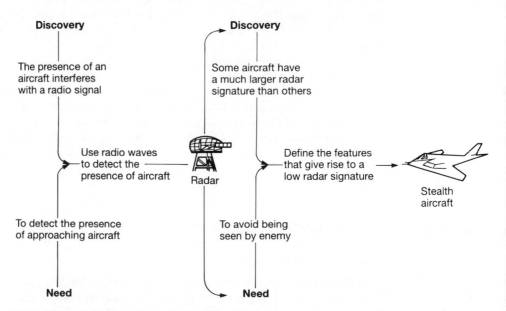

Figure 2.2 A discovery combined with a need leads to a new product, and the creation of one new product often leads to demand for another.

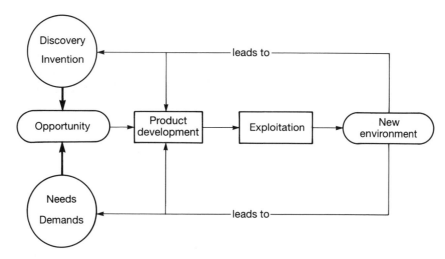

Figure 2.3 The cycle of innovation.

a new product. It will require development to generate something that can be exploited in the market-place but each time a new invention finds its way into industrial, military or domestic life the surrounding social, industrial and, possibly, physical environment is altered. Each alteration creates the potential for new needs that, in turn, present new opportunities. Computers offer one of the best examples this century; at the time the first machines were built, few, if any, of their inventors realized their potential or the impact that they would have; when first conceived, their industrial applications were thought to be very few. However, the invention of a computer that could store a program in its memory and the application of transistor electronics meant that a versatile machine could be built that was small enough to fit into a room in an office building. The age of computing was born and industry saw the application of computers as a way of making business transactions less labour intensive and thus cheaper; engineers saw it as a way of aiding the design process; and scientists saw it as an aid to processing research data. The very existence of computer technology and the opportunities for its use led to a demand for more computing; and that, in turn, has meant more, cheaper and smaller computers.

The emergence of compact, affordable computers led to new applications such as the means of home entertainment or education. Each advance in computer technology has opened up new opportunities for the exploitation of computing. Perhaps no invention will ever again quite equal the computer, for it is unique; nothing before has been able to behave in so many different ways. All depends on the instructions that are fed in. The diversity of its applications, in such a short space of time, is unparalleled in history and so are the opportunities that it has brought with it.

Product life cycles

For products other than some basic necessities there is a finite cycle during which they will have a place in the market before becoming obsolescent and finally losing appeal as more attractive products appear; Figure 2.4 illustrates this cycle.

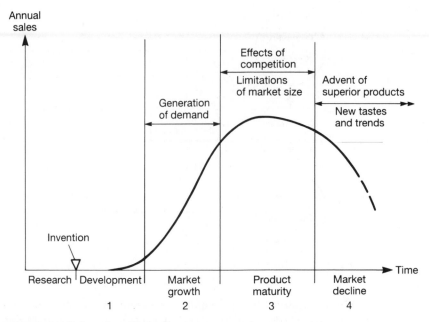

Figure 2.4   Typical product life cycle.

From the point that an invention capable of exploitation is made, the life of the resulting product can be divided into four major phases:

Phase 1 is the development of the product and during this period money will have to be invested, and all investment should be considered as being at risk. No return can be expected during this phase and, if development is not completed successfully, the investment will be lost.

Phase 2 begins at the point that the new product is introduced into the market and, if it is successful and has appeal, a period of market growth will follow as its usefulness is realized by an increasing number of consumers. During this period, product costs will usually be at their highest due both to the costs of start-up and a need to recover development expenditure. However, profit potential may also be at its highest as the initial supplier can usually demand a higher price before rival products begin to emerge.

Phase 3 marks the period where sales growth levels off as rival products capture significant shares of the customer base. Both the effects of competition and the eventual total size of the market will combine to limit sales to a stable, sustainable figure. At this stage, the product has reached maturity and, in general, manufacturing costs will be at their lowest. Eventually the profit potential will begin to decline if price competition becomes severe and more has to be spent on promotion.

Phase 4 sees the decline in sales and the eventual ending of production. This can occur when (a) the market has become saturated and the only demand is for replacement, (b) when demonstrably superior products arrive or (c) attitudes and tastes change such that the original appeal no longer exists.

Sometimes products can be given an extra lease of life by progressive development throughout the period of market maturity, and many organizations find this very worthwhile. It has many benefits, not least being that the risk associated with developing an upgraded product is much less than with a totally new one and a price advantage can be gained through both the learning experience and the use of equipment acquired on the earlier item.

Highly competitive markets with very sophisticated customers may force the pace of change by demanding design solutions that involve significant changes in technology; this is particularly true of the military field. It also applies to transport aircraft; the principal field of competition between aircraft types will be in the area that the airlines value most: direct operating cost per seat-mile. Besides the design of the airframe, the engine technology has an obvious bearing on this figure and it will be used as a case study to illustrate the effects of improvements in technology on product life cycles.

Case study 2.1: Product life cycles – the aero-engine for commercial applications

Although the driving-force for much of the progress in aviation has come from military applications, the pressure from commercial operators of aircraft for increases in both economy and performance has led to a series of developments in engine technology, each with a discrete product life and quite distinct from military uses. The principal engine types since the beginning of aviation are shown in Figure 2.5; it will be seen that five significant types of engine have emerged in the period and a sixth may be about to appear. Each type represents an improvement over the previous one and the rate and direction of this improvement can be seen clearly from two measures of engine performance:

(a) Power-specific weight – i.e. how much engine mass is required to produce one horsepower of output. Obviously there is pressure on engine designers to make the weight as low as possible.

(b) Specific fuel consumption – i.e. how much fuel is needed to produce either one horsepower or one pound of thrust for one hour. Again, there is pressure to make this figure as low as possible as it has a heavy bearing on aircraft direct operating cost.

Although these are not the only factors in the design and selection of engines, they are crucial. In this case study consideration will be given to how these factors have progressed over time and some of the issues that have influenced engine designers in their choice of the products that have been developed. Figure 2.6 shows how power-specific weight has changed over the period from the first practical aeroplanes. (Technically, piston engines are rated in horsepower, whereas jet engines are rated in pounds of thrust; these two terms are not strictly equivalent because the jet engine behaves differently in terms of its power when it is in flight (i.e. moving) to when it is stationary on the ground. However, for an assumed flight speed, a thrust–horsepower figure can be calculated and this has been done for a typical cruising speed of 550 m.p.h. in all cases. At such flight speeds, there is a marked reduction in propeller propulsive efficiency, but this has not been taken into account; in practice, it would tend to reduce the power-specific weight for gas turbines still further when compared to the piston engine/propeller combination.) The major trend lines through three principal types can be drawn; on a logarithmic

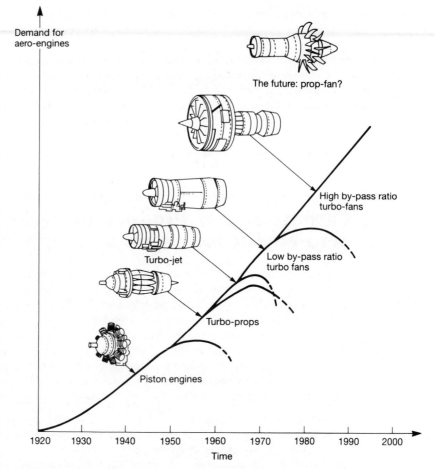

Figure 2.5   Product life cycles for the principal types of aero-engine.

plot these have tended to be linear and in the case of the piston engine to have exhibited the same trend over a long period. It also becomes clear that the case for changing from piston engines to gas turbines around the beginning of the 1950s was a very strong one.

Early aero-engines

Within a few years of the Wright brothers' first flight, various engineers attempted to produce a successful aero-engine that would combine high power with low weight. The problem was solved by the Seguin brothers of Paris with a somewhat perverse engine design based on a principle already devised for small engines for motor cycles. This was the famous Gnome rotary engine and it solved the weight problem by making the engine air-cooled thus saving the weight and drag of a liquid-cooling system; cooling efficiency was obtained by making the cylinders move through the airstream. High-strength, high-

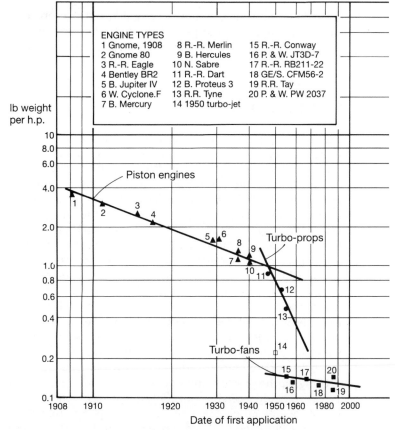

Figure 2.6 Plot of power-specific weight for various engines against time.

conductivity light alloys were not available so the engines were made in the newly invented nickel-chrome steel. Other French makers, as well as British and German firms, produced their version of the rotary engine and it became the most significant power unit for First World War fighters. Its rise to the pre-eminent position in aviation was spectacular and its demise was equally so. The rotary represented an ingenious solution to the problem of high power for low weight, given the available technology, but there are fundamental drawbacks to an engine in which most of the mechanism, particularly the valve gear and induction system, rotates and they severely limit its development potential. By the end of the war, it was clear that better efficiency could be obtained with a stationary engine using new materials and cylinder head designs.

Piston engine development continued with improvements in power-specific weight following a linear pattern; it can be seen from Figure 2.5 that by the late 1930s the pace of progress was diminishing to a point where significant improvements would be slow in coming. Points 7, 8, 9 and 10 are all important Second World War engines and are closely grouped; at the time they were designed, their designers already knew that they were approaching the limits of piston technology. Studies in the 1930s had already indicated that a practical limit to useful piston aero-engines would be in the 3500 h.p. class; and this in fact proved correct although was not achieved until the 1950s. However, throughout the period up to the Second World War progressive improvements were made, but with the pace of progress slowing, the time was ripe for the emergence of a new technology if significant improvements were to be made.

Gas turbines

The pioneering work of Frank Whittle must be among the greatest inventive work this century and what makes it so remarkable is that it was not one invention but two. First, he realized, together with other contemporaries in the 1920s, that the gas turbine offered far better prospects than the piston engine ever could for a light and efficient aero-engine with excellent power at altitude; however, the materials available at the time precluded the design of a satisfactory engine. Secondly, he saw that such an engine could be used to propel the aircraft through the air using the thrust from its exhaust alone rather than using a propeller. Whereas the gas turbine offered high power for low weight, its specific fuel consumption was significantly less good than the piston engine. Early jets were typically 50–100% more thirsty than equivalent piston engines at modest airspeeds. What jets did offer was high speed; freed from the effects of decreasing propeller efficiency at high forward speed, jets offered a new level of performance for fighter aircraft where speed was more important than economy and this was their first application. Progress in specific fuel consumption for gas turbines is shown in Figure 2.7.

Using jet thrust is not the only way of extracting power from a gas turbine. Where forward speeds below 500 m.p.h. are concerned, greater propulsive efficiency can be obtained through a propeller. However, due to the large difference in rotational speed between the turbine and the propeller, a reduction gearbox is needed and this contributes to weight, hence turbo-propeller engines have a higher power-specific weight than jets. The first successful use of gas turbine engines in commercial applications was in the form of the turbo-prop as its economic characteristics were better suited to the aerodynamic design of the day which was based on propeller-driven aircraft.

One manufacturer, the Wright Corporation, famous for the Cyclone engine used in the Flying Fortress, however, continued to believe in the development potential of the piston engine. It was to prove a fatal mistake. In the late 1940s and early 1950s they produced the turbo-compound engine, a piston engine with a large turbo-supercharger that extracted maximum energy from the exhaust gases by (a) supercharging the inlet air, and (b) extracting the surplus energy by coupling the supercharger back into the output shaft of the main engine. Coupling the intermittent flow of a reciprocating engine with the steady flow requirements of a turbo-charger under all flight conditions was a demanding engineering exercise. The engines were a masterpiece of mechanical complexity and found too few customers. By its failure to embrace gas turbine technology and, instead, pursue a technology that was at the end of its development life, Wright ensured its own demise as a supplier of engines to the world's airlines. The jet engine owes more to supercharger technology than to piston engines and it is significant that the place of Wright in the USA has been taken by General Electric, a supplier of superchargers during the Second World War.

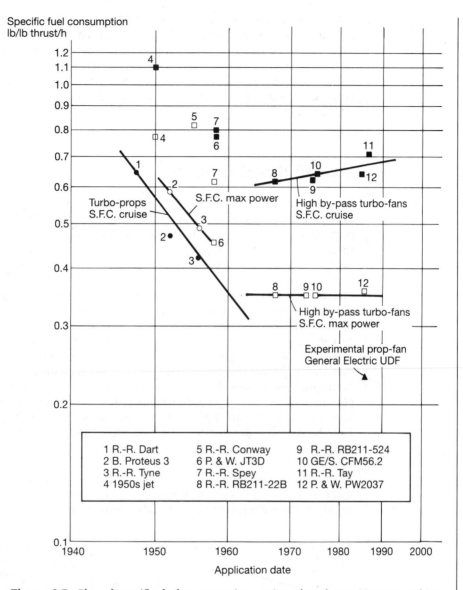

Figure 2.7 Plot of specific fuel consumption against date for various gas turbine engines.

Rapid advances in specific power were made with turbo-props during the 1950s, as can be seen from the steepness of the progress line shown in Figure 2.6. Although power-specific weight was above that of jets, specific fuel consumption at cruise was well below even the best of today's jet engines, as can be seen from Figure 2.7. Nevertheless, the turbo-prop had a relatively short life as the principal form of commercial aero-engine, and promising turbo-props that were designed and tested in prototype form (e.g. the Bristol Orion) offered even greater advancements in power and fuel consumption but never went into production. The reasons for this seem, in part, to lie in fashion. What the airlines had to sell was fast travel, and the fastest way to travel was in a jet. The advent of the Boeing 707 brought about reduced journey time with none of the cabin noise associated with propellers. The development of the by-pass jet, now called a low by-pass ratio turbo-fan, offered a considerable improvement in fuel consumption over pure turbo-jets. Suddenly the propeller-driven aircraft cruising at 400 m.p.h. looked old fashioned compared to the swept-wing 500 m.p.h. jets.

Future developments

To understand the rationale for further engine developments it is necessary to look at the two graphs shown in Figure 2.8; they show the changes in propulsive efficiency and specific fuel consumption with regard to aircraft speed for the principal types of engine. It will be seen that for speeds up to approx. 450 m.p.h. the turbo-prop is more efficient on both counts than all types of jet, but improvements in jet efficiency can be brought about by increasing the by-pass ratio, that is the amount of air that is allowed to pass around the engine compared to the amount of air that flows through it. Low by-pas turbo-fans typically had by-pass ratios around 2:1, but the greater the by-pass ratio, the better the propulsive and fuel efficiencies. A further benefit also derives from a high by-pass ratio, and it has come to be a very important one: low noise. By developing high by-pass engines with a by-pass ratio of 6:1, the engine makers could offer powerful, fuel-efficient and quiet engines. They also allowed the development of high-capacity, wide-bodied aircraft with low seat-mile costs: cheap mass transport had arrived. High by-pass turbo-fans have become the predominant type of engine in service on the larger commercial aircraft but progress in terms of overall efficiency is, like the piston engine before it, becoming very slow.

So what of the future: is it time for another product to emerge that will make a further significant improvement? The answer may well be 'yes', and it could lie in the direction of a further derivative of the turbo-prop. There can be

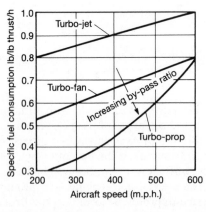
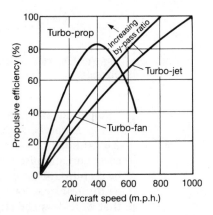

Figure 2.8 Plots of specific fuel consumption and propulsive efficiency versus aircraft speed for various gas turbine engine types.

little doubt that the turbo-prop was abandoned far too early in its development cycle and the rates of progress that were being achieved, shown clearly in Figures 2.6 and 2.7, are indicative that a great deal more potential still existed. The problems were the falling propulsive efficiency of the propeller with increasing flight speed, the weight of the reduction gearbox and the propeller noise. It would therefore seem that profitable lines of research and development lie in:

(a) a radical improvement in propeller design (a technology that has not received much attention since the advent of jets);
(b) devising an engine that does not need the reduction gear.

All the major engine makers have in fact been pursuing such lines of research and it is significant that new types of engines employing novel, rear-mounted contra-rotating propellers have been built and tested. They are referred to as 'prop-fans' and have an effective by-pass ratio of about 30:1. Both geared and un-geared designs have been devised, each using novel, curved multi-bladed propellers. It is significant that a prop-fan engine was tested in 1986 and produced the lowest specific fuel consumption of any aero-engine (Figure 2.7). It may be concluded from this that a rational study of design options and applied research into solving particular problems that have inhibited earlier development could lead to a new cycle of aero-engine development.

Conclusions from the study

The above case study is a brief history of a complex subject but a number of important points emerge that are useful in considering questions of (a) whether or not to develop a new product, (b) the time at which it should be introduced and (c) what avenues of research might be worth pursuing:

1. Continuous competition or demands from users for improved products stimulate innovative new developments.
2. Companies that fail to respond to market demands with improved products or choose the wrong path of technical development can cease to exist in that market.
3. Progressive improvements in the performance of a product tend to proceed at a rate that is constantly slowing. This is well illustrated by the straight-line nature of changes in significant parameters when plotted on a logarithmic timescale. The trend, once started, can often be detected after quite a short period.
4. A corollary of point 3 is that as the pace of progress slows, each new increase in performance becomes progressively more time-consuming and expensive to achieve.
5. Significant improvements tend to come about through radical new technologies rather than through progressive developments. However, the time from first invention to successful exploitation could be many years.
6. Where the performance of a product is largely governed by physical laws, the ultimate performance that is likely to be obtainable through progressive develop-

ment is often predictable well before it can be achieved in practice. (A point to ponder is whether or not this is true of products that are not bound by physical laws; for example, computer software may only be limited by imagination. Thus the ultimate applications of software may be impossible to predict and limited instead by the performance of the carrier technology.)

7. Not all technologies have been exploited to the full at the time they are superseded. If more development effort is put in hand, they could still have a significant place in the market, provided that the economics and customer acceptability are satisfactory. (Despite a number of advantages, the two-stroke engine disappeared from motor transport after the Second World War. However, Ford has recently revived the technology and is currently developing a two-stroke engine for cars with better efficiency than a four-stroke.)

8. Besides pure performance or economics, public acceptability in the form of changing tastes and trends, which could involve sensitivity to environmental issues, can markedly affect the demand for a product. It could accelerate sales or prematurely shorten the sales life.

Sources of ideas for innovative products

The process of innovation and product improvement is vital for the survival of companies that sell products as opposed to those that provide a pure service. For the most part, invention is relatively rare, whereas innovation through continuous improvement is much more common. The aero-engine example shows that after the rotary engine there really were only three significant inventions: the use of gas turbines, the use of jet thrust for propulsion and the discovery of the by-pass principle. All other improvements have been the result of continuous development based on these principles. Radical inventions such as the hovercraft come about on very few occasions. Even such machines as the helicopter, often associated with Igor Sikorski as its principal inventor, had a history of earlier rotary-wing craft from which to draw both inspiration and experience.

If companies are to survive by continuous product improvement and the creation of new products, one might ask if there are ways by which the process of innovation can be stimulated and what direction it should take. A number of methods have been evolved, as follows.

Technological trend forecasting

With **technological trend forecasting**, past and present trends in specific aspects of a product's performance are extrapolated to see what future developments might be possible and the likely timescale in which they might occur. Time-based logarithmic plots, as shown in Figures 2.6 and 2.7, are particularly useful but care must be exercised in choosing the parameters to plot. More important, in forecasting the future for one technology it may be necessary to consider the impact of another. For example, the application of computer technology to a product that currently does not make use of it could radically improve its performance and generate a huge demand. Such a system might be a computerized engine management system for small family cars. However, acceptance of such an application may rely on (a) the price of the computer, (b) the size of the computer, (c) the computer processing speed and (d) the reliability of the total computer–engine combination. Trend extrapolation based on these parameters could show the time at which the technology will have advanced to a point where such a system will become a worthwhile commercial possibility, hence the time at which serious research and dvelopment ought to be put in hand to have it ready for the market.

Market forecasting

Whereas technological forecasting looks at the pace of progress with respect to particular technologies or capabilities, **market forecasting** looks at how demand for new goods and services is likely to develop in the future. Technology trends tend to be governed by physical laws and, unless there are major breakthroughs, tend to settle into a measurable pattern of progress. Markets, however, are not so predictable, they develop according to circumstances and are affected by such factors as:

- Fashion, taste and national culture.
- Trends in work and leisure patterns.
- Amounts of personal disposable income.
- Issues of public concern: health, disarmament, pollution, etc.
- The emergence of new or rival technologies.
- Politically imposed constraints: tariff barriers, export of defence-related materials, etc.

Fashion, taste and cultural issues can be among the most difficult to forecast with long-term certainty. Products that have become popular in one country, such as citizen-band radios, in the USA, have failed to make anything like the same impact in the UK and Europe. However, making use of the concept of a product being 'fashionable' can dramatically improve sales. Babycham is a good example of fashionable marketing of a simple product, a light, sparkling wine made from pear juice with a resemblance to champagne. Putting the drink in a small individual bottle under the description 'champagne perry', serving it in a champagne glass with a cherry made it a fashionable drink, particularly with teenage girls. It gave the drink a 'smart' image, thus drinking Babycham was a signal that the teenage girl had joined the adult world; besides being a social drink it had acquired an esteem value thanks to fashion.

We are all influenced by fashion and taste to a greater or lesser extent; to remain aloof from fashion or continue with the style of an earlier generation would mark one out as an eccentric. Fashions can of course stem from the advent of new technology; its existence can create new behaviour patterns. For example, improvements in aircraft and aero-engine technology have brought down the cost of air travel to the extent that it is within the reach of all but the poorest in Western society; when combined with the construction of cheap hotel accommodation, it has made the foreign holiday a popular recreation. Spending a fortnight in Greece is a trendy thing to do, it signals a degree of affluence.

Trends in work and leisure patterns, as well as disposable income, are somewhat easier to define. Historic patterns in income growth and reductions in working hours are well known, along with a growth in employment of female staff; they have brought about changes in social terms and in the levels of ordinary peoples' expectations. People expect more leisure time and the things with which to enjoy it whether it is in the home (e.g. video recorders) or outside (e.g. sports equipment). There can be little doubt that these trends will continue for the foreseeable future.

Issues of public concern, particularly the environment and health, will have an increasing effect on the design of many familiar products. Potentially harmful products such as fluoro-carbon propellants will be forced out by popular demand or legislation. Exhaust gas emissions from cars will be brought under stricter control. Noise is increasingly recognized as both an irritant and a pollutant; the case for developing the high by-pass turbo-fan engine, already mentioned, was clearly influenced by the fact that it offered a huge reduction in noise level for greater power than previous jet types. Environmental issues generally, global warming and waste dumping will have to be taken increasingly seriously by all designers and manufacturers; increasing pressure for 'environmentally friendly' products will come from both public demand and legislation.

The emergence of new or rival technologies can radically alter the prospects for

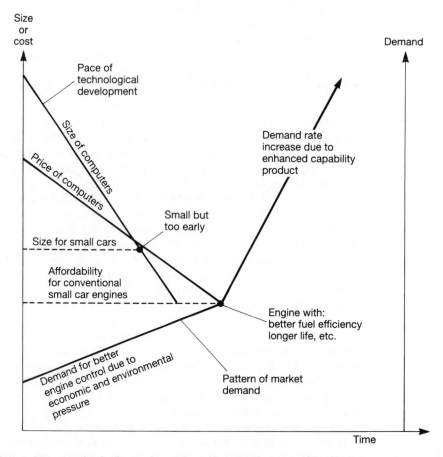

Figure 2.9 Trends, both in demands and technology, combine to create new market opportunities.

any product. The vinyl LP record is disappearing from record shops as the superior compact disc (CD) takes over. The CD has brought about a demand for new disc-playing equipment causing many people to replace their old hi-fi sets. The convenience of the CD format, allowing up to twice the playing time of an LP for no greater price, has led to an output of CDs containing collections of music from earlier eras which were not available previously on LPs. Companies holding the rights to those original recordings are thus finding a new lease of life for them due entirely to the CD. The video recorder not only has increased flexibility in lifestyle as programmes can be recorded if it is not convenient to see them when they are broadcast, but has also spawned an industry based on video films. Products that offer increased convenience will find a ready market in the future and will rapidly replace older, less convenient technology.

Trend analysis techniques, particularly regression methods or logarithmic plots, can be used to forecast trends based on history. They cannot be extended too far as individual trends will have to be combined if technologies converge and start a new trend; developments in motor car technology and developments in computing may coincide and create a new trend in engine fuel efficiency and car technology generally; Figure 2.9 shows a possible scenario.

A combination of technological development forecasts combined with a market demand forecast can lead to the identification of a new product that by its advent will alter the shape of the demand curve. Companies that spot these trends and correctly identify opportunities in advance stand to make greater profits than those that enter the market after the initial breakthrough has been made.

The Marketing Department in the majority of large companies puts considerable effort into forecasting the sales potential of its products through assessing past sales records and surveys of customers, but it may be less good at spotting emerging trends when they involve the development of technology outside the company's current activities. Here the Design Department should make a contribution. Only by a combination of the two will profitable opportunities for innovation be identified.

Suggestion schemes

One of the most valuable sources of ideas is the company workforce. A popular way of capturing the creative instincts that can exist at every level in a firm is through a **suggestion scheme**. The greatest number of people that spend their time being intimately involved with the company's products are its workers, and with so many eyes, hands and heads involved, it would be surprising if none had a useful idea on how things might be improved. Suggestions can range from minor improvements, most probably aimed at production efficiency and cost reduction, to radical ideas that could transform the product. Suggestion schemes have to be properly run and be seen to be fair to all. Sometimes they exclude the most creative staff by restricting their application to staff who are not managerial or involved with product design or engineering. The view often taken is that these staff are paid to be inventive in the course of their duties; this is a poor argument as they are as likely as any one else to see improvements or opportunities for new products that may be on the fringe of their normal work, yet get no reward for suggesting them.

Where a scheme is set up, it should have a judging panel that includes at least one high-level person, perhaps the company's Chief Engineer, as well as members from

Marketing and Production. The panel should have the power to make monetary awards for suggestions that are implemented. A suitable scheme might be: an initial lump sum at the time the company adopts the suggestion followed by payments based on either a proven saving or a measure of sales of the product. To be eligible, suggestions must be sufficiently removed from a person's normal duties for it not to be expected as part of his job; where disputes arise the panel arbitrates. Most companies include a clause in their contract of employment that gives them the right to exploit all inventions made by employees; this can be a deterrent to some staff coming forward with a truly novel suggestion, they may prefer to leave to develop the idea on their own. This can be overcome in a suggestion scheme by the company agreeing to pay royalties to the individual if a patentable invention can be turned into a profitable product.

Brainstorming

The method of creative thinking known as **brainstorming** arose out of the advertising industry; it is a useful aid to generating new ideas, and some of the 'wilder' ones may contain the seeds of some really innovative products. Brainstorming is most frequently used for problem-solving, and it is described in Chapter 6.

Delphi methods

Devised by the Rand Corporation in the USA, the **Delphi technique** aims to generate a view of the future by using the knowledge of experts in particular fields. The name derives from the Oracle of Delphi, in Ancient Greece, that was supposed to foretell the future. The unique feature of the method is that the panel of experts are not called together as a team to formulate a view of the future: this approach was decided upon as it has been observed that committees often become dominated by a few strong personalities and the resulting conclusions may be biased towards a particular viewpoint. It can also prove difficult to assemble a panel of experts if they are widely separated and work for different organizations. Noted academics, specialist writers or leaders of research organizations could form a suitable panel; leading industrialists may be less keen to participate for reasons of commercial confidentiality. Questionnaires are circulated to the team members, who may not be aware of each others' identities, and each is invited to make his or her own prediction of future progress in a particular field. As far as possible, projections must be quantified and the questions must be framed accordingly – e.g. what proportion of all households do you expect to have a personal computer by the year 2000? After the first round of replies, the results are analysed statistically and the results re-circulated and panel members are asked to reconsider their views in the light of the new statistics. If their view lies outside the interquartile range, they must either revise their opinion or give their reasons for their extreme view; this will be seen by the other panel members. This process can be repeated for a third or fourth round until a consensus view is obtained. Results of Delphi studies are given in the form of timescales and probability levels for the feature being forecast. Some large corporations have used the method for assessing long-term trends and the development strategies that may be open. Research by the Rand Corporation indicates that with current trends the panel does tend to move towards a consensus view, which tends to be generally correct. There is usually less accuracy when forecasting new developments.

Functional and morphological analyses, relevance trees

A group of techniques has arisen which bear a certain resemblance; they seek to establish the functions that are necessary to perform a particular task and then generate alternatives that could be worthy of investigation. **Functional analysis** is often used in the context of value engineering – i.e. it is applied to an existing product. However, it is just as relevant to the search for new products or further development of existing ones. It examines the functions that every element of a product performs and can provide a springboard for finding new ways to accomplish them.

Morphological analysis takes functional analysis one step further by inviting the analyst to list all the ways by which each function could be performed if there are no constraints on feasibility. All combinations of functions and solutions are then examined for feasibility; from this process concepts for novel products may emerge. Technical feasibility studies would be the next step for those concepts that look most promising.

The generation of **relevance trees** is somewhat similar to morphological analysis, except that an objective may be stated as the end-goal rather than a particular product. For example, functional analysis may be applied to the components of a central heating system, whereas a relevance tree may take as its goal the subject of efficient home heating. Solutions that might be considered are solar panels, wind generators, wood-burning stoves, etc.; the functions that each has to perform and their attributes are then displayed on a tree diagram, each attribute being ranked according to its relevance to meeting the objective. By tracking the paths on the tree which show the greatest relevance, new combinations of technologies that could lead to the objective may be discovered.

General market intelligence

Overall awareness of what is happening in the market and the advances that are being made in technology cannot be overstated as a source of inspiration. Possibly the most useful source of intelligence is regular contact with customers and suppliers. Other actions to increase awareness include:

- Encouraging individual and corporate membership of relevant professional bodies and trade associations.
- Subscriptions to trade journals.
- Attendance at exhibitions, trade fairs and seminars.

Strategies for innovation

The pace of innovative progress varies greatly between industries and also between companies. The reasons for this depend on the maturity of the technology, the level of competition and the nature of the company itself. Companies with broad product bases, such as those in the field of consumer electronics, will need to pursue a vigorous policy of innovation and development as a vast scope currently exists for the incorporation of electronic technology in household goods. On the other hand, the pace of innovation and development in one-product companies with well-established technologies, such as tyres or automotive transmissions, will be relatively slow; where it is applied, it may well be directed at reduced production costs, improved reliability, longer life, etc. rather than a totally new concept product. Whatever the industry, four basic strategies can be adopted:

1. Continued development of existing products.
2. 'First in the field' with a new product.
3. 'Follow the leader' with rival products.
4. Longer-term research into new product ideas.

Continued development of existing products

This is one of the most favoured approaches to innovative work; it has many advantages, but for survival, it may have to be allied to other strategies. All products other than some of the most basic have finite lives in the market and, ultimately, they will be replaced with more effective items. However, the lives of most products can be increased by a series of progressive developments unless they are overtaken by some vastly superior technology in the way that the home-movie camera has been displaced by the video camera. The developments need not be breakthroughs in technology, but merely carry an enhanced capability or increased customer appeal. The airliner manufacturers have been among the greatest exponents of this approach, keeping basic designs in production for 25 years or more. Improvements that have been adopted include increased passenger-carrying ability through fuselage 'stretches'; the fitting of more powerful, fuel-efficient engines; improvements in avionics allowing reductions in crew levels; and better 'management' of the aircraft systems. While fuselage stretches involve basic aircraft engineering, the fitting of improved engines or avionics is a case where advances in those two technologies can be used to enhance the overall product capability with relatively low risk, particularly in terms of development capital and without forcing the pace of technological progress.

Enhanced capability products can be attractive propositions both for the producer and the customer for the following reasons:

To the producer
- The technological risk is low.
- The market risk is low as the acceptability of the product is already established.
- Existing capital equipment and tooling can often be used.
- Products can be offered at low cost because operator times are low due to previous learning, as well as using 'depreciated' capital equipment.

To the customer
- The product characteristics will be well understood.
- Reliability and maintainability will be proven.
- There will be reduced operator, training and maintenance costs if earlier versions have already been acquired.

The 'first in the field' strategy

This approach is sometimes called an 'offensive marketing strategy' as it is one that aims either to create a new market or capture a market from rivals with a product that represents a significant advance over previous ones. A recent example is the introduction of electronic cameras which can capture a still picture that is viewed on a TV screen. They have yet to make a great impact as the pictures do not have the convenience, cheapness or quality of a picture printed on paper but the existence of these cameras poses a threat to conventional silver-based photography; if development effort is put into the areas mentioned, the market leadership for personal pictures could pass from the film manufacturers to the electronics firms unless there is a breakthrough in film technology.

A 'first in the field' strategy implies the highest level of risk-taking for the following reasons:

- The highest levels of R & D expenditures are associated with novel products as the greatest degrees of uncertainty exist.
- Unproven technology may show itself to have inherent drawbacks that either render it unsuitable for its intended use or are prohibitively expensive to eliminate.
- Market acceptability may not be established at the outset and preferences may change during the development cycle.

However, there are some significant advantages from a successful offensive strategy:

- Due to the absence of competition, higher profits are associated with products when they are first introduced into the market, particularly if market growth is rapid.
- With a really novel product, it is possible for comparatively small organizations to challenge the largest (note the success of the Apple microcomputer).
- An enhanced company profile may result due to it being perceived as a market leader, which could lead to increased sales of other products in the company's range through a 'halo' effect (upon the introduction of Concorde services, British Airways noticed an increase in demand for their subsonic flights due an to enhanced image generated by Concorde).
- Opportunities may exist for licensing the product and thus reaping additional profits for little extra outlay.

The cost of marketing and promotion of new products should not be overlooked; it could become costly as there is no previously established reputation to act as a springboard for sales. Timing the entry into the market will also be a critical factor, but events may not always be under the control of the producer. There is little doubt that more Concorde aircraft would have been sold if it were not for the steep rise in fuel prices that occurred due to Arab-Israeli conflicts in the early 1970s.

The 'follow the leader' strategy

This approach to new product introduction is referred to as a 'defensive marketing strategy' as the principal objective is to defend a proportion of the market by developing products that rival those of the market leader. Risks are lower than with the offensive strategy since both the technology and the market will have already been explored. Even with the protection of patents, a rival company's technology can be exploited either, amicably, through licence agreements or, less so, through indigenous design of similar but not identical products. The risks associated with a defensive strategy are that profits may be low as competition in the market will already exist and, if it comes to be recognized that this is the principal strategy, initiative and innovation within the company may be stifled.

Long-term research into new ideas

Long-term research should be seen as essentially speculative. The further we attempt to peer into the future, the less clear the picture becomes, thus long-term research may have to be conducted on a broad front. Much of the work will be concerned with feasibility studies, looking at emerging market trends and technologies. The identification of critical techniques will be an area of particular concern. Only a few of the avenues of research should get as far as the construction of a prototype or test example. In many cases, it will be restricted to a technology demonstration item containing only as many features as are necessary to test the particular technology. It is also likely that a significant number of these experiments will be abandoned after test; even though feasible, drawbacks will be seen that make further development unattractive. Nevertheless, a successful long-term R & D programme should lead to a small number of new ideas that can be translated into new products. These ideas could be used either as:

(a) part of a continuous product enhancement strategy; or
(b) if radical enough, as the basis of an offensive new product drive.

Although much of the long-term research expenditure will turn out to be fruitless, its value should not be overlooked. Without it, the impetus for inventive work may dry up and the most creative brains may leave the organization. Also by pursuing long-term R & D over a broad front, an insight may be gained into many technologies, even if only at a superficial level. It could be that a technology rejected by one organization could be made into a workable product by another, perhaps through the application of an even newer branch of technology. However, the insight gained by the abortive work done in the first organization could still be of value if a defensive strategy needs to be adopted or if a collaborative venture looks attractive.

For many organizations, an optimum approach would be a combination of all four strategies and this is done by the very largest companies. Smaller organizations, however, may not have the finances to support innovative work on all fronts. It then becomes a matter of company strategy as to how it chooses to spend its resources. To adopt strategies based on development of existing products and a generally defensive approach to new products may ensure a long-term place in the market but with a low level of profitability. Survival, though reasonably certain, may always be a struggle. To put everything into the development of something radically new may lead to riches if the product succeeds, but if it fails it could bring down the company if there is nothing left to enhance existing products. Similarly, too much emphasis on long-term research could lead to wasted money if too few useful ideas result.

Some factors to be considered in choosing a strategy

The principal factor used to decide upon the desirability of any project, whether innovative or not, is the expected return from the investment. Whatever strategy is adopted, this test should always be applied; however, it cannot be applied outside of the context of the company itself and the world in which it exists. It is these additional factors that shape the decisions as different conditions will indicate different optimum strategies. Significant factors that should be taken into account in formulating a strategy are:

1. Corporate objectives, which could be:
    - the maintenance of a set share of the market
    - increased growth or profits
    - social or environmental responsibility
    - improved efficiency
    - diversification or concentration.
2. Position in the market, which could be:
    - expanding or declining
    - perceived high or low profile.
3. Life of existing products, which could include:
    - those with long lives still to come
    - those approaching the end of their lives
    - those in need of an up-grade to extend their lives.
4. Existing and potential competition, which could come from:
    - existing suppliers in the home market
    - new overseas suppliers
    - new or emerging technologies in the hands of rivals.
5. Design and technology strengths and weaknesses, which could be:
    - extensive or limited research facilities
    - broad-based technical skills or narrow disciplines.
6. Plant capability or capacity, which could be:
    - modern or old general manufacturing capability
    - modern or old special-purpose production lines
    - excess or limited production capacity
    - extensive or limited use of subcontractors.
7. Level of development funding, which could be:
    - extensive due to company size and fast-moving nature of industry
    - relatively small due to nature of industry, fierce price competition but little innovation.
8. Market forecasts, which could show:
    - expanding or declining opportunities for existing products
    - opportunities for new product types.

9. Technological forecasts, which could show:
   - an accelerating or declining pace of progress over the industry
   - the pace of development of rival technologies
   - the pace of development of complimentary technologies
   - gaps in technologies that could be developed or exploited.

With such a complex array of factors, there can be no single strategy that is best for all conditions. The important point is that all the factors listed should be examined carefully with as little bias as possible when formulating a way forward. It is equally important that a conscious choice of strategy is made and that it is communicated to and understood by all involved. The alternative is to have no real strategy, implying an opportunistic, *laissez-faire* approach. This may work for some organizations, particularly if they have the facilities to develop rapidly a new idea into a product and bring it to the market. Such an approach could, however, lead to a waste of resources on ill-founded projects or missed opportunities due to a failure to concentrate efforts in a particular direction at a critical time.

Some factors to be considered when assessing a new product

Ideas for new products may come from internally derived sources but occasionally ideas come from outside when an approach may be made from a private individual or another company which lacks the particular technology involved. All product ideas should be examined, nothing should be rejected out of hand; even the most outlandish idea may contain the seeds of a successful product, provided that the right approach is taken to development and marketing. A screening process is necessary and here a checklist and scoring system can help. The major factors to be taken into account are similar to those used for assessing the whole product development strategy and will be influenced by the strategy that the company has chosen to adopt.

A simple example of a product checklist and scoring system is given in the New Product Evaluation Sheet, shown in Figure 2.10. Various product evaluation techniques have been devised; these tend to involve a method of applying weightings to specific product or project attributes and then attaching a score according to how well each attribute conforms to the company's objectives. In this example a new product is evaluated both for its positive and negative aspects. Positive factors stress the benefits in terms of profits, image, strategy and technological advantage. Profit is given the largest weighting as it is the principal reason for investing in new products; the contribution to corporate image, in this case, is given the lowest weighting but this may not always be the case, especially if the firm is looking to enter a new field or expand its customer base. Exposure to new technology and the experience derived is considered a benefit as is the strategic fit in the overall programme and the company will need a succession of new products to remain competitive. The negative effects are due to the risks associated with failures in the development and production phases and the timing of the eventual profits. The risks can be broken into two elements: (a) the amounts of capital associated with the development process and the production machinery, including the cost of borrowings, and (b) the risks that either the development will result in a technical failure or that the product

NEW PRODUCT EVALUATION SHEET					

Application no. _P-171_	Product description		SYNTHETIC STEAK FOR ARMY USE	Recommendation:	
Date _20/3/93_	Project reference			SECOND STAGE FEASIBILITY STUDY	

Positive factors		Weighting (W)	Scoring guide			Assessed score (S)	Result W x S
			High (Good) 1.0	Medium 0.5	Low (Poor) 0.1		
A	Profit over ten year period	60		X		0·5	30
B	Contribution to corporate image	5		X		0·5	2·5
C	Strategic fit in overall programme	20		X		0·5	10·0
D	Technology benefits	15	X			1·0	15·0
E	Total score of positive factors: A + B + C + D						57·5

Negative factors		Weighting (W)	Scoring guide			Assessed score (S)	Result W x S
			High (Poor) 1.0	Medium 0.5	Low (Good) 0.1		
F	Development cost as a % of budget	100	X			0·85	85
G	Risk of technical failure	25	X			1·0	25
H	Development risk					$\frac{F \times G}{100}$	21·25
J	Capital for production as a % of budget	100		X		0·65	65
K	Risk of failure in market	50			X	0·2	10
L	Production risk					$\frac{J \times K}{100}$	6·5
M	Discount due to time at which profits accrue	25		X		0·65	16·25
N	Total score of negative factors: H + L + M						44·0
	Overall total score: E − N						13·5

Figure 2.10 New Product evaluation sheet.

will not make the anticipated sales. Multiplying the risk factor by the relative amount of capital involved produces an overall score for the risk element. Provided a thorough feasibility study is carried out, few projects will fail for purely technical reasons; given enough time and development effort, the technology can usually be made to work. The failures tend to occur in the market where the effects of timing, competition and alternative technologies may all combine to reduce sales to a fraction of that anticipated at the outset, hence the higher weighting given to this element compared to the technology. The timing at which the anticipated profits will arise is also a negative factor as the further away they are, then the less future earnings are worth. Before this evaluation can be performed, much preparatory work will be needed to produce estimates of costs, timescales, markets and profits.

Within the evaluation sheet both the weightings attached to each factor and the scoring guide can be adjusted to suit circumstances. In the example shown in the figure, they are set to give an overall total score of zero for products that have equal assessments both for the positive and negative factors; to be attractive any new product must score an overall positive value. The scoring guide can be adjusted from time to time to suit the company's current development strategy; thus reducing the scores associated with the positive factors to high = 0.9, medium = 0.4, while raising the scores for the negative factors to medium = 0.7 and low = 0.3 would stress the risk aspect and make fewer products look worthwhile. Had these scores been used in the example, the overall total score would have been -5.5 and this product would be rejected, at least for the time being. In a period when the bulk of the development funding is already allocated to a major new development, such a view of new product ideas may be the best approach. Alternatively, if profits are high from current sales but the perceived life of current products is relatively short, there is an incentive to invest in new products. In this case, the scores can be adjusted to give higher values to the positive factors and thus make more new ideas look worthy of further investigation.

The weightings can also be adjusted to take into account strategic decisions regarding such things as the relative importance of short-term high profits or improved technology and corporate image. This evaluation method can thus be used as an instrument of corporate development policy as any new product can be assessed in the context of the current strategy, reflected in the scoring and weighting, and only those that fit the requirements most closely will proceed to further evaluation and prototype testing. Corporate policy may of course change over a period and products rejected under one set of circumstances may look more attractive later on; it may thus be worthwhile re-examining old proposals when a significant change of policy or technology occurs.

Sources of funds for development projects

Many innovative projects are financed internally from budgets set up for that purpose and derived from the company's operating revenue. However, from time to time it may be necessary to seek additional funds to carry through a development programme where the capital needed is beyond the scope of the current budgets. The funding of projects is one aspect of the company's overall business strategy and the source and application of money is part of that plan. The overall question of company finance is beyond the scope of this text, and the task of raising money often falls outside the scope of the Project Manager as it is most frequently given to the Finance Director. Broadly, funding and financial assistance can come from four major areas:

1. Professional lenders and investors.
2. Grants from government bodies.
3. Interested parties.
4. Private, non-professional investors.

Professional lenders and investors

These can be divided into two classes: those interested only in lending money: (i.e. banks), and those that lend money on the basis of making an investment in the company (i.e. the venture capital funds). Banks can provide money in two forms: (a) overdraft facilities, and (b) long-term loans.

Where sums of money are relatively small and only required in the short term, an overdraft should be considered; these are simple to arrange and comparatively cheap. The disadvantage with an overdraft is that if the bank sees fit it may demand instant repayment or part-repayment. This may not happen very often but if it does it can be very embarrassing for the company concerned. Some form of security for the overdraft may be required; for small companies this may be the personal guarantee of the owner, alternatively property may be needed.

Where longer-term financing is needed, loans can be arranged for periods up to 30 years. Arrangements vary from bank to bank and interest charges will be several percentage points above bank base rates. Security will be required as a loan guarantee and there will be a charge for setting up the loan. Evidence of a sound business plan with full details of development costs, market forecasts and projected profits will also be needed.

Venture capital funding is a recent innovation in financing methods having been started in the UK in the late 1970s. These funds exist to invest in industry by making money available for promising ventures in return for interest payments on the capital advanced and a share of the business. The money they have to invest comes from many sources, including insurance companies, pension funds and investment trusts. The primary interest of the venture capital funds is those companies with high prospective growth rates not as yet floated on the equities market. They will look most favourably at proposals with high expected margins and large markets backed by an experienced and committed management team. Investment funding is provided in return for ordinary shares in the company; thus some measure of control is lost although few venture capitalists will wish to take a controlling interest. Their expectation is that the company will grow sufficiently over a three- to ten-year period for it to be floated on the stock market when they can sell their shares and make a gain on the original investment. If the equity stake in the company is large, there is always the risk that when the fund sells its shares they could fall into the hands of an unwelcome rival who would have sizeable voting powers. The fund may also require their own appointed director to be on the Board, to look after their investment. There will also be setting-up charges, research and legal fees that must be borne by the client company. Individual funds will set both minimum and maximum sums that it is willing to invest in any one company. There are a few funds that specialize in small sums of money, approx. £5000, but the minimum investment tends to be £50 000 although many funds have higher limits; maximum investments can be as high as £100 000 000. As individual funds limit the amount they invest in any one venture, a consortium of funds must be set up if very large sums are needed; it will be up to the client company to arrange this. Venture capital funds vary in terms of their investment policy. Some specialize in narrow industrial sectors, while others take a broader view. The amounts of money available for investment at any given time varies between funds and some research into the best fund to approach will be necessary. A directory of UK venture capital funds is published by the British Venture Capital Association.[1]

Finance can also be raised through the stock market; if a company has grown sufficiently to make it worthwhile becoming publicly quoted, then capital can be raised through floatation. The initial cost of 'going public' can be high and must be taken into account. For companies that are already publicly quoted, rights issues are an attractive proposition; under this arrangement existing shareholders are invited, as of right, to buy additional shares in proportion to their existing shareholding. As an inducement, the additional shares are usually offered at a price below the current market value, so that shareholders can make an instant capital gain if they take up their rights and buy the shares. The success of a rights issue can be underwritten by arranging additional investors who are prepared to acquire any shares left over from shareholders that did not exercise their rights.

Grants from government bodies

For most countries, the continued growth of its industrial base is a matter of public priority and governments will provide grants to enable industry to develop, modernize and innovate in areas that are in the national interest. In the UK both the Department of Trade and Industry (DTI) and the Commission of the European Community (EC) operate schemes to encourage the development of innovative technology. In general, they are aimed at research and development for technologies that are exploitable as products rather than pure research. Special schemes exist to promote development work in key technologies. The schemes tend to run for several years and new ones are introduced as earlier schemes come to an end. Schemes running in 1991 included:

- SMART, Small Firms Merit Award for Research and Technology. This is an annual competitive award, sponsored by the DTI, for innovative technology for firms smaller than 200 employees. It is divided into two stages and there are limitations regarding the amount of capital awarded at each stage.
- LINC Collaborative Research Initiative. This scheme is designed to promote collaboration between industrial and science based partners in key areas of science and technology. The projects normally involve at least two companies and one publicly funded research organization. The grant can cover up to 50% of the eligible expenses.
- The DTI sponsors projects involving some key technologies, examples of these schemes are:
  - Advanced Robotics Initiative, which is aimed at promoting the development and use of robotics in industrial applications;
  - National Electronics Research Initiative, covering collaborative research projects involving at least five firms in the electronics industry.

The European Commission also sponsors development work in specific technologies, in particular, information technology, nuclear energy and the environment. Sponsorship programmes include:

- ESPRIT, European Strategic Programme for Research and Development in Information Technology.
- RACE, Research and Development Programme for Advanced Communication Technologies for Europe.
- Management and Storage of Radio-active Waste.
- Non-Nuclear Energy Research and Development Programme.

Funding, as with DTI grants, is normally up to a maximum of 50% of costs. Applications for EC grants in the UK are handled by the DTI.[2] More information on government grants can be found in *Tolley's Government Assistance for Business*.

Interested parties

Organizations that are potential customers for a new product may be prepared to finance some or all of its development. In some cases, they may be willing to sponsor basic research but a commercial or potentially useful end must always be in view. In the public sector the defence ministries are among the largest purchasers of advanced technology goods and services. Without support from government sources, the huge advances in electronics, radar, aerospace, etc. could not have been made. Product ideas that have a direct application to defence issues can have some of the basic development work sponsored by the ministry. The research establishments associated with the various branches of the armed services have budget allocations for extramural research and will sponsor relevant ideas. Basic development work can be funded but the sponsor will normally expect free use of all reports, designs and drawings that emerge. The position is usually negotiable, particularly if the company's own private investment has already been substantial.

Some defence equipment is developed privately by individual companies who seek to sell it to defence organizations at home and abroad but the more significant programmes are funded directly by the government. For a programme to reach this stage its feasibility will have to be proven and the military need for it established. The basic product specification will be contained in an 'Operational Requirement'. In the majority of cases, defence organizations seek competitive bids from companies with the capability to satisfy the requirement. Thus initial development of an idea could be funded by the ministry but, if it has enough promise to form the basis of an operational requirement, it could be disclosed in an open competition to develop it for service use. Although its established expertise should give it an advantage, the company that has had the original idea and carried out the initial development could lose to a rival that takes an aggressive view over price.

The defence market is becoming increasingly international and companies need not confine themselves to their home market in the search for funding. The vectored thrust Pegasus engine that made possible the revolutionary Harrier V/STOL fighter received 75% of its development funding from the US Mutual Weapons Development Program.

Defence organizations can be large, complex and bureaucratic, and obtaining funds may require an intimate understanding of the departments and personalities involved, as well as the budgeting, timing and applications procedures. In the USA firms of consultants have sprung up specifically to help and advise companies that wish to promote ideas and products to the US Department of Defense. Their understanding and the help they can offer can be invaluable to overseas companies wishing to enter that market.

Industrial organizations that can see the application of a new idea to their own product range may also be willing to sponsor development. If sponsorship is given, they may expect rights to manufacture the product themselves or seek competitive sources of production. However, if the ideas are protected by patents, the company that made the invention can still expect royalties from items made by third parties, even after sponsorship. Intellectual property protection is thus important before approaches are made to potential sponsors; furthermore, a careful study of suitable companies, their record, financial soundness, marketing methods, etc. must be made. For good ideas this method can be very successful; one good example is the popular 'Workmate' portable workbench, an idea created by a British inventor but developed and marketed by Black and Decker. Compared to the bureaucracies inherent in government departments, industrial companies can be less structured and more opportunistic in their view of proposals for new products; their approach to negotiating exploitation and intellectual property rights may be less rigid but the commercial motivation to strike a deal which benfits the sponsor will be just as great.

Occasionally an idea for an improved product will involve a new technology not possessed by the originating company. Firms that have the required expertise may be persuaded to develop the necessary technology at no cost to the requiring company if a worthwhile market can be foreseen for the new product. Both a detailed technical specification and a good marketing case must be established before serious approaches are made. Company reaction varies enormously, but initially it is likely to be cautious. If the idea is taken up, all that may be offered is an initial design study, possibly followed by one or two 'breadboard' prototypes to test functionality. This work may have to be fitted into the existing research and development programme and proceed on an 'as and when' basis, with work starting on little more than a handshake and a confidentiality agreement. This may be frustrating for the originating company but in many organizations R & D programmes are fixed a year in advance, and if one wants a firm to do speculative work on a no-charge basis, then 'as and when' may be the best that can be expected. Once the prototype phase has passed, and provided that interest still exists, the whole arrangement between the two companies should be put on a more formal footing, with an agreed timescale, specification and contracts for deliveries. Intellectual property issues, marketing rights, royalties, etc. should also be resolved. Each party should secure the rights to the other's designs, so that if, at the end of a successful development programme, one party decides not to proceed with production, the design can be procured by the other to allow production to go ahead. When a problem does arise between companies collaborating on a venture, it can often stem from lack of formal understanding and agreement between them at the start.

Non-professional lenders or private investors

Private individuals, often local businessmen, may be prepared to back a new project with money of their own. Personal friends and contacts may also be useful as a source of cash but the sums of money may be relatively small. If, however, all that is needed is a few thousand pounds, this is worth considering. Employees may also be prepared to invest in a new project as they may see a benefit from continued employment in a profitable firm and a return on their investment. It should be made clear to all involved that money put into a project to create something new is speculative money, a profit is not guaranteed and it could all be lost. Many private individuals do not think in these terms, seeing money invested as being like money in the bank which, in this case, it is not. Private businessmen are much more used to the concept of risk money and may well favour backing new development work in return for a share of the profits as an interesting and, possibly, more profitable way of investing surplus cash. There may even be tax incentives; in the UK there is a business expansion scheme aimed at private individuals that wish to invest in small businesses that are not publicly quoted. Investors can obtain full tax relief at the highest rate on what they invest in newly issued shares; provided the shares are held for more than five years, they are free of capital gains tax on disposal. The scheme is designed to attract outside investors and thus directors and employees are not eligible.

Where large sums of money are needed, a syndicate of businessmen and investors may have to be put together. Potential investors may be found through advertising in the local, national and trade press. Firms of accountants that may act as advisers to businesses about their investments or firms of consultants that help companies to raise finance can be another source of possible investors. LINC (Local Investment Networking Company)[3] operations are being set up in the UK on a regional basis by a growing number of enterprise agencies. They issue regular bulletins to interested investors that list companies looking to raise finance. Currently they deal with sums of money less than £100 000, and firms should apply to their local agency if they wish to be included in the bulletin.

Summary

The process of innovation and adaptation is essential to the survival of any organization, to stand still is, in effect, to go backwards as there will always be rival organizations going forwards. All products have a finite life cycle – they will be displaced in the market by changing tastes and the emergence of superior products; therefore firms must pursue a policy of creating new products that will meet changing needs, and for this some speculative research and development will be needed. Changes, however, mean new opportunities and firms that can spot trends both in the market and the technology can take advantage to improve their position in the market, together with their overall profitability. Analytical techniques have been developed that can assist in evaluating trends and pointing out the scope for new products.

Ideas need stimulation as pure invention cannot be relied upon to come up with suitable products in an acceptable timeframe. Many firms therefore pursue a policy of both speculative research and development of existing products. Truly novel ideas, when they emerge, may call for development expenditure over and above that which would normally be allocated to product development. This need not be a stumbling-block as there are a variety of ways to attract investment and each should be considered on its merits if funding is needed.

Contacts

1. British Venture Capital Association, 3 Catherine Place, London SW1E 6DX, Tel: 071-233 5212, Fax: 071-931 0536.
2. Department of Trade and Industry, Innovation Enquiry Line, Tel: 0800-44 2001.
3. Local Investment Networking Company (LINC), 4 Snow Hill, London EC1A 2BS, Tel: 071-236 3000.

3

Getting organized

Projects in one form or another have been around since Stonehenge and the Pyramids were built, so somebody must have organized and managed their execution. However, one thing is certain; whoever did it was not called a Project Manager. We may surmise that the men who masterminded those prodigious feats must have possessed project management skills in abundance, but management would have been a secondary role. Stonehenge, no doubt, came under the control of the local religious leader, while the Pyramids would have been the responsibility of the chief architect to the pharaoh.

Project management, the approach for today

The concept of a Project Manager is a recent one, despite the existence of projects throughout history. If 'projects' have been undertaken for such a long time and without the need for the separate role of project management, one can argue that things must have changed to the extent that the need has arisen in the recent past. The birth of project management must surely indicate an awareness of the special skills that project work demands – but if it is so special why was it never recognized before? The creation of the Project Manager can be seen as a response on the part of industry to the growing difficulties that current projects pose. Projects have already been defined as one-off activities with a well-understood end-goal, and that fact alone might have warranted the creation of project managers but historically it did not; it would seem that architects, engineers and even priests were able to encompass all the management activities necessary within their own disciplines and daily routines. Other factors must therefore be at work, and chief among these is the growing complexity of contemporary products. Gone are the days when it was necessary only to look at a piece of machinery to see how it worked; products are now 'systems' composed of many different technologies, all dependent upon the other. Some products may be so complex that no individual could hope to understand them in every detail: complexity has brought specialization. But complexity and specialization too bring new requirements, in particular, coordination and control. The Project Manager is the living expression of that need to bring together, to coordinate and control individuals in different disciplines, in pursuit of a common goal.

Other changes have also been at work, all of which have promoted the role of the Project Manager:

1. Contractual relationships between companies have tended to become much more formalized – the days of the gentleman's agreement are over. Projects are now perceived to embody much higher risks than previously: the product may not work as specified, the plant may not be opened on time and a competitor may be first in the market. Whichever of these may be the case, a loss in financial terms can be assigned to the project. Client organizations naturally wish to protect themselves from losses and this has resulted in contract terms and conditions that are explicit and, in some cases, penal. Given the complexity that may exist in a product, it becomes clear that a role exists for people who can devote all their energies to interpreting clients' wishes, coordinating efforts in order to bring those wishes into being and, at the same time, comply with the contractual arrangements. The Project Manager fulfils that role.

2. The advent of high-speed computing has brought with it a series of new techniques for the control of business activities. The techniques owe little to engineering or science, but have their roots in management theories and mathematics; they are not necessarily intuitive and have to be learned. To apply them requires a specialist in the new methods. Project Managers are such individuals, trained in the practice and able to apply the control mechanisms.

3. Teams accomplish more than individuals. The systems nature of many modern products brings with it a need to draw together personnel from different disciplines and organizations and to focus their efforts onto a single objective. One thing that has been demonstrated clearly in almost every sphere of human endeavour is that team spirit adds a dimension to the effectiveness of individuals. Being part of a team gives an extra meaning to people's working lives, allowing them to identify with a common goal. The formation of project teams that pool their efforts in a shared cause is a logical business strategy that is efficient in terms of communication and understanding while releasing this extra energy for the common good. To be effective, however, a team needs a leader to set a direction, to motivate and inspire and to coordinate and control. Without a leader the team will loose its sense of direction and eventually a sense of purpose. The Project Manager provides that leadership: without him, either the team will not function, or if it does, there is no saying where it will go.

The above points are becoming recognized throughout industry as reasons why a project-based approach to managing the process of going from 'state A' to 'state B' is right for the climate of today. However, managing by projects represents a break with long-held traditions and its introduction can cause problems at all levels within a company. Among these problems are those that concern the responsibility and authority given to Project Managers.

The Project Manager lives, in a sense, in limbo; he has authority but not complete authority, and responsibility but not complete responsibility. His position is ambiguous; while he may be given responsibility for the completion of a project, his formal authority over any individual may be limited, he may be able to act only with the consent of others. To survive and be effective he may need to cultivate a quality that is not necessarily a property of management *per se* – namely, influence.

Conventional company structures tend to group specialists in similar disciplines under one functional head; typically all design, test and drawing office staff report ultimately to the Technical Director, marketing and sales staff report to the Sales Director, etc. This does have the merit of having a specialist in the subject as the head of each function, who is able to direct and advise staff from a position that is both defined by that head's status within the organization and by accepted competence in the discipline. The project structure calls upon all the disciplines but the Project Manager must work through the functional heads.

Authority, power and influence

Authority is the essential element that divides managers from their subordinates, a dictionary definition shows it to be: *the rightful power to command or enforce obedience in others*. Authority only has meaning in the context of a group that is organized such that there are recognizable superiors and subordinates. Authority implies legitimacy, it is an enforceable right; people who defy authority risk punishment. In groups where there is no recognized superior and subordinate relationship, there is no authority, only influence. Influence may cause people to act in a way that resembles a superior–subordinate relationship but that is because of choice; it could change if circumstances change. Ultimately, authority derives from the right of private ownership; whoever owns a company has the right to do with it as he or she wishes and others to obey. Nevertheless, groups without clear issues of ownership (for example, clubs and societies) find it difficult to function without a system of authority being created. One of the first things clubs may do is to create a committee to run their own affairs and to vest in it the authority to spend money, organize events, etc.; in this situation, people accept authority voluntarily and for good reasons. Authority allows decisions to be made and acted upon; without it, there would be no cohesive force that binds together the group in pursuit of its goal.

Authority, ultimately, resides at the top of any organization but it can be delegated to subordinates by those who have that authority; anyone with delegated authority has the same rights of action and obedience as the owner. This process of delegated authority reveals itself in the organization structures and reporting chains that companies adopt. A departmental director has authority over the actions of his staff; this is clearly defined by his position in the organization and is the basis of his legitimate authority.

Power derives from authority; but whereas authority is a right, power is: *the ability to act and control others*. It is the practical exercise of authority. However, right and ability are two different things: authority may have a legitimate or legal basis, but power need not. For example, the use of threats with no legal basis can be the basis of one person's power over another; it does not have to take the form of threats, however, admiration could be just as effective for the exercise of power. The most visible signs of power in any manager are the rewards and punishments at their disposal: the greater or more drastic these are, the greater is their nominal power. Employees will be aware of their manager's power through the latter's ability to award pay rises and promotions or demotions and dismissal; how effective these are may depend on how seriously they are taken. To be taken seriously they must exist in a relationship where both parties have a mutual interest in making the relationship work – i.e. subordinates must accept the authority and powers of the superior because it is in their interest so to do. Likewise, superiors should not use their power in a way which is detrimental to the subordinate without good reason or they may lose the subordinate.

Authority derived as of right, and the power that comes with it, are only two facets of the control that can be exercised: the third is influence. This is a 'soft' quality, in that it does not necessarily derive from either authority or power (which are aspects of the organization structure), but from the respect in which an individual is held. This may stem from personal qualities or professional standing, or a combination of both. Influence manifests itself in the willingness of individuals to follow the lead given or to consult before taking action. It can be just as powerful a tool for directing others but it resides in the individual, not the organization. The degree to which individuals can exert influence over each other, and the way in which this is done, will shape the subculture of the company; this is the informal structure, beneath the formal organization, by which things actually happen. Subcultures exist in all organizations of any permanence; they reflect the attitudes, values and practices of the individuals. This informal structure and the practices that go with it arises from the fact that organization structures and procedures manuals define only a small part of the total business situation, they do not define the solutions to most of the everyday problems that arise – these are solved by the individuals themselves and the ways in which they do it are as varied as the people involved. The solutions they arrive at, the relationships that they form and the handling of individuals all contribute to the culture of the company and the behavioural norms. Some individuals, through their approach, experience and personal qualities, will be able to exploit this to their advantage. They will be able to exert influence, even if they do not have legitimate authority; their position in the informal structure may be much more significant than in the formal one.

Responsibility and accountability

The exercise of authority brings with it two other properties: responsibility and accountability. One who directs the work of others cannot remain aloof from the results of their actions, he or she is both responsible and accountable for what is done. Responsibility implies that the individual is formally associated with the actions that are directed and their outcome; one who accepts responsibility takes on culpability for what transpires. Accountability, however, implies the requirement to report to others for actions taken and their outcome; one who is accountable is in a subordinate–superior relationship, and a person who is accountable to no one is a free agent, he or she may do as they please without explanation. Although these two facets are closely related they are different, in that responsibility can be delegated but accountability cannot. Thus anyone who delegates authority also delegates with it the responsibility for its use, while retaining accountability for the quality with which that authority has been exercised; he cannot absolve himself from the initial decision to delegate. To attempt to delegate responsibility as well as account-ability leads to the abdication of management.

Project Managers and project structures

For the most part, persons working in company structures have only to look in two directions: upwards to their superior for direction, and downwards to their work which may involve the direction of subordinates. However, the Project Manager is in a different position where he is required to manage a project that is being carried out on the behalf of another; in this case, he has to look three ways. He is responsible to his superiors who authorized the project and have given him his mandate; he is responsible for his team who look to him for direction; and he must also deal with the customer, that person or organization that is sponsoring the project. He will be responsible to the customer or sponsor to the extent that he will be the first point of contact for all routine reporting matters and any instructions that the customer may wish to give will initially be through him. He thus bears a triple responsibility: first, to complete the project satisfactorily and within its budget; secondly, to lead the team; and thirdly, to present the public face of the company to the customer. This is a more demanding role than is usual and is much more akin to that of a managing director, who also has a triple responsibility to the shareholders, the employees and the customers. Figure 3.1 shows this three-way split. Individuals who take on the role of a Project Manager should be chosen for their ability to handle the situations that arise from all three roles.

Company structures have been – and mostly still are – organized along functional lines, with each discipline grouped under a functional head. Reporting chains are vertical, with issues being raised upwards through the reporting chain then down-wards to the individual. The weakness of this approach in terms of efficiency have

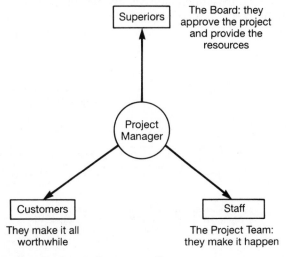

Figure 3.1 The Project Manager's three-way split.

been recognized and the 'project' approach is increasingly becoming normal in dynamic companies that thrive through constant adaptation and innovation. The 'project' challenges the conventional structure but it does not replace it, rather it co-exists with it but that existence can be uneasy. With 'projects', the emphasis is less with the vertical reporting chain and more with the horizontal: communication is cross-functional, multi-disciplinary teams are created and the Project Manager is a new force in the organization structure. The Project Manager, however, exists out-side the conventional structure, yet has both responsibility and authority. How much of either is acquired and the effectiveness of the role will depend on how 'projects' are viewed within the organization and the status he or she is accorded.

Small and simple projects

With small or simple projects, the Project Manager may be primarily a planner, coordinator and administrator. This role has been created to provide a cohesive, directional force to a series of tasks that otherwise would go on in a piecemeal fashion, and also to report progress to interested parties. Normally he or she will be dedicated to project management work although they may have several different projects on the go at the same time. He will be required to produce a plan for the project's tasks, possibly also a budget and then ensure, as far as he is able, the progress of that plan. The Project Manager may in fact have no direct control over any staff engaged on the project except, perhaps, for an assistant or two, seconded from his own functional department. His position of authority is relatively weak and much of his time will be spent in negotiation and discussion with the functional heads on whose cooperation he depends. He may well form committees or call meetings of members of the relevant disciplines to discuss progress and also issue minutes that detail the actions that have been decided upon. The Project Manager may also have a separate role that takes him outside the organization to deal with the client or customer. A typical structure is shown in Figure 3.2. Project Managers in this situation may report to an Operations Director or Projects Director if sufficient projects are undertaken to warrant such a position. With technically orientated projects, the Project Manager may report to the Technical Director or, possibly, the Marketing Director if projects are heavily biased towards satisfying specific customer needs.

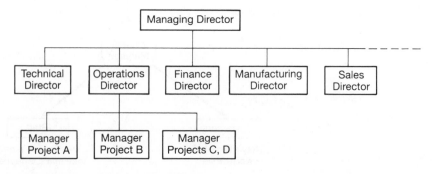

Figure 3.2   Organization for small projects.

Despite the weak authority of the Project Manager in absolute terms, many organizations use this form of project management and find it successful. In this case, the success of the Project Manager in eliciting the cooperation needed depends heavily on the power he or she can project through the influence they generate. It is a difficult role to play and the individual must be carefully chosen. His power, in part, derives from the legitimacy of his role; it is an appointed position with terms of reference that can be understood by all with whom he deals and also from the personal influence that he creates by his conduct. To exercise influence he will need to set up appropriate channels of communication to the functional heads; he must be able to transmit the concept of the project goal and emphasize its importance. To achieve it he will need to consult with and persuade them but, most important, he must form alliances based on trust and cooperation. Conflicts of interest will arise and cooperation may be less than willingly given which, in turn, derives from individual attitudes or the company's way of operating. For example, the Production Director may have a productivity bonus based on value of throughput as part of his salary package and this may militate against giving priority to prototype work when large-scale production orders can be tackled. Where cooperation is not forthcoming, he has the recourse of going upwards through the formal chain of command, but this should be used only as a last resort. Once that route is taken, cooperation may follow but trust may be lost for a long time.

Where projects are simple undertakings, the approach outlined is economical in terms of manpower as special teams do not have to be created and it does not significantly conflict with the formalized structure. It does, however, rely heavily on both the qualities of the Project Manager and the degree of backing he is seen to be given by his superiors.

As projects get larger, and the interactions between disciplines become more complex and interdependent, the Project Manager who acts primarily in a coordinating role may find it increasingly difficult to function. Relying on cooperation from those over whom he has no direct control may prove insufficient to achieve the company's objectives. When this arises, the responses have tended to be of two forms: (a) the creation of a 'matrix management' structure within the company or (b) the formation of a separate semi-autonomous entity to undertake the project.

Matrix management

This is, perhaps, the most popular way to run a project, and the use of the term **matrix management** has become synonymous with the project environment. Its principal feature is the division of responsibility for the day-to-day activities of an individual on the one hand, and the quality of the work on the other hand. These are shared between the Project Manager who gives day-to-day direction and the functional head who is primarily concerned with the quality of the work done and the professional development of staff. Figure 3.3 shows the principle of matrix management.

Project Managers are appointed to lead specific projects and draw staff from the functional departments as in the simple project case, the difference being that staff, by agreement with the function head, are dedicated to the project. They cannot be removed from the project team without the agreement of the Project Manager and they take their directions from him without reference to their functional superior.

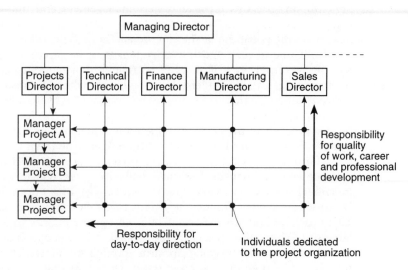

Figure 3.3 The matrix management structure.

Often, when a matrix structure is introduced, the project team is brought together in one location. This creates a project identity, shortens lines of communication and, to some extent, severs links with the parent department. There is clearly a loss of authority on the part of the functional head, while the Project Manager gains a new, legitimate and elevated authority.

This loss of authority can lead to friction if it is not properly handled, and responsibility for that will rest with the Managing Director. In fact giving up day-to-day direction frees the functional head to concentrate on the development of policies within his or her department, as well as developing the qualities of the staff. Nevertheless, some functional heads find it difficult to divorce themselves from the detail of the work undertaken by their staff – this stems from a background of working their way up through their discipline, and it may reflect where their true interests lie. There is a difference between a Production Director who can look ten years ahead, plan and implement a programme of improved productivity and a Production Manager who keeps production running to schedule day in and day out, or a Technical Director who can assess improvements in technology, direct re-search into profitable avenues, while developing a design skills base, and a Chief Engineer who can devise good engineering solutions to today's design problems. It is not uncommon to find people in the director's position who have been promoted due to fine performance in their former role, which they may find hard to give up. A director needs not only technical competence, but a broad vision of the future, together with insight, planning ability and the drive to ensure the firm gets to where it should be. The matrix structure will be accepted by such people as it allows them to concentrate more of their creative energies on a better tomorrow, which is the real role of a director. Those less well suited may, however, find that the loss of authority over detail has robbed them of an essential element of their work enjoy-ment. Introducing matrix management may be the time for a new assessment of the roles, responsibilities, aspirations and suitability of individuals at all levels.

Project management forms a separate discipline from the technical background from which many managers are drawn; a move into project management often involves a transfer of divisions within a company. With a matrix structure, the Project Manager's role embodies a marked improvement over that of coordinator for a simple project, but it brings drawbacks as well as advantages. He will be able to take a much more commanding role, driving the project in the way he deems best without having to agree all issues with a variety of functional heads. His status and authority is raised as he will have staff from all disciplines who take their direction from him, and he will be much more closely identified with the project. The project becomes his, personally; both self-esteem and career progress may be intimately bound to it. This, however, can raise questions both of objectivity and personal security. Could a Project Manager be expected to recommend cancelling his project, even though there could be a good business case for doing so when the prospect, however faint, of a success still remains? Should the project fail, even for reasons beyond the Project Manager's control, he may be stigmatized – he may be seen as having allowed the project to fail. This may have nothing to do with a matrix structure, for a project may fail because the customer backs out, but managing the customer and keeping him interested may be seen as part of the Project Manager's job. Premature termination of a project can have a serious effect on the manager's career if no new projects are available for him to manage. People who have spent any length of time in project management sometimes find it difficult to return to their former discipline with the loss of status that some find impossible to accept.

The Project Manager working in a matrix structure needs diplomatic as well as managerial skills, for he is in a potential 'conflict situation' with the functional heads with whom he must work. Project Managers are usually required to provide written progress reports on their projects to their superiors, and these may reach the Managing Director. It is inevitable that there will be occasions when the work of one department will fall short of what is needed; this will eventually be reported and may cause embarrassment for the particular functional head. The growing introduction of cost and schedule performance measurement systems for project control will make reporting of effectiveness and progress even more pointed and quantified. Function heads may thus see Project Managers as being in a position to 'point a finger' when things do not go as they should. In this situation, the Project Manager may feel torn between objectively reporting a situation (thereby protecting himself) and not wishing to make an enemy of a person who could, if he chose, make life difficult. There will be occasions when things need to be said if progress is to be made; at other times things may be better left unsaid on the basis of the gentleman's agreement, that matters will be put right. The ability to cope with such situations and to exercise human skills, together with a degree of judgement, is of paramount importance. Where matrix management is implemented, the individual filling the Project Manager's job needs to be chosen for such qualities as these, as well as the technical aspects of project control.

For more junior staff working in the project team, things can become confusing. Matrix management is commonly criticized as 'the set-up where everybody has two bosses'. This is a valid point, for although it should not happen, conflicts either of loyalty or of direction can and do arise for the individual, particularly if the function head is the sort who likes to interfere as a way of demonstrating authority. For example, a function head may feel that more development and testing work is needed on some aspect of a design, whereas the Project Manager's position may be that there is no more money available and he feels sufficient confidence already exists. Rather than confront the Project Manager directly, some function heads may choose to fight this battle by giving instructions, to staff allocated to the project, about the quality or completeness of the work. Another problem that can arise is that of over-commitment; function heads may find themselves in a position where they do not have sufficient staff to meet all the demands – perhaps, because they have a fixed budget for staff numbers. They may then be forced into switching staff from project to project in an effort to satisfy the requirements of several Project Managers. This is frustrating for the Project Manager and unsettling for the staff, who may become unsure of what their real objectives are. Matrix management implies a degree of permanence in the project structure and its staffing; it is not so economical as the departmentalized arrangement and budgetary provision should be made for enough staff in each project. Where the numbers of staff in each discipline are small, such as ones, twos or threes, then matrix management may be somewhat impractical and will be seen as costly in staff terms. It is thus more suitable for bigger companies and the larger, longer-term and more complex project.

Despite these drawbacks, individuals working in matrix structures often like it as they develop a sense of identity with the project goal and receive stimulation from outside their own discipline through other team members. They can develop a sense of being part of something greater, in which they have a personal, if small, stake. Functional heads can use this to their advantage; by noting the skills and progress of each individual, they can use the opportunities that each new project brings to direct staff into tasks where their experience is broadened. Most individuals will respond to this and see it as evidence of management taking care of their personal development.

Matrix management shows some clear advantages but it is nevertheless a compromise solution; although most of the disciplines of the company may be represented in the matrix structure, some important ones may be left out because it is simply too difficult or not the policy to include them. Purchasing is one example of a function that may not appear in the matrix because it may be the policy that all purchasing is done centrally and the buyers may be in a different building or even a different factory. Manufacturing shops are another case where development prototype work may have to take its turn in the queue, along with routine, profit-making production work, and priorities will be set by the shop's own management. In this case, the Project Manager has no more authority than the manager in the simple project case; here he will have to use his influence rather than ability to direct in order to ensure progress.

The semi-autonomous project group

Whereas the matrix structure may be something of a compromise, the **semi-autonomous project group** removes that disadvantage by creating an organization within a company that has all the facilities at its disposal to develop, produce and market the product. The project group functions as though it were a small, independent company but within a larger organization, all its attention being directed on just one product. Staff seconded to the project group are relieved of all other responsibilities and report to the Project Manager who may be given director status. The Project Manager will be in a similar position to the Managing Director of a small company, with complete discretion over how money is spent within an agreed budget; he is able to recruit staff where necessary and contract for outside work. He will usually be responsible for marketing and have discretion to set prices and

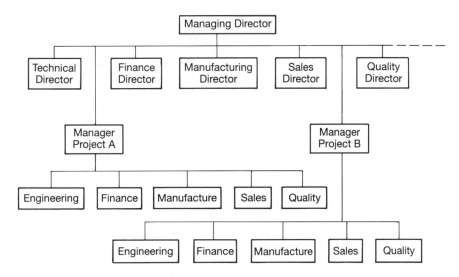

Figure 3.4   The semi-autonomous project organization.

establish production schedules. His principal reporting responsibility will be for the money spent and profit made; he will be expected to achieve targets agreed with his superiors on the main board. The organization structure for the semi-autonomous project group is shown in Figure 3.4.

It will be appreciated that there is a duplication of staff in many areas, and it would seem to be the least efficient in labour terms compared to the other methods, but some large companies have taken this approach and found it successful. One of the first was the du Pont chemical company which coined the term 'venture management' in the 1960s, to describe the fact that each project was seen as a venture aimed at making a profitable return over the whole product cycle. Product management is also a term that is coming into use to describe a total responsibility from the birth of the product concept to the ending of production. Although initially associated with sales personnel, the concept of the Product Manager is starting to be recognized as a much wider role, and in some industries the term Product Manager will come to replace Project Manager. Johnson and Johnson in the USA has taken the semi-autonomous group even further by creating hundreds of small divisions, each run by a committed 'Product Champion'.

The creation of semi-autonomous project groups marks a complete break with the more traditional, functionally organized companies; the roles of the function heads are further reduced in terms of any effective control over staff in their discipline. Given the rapidly changing nature of contemporary business, there will still be a role for the function head, but it will tend towards a broadly based role that concerns more general matters of policy, strategy and shaping the organization to meet the challenge of the future.

There are good reasons to believe that the semi-autonomous project group will become more popular and accepted in the future; some of them are:

- *Changing patterns of work*
  In the future people will tend to work more for themselves, less for large corporations. Some of the traditional benefits of long service with big companies, such as

pensions, extra holidays, etc., are becoming less valued by employees as they perceive a business world with far less certainty; too many have experienced reorganizations and redundancy to have much real expectation of a lifetime career with one employer. The more able and adventurous will develop and market their own specialist skills. Projects will be specially formed to exploit one product using such specialist people, who will remain with it only as long as is necessary. Modern information technology systems will mean that many will work from home for much of the time.

- *Changing nature of companies*
  Currently many companies, particularly large ones, are examining the nature of their organization. Above all, there is a drive to reduce the costs of running the business and thus offer more competitively priced products. One area that is coming under scrutiny is middle management; layers of middle managers are a feature of the more traditional structure. With the semi-autonomous group, there is no need for them; the project group contains only as much management staff as it needs to function and it reports directly to the Managing Director. Projects are temporary affairs, they exist only as long as the project has still to be completed – once it is finished the group is disbanded – thus some of the costs and commitments associated with permanent staff may be avoided. We may in the future see companies divesting themselves of much of their permanent staff and instead turning into organizations that exist by creating the conditions where they can sponsor more entrepreneurial groups of well-paid specialists, brought together to successfully conclude a project. That does not mean the end of the large company – these will still function where large investments in research or production facilities are required or where the product is massive and complex, what will change is the large permanent staff base.

- *Changing levels of aspiration*
  Rising education standards and generally greater awareness have brought with them rising levels of expectation and aspiration. People expect to gain more in terms of job satisfaction and this includes a desire for some greater degree of influence in the conduct of their working lives. The short lines of control and communication in the semi-autonomous group mean that individuals can exercise a greater degree of influence over the project than would be the case in the traditional structure. Personnel can identify more closely with both the project goals and the outcome, their degree of commitment can be expected to rise and this will be recognized as valuable to the parent organization.

Faced with running a semi-autonomous group, the Project Manager may have to be much less of a specialist than with matrix or simple project structures. Within a broadly based, entrepreneurial frame, he must be able to see both the nature of the developing product and of the market while, at the same time, balancing these two requirements. He will need the skills of leadership rather than technical skills, and business acumen rather than pure administrative ability. He will have to worry much less about exerting influence with function heads and much more about influencing potential customers, his identification with both the project and the product will be total.

A derivative of the semi-autonomous group is the **joint venture group** or **company**, specifically set up to manage a project where two or more organizations wish to collaborate in a venture. This arrangement is popular where large, multi-national projects are undertaken. When two or more companies decide to collaborate, the matrix type of structure across the whole project is impossible. Matrix structures may exist within each company for their part in the project but it would be difficult to bring them together as a whole – there are just too many complications where individuals work for different organizations, possibly in different countries, with different terms, conditions, cultures, etc. However, a complex project needs more coordination and control than a simple one and the response can be of two forms:

1. One company, usually the one with the larger stake in the project (often financially but possibly technologically) takes on the direction of the whole project and the other companies accept the direction given. Here the leading company is acting as a '**prime contractor**' and may appoint a Project Manager to look after the overall direction of the project, who is quite separate from a Project Manager in the same company who manages that company's contribution to the product.

2. A controlling group is formed from members of all the participating companies. At the simplest, they could form a steering committee that meets to assess progress and give directions. At the other extreme, they could constitute a Board of directors for a joint venture company; members of the joint venture Board would normally be directors or senior managers within their parent companies. Where such companies are formed, the Managing Director will act as the overall project manager, setting the direction of the project and enjoying a great deal of autonomy. However, he or she is still accountable to the companies that created the joint venture and a high-level committee may be formed to monitor progress.

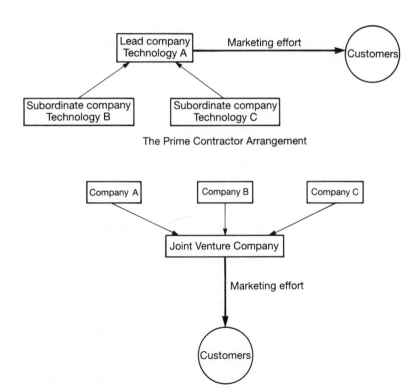

Figure 3.5 Organization structure where cooperative ventures are involved.

A number of legal options are open for the pursuit of joint ventures, including contractual joint ventures, in which a contract to work together is agreed between the companies but no separate legal entity is formed, partnerships and joint venture companies. In the latter case, a company is formed which is a separate legal entity and in which the cooperating companies are shareholders. The company will operate in the normal way for accounting and tax purposes; the individual companies will be liable to the extent of their share capital involvement, although they may be asked to provide additional indemnities to third parties if the assets of the joint venture company are small but the undertaking is large. These structures are shown in Figure 3.5.

One final structure that should be mentioned is the **task force**: this lies somewhere between the matrix structure and the semi-autonomous group. Usually it is constituted on a short-term basis with a very specific goal in mind; members are dedicated solely to the force and the group is given considerable authority to act. This approach has become associated with 'Simultaneous Engineering' and is discussed more fully in Chapter 5.

Leadership and the individual

Facets of leadership

Without a leader the project will get nowhere, responsibility for leading the project is vested in the Project Manager. He or she may be able to delegate many aspects of their job, but leading is one thing they cannot: it is their principal function. The Project Manager is there to:

1. set the direction of the project;
2. define and explain its objectives to the participants;
3. create the framework in which the project can flourish;
4. control the activities of the participants towards meeting the goal.

Four distinct facets are mentioned, each is separate but indispensable to the task of leadership.

When projects are started, there will usually be well-understood or simple-stated goals, such as 'maximize profit', 'achieve $x\%$ of the market', etc., but to take such statements and translate them into a plan of action that has some chance of success will be the first task of the Project Manager; almost certainly, it will precede the formal launch of the project. There are always a number of ways that any task can be accomplished and it is for the Project Manager to define the most suitable one, it is this that sets the direction of the project. The Project Manager will not plan that task in every detail, but must be able to define, in outline, all steps that are necessary. Some aspects will be established from his own knowledge and experience, but in others advice must be sought. He must be aware of his own limitations and know when to accept advice himself. In the end, his should be the final decision on the shape of the project, the timescales and the tasks – but it need not be. Most project plans are scrutinized by either client organizations or Boards of directors; in many (most) cases, they will accept the recommendations of the Project Manager but for various reasons choose a different direction. The Project Manager must accept this and adapt his view. The direction that is taken, once the project starts, is largely in the hands of the Project Manager: he must be alive to changes in circum-stances or deviations from plan but that central direction must always be in mind; his actions must be focused on it and he must be able to instil it in others.

A project brings together individuals in a common cause and, to be a success, all must take up the cause. The leader must provide the inspiration for others to follow – but the followers need to be believers in the first place. The Project Manager is thus both a 'prophet' and a 'salesman': few will become converts without question, most will need to be persuaded. Above all, he must be a communicator, for this he needs to be able to explain to his team, in language they can understand, the objectives of the project, the role that each has to play and the importance of their contribution. He must – by personal example and perceived commitment – be able to convince people of the value of the project, both to the organization and to themselves. Only when people understand and accept the objectives of the project as being their own objectives will he have succeeded; but when it is achieved, he will have laid the foundation for success.

Projects do not exist in a vacuum, they live in a multi-dimensional world that is at once technical, physical, cultural and political. The Project Manager needs to manage these dimensions, which sometimes coincide and at other times conflict, so that the project can succeed and flourish. He must set about creating the environment in which the necessary staff are brought together and in which they can work to the best of their ability. The staff will look to him to provide for certain of their needs; if they are not satisfied, then he will be diminished in their eyes. Basically they will expect their physical and technical needs to be looked after – i.e. good working conditions and the right technical equipment and mix of technical skills. They may already be satisfactory – but if not and he cannot satisfy them, he will either be seen by his team as not caring or having insufficient influence to make his point felt.

The culture of the company and the politics associated with the project are other dimensions of the environment. The company culture can be the hardest to deal with, it embodies the attitudes, values and practices of the organization and can be very deep rooted. It has been noted that in companies that were originally family businesses, the family culture can persist for a generation or more after the original owners have sold out and the firm has become a large public company unconnected to the founders. The Project Manager's first task is to recognize the culture for what it is; it may be beneficial if the accent is on adaptability, responsiveness and inven-tiveness, but less than helpful if it lays a strong emphasis on departmental loyalty and strict adherence to procedure. Brave Project Managers may try to bring about a cultural change on their project but without backing from the most senior level they are unlikely to succeed. To try to change the culture and fail may do more harm than good and the person that suffers most could be the Project Manager – he may be perceived as not fitting in.

If culture is a hard battleground on which to fight, politics is much more fruitful. All projects exist against some form of political background – it may be national politics if a military project is involved or company politics in the private sector, or sometimes both. Whereas attitudes and values tend to be ingrained and slow to change, politics is primarily about opportunity and self-interest, for example: who is to be in charge of whom, who gets the largest budget allocation, which project might be cancelled, etc.? Where opportunities are concerned, people can be more flexible and reactive; they will be much more open to negotiation and will adapt where they see advantages for themselves, provided that it remains within their cultural frame-work. If the Project Manager is sensitive to these issues, he may be able to use it to his advantage by identifying the persons with the real influence, forming alliances with them and fostering mutually co-operative arrangements. It is the exercise of influence from a weak position of legitimate power that will characterize the Project Manager who can read the politics of the project environment, and it is often for just this quality that senior Project Managers are chosen. The ability to influence an important but difficult client, or to hold a joint venture project together in the face of both internal or inter-company pressures, may be seen as among the most important attributes; failure in these areas can lead to failure of the project overall. The project can certainly be damaged if it is seen to be a political object over which others are fighting for influence or resources. The Project Manager must, as far as he is able, shield his team from such damaging influences; if it becomes apparent that the project is a political football, it can easily destroy the morale of the team as they become unsure of what the real objectives are and what their future might be.

Having set the direction, it needs to be maintained: the project will not necessarily steer itself towards its goal. Without course corrections, the project may wander off in a new direction of its own. Holding the project on course is the process of control – it is the action by which the Project Manager ensures that the instructions he has given are carried out as intended. A failure to establish proper control mechanisms is to hand the process of leadership to others. It implies that there are no constraints on the actions of the team members. When this occurs, projects are described as 'out of control' or 'leaderless'. The Project Manager exercises control in a number of ways, both formal and informal. Chief among the formal methods is the reporting struc-ture that he sets up, and in so doing he delegates some of his authority to others below him but within specific boundaries. The price for this authority is that the delegate must report on the actions taken and the progress. The Project Manager has the power to set reporting standards and he should see to it that they are enforced. A Project Manager may lose the respect of his staff for a number of reasons but demanding good and timely reports is not one of them; a failure to ensure that reporting standards are met may be seen as evidence of lack of interest or under-standing on the part of the manager and that is far more damaging. The project is more than just a collection of individuals who report to a manager, it is a collective effort. The leader, through the actions taken and directives given, can bind the team together or allow it to degenerate. Calling the team together at regular inter-vals generates a sense of cohesion; it allows decisions to be formulated on the basis of consensus and also lets team members report on their progress, as well as hearing the progress of others. No one wants to let the team down and be seen in the eyes of colleagues as not pulling one's weight. Simply by creating the conditions where team members not only report to the Project Manager, but to the team itself, can result in a self-controlling mechanism.

Team building

Team building has been widely discussed in contemporary management texts but it should be viewed with a little scepticism. Team selection is a favoured topic and suggestions are put forward about choosing the right mix of personality types to compliment one another. While nobody would deny that the right mix of personal attributes is desirable in the team members, it is often a matter over which the Project Manager has no control. In most cases, the people allocated to the project are those that have the required technical skills and are available at the time the project starts. Unless the company is very forward-looking, it is unlikely that any were tested for personality traits at the time they joined. However, a project can succeed with a mix of personal traits that is less than ideal but personality clashes can reduce team effectiveness if they go unchecked. Where they are detected, the Project Manager should confront the individuals over the reasons for their differences – if they cannot be resolved, the best solution is to change one or other person when a suitable replacement becomes available. Team morale is another well-discussed subject; in general, if people are given good pay and conditions, secure prospects and interesting work, morale will not be a problem. To keep up morale, the Project Manager's strongest card is his own enthusiasm and force of personality, but where pay and working conditions are poor and the project is starved of cash or its future appears clouded, morale will simply drop. The power of the Project Manager to do much about it may be limited.

Leadership styles

What style of leadership to adopt is a question that all Project Managers should ask themselves, but few actually do. To some extent, the style goes with the individual, it is an extension of his personality, interests and how he perceives his work. Nevertheless, choices are open to the manager if he is perceptive enough to see them. In general, two styles are possible: permissive or directive, but the choice will depend on the manager's position and the nature of the project. Three principal factors determine the position of the leader with respect to both the task that faces him and his team:

1. *The degree of task structure*
   This defines the organization, the goal and the plan to achieve it. Where these are highly formalized and defined in detail, the task is well structured and this would be expected of a development project. A pure research project designed to explore new and creative approaches would be far less structured at the outset, but it may acquire a more structured approach as it moves towards a conclusion.
2. *The leader's power position*
   This is defined by the authority accorded to his position as defined by the type of project organization and the influence he can exert.
3. *The leader's relations with team members*
   The leader may either be liked or disliked, accepted or mistrusted.

The characteristics of the leadership approaches are:

1. *Permissive, democratic*
   With this approach, the leader adopts a style that allows free discussion, decision-making on a group basis and an approach that encourages good interpersonal relationships among the team.
2. *Directive, autocratic*
   With this approach, the leader concentrates on achieving the goal through directing and controlling the tasks and is less concerned with the views of the people involved.

3. *Laissez-faire, abdicative*

With this approach, the leader outlines clear goals to the team but they are then free to pursue them in any way they choose.

Which of these approaches to choose to get the best results from the team will depend on the combination of factors 1–3. Table 3.1 gives the style of leadership that is appropriate to effective achievement of the project goal for each combination of situation factors.

Table 3.1 shows that for most of the common situations found in project teams a directive, controlling style of leadership is likely to bring the best results. Where the leader is in a very good position, such as situation 1, the team is waiting to be led and is ready to accept direction. It is this situation that all leaders should hope to achieve – if they are not already in this position, they should look to how best they can create it. Situations 2 and 3 also require a directing style. In 2 the leader should adopt firm control to create a sense of power by exerting influence over the group and creating the illusion of situation 1. In 3 he should concentrate on creating a more structured approach to the task through goal-setting, planning and ensuring the tasks are carried out, again moving to situation 1. In a less good position, such as 4, where the leader is accepted but the task or goal is not well defined and his power weak, a permissive style may be more appropriate, thus drawing the team together and allowing group members to participate in generating ideas and goal-setting. This may lead to creative or new approaches, as well as general agreement as to what the objectives are – and from there a more structured approach can be evolved which, ultimately, will require a directive style to ensure success.

In situation 5, where the task is well defined, the leader's position is strong but he is not well liked or accepted, he may do better by adopting a permissive style that concentrates on building an improved relationship in which members do not feel threatened but feel more valued and are encouraged to cooperate. Cases 6 and 7 are more difficult for the leader and the choice of approach will be down to the individual. In case 6 he might initially try a permissive approach with a view to improving his standing but that may only emphasize his weak position of power, or he could try a more directive approach and thereby create a power situation but at the risk of becoming even less popular. With case 7, a directive style would initially concentrate on giving the task a structure, and the leader has the power to do this; once a structure is established, he may wish to concentrate on improving his team relationship. Case 8 is the worst possible for the leader and here a directive style is appropriate. Without it, the team will fall apart, only active intervention will ensure that the team is focused on the goal; the leader has nothing to lose by adopting it.

Table 3.1 Optimum leadership styles for alternative team situations

No.	Leader/member relations	Task structure	Power position	Optimum leadership style
1	Good	Structured	Strong	Directive
2	Good	Structured	Weak	Directive
3	Good	Unstructured	Strong	Directive
4	Good	Unstructured	Weak	Permissive
5	Moderate to poor	Structured	Strong	Permissive
6	Moderate to poor	Structured	Weak	No clear choice
7	Moderate to poor	Unstructured	Strong	No clear choice
8	Moderate to poor	Unstructured	Weak	Directive

This brief guide is certainly an oversimplification of the situations that actually arise, each must be judged by the manager on its merits at the time. The actions he takes may depend not only on his perception of the situation, but also on the degree of confidence he has in (a) his own ability to control the project, and (b) the backing he will receive from his superiors. If the leader does not feel well supported from above, he will find it difficult to feel confident in whatever actions he takes or style he adopts.

Leadership qualities

There can be little doubt that some people make very much better project leaders than others. Two individuals may possess the same technical background and ability, yet one will adapt to the leader's role much more easily than the other. The ability to lead is a quality that is quite distinct from technical abilities and it derives, in part, from the personality of the individual. To some extent, leadership can be taught and it is also an acquired skill – the more you do it, the better you get – but a part of it too is inherent in the individual at the start. Leadership implies the ability to influence and direct a group towards some common goal. It contains within it the concept of power over the direction of the group and over individuals. However, the leader also takes responsibility for the direction he gives and the outcome that transpires. Whereas most people have some desire, however small, to exert some influence in their working lives, not all can live so happily with the responsibility that goes with it. Such people do not make good leaders, fear of responsibility generates a timid approach to situations and this soon communicates itself to the team.

The personal qualities that mark out the good leader are:

1. *Enthusiasm for the job*: this applies both to the task of leading the project and to the project itself. The success of some very novel projects has been credited in some part to the leader who has taken on the role of 'Project Champion', totally committed to its accomplishment, able to sell the concept of the project both to directors and customer organizations and inspiring enthusiasm in the project team. A person may be promoted to the post of Project Manager but it is hardly possible to order that person to become a 'Project Champion', that is something that springs from within and may lie with the individual's own level of desire for success.
2. *Technical understanding*: with today's complex products, it is not possible for a Project Manager to understand all aspects of the technology of a new product. In practice, it is not necessary and he does not need to be able to generate solutions to technical problems (although that can be useful); but the Project Manager must possess sufficient understanding to enable him to communicate with the technical staff on their terms and also be able to grasp the implications of what is being said to him on technical issues. A Project Manager with no real understanding of the technology involved may have difficulty in inspiring confidence in the team. He may be seen purely as an administrator with little else to contribute to the project by way of advice or insight into the development process.
3. *Broad vision*: the Project Manager must be able to see the whole picture, his is the responsibility for pulling together into a cohesive whole all the strands of the

project: technical, marketing, production, etc., and ensuring that each has the appropriate priority at every stage of the project. A manager who interests himself primarily in one specialism at the expense of other important aspects of the project will be less likely to create conditions for success than one who can take the broad view and see the contribution of each specialism for its place and its worth.

4. *Goal-setting ability*: people need the stimulus of a target or goal, there may be a number of these at various points in the project. It is unlikely that the Project Manager will plan the project in all its detail, but he must be able to assess plans for realism and achievability, set meaningful goals and communicate these to the team members. He must also show interest in progress and foster the view that goal achievement is important.

5. *Ability to delegate*: the manager cannot do it all himself, his role is to direct the work of the team, not do their work for them. For many people who come into management roles in mid-career, this is one of the most difficult aspects with which to come to terms. To succeed as a leader the individual must give up much of his direct authority to others and be able to trust them to use that authority wisely. He must be able to feel comfortable in this situation but he can help himself by setting up a reporting structure so that he is always informed of routine matters but consulted only when his personal input is needed.

6. *Interpersonal skills*: like all managers, the project leader achieves results through other people, to get the best from a team the leader needs to exercise a degree of sensitivity to individuals. He should be alive to the personal aspects both of his team and others within the organization upon whom he depends for success. He should be able to recognize personal contributions and give praise where it is due; where things are not as they should be he must be able to express a tactful disapproval. Some managers have performed well with a very blunt, even rude, attitude and occasionally it is necessary where team members lack individual drive or are in the habit of taking refuge in excuses. However, such an approach needs to be used with caution where highly educated or sensitive people are involved – it can result in resentment that may become deep-rooted and backfire on the manager.

7. *Tolerance of fortune*: despite the best-laid plans, innovative projects are always a hostage to fortune; there will be failures as well as successes along the way but the leader must show tolerance in the face of frustration. He must not be shattered by setbacks or defeat, should accept victories without excessive emotion and be able to 'keep his head when all around are losing theirs'.

The structure of the project team

Every project will have its own structure dictated by the objectives of the project, its size and complexity. With simple projects where the Project Manager acts as a coordinator, it may be difficult to define a formal structure other than for one or two staff that report to him directly; but with more complex undertakings and with a greater sense of permanence, teams will be formed expressly for the purposes of completing the project. In general, project teams are structured in a way that resembles the structure of the parent company. A matrix management arrangement may be in place and staff will be drawn from their specialist disciplines; the Project Manager may wish to group staff in related disciplines under a Section Leader or

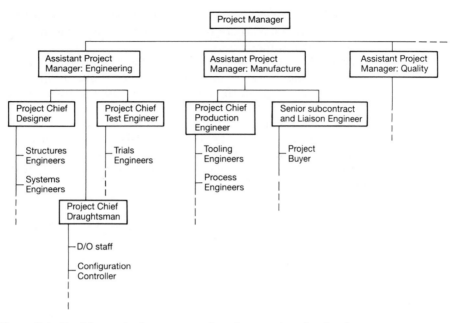

Figure 3.6   Partial organization structure for a large engineering development project.

Assistant Project Manager reporting directly to himself. Just how many assistants are needed will depend on the scale of the project and, possibly, the reporting structure of the company itself. For example, it may not be politic to have someone in one division reporting to the Project Manager through a person from another division, although in some companies it may work if there is sufficient agreement and cooperation between divisional heads. A part of the reporting structure for a large engineering development project is shown in Figure 3.6. It will be seen that it represents the company structure in miniature – but not all the functions of a company need appear, for example, accounting may appear in a matrix structure but finance is unlikely to be included.

Summary

The 'project'-based approach to the creation of new products or undertaking new ventures is increasingly being recognized as the style appropriate to today's conditions. This stems from a number of factors but chief among them are the growing complexity of modern products, the more formalized contractual arrangements that exist between project sponsors and contractors, changing patterns of work and new levels of individuals' expectations. Companies have responded in a number of ways but with larger projects the matrix style of organization has become popular. It marks a break with tradition as responsibility for day-to-day direction of staff is vested in the Project Manager rather than the functional head. Introducing a matrix arrangement can cause some problems, but firms that have employed it have generally found it successful. For more entrepreneurial projects, forming a semi-autonomous project group can also work well; with this arrangement, the project group takes on the overall profit responsibility for the project and thus diverges further from the parent organization. There is good reason to think that this approach will become more popular in the future.

Project Managers are a new breed trained in the techniques of project management and able to survive in a world that has at once technical, financial, schedule, political and interpersonal dimensions. They are the driving-force in the project, for it is they who must provide the leadership that is vital for success. Leadership has many facets, it requires enthusiasm that communicates itself to the team, the ability to set the direction of the project and vigilance to ensure that the project remains on track. It is not a role that all can handle well, Project Managers should be chosen with some care and good ones should be recognized for their worth; if lost, they may not be easily replaced.

4

Planning: the way ahead

- Organizing the planning function
- Setting out the plan
- Bar charts and logic
- Network analysis
- Networking in practice, faults and cures

Without a properly laid-out plan, nothing can proceed in an orderly fashion – no doubt, a true enough proposition, yet historically management in the UK has paid too little attention to planning and earned for itself a world-wide reputation for late delivery, frequently termed 'the British disease'. The reasons for this attitude are beyond the scope of this text, but may be a mixture of:

- a belief that management is more of an art than a science;
- a lack of understanding of modern planning techniques;
- setting out a plan implies stating a set of goals against which the performance of the manager may be judged.

None of these are valid reasons for not taking planning seriously.

Organization for planning

The amount of effort and the organization of the planning function will depend on the company and the scale of the project. Projects are usually planned by: (a) the Project Manager; (b) a project planning group or engineer attached to the project; or (c) a central project planning facility.

Planning by the Project Manager

This is common where projects are relatively small or of short duration. Here the objective will be clearly defined and well understood by the manager, who will need to assess the tasks required to complete the project and the necessary resources in terms of capital and labour. In such an arrangement, planning will often be set out in the form of a chart or planning sheet and by negotiation and discussion with the various departmental managers a workable schedule of activities will be derived. When this is complete, the Project Manager may then send out work authorization requests which will allow the departmental managers to carry out the tasks. He will need to progress the tasks as they occur and liaise regularly with the departmental heads.

Planning by an engineer or group dedicated to the project

As projects become larger a dedicated team of individuals may be seconded to the Project Manager that takes its day-to-day direction from him. A part of that team is likely to be a project planning engineer or, in the case of a very large project, a team of planners. Their work will include assessing the tasks and their durations, assessing resource levels, creating schedules, charts and networks, issuing plans, monitoring progress and reporting to the Project Manager. In this arrangement, the Project Manager will have an interest only in the project plan at a broad level, setting out the general framework of activities, objectives and timescales for the planning engineers to turn into detailed activity plans. He may well have sought the advice of the planning engineers at the outset of the project as their experience of the order in which things have to be done, together with an appreciation of the likely durations and staff demands, may have a direct bearing on the concept of the project. When this experience is available, no Project Manager should fail to make use of it; realism at the outset can temper over-optimism and save embarrassing situations later on. The planners will remain with the project only as long as the project remains in being.

Planning by a central planning group

This approach is used by some very large or multinational companies and is often applied to capital projects. Here a central organization is required to interpret a high-level master strategy and turn it into a series of specific project plans. Materials may be purchased on a worldwide basis or competitions run for the supply of capital equipment.

There will be a Project Manager dedicated to the project and he will work on location receiving the materials procured through the central organization and implementing the plan. In some cases, the planning organization may not be in the same continent as the place where the work is carried out, hence regular and efficient progress reporting will be one of the Project Manager's main responsibilities.

Total responsibility for planning cannot, however, be left entirely to a remote group and there may be some activities which are entirely under the direction of the manager on site, for example, hiring of local labour. In such cases, with large capital projects, additional planning engineers will be needed on site to make more detailed plans, as well as communicating with the central group.

The role of planning in a development project

We shall consider planning by an engineer or group dedicated to a project, as outlined above, as this is often the case found in medium- to large-scale development projects and the principles are equally valid for smaller activities. The functions of the planning group will be:

- To translate the overall project goals into a series of identifiable activities which can be set out in a logical way that will achieve the desired end.
- To communicate the plan of activities to the staff responsible for carrying out the activities.
- To monitor the progress of activities and report to the Project Manager.
- To revise the plan in the light of events as they occur, in such a way as to preserve the overall objectives.

To perform these functions, the planning group will need to interface with the departments responsible for carrying out the tasks, principally Design, Manufacturing and Test. The group may also have to deal regularly with the Accounting Department for establishing costs and budgets; other departments, such as Quality Assurance and Marketing, may also have an input into the planning function as the project progresses. The relationship of the planning group to the other principal functional areas is given in Figure 4.1. It will be seen that planning is at the centre of a series of feedback loops running both in the upwards direction to the Project Manager and downwards through the functional disciplines. Overall programme objectives, timescales and costs will be set by the Project Manager but the creation of the plan that meets those constraints will require inputs to the planning process from the departments that carry out the work; typically these will be:

- lead times, costs and output rates from Manufacturing;
- trials definitions and test hardware demands from the Trials group;
- design philosophy, design tasks and manpower consumptions from the Design group;
- budgets from Accounts.

The function of the planners is to assess these inputs and then put them together in such a way that the objectives can be achieved. This may not be an easy task as when the first inputs are received there are likely to be problems with both the overall timescale and costs. Few projects of some size or complexity are planned successfully at the first go, much discussion will be needed between the planner and the responsible function heads. Design engineers tend to be cautious and may decide that they would like a large number of prototypes each to test a specific feature before the final system is assembled and tested. Trials engineers may generate demands for hardware that can be excessive and come too early in the programme for design and manufacturing processes to be complete. Manufacturing

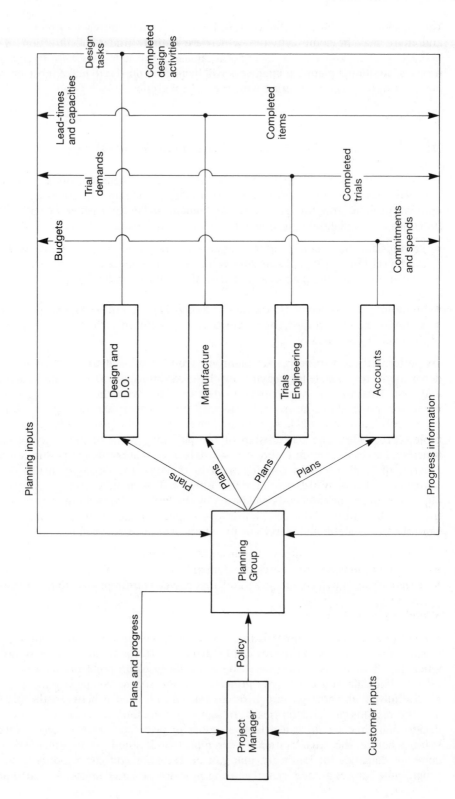

Figure 4.1 Functional relationships of the planning group.

engineers are sometimes over-optimistic about the time it takes to get things made, forgetting the difficulties and time penalties that come from the modifications, concessions and scrap that accompanies the manufacture of all newly designed items. The planning engineer must take a balanced view of these initial requests, challenging those areas that seem excessive while adding some contingency where experience says more time or effort is likely to be needed. As far as is possible, experience from past projects should be drawn upon; unless significant changes in operating methods are planned, a company's history is the best guide to its future.

No plan will ever remain static throughout the life of a project; however well conceived the original plan is, there will always be deviations that call for revisions. Regular assessment of progress is an equally vital element of the planning cycle and the planning group must continuously compare achievement with the plan. Where significant differences arise, this must be reported to the Project Manager. Besides reporting, the planning group will be required to suggest revisions which will ensure that the overall objective can still be achieved. The Project Manager's approval may well be needed to implement the new plan as it may call for changed priorities, more expenditure, overtime working, or any of a host of other possibilities.

Setting out the project plan

At the outset of projects, overall objectives will usually be fairly well established. Goals may not be known exactly, however, as market opportunities may play a part in the strategy and the precise objectives might vary as the project proceeds. If the object is to launch a new product, then completion of the development programme and the satisfactory conclusion of testing will be one clearly identifiable goal; the implementation of the production programme will be another. Along the way, a series of steps must be taken that form a logical progression, where each step builds upon the previous one and taking into account the time constraints while, at the same time, minimizing technical and financial risk. In the first instance, a feasibility study is usually carried out and in this phase the technical feasibility, potential market and financial risks and rewards are assessed. If the study shows both an acceptable risk and return, then the development programme can be set out observing the constraints and sub-goals. A convenient way of doing this is by the use of a logic and sequence diagram. Figure 4.2 shows an example for the prototype phase of a new product. In the figure the targets to be achieved during the programme are set out along the upper edge, these may be defined by the Marketing Department. Some targets may be fixed in time, such as the presence of a trade show, while others, such as customer demonstrations, are dependent upon the customers' reactions. Along the bottom edge are the constraints on progress; here they are Board-level approvals for continued work based on sufficient confidence in the programme. In the central area all the major activities are drawn in boxes with arrows used to link the activities to show the logic of the tasks. At the right-hand edge by the head of an arrow leading from a significant activity is written the particular item of knowledge to be gained from the completion of the activity. If the diagram is drawn with all the logic arrows pointing towards the bottom edge, then the listing of the knowledge gained will be arranged in the order it will be obtained. This can be particularly useful if significant decisions have to be taken at key points in the project. A look at the list of items of knowledge that appear above the head of

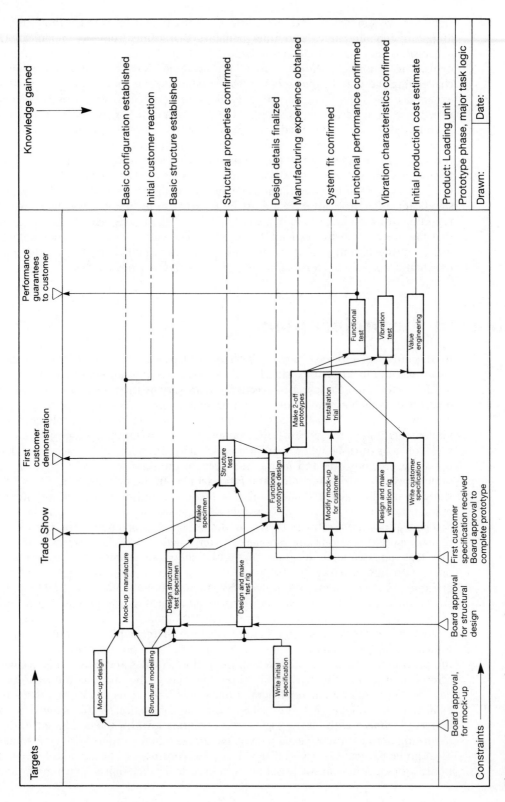

Figure 4.2 Logic and sequence diagram.

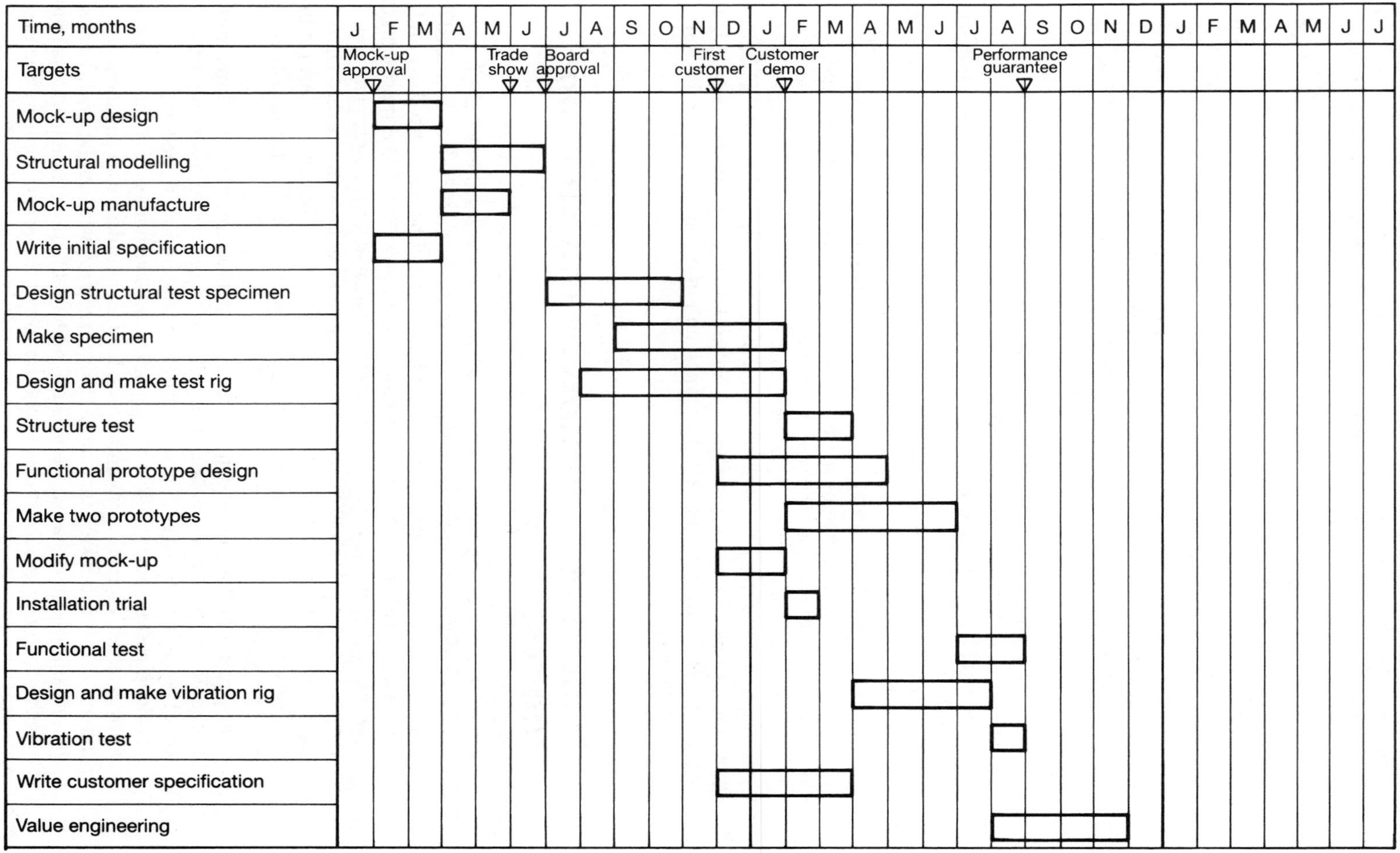

Figure 4.3 Bar chart drawn from the logic of Figure 4.2.

the arrow leading from the activity relating to the decision point will show what areas of the design are confirmed in terms of feasibility or performance, while those items listed below the arrow represent the areas of knowledge still to be established. These latter items represent the areas of uncertainty that should be examined at any decision point.

In this initial treatment of the project programme, no account has been taken of the likely durations of any of the tasks, the only time elements apppear in the dates fixed for any of the targets or constraints. The next step is to lay out the programme on a time basis; for this, the conventional representation is the **bar** or **Gantt chart**. The chart is normally drawn in two sections: a left-hand column which contains the activity description, and a larger right-hand area marked out with a horizontal timescale. Each activity is drawn against its activity description using a horizontal line or bar to represent the timing and duration. Figure 4.3 shows the bar chart constructed from the logic of Figure 4.2; the targets and constraints are marked along the top edge. An assumption has been made about the date by which a customer will have been found with sufficient interest to warrant the modification of the mock-up.

The bar chart has become a familiar and popular method of project control and most of the modern computerized project management systems have the ability to produce bar charts in a format similar to that shown in the figure. Representing the activities on timescales makes it easy to see their relationships and spot logical or planning difficulties before the plan is finally approved and put into operation. The weakness of the simple bar chart representation lies in the fact that although the interrelationship between activities in time is shown, the logic that lies behind it is not represented. To overcome this the linked bar chart is sometimes used. In this chart arrows are used to connect the completion of one activity with the start of the succeeding one.

Example 4.1: Prototype construction and test

Figure 4.4 shows a linked bar chart drawn to represent the design, manufacture and testing of some prototypes. A similar format to that described has been used but an additional table has been created beneath the chart and, in this case, it has been used for manpower planning. The visual representation that the bar chart gives makes it particularly suitable for resource planning. The format shown with an area for constructing a table beneath the bar chart is a convenient and popular planning tool. The bar chart showing the logical links also serves to show clearly any difficulties or undesirable features that may exist in the plan.

Inspection of this initial plan can lead to a better one: in the example shown in the figure there is a gap in testing activities from weeks 39 to 46; if this gap could be closed, the overall project duration could be shortened with a possible saving in cost through project management involvement over a shorter period. Furthermore, there is a potential overload in the design department as it is known that it is unlikely that more than three designers can be made available for anything other than a very short period. In this example the activities which effectively govern the overall duration of the programme are the design

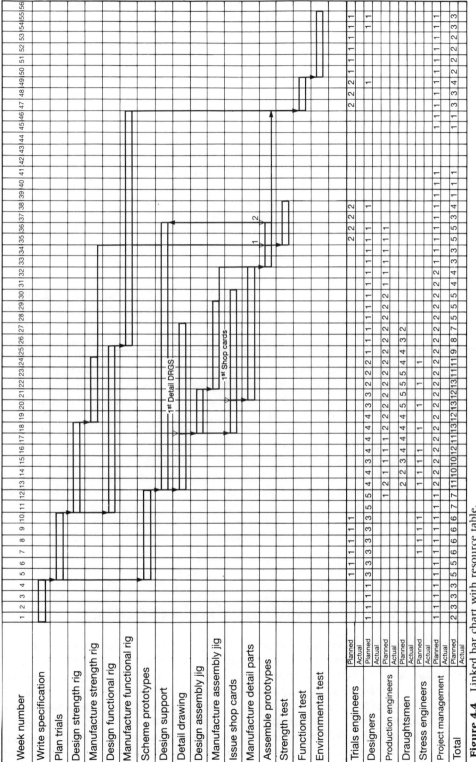

Figure 4.4 Linked bar chart with resource table.

and manufacture of a functional rig. This is a complex, automated device designed to function the prototype through many operational cycles continuously; straightforward functioning can, however, be done without the aid of the rig. The strength test will result in the destruction of the item under test but the strength rig is a much simpler item to design and manufacture than the functional rig. No special rigs are needed for environmental testing as existing test chambers can be used.

The difficulties can be overcome by rescheduling the trials, so that the first activity is now the environmental test – this can start as soon as the first prototype is available. The manpower demand in the design office can be eased by noting that the design and manufacture of the strength rig can be moved to week 34 without affecting the overall programme. At the end of the environmental testing, the prototype can be inspected and refurbished and then used for the strength test. The second prototype will have to wait for the functional rig to be completed before the functional testing can begin.

Using the reasoning derived from the plan in Figure 4.4, it has been shown in Figure 4.5 that the project can be completed in 49 weeks rather than the original 55. Furthermore, the demand for designers has been reduced to three except for a two-week period where it goes up to four. Figure 4.5 also illustrates the use of the bar chart for demonstrating progress and highlighting critical areas that need management attention. Progress is indicated by shading the proportion of the activity bar that represents the degree of progress achieved. When a line is ruled in to represent the time at which progress has been assessed, the project position becomes clear. In the example the project is running three weeks behind schedule, both in terms of detail drawing and the manufacture of detail parts. Although the design and manufacture of the assembly rig is four weeks behind, there is a three-week period by which the manufacture can move back without holding up the start of assembly work. A comparison of the planned and actual staffing level given in the table below shows that the overall number of staff made available has not met the plan and in the four weeks prior to 'time now' staffing has fallen considerably, particularly in respect of draughtsmen and production engineers.

The usefulness of bar charts is shown by their popularity with Project Managers when conducting the weekly or monthly progress review. Departmental heads or section leaders responsible for executing the various tasks can see at a glance the effect of failing to complete the work on time.

Scheduling activities with limited resources

The example above has touched upon the problem of limited resources influencing the practical order and timing of activities. The resource constraints may be staff, cash, test rig availability or any other item in limited supply. The problem becomes one of constructing a programme which satisfies the end-goals, yet does not violate the resource constraints. The essential approach is to move those activities that can be moved without affecting the project end-date until an acceptable programme of start and finish dates is achieved. This may not always be possible, in which case either more of the required resource must be made available or the project end-date

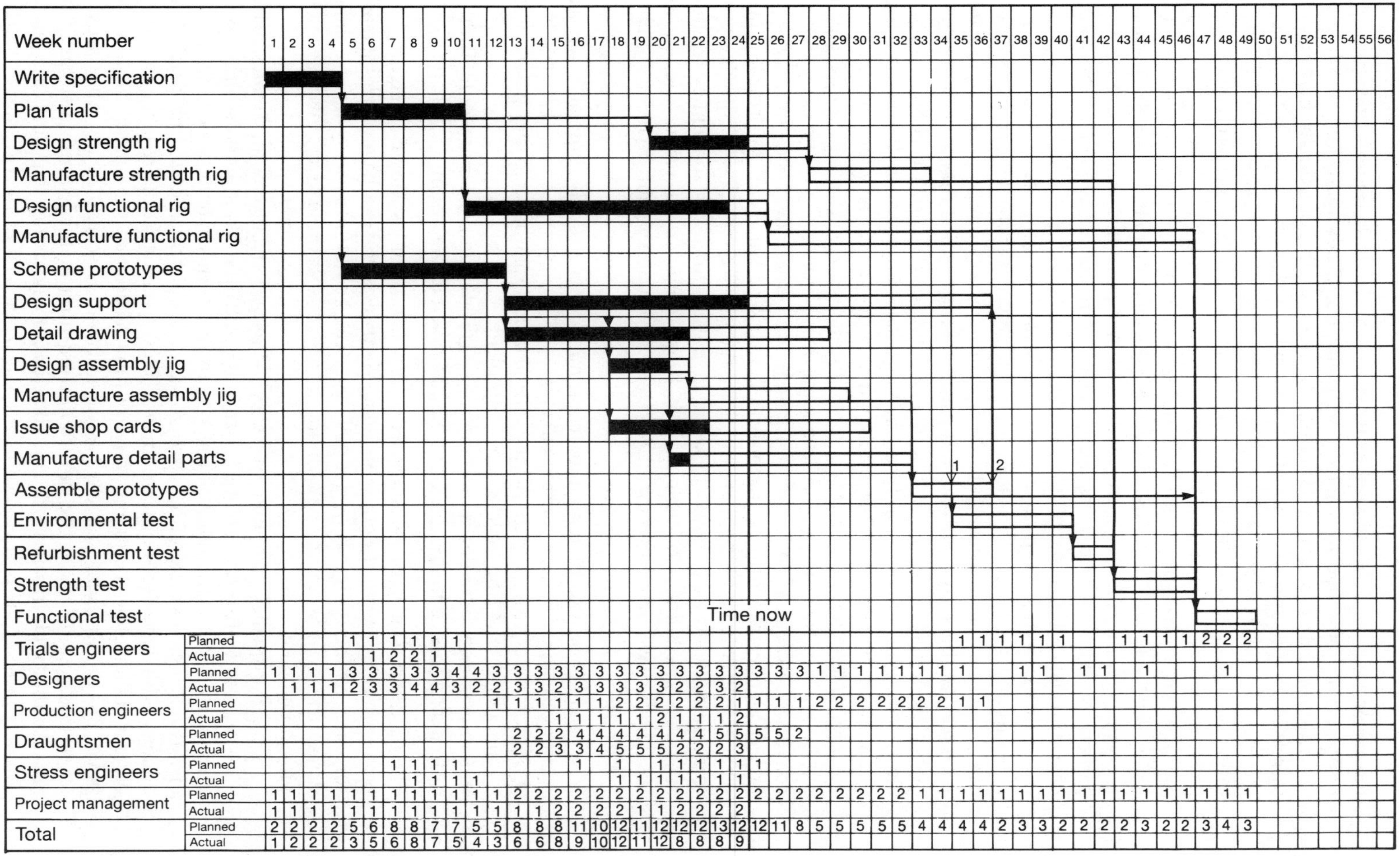

Week number: 1 2 3 4 5 6 7 8 9 10 11 12 13 14 15 16 17 18 19 20 21 22 23 24 25 26 27 28 29 30 31 32 33 34 35 36 37 38 39 40 41 42 43 44 45 46 47 48 49 50 51 52 53 54 55 56

Task rows:

- Write specification
- Plan trials
- Design strength rig
- Manufacture strength rig
- Design functional rig
- Manufacture functional rig
- Scheme prototypes
- Design support
- Detail drawing
- Design assembly jig
- Manufacture assembly jig
- Issue shop cards
- Manufacture detail parts
- Assemble prototypes
- Environmental test
- Refurbishment test
- Strength test
- Functional test

Time now

Resource rows (Planned / Actual):

- Trials engineers
- Designers
- Production engineers
- Draughtsmen
- Stress engineers
- Project management
- Total

Figure 4.5 Linked bar chart showing revised logic and progress.

moved backwards. Some resources may be flexible to the extent that most of the resource may be made available, given sufficient notification, and possibly at increased cost. For example, the staffing of the drawing office may be temporarily increased by the use of contract draughtsmen, while machining capacity can be increased by subcontracting out the work. Where subcontractors or temporary staff cannot be used, then overtime or weekend working will increase capacity. Some departmental managers object to overtime being scheduled into project plans, insisting that as they have the right to authorize overtime, then it is theirs alone to use when they feel the need to recover a difficult situation. One cannot help but sympathize with this view as regularly scheduling overtime and weekend working, particularly where several projects are being planned independently, can lead to a dangerous level of over-commitment.

The first step in solving the resource problem is to generate the demand profiles either from the bar chart or using a computer network analysis program (as described in the next section) and compare them with the known availability of the required resources. In this respect, it should be firmly borne in mind that the requirements of one particular project may not be the only demand, and the Project Manager should always discuss this with the departmental head concerned. In the short term the position may be reasonably clear and potential overloads easily identified, but in the medium to long term this may be very difficult as the precise timing of events may not be known. New and unforeseen work may arise in the intervening period or, conversely, expected work may not materialize. Where overloads can be seen, the project planner can inspect the project network or bar chart, in order to: (a) see what activities have 'float' that will allow them to be moved, and (b) give priority to those activities that should be done first. This process is sometimes referred to as 'hand scheduling', to distinguish it from computerized scheduling. Although it can be a very loose process in terms of scheduling rigour, it has a number of advantages:

- It need not be a particularly time-consuming process if only those activities where an overload occurs are considered.
- A more creative approach may be taken such as splitting activities where possible and also altering the logic where convenient.
- Subtle priority differences or knowledge of local conditions that would be difficult to define to a computer program may be taken into account.

The bar chart format when combined with a tabulation as shown in Figure 4.4 can be a convenient way of doing this, and when revised dates have been established, the chart can be re-drawn or the new dates can be put into the system as 'imposed dates'. The analysis routine will call up the activities at these dates, this may alter the project end-date.

The better-quality computer packages for project management, besides network analysis, also feature the ability to schedule activities taking into account resource constraints. A full description of the way in which this is done is beyond the scope of this text, but two algorithms are possible: 'serial scheduling' and 'parallel scheduling'. With **serial scheduling**, the activities in the network are taken in start-date order and then allocated to a resource or moved backwards in time until each can be fitted into the available capacity; as each activity is scheduled no other activity is taken into account. With the **parallel scheduling** method slices, in terms of time, are taken through the network and all activities whose start dates indicate that they can take place at the particular time are scheduled against their resource availability or moved backwards. Each method will produce a feasible schedule if the resources allow but the schedules need not be the same. It is a general feature of scheduling that for any given set of circumstances there may be many possible schedules.

Whichever algorithm is used, if there is a capacity problem, then the programs will generally produce schedules of two types: either the project end-date is held but showing inevitable overloads in resources in some areas or no resource limitations are violated but the end of the project is allowed to move backwards. In a practical situation most project planners would request both schedules to assess what the options are and the scale of the overload or likely slip in the end dates. At this point a little intelligent 'human logic' can be used to re-assess priorities, alter the logic or re-define the activities in an attempt to solve the problem. The ease with which the computer can re-schedule once the revised logic is put into the system can greatly speed up the process of finding a workable schedule. With on-line or PC-based systems, scheduling can thus become an interactive human and computer process.

Network analysis

Introduction and origins

Network analysis is the most significant technique to be introduced into the field of project management in the period since the Second World War. It came into vogue during the early 1960s and was hailed as the panacea for all project management ills. Such a precisely analytical technique would, it was claimed, allow the Project Manager total control and complete knowledge – gone would be the days of slippage and overruns. Things of course are never that simple, and although the technique has helped greatly in controlling large projects, it cannot compensate for slippage due to under-resourcing, unforeseen difficulties, cash problems or poor management. Although the technique has not been succeeded by any radically new method, its popularity did seem to decline with some Project Managers during the mid-1980s. The reasons for this will be discussed later, when it can be judged for its true value among the range of management methods.

The technique referred to variously as network analysis or **critical path analysis** (CPA), was invented in the USA where two independent developments during the late 1950s resulted in the general concept of using networks for project control. The US Navy's Special Projects Office devised PERT (Program Evaluation and Review Technique) in conjunction with the Lockheed Corporation and the consultants Booz-Allen and Hamilton. The first successful application was in the control of the Polaris nuclear missile development programme. During the same period the du Pont Chemical Company in conjunction with Reamington-Rand produced the 'critical path method' (CPM) for use in controlling new projects and plant maintenance programmes. In both these developments it was recognized that with a large amount of data to be manipulated the success of the technique depended on the use of a computer. Initially, large mainframe computers were necessary and hence use of network analysis tended to be restricted to those large organizations that could afford it. However, the greatly increased computing power of the personal computer has meant that the software capable of applying the technique is now available at very low prices – so low in fact that unless the projects are very small every Project Manager should have access to suitable software. Network analysis forms the basis of the majority of contemporary project management systems; a knowledge of it is fundamental to understanding and using them, hence an explanation of the technique is given in some depth.

The characteristics of networks

The **network** or **linear graph** is a stylized representation of a set of activities and events. It has a direct relationship to the bar chart as lines and logical links are used to represent a series of activities, but whereas the bar chart makes use of time as a scale factor, time is not represented diagrammatically in a network. Two conventions have arisen for drawing networks: **activity-on-arrow** and **activity-on-node**. We shall consider 'activity-on-arrow' networks as they have been the more popular until recently. The growing use of the computer packages that have tended to favour the 'activity-on-node' notation indicates, however, that activity-on-arrow will eventually be displaced. The activity-on-arrow method is the more generalized version and, once learned, converting to activity-on-node is relatively easy; this is not true in reverse.

With activity-on-arrow, the network consists of a series of '**nodes**', each representing an '**event**', which are joined by a series of arrows or '**arcs**', each of which represents an '**activity**' either leading to or arising from an event. The simplest possible network is one which consists of two nodes lying at either end of an arc representing a single activity, as shown in Figure 4.6.

All networks have a starting node or '**source**' and a finishing node or '**sink**'. When a series of arcs and nodes are drawn, the result is a more complex network, which if it has two or more arcs arising at or departing from a node, will have several possible routes through it from the source to the sink. Figure 4.7 shows a network with four nodes joined by five arcs or activities. Three paths exist through the network, the first is from Node 1 to Node 4 by way of Activity 1 and Activity 2 then Activity 5. The second path makes use of Activity 3 to go from Node 2 to Node 3, while the third is via Activity 1 to Node 2 and from there to the sink node via Activity 4.

It is a necessary feature of a network that the order in which the activities are drawn and the way in which they relate at the nodes correctly represents the order of events under study. The property that some activities necessarily follow other activities, while some activities can proceed in parallel with others, is termed the '**logic**' of the network. Figure 4.7 shows a network where each activity after Activity 1 springs directly from a node, the logic of the network could thus be described as:

(a) The network starts with Event (node) 1 followed by Activity 1;
(b) Activities 2, 3 and 4 cannot start before Activity 1 is complete;
(c) Activity 5 cannot start before both Activities 2 and 3 are complete; and
(d) Event (node) 4 cannot happen before Activities 4 and 5 are complete.

Now consider the following set of conditions:

(a) Activities 1 and 2 can start at the same time;
(b) Activity 3 cannot start before Activity 1 is complete;
(c) Activity 4 cannot start before Activity 3 is complete;
(d) Activity 5 cannot start before Activities 2 and 3 are complete;
(e) Activity 6 cannot start before Activity 4 is complete; and
(f)   the task ends when Activities 5 and 6 are complete.

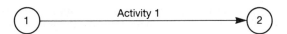

Figure 4.6 Simple network.

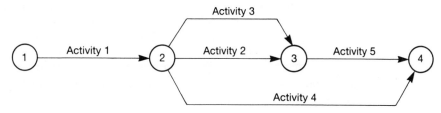

Figure 4.7 A network of several paths.

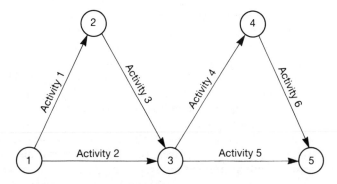

Figure 4.8 Incorrect network for conditions.

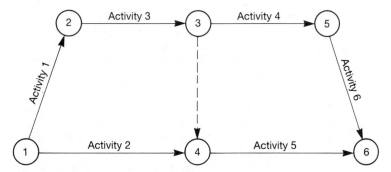

Figure 4.9 Correct network with dummy activity.

It might, at first glance, appear that the conditions can all be satisfied with a network of the form shown in Figure 4.8.

However, in Figure 4.8 this would be wrong as the implication for Activity 4 is that it cannot start before both Activities 2 and 3 are complete. In fact this set of conditions cannot be drawn as a network without the inclusion of an additional symbol which preserves the logic of the activities but is not an activity itself. Figure 4.9 shows the correct network that results and it includes a '**dummy**' activity joining Nodes 3 and 4; it is necessary to satisfy condition (d), on the previous page.

If the dummy were removed, it would be implied that Activity 5 need only wait for the conclusion of Activity 2 before it could start and this is clearly not the case as (d) states that both Activities 2 and 3 must be complete before the start of Activity 5. Dummy activities are conventionally shown as broken lines to indicate that they do not represent an activity; they have no duration, nor do they consume any resources.

In the simple examples shown in Figures 4.7–4.9 the activities have been given numbers and so have the nodes. In practical networks the activities are usually given descriptions that define the tasks they represent, while the nodes are always numbered or coded. It is common practice to number the nodes sequentially, so that the node at the head of an arrow has a higher value than the node at the tail. This allows elementary checks to be made on the network to ensure that no loops exist. A '**loop**' is a condition where a series of arcs and nodes leading from a particular node eventually leads back to itself. In practical terms, it means series of tasks forever repeating with no conclusion and is thus nonsense in the context of a project with a defined start and end. Any network that contains a loop cannot be analysed; if it is noticed that any node at the head of an arc is lower in value than the node at the tail, it is a warning that a loop may exist. The practical difficulty is that once the nodes are numbered, it can become difficult to add further arcs and nodes without having to completely re-number. One method that can help is to take the node numbering from a grid reference on the paper on which the network is drawn. (This convention has been used in Figure 4.13.) The only restriction upon drawing the network using this method is that no arcs should have their heads pointing to the left; provided that this convention is remembered, additional activities could be drawn in, if space permits. With large networks drawn on many sheets or networks subject to frequent changes, this convention can also become difficult and, in this case, a random numbering system may become necessary, the only condition being that no two nodes should have the same number. Computerized network analysis techniques make use of the tail node number, often termed the '**preceding event code**' and the head node number called the '**succeeding event code**' to define the activities that lie between. The codes need not be sequential, but computerized analysis usually has the ability to check the network for the presence of loops.

The practical use of networks is finding the overall project duration from a set of tasks and establishing which activities lie on the path that determines that overall duration. For this to be possible, the network must satisfy the following conditions:

- There is a single starting node and a single finishing node.
- There is at least one arc between each node.
- A path, or paths, exists from the starting node to all other nodes.
- There are no loops.
- There is no node other than the finishing node from which no activities or dummies spring (i.e. there are no '**dangles**').
- All activities other than dummies have known durations.

There is another type of activity termed a '**hammock**' which has no particular duration but takes on the duration of a series of activities to which it is linked. An example of such an activity is design support during the construction of a prototype – as long as the construction of a prototype continues, support will have to be given. When the duration of all the activities is known, the network can be analysed to find the overall duration, this is defined by the longest path through the network and

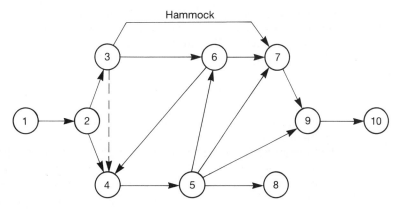

Figure 4.10 Features of a network.

is termed the '**critical path**'. Any delay in the activities on the critical path will increase the overall task duration. Figure 4.10 shows the features of a network.

Figure 4.10 incorporates the features and characteristics discussed:

(a) a dummy activity links Nodes 3 and 4;
(b) a loop exists between Nodes 4, 5 and 6;
(c) a hammock activity joins Nodes 3 and 7;
(d) a dangle exists between Nodes 5 and 8.

Point (b) would have to be corrected by revised logic before such a network could be analysed. In a classical analysis point (d) would also have to be corrected but contemporary computer systems now allow dangles.

Establishing activity durations

It was one of the conditions for the analysis of networks that all the activities must have known durations unless they are dummies or hammocks. However, this particular condition can cause problems as the durations are not always known well enough in advance. It was with this in mind that the originators of the PERT system thought to add an element of sophistication. In essence, the PERT system allowed three estimates to be made of each activity duration, the shortest or most optimistic duration, the most likely duration and the longest or most pessimistic duration. These three estimates are then combined to give the activity duration to be used in analysis according to the formula:

Expected duration, $$D = \frac{S + 4M + L}{6} \tag{4.1}$$

where: S = shortest duration;
M = most likely duration;
L = longest duration.

This formula was derived from an analysis of a particular case of the Beta distribution which, at the time the original work was done, was felt to represent the spread of durations. This formula works with any symmetrical distribution; also calculable is an estimate of the variance of the expected duration using the formula:

$$\text{The variance of the expected duration, } V_d = \frac{(L - S)^2}{36} \tag{4.2}$$

By using the additive properties of the variance as an estimate of the spread of durations, it was hoped that some greater measure of confidence could be placed on the estimate of the overall project timescale and the probabilities associated with an overrun in planned duration. None of the above sophistication was applied to the estimates in the original critical path method where a single estimate of activity duration was used. In practice, the single estimate has proved to be much more popular and little use seems to be made of the PERT three-estimate method. A criticism of the PERT formula is that it tends to underestimate the most likely duration and has led to a revised formula being suggested:

$$D = \frac{S + 3M + 2L}{6} \tag{4.3}$$

In this case, more weight is given to the longest duration and this would certainly conform with common sense as activities can always be extended by many times the amount that they can be shortened. Despite the historic lack of interest in the PERT three-estimate method, it is now being revived in the context of risk analysis.

The method for finding the critical path through a network is illustrated by an example, as follows.

Example 4.2: Analysis of a simple network

Consider the design, manufacture and assembly of an item of equipment whose logic and durations are indicated as follows:

(a) Design scheming of the item can be done in two weeks.
(b) When the scheme is complete, quotations can be obtained from tool suppliers for an assembly fixture; quotation time is four weeks.
(c) After the schemes are passed to the drawing office, detail drawing will take five weeks.
(d) After all the quotes for the assembly fixture are received, a final decision to order must await the completion of the detail drawing set; the assembly fixture is expected to take twelve weeks to deliver.
(e) When the drawing set is complete and passed to the Planning Department, the material can be ordered and this is expected to take five weeks to deliver.
(f) Manufacturing planning and raising of shop cards is expected to take two weeks after completion of the drawing set.
(g) After issue of the shop cards, manufacture of the detail parts will take six weeks from the date of delivery of the material.

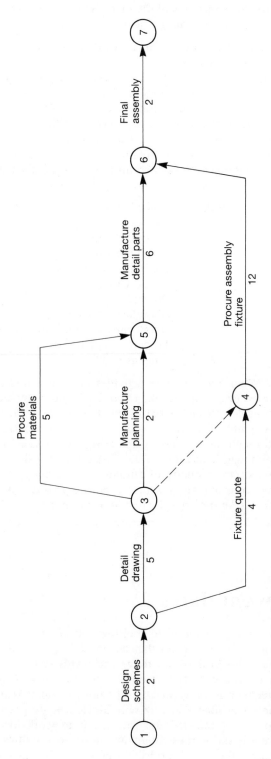

Figure 4.11 Network of design, manufacture and assembly project.

(h) Final assembly of the item will take two weeks after receipt of the assembly fixture and all the detail parts.

Figure 4.11 shows the network that describes the pattern of work in the example. Readers may satisfy themselves that it meets all the conditions. The duration of each activity in weeks is written under the appropriate arc. It will be noticed that the length of the arc bears no relation to the activity duration and there is no duration associated with the dummy between Nodes 3 and 4.

The total task duration is given by the longest path through the network. This is termed the critical path and the activities that lie along it the 'critical activities'. It can be found by working forward from the starting node. By considering each node in turn, we can make use of the rule that no activity can start earlier than the preceding event (node) can be completed:

Node	Dependent activities	Longest duration
1	—	—
2	Design schemes	2
3	Detail drawing	5 + 2 = 7
4	Assembly fixture quote	4 + 2 = 6
	Dummy from 3	7*
5	Procure materials	7 + 5 = 12*
	Manufacture planning	7 + 2 = 9
6	Detail parts manufacture	12 + 6 = 18
	Procure assembly fixture	12 + 7 = 19*
7	Final assembly	19 + 2 = 21*

When two or more activities meet at a node, the activity path giving the latest event time is taken and this is shown by an asterisk (*). The critical path thus lies through Final Assembly to Node 6, then through Procurement of the Assembly Fixture to Node 4, then via the Dummy to Node 3 and hence through Detail Drawing and Design Scheming. In this case, the dummy activity although it has no duration allocated to it lies on the critical path. This is an important property of dummies, for although they have no duration and do not consume any resources, they do preserve the network logic, and that logic may take the critical path along a dummy.

Expected event dates

The simple operation to find the critical path is not the only analysis that can be done. All the activities that do not lie on the critical path have the property called 'float', that is they can move backwards in time or be extended without affecting the critical path. The amount of movement or float is, however, limited for if the movement is too great, then the non-critical activity will, itself, become critical. The amount of float that any non-critical activity possesses can only be established by two sets of calculations. The first is to work forward from the starting node to establish the earliest point at which all activities will start and finish. This will establish the overall project duration and thus its end-date; the second calculation is

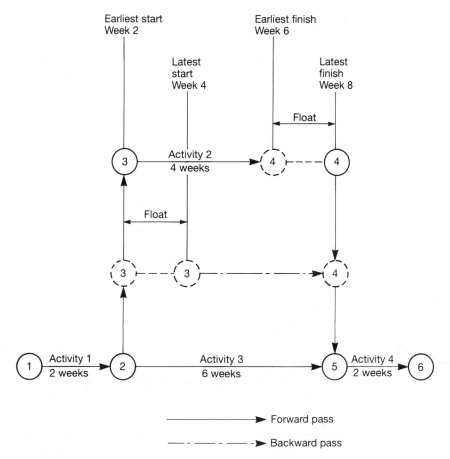

Figure 4.12   Illustration of float.

to work backwards from the end-date through the network to determine the latest points at which all the activities can start and finish. These two processes are termed the **'forward pass'** and **'backward pass'** respectively. At its simplest, the principle is illustrated in Figure 4.12 which shows an activity with float.

In this network the overall duration is ten weeks and the critical path lies through Activities 1, 3 and 4; Activity 2 can start with the completion of Activity 1, but it does not need to end until Activity 3 is complete as Activity 4 depends on the completion of both 2 and 3 before it can start. A forward pass would indicate that the earliest date at which Activity 2 could start is at the end of week 2, and the earliest point at which it could finish is four weeks later at week 6. Working backwards from the end-date of week 10, the latest point at which Activity 2 can finish without itself becoming critical is week 8, and the latest point at which it can start is four weeks earlier at week 4. The float can be seen diagrammatically as the amount by which the activity can either be delayed in starting or be late in finishing without, itself, becoming critical.

The term 'float' is usually taken to mean the amount by which an activity can move; the nodes or events, although tied by the activity duration, can move by

Table 4.1   Forward pass calculation

Activity no.	Activity description	Start node	Finish node	Duration (weeks)	Dependent activities	Earliest start week	Earliest finish week
1	Design schemes	1	2	2	—	1	2
2	Detail drawing	2	5	5	1	3	7
3	Assembly fixture quote	2	4	4	1	3	6
4	Manufacture planning	3	5	2	2	8	9
5	Procure materials	3	5	5	2	8	12
6	Procure assembly fixture	4	6	12	2, 3	8	19
7	Detail parts manufacture	5	6	6	4, 5	13	18
8	Final assembly	6	7	2	6, 7	20	21

Table 4.2   Backward pass calculation

Activity no.	Activity description	Start node	Finish node	Duration (weeks)	Dependent activities	Latest start week	Latest finish week
8	Final assembly	7	6	2	—	20	21
7	Detail parts manufacture	6	5	6	8	14	19
6	Procure assembly fixture	6	4	12	8	8	19
5	Procure materials	5	3	5	7	9	13
4	Manufacturing planning	5	3	2	7	12	13
3	Assembly fixture quote	4	3	4	6	4	7
2	Detail drawing	3	2	5	6, 5, 4	3	7
1	Design schemes	2	1	2	2, 3	1	2

Table 4.3   Calculation of total float

Activity no.	Activity duration	Earliest start week	Latest start week	Earliest finish week	Latest finish week	Total float
1	2	1	1	2	2	0
2	5	3	3	7	7	0
3	4	3	4	6	7	1
4	2	8	12	9	13	4
5	5	8	9	12	13	1
6	12	8	8	19	19	0
7	6	13	14	18	19	1
8	6	20	20	21	21	0

different amounts at the head or tail of the activity depending on the logic of the network. Movement in the events is generally referred to as 'slack' to distinguish it from float in the activity as a whole.

Referring to the example given in Figure 4.11, the earliest start and finish dates derived from a forward pass are given in Table 4.1. The reader can follow the build up of the start and finish dates by reference to the figures. The earliest finish week is assumed to be the end of the week concerned. Thus the earliest start week is taken as the beginning of the week following the completion of the preceding activity. As the overall duration has been found to be 21 weeks, a backward pass can be done by working backwards through the network from week 21, and this is given in

Table 4.4 Calculation of free float

Activity no. (A)	Duration (B)	Earliest start week (C)	Suceeding activity no. (D)	Earliest start week (E)	Free float (E-C-B)
1	2	1	2	3	0
2	5	3	4	8	0
3	4	3	6	8	1
4	2	8	7	13	3
5	5	8	7	13	0
6	12	8	8	20	0
7	6	13	8	20	1
8	2	20	—	—	0

Table 4.2. The same rule is applied, in that the start week assumes the beginning of the week and the finish week assumes the end. From these two tables a composite can be created that will allow the calculation of the float associated with each activity, as shown in Table 4.3.

The '**total float**' is calculated by subtracting the activity duration from the time available between the earliest start date and the latest finish date. In Table 4.3 one must remember the convention regarding the start and finish points at the beginning and end of the weeks in order to get the correct total float figure. Activity 4 can start at its earliest at the beginning of week 8 and finish at the latest at the end of week 13, a total of six weeks; the activity duration is two weeks, hence the total float is four weeks. Activities with no float lie on the critical path.

The total float as defined above is not the only float that can be calculated, but it is by far the most widely used. Another float sometimes used is the '**free float**'; this is calculated by subtracting the activity duration from the time between its earliest start date and the earliest start date of the next activity. If this results in a positive value, this is the 'free float'; if the result is zero or negative, the free float is zero. The free float can be defined as the time by which an activity can move backwards without affecting the ability of any subsequent activity to start at its earliest time. The free float for the activities in the example can be calculated by consideration of each activity and any one of its immediate successors as given in Table 4.4. Other types of float have been identified: 'independent float', 'interfering float', 'late free float', etc. No practical use seems to have been found for these values.

Example 4.3: Prototype manufacture and test

Figure 4.5 in the section dealing with the drawing of bar charts gives an example of a small project dealing with the design, manufacture and test of some prototypes. Figure 4.13 shows this project translated into a network. In this example the nodes have been numbered using the grid references from the borders of the drawing sheet. The network given in Figure 4.13 must be analysed by a forward and backward pass.

The bracketed dependent activities indicate the activities which govern the start of the given activity, in each case it is the activity with the latest of the earliest finish dates. Thus the start of activity 16 is governed by the finish of

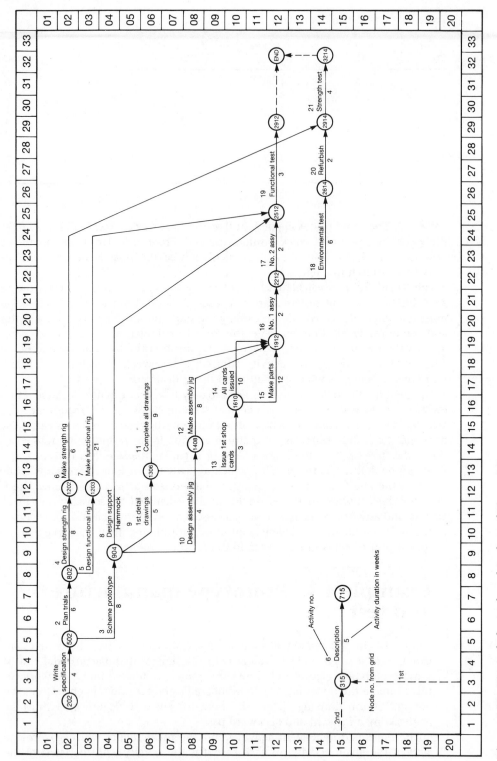

Figure 4.13 Network drawn from bar chart of Figure 4.5.

Table 4.5 Forward pass calculation

Activity no.	Description	Start node	Finish node	Duration (weeks)	Dependent activities	Earliest start week	Earliest finish week
1*	Write specification	202	502	4	—	1	4
2*	Plan trials	502	802	6	1	5	10
3	Scheme prototype	502	904	8	1	5	12
4	Design strength rig	802	1202	8	2	11	18
5*	Design functional rig	802	1203	15	2	11	25
6	Make strength rig	1202	2914	6	4	19	24
7*	Make functional rig	1203	2512	21	5	26	46
8	Design support	904	2512	Hammock	3	13	36
9	1st detail drawings	904	1306	5	3	13	17
10	Design assembly jig	904	1408	4	3	13	16
11	Complete drawings	1306	1912	9	9	18	26
12	Make assembly jig	1408	1912	8	10	17	24
13	Issue 1st cards	1306	1610	3	9	18	20
14	All cards issued	1610	1912	10	13	21	30
15	Manufacture parts	1610	1912	12	13	21	32
16	Assemble no. 1	1912	2212	2	11, 12, 14, (15)	33	34
17	Assemble no. 2	2212	2512	2	16	35	36
18	Environmental test	2212	2614	6	16	35	40
19*	Functional test	2512	2912	3	(7), 8, 17	47	49
20	Refurbishment	2614	2914	2	18	41	42
21	Strength test	2914	3214	4	6, (20)	43	46

Table 4.6 Backward pass calculation

Activity no.	Description	Start node	Finish node	Duration (weeks)	Dependent activities	Latest start week	Latest finish week
21	Strength test	2914	3214	4	—	46	49
20	Refurbishment	2614	2914	2	21	44	45
19	Functional test	2512	2912	3	—	47	49
18	Environmental test	2212	2614	6	20	38	43
17	Assemble no. 2	2212	2512	2	19	45	46
16	Assemble no. 1	1912	2212	2	17, (18)	36	37
15	Manufacture parts	1610	1912	12	16	24	35
14	All cards issued	1610	1912	10	16	26	35
13	Issue 1st cards	1306	1610	3	14, (15)	21	23
12	Make assembly jig	1408	1912	8	16	28	35
11	Complete drawings	1306	1912	9	16	27	35
10	Design assembly jig	904	1408	4	12	24	27
9	1st detail drawings	904	1306	5	11, (13)	16	20
8	Design support	904	2512	Hammock	19	16	46
7	Make functional rig	1203	2512	21	19	26	46
6	Make strength rig	1202	2512	6	21	40	45
5	Design functional rig	802	1203	15	7	11	25
4	Design strength rig	802	1202	8	6	32	39
3	Scheme prototype	502	904	8	8, (9), 10	8	15
2	Plan trials	502	802	6	4, (5)	5	10
1	Write specification	202	502	4	(2), 3	1	4

activity 15, that having a later finish date than activities 11, 12 or 14. By working back from the end-activity through the earlier dependent activities, the critical path can be found and this is shown by the activity numbers marked with an asterisk. The combined result of the forward and backward passes are given in Table 4.7. As will be expected, all the critical activities have zero float. The hammock activity has a potential duration of 33 weeks; if scheming is completed at the earliest point and assembly of the second unit is delayed until week 45, five of the activities exhibit free float. Because of the relative rarity of the free float and its limited use, many computerized network analysis routines do not calculate it.

Table 4.7   Combined result and float calculation

Activity no.	Activity duration	Earliest start week	Latest finish week	Total float	Suceeding activity no.	Suceeding activity earliest start	Free float
1	4	1	4	0	2, 3	5	0
2	6	5	10	0	4, 5	11	0
3	8	5	15	3	8, 9, 10	13	0
4	8	11	39	21	6	19	0
5	15	11	25	0	7	26	0
6	6	19	45	21	21	43	18
7	21	26	46	0	19	47	0
8	—	13	46	—	19	—	—
9	5	13	20	3	11, 13	18	0
10	4	13	27	11	12	17	0
11	9	18	35	9	16	33	6
12	8	17	35	11	16	33	8
13	3	18	23	3	14	21	0
14	10	21	35	5	16	33	2
15	12	21	35	3	16	33	0
16	2	33	37	3	17, 18	35	0
17	2	35	46	10	19	47	10
18	6	35	43	3	20	42	0
19	3	47	49	0	End	—	0
20	2	41	45	3	21	43	0
21	4	43	49	3	End	—	0

Activity on node or precedence networks

All the foregoing networks make use of the convention that the activity in question is designated by an arrow. Nodes are used to signify events that mark the start and end of activities and provide a numbering system for indicating the network logic. It was stated that until very recently this has been the preferred notation, but with the advent of relatively inexpensive computer systems, the alternative 'activity-on-node' or 'precedence' network has become popular. The attraction stems from the ease with which the network can be constructed on the computer screen and the ability to dispense with dummy activities while still preserving the logic. To distinguish the precedence network, rectangular boxes are commonly, though not exclusively, used to designate the activities, the activity codes being contained within the box. The appearance of the network is thus altered.

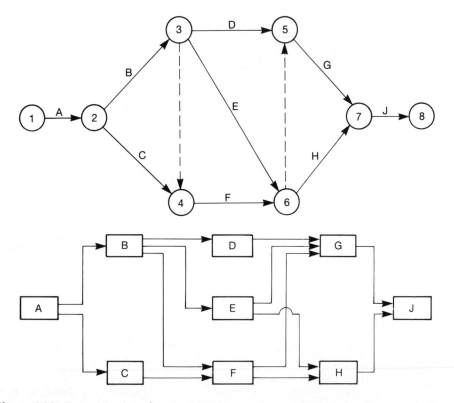

Figure 4.14 Representation of an 'activity-on-arrow' network as a 'precedence' network.

Figure 4.14 shows the conventional 'activity-on-arrow' network featuring two dummy activities. Beneath it the same set of activities are drawn as a 'precedence' network. The representation looks sufficiently different for it not to appear obvious that the two diagrams define the same set of conditions. Examination of the logic will show that they are exactly equivalent, for it will be seen that:

- the completion of activity A leads to the simultaneous start of activities B and C;
- when activity B is completed, D and E can start;
- activity F can only start when both C and B are complete;
- activity G cannot start before D, E and F are complete;
- activity H can start when E and F are complete; and
- activity J can start only when G and H are finished.

Analysis of a precedence network is identical to an activity-on-arrow network and because of this some computerized network analysis packages allow either method to be used.

Alternative logic

In all the examples shown previously, the only type of relationship between activities has been that the finish of one activity leads to the start of another. This is not

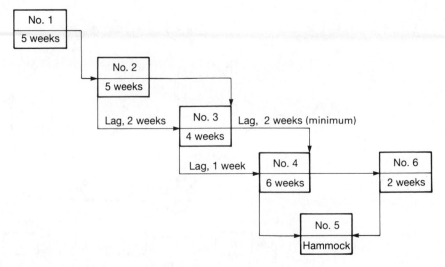

Figure 4.15 Activity relationships in a 'precedence' network.

the only possible relationship; it may be that the finish of one activity leads to the finish of another – i.e. one activity cannot finish before another activity finishes. For example, in a manufacturing situation all works orders cannot be issued before all drawings have been issued. This is referred to as a **'finish-to-finish relationship'** and it is used where this type of definition is more logically convenient or correct. With precedence networks, the type of relationship has to be specified. This is done through the arrangement of the arrows that link the activity boxes.

Besides the start and finish relationship, there may also be time relationships that need to be specified in order to preserve the timescale element of the network. For example, it may be known from previous experience that the first detail drawings tend to emerge from the drawing office four weeks after the start of drawing work. Works orders for parts cannot begin to be produced until the first drawings are issued, hence the logic would be that generating works orders can start four weeks after the start of detail drawing; this would be deemed a **'start-to-start activity relationship'** with a four week **'lag'**. When a series of activities are all linked in such a way that the start of each one is dependent upon the start of its predecessor, usually with a lag between each, it is termed a **'ladder network'** because of its appearance on the page. Figure 4.15 shows examples of the various relationships in the precedence format.

Figure 4.15 shows a network with the following features:

- a finish-to-start relationship exists between Activities 1 and 2, and 4 and 6;
- a 'ladder' exists between Activities 2, 3 and 4;
- lags are indicated between the starts of Activities 2 and 3, and 3 and 4 but not between 4 and 5;
- a start-to-finish relationship exists between Activities 5 and 6.

Networks in practice

Network analysis has become firmly woven into the fabric of project management but the practice of using it is somewhat less analytical than the originators intended; this has stemmed from:

- The grade of labour employed to construct and manage networks is often not of the same calibre as the mathematicians who devised the original method.
- The sheer size and complexity of many real-life networks.
- The difficulty in drawing a network which represents the plan with complete accuracy.
- The difficulty in interpreting a large network.
- The lag in updating the network with actual progress.
- Precise analysis is not always needed by senior management, nor are its implications fully understood or trusted.

Furthermore, some Project Managers have expressed a positive dislike and mistrust of networking when used as a control mechanism for their project. Despite the claimed benefits, there are clearly difficulties; broadly speaking, the problems can be summed up with the following typical comments:

(a) 'Networking is expensive in terms of the number of staff and computer costs.'

British management historically has not paid much heed to planning, and if a project is running into cost difficulties, one of the areas that is often cut back is project management. When this happens, the cost of operating a network often attracts adverse attention. Computer costs of networking may have been relatively expensive a decade ago but with the falling prices of computer hardware and software the computing cost argument is rapidly diminishing.

(b) 'Networks seem to follow events rather than predict them.'

It is a fact of all planning activities that plans only say what should happen, not what will happen; when events deviate from the plan, there will always be an element of information arriving after the event. Part of the problem, however, stems from the duration of the reporting cycle, that is the time taken to update the network and produce a new output that is completely validated and error-free. In some cases where the networks contain many thousands of activities and rely on inputs from subcontractors that are themselves using networks, the reporting cycle can often take a month or even longer. Obviously, project managers will become frustrated at being presented with out-of-date information too late to influence decisions that have already been taken.

(c) 'Networks always present information in a form that cannot be understood or which does not make the position obvious.'

This is one of the most valid criticisms of networking, particularly where large and complex networks are involved. Networks are an abstract representation of events in which the time element is reduced to a numerical value and the networks are not necessarily drawn on a scale which has any relationship to the pattern of events. Consequently, attempting to establish the relationships of activities in time terms can be very awkward and misleading. This author has been presented with a dozen AO size drawing sheets each containing 100 or more activities and has been told 'this is the new project plan'. Not surprisingly they were consigned to the bottom drawer of the filing cabinet and never looked at again.

All of the criticisms contain an element of truth and there has been a move back to the use of bar charts for project control. This move has been helped by the development of computer packages that can draw networks on a timescale basis and thus combine the benefits of both methods. None of the criticisms imply any inherent flaw in network analysis, therefore much of the difficulty must have stemmed from the way in which the networks have been used and presented; in this respect, practising network analysts must bear some of the responsibility.

The faults in the operation of networks are:

(a) 'Networks are often too large and complex to be meaningful.'

One cannot escape the fact that many projects are large and complex, therefore the plans that accompany them must reflect that fact. Having said that, efforts can be made to simplify the logic or restrict it to its most relevant interrelationships. Adding additional detail or subdividing activities unnecessarily should be resisted. In general, the farther away in time any events are from the time at which the network is compiled, the more general should be the activities. As events approach in time, a more detailed breakdown can be applied, so that control is only exercised when it can be effective. Similarly, activities which lie along the critical path can be broken down and expanded for more detailed control; activities with large floats can be treated in more general terms. The level of detail in the estimate of activity durations can be adjusted accordingly; for example, activities in the next three months can be scheduled in days, activities four to 18 months away scheduled in weeks and activities at 19 months and beyond scheduled in months. This may cause problems with some computer programs where the unit of time has to be constant throughout the network, but the principle can still be applied when deciding on the size of an activity to be represented. In a development project many things can happen in a year, and a program may look very different 12 months on from its conception; therefore it is not worth spending a lot of effort on detail which may change considerably.

(b) 'Faulty reasoning sometimes occurs in the operation of networks stemming from oversimplification or incorrect simplification.'

On the face of it, this would seem to be a fault due to an attempt to cure the problems indicated at (a), and in part it is. In order to make complex networks more easily understood by senior management some projects use a tier system of networks, where each higher tier or level is a summary of the lower ones, as shown in Figure 4.16.

In the tier system the Level 1 network is sometimes called the 'management' level, the Level 2 and 'planning' level and the Level 3 the 'working' level. If the Level 3 network is large and complex, it is inevitable that some compromises are made in the logic when summarizing the Level 3 to arrive at the Level 2 and further compromises made in creating the Level 1. Besides combining activities, some of the logical interrelationships are broken. Thus the Level 1 network may be a crude representation of the true situation. This is not a problem if the network is only used to provide top management with progress information and the critical path. It can, however, cause real problems if combined with the 'top-down, bottom-up' control system, as shown in Figure 4.17.

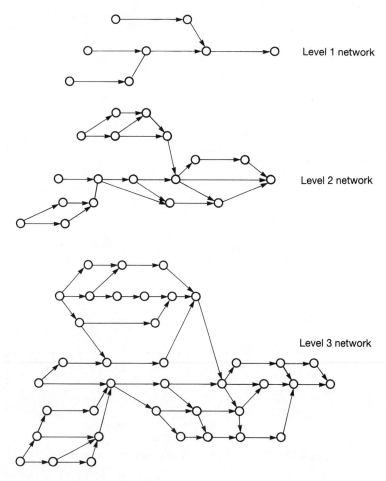

Figure 4.16 Tier system of networks.

'Top-down, bottom-up', in the ultimate, is the only way that projects can be run as no manager can be in possession of all the facts about the project. The difficulty comes in the particular application to networks if the Level 1 summary is used by the Project Manager for frequently re-planning the project. Whenever the project has problems, re-planning will almost certainly be necessary, but a Level 1 summary network may not be the best medium. Changes may be introduced that appear reasonable in summary form but can prove difficult to implement when it comes to expanding the network downwards. Because some of the logic links may have been cut to produce the Level 1, reintroducing them to preserve the real logic can become awkward and may indicate undesirable or even impossible new situations. This has then to be referred back to the Project Manager for further clarification and more changes. In the meantime, data is being received about progress against the earlier logic; this now has to be fitted in, often in a hurry, to meet the end-of-month update. With the revised logic half complete, the output reports inevitably have errors and these eventually get picked up by the departmental heads who have to carry out the actions;

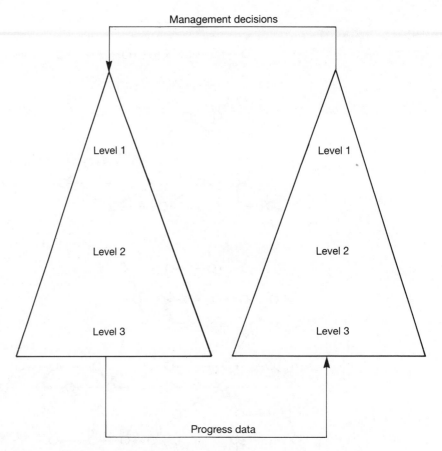

Figure 4.17   'Top-down, bottom up' control system.

consequently, there are more arguments for changes at a detail level. Confidence in the network and its reports begins to decline and individual managers begin to make their own plans.

By this process, an orderly plan can degenerate into a muddle with frustration at every level and lead to the criticisms listed earlier. The solution lies partly in the recommendations given at (a) – i.e. simplicity and keeping the network to its essential elements. Secondly, the network should be constructed on a modular basis, as far as possible, so that summary networks can be created from the lower-level network modules with as few compromises in the essential logic as possible. Thirdly, some Project Managers have chosen to replace the Level 1 network with a bar chart representation to ensure that when high-level replanning is done the correct interrelationships in time terms are clearly represented and understood.

(c) 'Networks are sometimes used for tasks for which they are not well suited, in particular, the scheduling of material flows under finite capacity conditions.'

Attempts have been made to use networks as a production control system in projects which demand a large volume of hardware to be manufactured, and that hardware has to pass from one subcontractor to another, each with a different output capacity. Problems of this type are much better dealt with by Material Requirements Planning systems which have the ability to hold build sequences and explode them into supply schedules for each component in line with a Master Supply Plan. In essence, MRP systems have the ability to synthesize schedules that are logical and complete from simple high-level plans. Networks cannot do this, the logic has to be complete and contain all the supplies detail for the lowest level of control at the start – but this has to be done before the network can be analysed; the computer systems only perform analysis, they do not perform synthesis. This author was involved in a project which involved a number of subcontractors developing and manufacturing large numbers of parts in varying standards. Initially, networks were used in an attempt to create the supply schedules for each subcontractor. In so doing, the network grew to about 16 000 activities, by which time it was completely unmanageable, but the supply schedules were so incomplete that they could not be issued. An analysis of the total supply position indicated that for a full definition the network would have to be expanded to about 25 000 activities. This situation was the worst of both worlds: a network too large to be manageable, yet too small to be complete. The problem was cured by the adoption of a specially created MRP system to deal with all the supplies, whereupon the main network was reduced to 4000 activities, with a consequent reduction in staff, and overall control of the project improved dramatically.

(d) 'Networks used to control subcontractors, who are themselves working from networks, have special dangers.'

In any project involving a prime contractor that relies on subcontractors to develop and supply parts, control and integration of those subcontractors can be one of the major challenges to the project management. In the project referred to at (c) above, the prime contractor required each subcontractor to generate a network showing his major activities and submit it to the prime contractor for integration into a Master Network of the combined input. In this way, it was hoped total control could be gained over all subcontractors and the progress of each could be measured. The project had many technical difficulties and an ambitious timescale; it was therefore decided at the most senior level that no subcontractor should have sight of any other subcontractor's plan in case it raised the temptation to 'hide behind' a perceived slippage. However, more than half the subcontractors relied on other subcontractors for the supply of parts but each was forced to do its planning independently without knowledge of what it could expect to receive or precisely when it was required to supply. Inevitably the integration progress proved to be almost impossible as each subcontractor made his own assumptions. It was eventually recognized that withholding relevant information, even if it does indicate a slippage, only leads to confusion, argument and a lack of direction. Once the prime contractor took a more directing role by using the MRP system to generate a set of integrated schedules that were all mutually compatible, the rest of the planning followed suit and the networks were easily integrated.

Network analysis is now resurgent in the field of project management systems largely because of the new range of PC-based project management packages that have come onto the market in the past few years. Their relative cheapness and power, combined with their ability to generate time-based bar charts, has generated renewed interest. Some of the latest systems also incorporate cost and schedule performance measurement techniques which adds to their potential. In using these new packages all the lessons learned from previous experience of networking still have to be taken into account.

The next generation of systems may incorporate Generalized Network Models which will allow variable durations and more subtle logical interrelationships such as the 'not earlier than' and 'not later than' type. Project Managers must become familiar with the network representation as it does not seem likely to be displaced as the primary system for defining the project plan for the foreseeable future.

Summary

Good planning is essential to the successful execution of any project, yet historically this has been an area of weakness in project management in the UK. The advent of affordable and refined project management software, combined with the more generally accepted principles of how projects should be run, has meant that planning is now being taken more seriously. Network analysis forms the basis of all contemporary project management software and a knowledge of the technique is vital to all practising Project Managers. Networking, once hailed as the panacea for all project ills, declined in popularity for a time as deficiencies were discovered, but these stemmed more from its application than any fault in the method. Some of the difficulties have been overcome by the current software which is much more sophisticated and versatile than earlier systems. There are, however, limitations to the type of control problem that can be dealt with by network methods, and here other approaches need to be taken.

The Project Manager is now better served with extensive, affordable and sophisticated planning tools than at any time in the past. Starting with a realistic and achievable plan is the first step on the road to project success, and there is no reason why it should not be done.

5

Success by design

More than any other factor, the design of a product will influence the outcome of the project venture. At its simplest, a well-designed product that can be made for a competitive price will always sell better than a poor and expensive design. Getting the design right at the outset is fundamental to success; in consequence, it should be given the highest priority in the Project Manager's approach to his task, but just what is the 'right design'?

The answer is quite simply the design that appeals to the most customers. First and foremost, it must satisfy the requirements of the user. To do that it does not need to be the most technically sophisticated, although good performance is necessary; nor does it have to be the cheapest, but a low price does help. Furthermore, it must appear on the market at a time when the demand is there. Innovation can show the opportunities for new products, but once found, they still have to be translated into profitable products through the design process.

It is probably true to say that for every product design deemed to be successful, there is one, if not more, that is unsuccessful. Lack of success may be either technical, if the product does not work as intended, or commercial, if it does not achieve an acceptable return on the investment. A technical failure will always lead to a commercial failure but technical success is no guarantee of a commercial one. To be a commercial success a product must have appeal by whatever standards the customer chooses; it must satisfy the customer's needs in a way that is acceptable and at a price that he or she can afford. These points may seem obvious, so why are so many design projects unsuccessful? The factors involved in the design process might give us a clue.

Factors that influence design

Engineering may be tied to the laws of physics but design is still a creative and imaginative process. The designer has to produce a solution to a problem, where nothing has gone before. There are always several ways in which any task can be accomplished, but the design that emerges for any specific application will be influenced by several factors:

- The design specification.
- The available corporate technology.
- The experience of the design team.
- The prevailing design culture.

The design specification

The **design specification** is the starting-point for all design work, it should lay down the basic parameters of performance and cost. It needs the utmost thoroughness in its preparation; if the specification is flawed in some way, everything that springs from it will have that flaw built in. Design specifications tend to evolve in two ways:

1. An organization identifies a need for a product that it wishes to acquire and approaches a contractor to design and make it for him.
2. Through research activities a vendor identifies a market opportunity and sets about designing a product that will satisfy it.

These two paths are fundamentally different. In the first case, the market is assured as the design specification springs directly from the customer; it is for the contractor to create a product that will meet the requirement. This is a characteristic of many public sector projects, particularly in the aerospace and defence sector where the military organizations specify the requirements for a new piece of equipment and civilian contractors design and produce it. Despite the assurance of the market, such projects are not without risk as it is common practice to run some form of competition among alternative contractors. To participate in the competition some private capital may need to be injected. Private sector development projects, on the other hand, are usually aimed at the market as a whole; specific customers may be identified during the design and development phases and their input sought. Just how much value is placed on this input is a matter for the contractor to decide rather than the potential customer to demand.

Public sector programmes often arise from work done in the private sector to define new products that are becoming possible through advancing technology, the final specification may be an amalgamation of this work and that done in the government's own research laboratories. With such projects, the design specification tends to be very closely defined, particularly in respect of the features to be included and the expected performance; these can be the subject of contractual guarantees. With military projects, each new generation of products tends to represent a significant advance over the previous one and the resulting specifications can be very demanding in technical terms. Overly demanding specifications have been the root cause of many military project failures in the period since the Second World War; to avoid a failure both the customer organization and the contractor may have to adopt a flexible attitude towards the trade-off between practicality, cost and performance.

The fixed-price development contract, which is becoming prevalent, seems particularly inappropriate in the circumstances. In projects where the technical risks are not great, the designer may have little scope for making significant changes to the specification, but the designs that result can vary greatly from one contractor to another.

With private sector projects, there is much greater freedom in formulating the specification. The principal instigator should be the Marketing Department although that is not a hard-and-fast rule as new product ideas can spring from anywhere within a company, particularly the Research and Design departments. Designers are, by nature, problem-solvers and innovators; their contribution is fundamental to new product development but the Marketing Department must be able to define what will sell and it is not always the most technically brilliant product. Appearance, ease of use, reliability and a competitive price all come into the design specification and they must carry a weighting that matches their perceived importance. It is for the Marketing Department to define these weightings and the designers to create a product to match them.

Product specifications are not created simply; there will and indeed should be much debate among the Design, Manufacturing and Marketing staff before the first draft specification is issued. This discussion is vital, it is an opportunity for free thinking where all parties can view the proposal and express their opinions. Some of the early thoughts may be challenged and replaced either by more advanced or more basic solutions. Once the design process begins, it is inevitable that some changes will be introduced to the specification but the process of change must be controlled.

Capability and experience

Both the available corporate technology and the skills and experience of the design team represent constraints on the design solutions that are likely to be generated. For example, an organization that has considerable experience in designing items as light alloy castings, and has a large capital investment in a foundry, may find it difficult to consider designing a new range of products as plastic mouldings, for it may have neither the detailed design expertise nor the factory facilities. There may be corporate pressure to design for in-house manufacture using existing facilities. There is nothing wrong with such an approach, provided that the limitations it imposes upon design are recognized. It is important therefore that as the product specification and the detailed design evolve, they are constantly tested against what is seen as the best practice of competitor companies. A study of rival products can open eyes to the design possibilities that exist. Research and design consultancies can supply the expertise that firms may be lacking and use should be made of them. Most suppliers of goods and services are willing to provide advice and assistance if it means that their product or service is going to be included in the design specification for a new item. No organization needs to be bound by its own capabilities, additional skills can always be bought from outside.

The cultural impact

Even if the design specification is correct in general terms and matches the perceived customer requirement, things can still go wrong if control of the design process is poor and the culture within the Design Department is at odds with the business objectives. A study in 1986 by McDonough and Leifer on the success of new product development projects has highlighted how both these factors have a strong bearing on the success of the project as a whole.

Within any company a variety of different cultures exist; in part, they derive from the professional training that individuals have received in their early years and the role they take on in their current positions. Board members should have a 'business culture' that sees the world in terms of the opportunities that exist, the gains that are to be made and the risks involved. Accountants may have a less visionary culture that stresses accuracy, monetary quantification of management issues and avoidance of risk. Designers are different again, their culture stresses innovation, creativity and problem-solving ability, it can be termed an 'R & D culture'. All of these cultures co-exist within any organization, and it is the mix and tension between them that provides both the creative drive and the hard-headedness that are necessary for a company to survive. A company may set out written procedures that define its way of working, but culture dictates the way things are actually done. Culture defines the unwritten rules of behaviour by which employees recognize what is appropriate or acceptable within their group, and what is not. The problem comes when the culture of the department is not aligned with the objectives of the business as a whole. Whereas a culture that values inventiveness and problem-solving is an essential asset to any company, its effectiveness may be reduced if it does not align itself with other, equally important, values.

Professionals in one discipline may see their own goals as being those of the profession as a whole. This may lead individuals to pursue activities that they see as increasing their professional standing, perhaps, by performing research that leads to published papers, but which have only a marginal bearing on the company's goals. McDonough and Leifer found that projects that involved developing novel products tended to be more successful in organizations where the 'business culture' was dominant over the 'R & D culture' in the Design Department. The business culture stressed the commercial viability of the product at every stage, and when a technical decision was necessary, commercial necessity took precedence over technical sophistication. Where projects to develop new products were less successful, the R & D culture prevailed; inventiveness was pursued at the expense of the original specification with the result that the product no longer met the business requirements that were the reason for starting the project in the first place. The quotations below illustrate the point:

> 'The program grew. [We were] forever changing the moulds. There were lots of design changes, when we finally got it, the costs were out of line.'

> 'This project was not very successful. It was too sophisticated. We needed to develop a less costly, less sophisticated product. The project went on and on.'

> 'Our current product is the best in the world. Unfortunately, this is not what we wanted. We have the Cadillac; but we wanted the everyday market.'

Such comments demonstrate that in these projects the design engineers were more interested in advancing the state of the art than they were in producing a commercially viable product. Advancements in technology may be vital to the survival of the company but, in these cases, the R & D culture of technology for its own sake had taken over to the detriment of the project as a whole. Cultural attitudes stem from early industrial training, they tend to be reinforced and ingrained through membership of a group of like-minded individuals. To attempt a cultural change may not be a very rewarding experience; it might have the effect of causing valued individuals to leave. Instead the R & D culture needs to be kept in check through close control. If the business culture is not reinforced by the appropriate leadership style, the R & D culture tends to prevail and, in consequence, the project suffers.

These issues raise the question of the Project Manager himself; his first objective must always be the commercial success of the venture. For this, a business attitude is essential yet some companies insist on drawing their Project Managers from the Technical or Engineering division. They reason that as manufactured products are an engineering job, an engineer is the best person to lead the project, in effect, they are saying that the first priority in a project is an engineering success. In fact, the first priority should always be a commercial success and a technical specialist, however competent in his field, may not be the best choice to ensure that. Project leaders that are primarily concerned with the technology may become fascinated by its possibilities and fail to see the broader picture, they may not take time to establish proper control procedures or set up lines of communication to other departments whose input is necessary as the following quotations show:

> '[The project] broke some technical boundaries but these were not of great benefit to the end-user. The leader needs to have a broad scope and this leader didn't have it. He wasn't concerned so much with sales.'

> 'He will not get a direction from Marketing, he will set one as project leader. [The project leader] said, "here's what I'm going to do, take it or leave it".'

> '[The project leader] was not flexible; it had to be done his way. [The design] was done only 1–2 months late but it took 6–9 months to get it through manufacturing.'

In each case, the statement clearly reflects the narrow, parochial attitude adopted by the Project Manager. With more successful projects, a broader and more businesslike approach was taken by the manager who ensured that design specifications were set out at an early stage with the full involvement of both Marketing and Manufacturing. Boundaries were drawn around packages of work and the designers were expected to conform to them, deviations from specification were only allowed with the agreement of the whole team. In short, a business culture that stressed (a) commercial value above novelty, and (b) practicality above inventiveness was imposed upon the designers; it did not replace the design culture or make them designers in any lesser sense, but it focused their efforts on achievability and directed them towards a more profitable goal.

The design cycle

The design process can be divided into a number of major phases:

1. Preliminary research and development: this may involve purely speculative work on concepts for new products or improvements to existing ones. Much of this work will be abortive, some lines of investigation will not show sufficient merit to warrant further work but, for a few, the work will show enough promise for it to be taken to the next stage. This is usually a feasibility study in which the technical aspects are studied in greater depth with a view to discovering any potential

problems that could render the idea impractical; an outline product specification is normally prepared, together with an assessment of the market and the profit potential of the project. The proposal that results will require either customer or company money to get it any further and many product proposals fail at this stage; the enthusiasm of the researchers may not be shared by the more cautious or pragmatic Board members.

2. Product definition: this requires the development of a full product specification. Whether the specification is generated internally or is inspired by an enquiry from a potential customer, this phase can be crucial to the overall success of the venture. The specification needs to be realistic, achievable and to meet the needs of the customer. If it is deficient in one or more of these areas, then the project will fail; however, it is not always possible to test these properties in absolute terms at the start. Enthusiasm and imagination can colour judgement; for the most part, innovative projects are characterized by an over-optimistic view of what can be achieved. Marketing staff may perceive opportunities for products with all the 'bells and whistles' and fail to test the strength of real demand, while designers often adopt a 'can do' attitude, seeing each new proposal as a challenge and an opportunity to demonstrate their innovative skills. Without enthusiasm and a positive approach, nothing useful will be achieved; but as far as possible, each assumption concerning either the market or the technology should be tested. Market research studies can be done and consultants or specialist researchers can be called in to advise on novel aspects of the technology. It may be possible to acquire rival products for examination and manufacturing specialists should be able to advise on production techniques to be embodied in the design, as well as the likely order of production cost. When this investigative work has been done, the draft product specification can be compiled – but not before.

3. Prototype design: the approach taken to this phase can vary greatly according to the product and the company. Where relatively simple products are concerned or there is a history of similar products, the production item may be designed at the outset in more or less its final form. Some of the parts may be designed to be made on 'soft' tools, or substitute materials may be used if it cuts down prototype costs or reduces the timescale. Where complex and novel products are concerned, the technology will be considered more important than the production features and a series of prototypes may be designed, each to test some specific aspect. Prototypes are often made without special tools, hence some of the design features will be quite inappropriate to a production design; for example, machined-from-the-solid parts may be used where castings or forgings would be substituted in the production version. Some features, such as internal systems, may be designed as 'breadboard' assemblies that are never installed in the prototype item, but tested for functionality on the bench. The principal function of the prototype phase is the demonstration of the technology; the Americans sometimes refer to this phase as a 'demonstration and validation' exercise. Any problems that appear can either be rectified and the modification tested at this stage or modifications can be specified for incorporation at the next phase.

4. Full-scale development: this phase is also known as 'engineering development' or, in the USA, 'design maturation'. It is often the most expensive period in the whole development cycle: one-half to two-thirds of the development budget may be spent on this activity. The successful completion of the prototype phase is an essential precursor and often some form of progress review takes place before any commitment is made to starting full development. The objective is to take the

prototype design and turn it into an item that can be produced in quantity, at a profit, and one which will perform reliably in service. There are often many more challenges during this phase than there were during the prototype phase. For the first time, a fully representative test example will be constructed that includes the full set of systems and this may then be subjected to extremes of performance or environment. It is at this point that design weaknesses, if they exist, will show up. At the same time, design-to-cost or value engineering exercises may be in progress, and there may also be inputs from potential customers. These will generate the need for further changes. This process, in which changes are instigated from various directions coupled with the need to prove that the changes are effective and do not create other problems, is the reason why this phase of development can become the most time-consuming and costly. The objective of this phase will be the creation of a set of drawings and specifications that define a product that can be produced satisfactorily; until that objective is secured, development cannot be said to have ended.

5. Pre-production: some organizations manufacture a pilot batch of items that are as near to production-standard items as can be achieved without actually having to commit to the mass production tools and assembly lines; they are called 'pre-production units'. The reason put forward for building a pre-production batch is that, as far as possible, it proves the production drawings and processes. The value of such items is questionable; they tend to represent a halfway-house between the development and production-standard items and data collected from them may be representative of neither. However, they are sometimes used for customer demonstration or acceptance purposes, or they may be used for some extended testing to be done over a long period, perhaps, for building up a databank of potential failures in advance of any items in customer service. The case for making pre-production items needs to be examined carefully; because they are often a hybrid standard, a considerable amount of design effort may have to go into creating a special drawing set to define them and this may be of no value for production purposes.

6. Production: this is the repeated output of items for sale. Whereas design activities associated with this phase will be relatively small, there will always be some support required for production. Mostly this will amount to designing modifications and controlling their introduction and resolving customer queries or sentencing concession applications for non-conforming batches of components.

The relationship between these phases is shown in Figure 5.1, together with a series of project review points; these are positioned at times when:

(a) a significant increase in expenditure is required in order to go to the next stage;
(b) the design group will experience a hiatus in work if continuity is not maintained.

Project reviews are an opportunity to assess the progress that has been made and the prospects for the future. The inclusion of so many review points can be considered a cautious approach, it typifies public sector projects. Here public money is at stake, and the way that money is spent can be subjected to investigation by government accounts committees, these tend to be well-publicized affairs. Furthermore, the whole basis of letting development contracts is one in which the amount of work to be done is clearly defined and costed proposals need to be approved before the project can go from one stage of development to the next. This method has been adopted for advanced technology projects where there is a high risk of either a

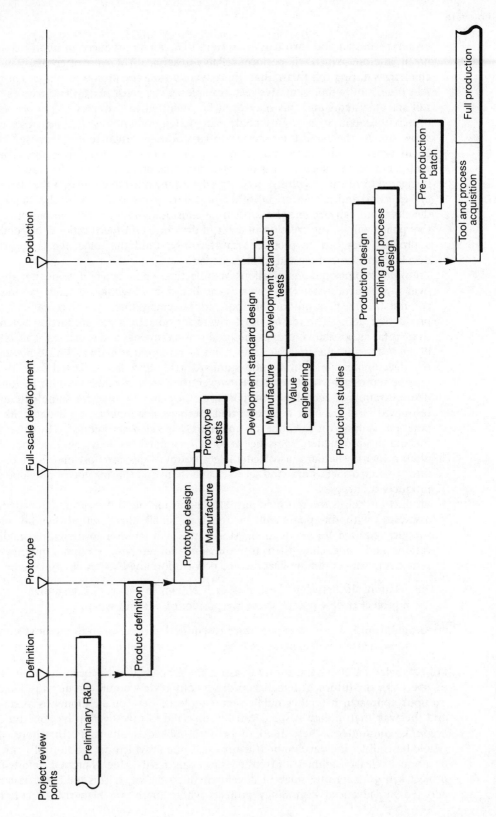

Figure 5.1 Phases of a typical development project.

technical failure or a change of policy that may dispense with the requirement. It minimizes the sponsors' cash exposure; if a project looks like running into severe difficulties, they have the option to stop before greater sums are spent.

The criticism of this approach is that it can lead to excessive development time-scales and, in a world of increasing competition, reducing the time from project inception to having the product on the market must generate an advantage. Comparisons have been made between the timescale for European development projects and that for Japanese projects; the evidence suggests that, for equivalent work, Japanese projects are completed in two-thirds to three-quarters of the time that European firms take. This is not the only difference; the products that emerge have demonstrably higher-quality levels than their Western counterparts. This comparison cannot be ignored and studies have been launched to examine the methods employed.

Simultaneous engineering

One thing that has been noticed as a clear difference between the Japanese approach and that taken by Western companies is the broad front on which all the project activities advance. This method has acquired the title of **simultaneous engineering** (SE) and it appears to challenge the more conventional order of working. However, a closer examination of simultaneous engineering may reveal that some of the reasons for its claimed success lie in the human and organizational aspects of the task as much as in the timing of events. Simultaneous engineering lays great stress on all departments involved in the job being brought together as a team from the very outset of the project. It ensures that the end-producers are a part of the design team from inception and that the Quality Assurance Department have an input to the design and are not merely inspectors who pass or fail the end-product. 'Simultaneous' is thus better thought of as referring to the input of all the disciplines in the project taking place at the same time rather than all the activities going on together. There is always a logical order in which things can be done and it does not differ greatly from one project to another; to attempt to work in a way that defies this logic would be risky and potentially very costly. What can be done is to speed up the process of performing each activity. To aid this process a **task force** is created that is concerned solely with the particular project, and this task force is allowed a considerable measure of freedom to manage its own activities. It must, however, have a clearly defined goal. It is claimed that the newly found freedom and product identification generates new levels of enthusiasm and commitment in the task force. Other inputs are also sought, in particular, those of supplier companies, and they are encouraged to join the team and work on an equal footing with the company's own engineers.

One could look at SE as an example of the 'project' approach to the creation of new products given a new name. In fact, it has all the elements of the project team approach, taken somewhat further than is customary in Western companies. There can be little doubt that commitment on the part of the task force members is a vital ingredient, and firms that have adopted simultaneous engineering claim great success. It does appear to release both creativity and energy that was hitherto dormant. Very large corporations such as Ford, Digital Equipment, General Motors (Opel), Rolls-Royce, Rover Group in Europe and several US machine tool vendors have introduced

SE. Results can be impressive: Digital Equipment halved their previous 30-month cycle time for product development. The benefits are not only in development time as reductions in product costs and improved quality and performance levels have also been seen.

Simultaneous engineering represents a break with previous cultural norms that have persisted throughout Europe and the USA and they may still prove a barrier to its introduction. Among the obstacles to be overcome are:

- The task force that draws together many members of the company in a semi-autonomous group may be seen as cutting across traditional lines of authority and responsibility. Senior management have to accept that some measure of day-to-day control is lost; however, they do not have to loose touch as they can still impose strict reporting criteria on the force.
- Putting dedicated staff into a team that is formed at the start of the project and remains together for the duration may be seen as expensive or consumptive of scarce resources. In large organizations such as those mentioned, there may be a small increase in staff costs, but this is more than offset by the gains. However, in small companies where specialist staff are employed in ones and twos the dedicated team method can be impractical. Using outside consultants or 'guest engineers' can offset this problem as they can be used on an as-and-when basis and the fresh input they often bring can add to the creative powers of the team.
- Involving suppliers in the design process can also pose problems. Traditionally many firms have not involved suppliers in the design of products for reasons of commercial confidentiality and price. They have been unwilling to let suppliers know much about what they are doing in case that knowledge could help a supplier design something of benefit to a rival and it has also been the accepted practice to play rival suppliers off against each other in order to obtain the best production prices. For SE to work these attitudes will have to change but a history of competition amongst rivals can still leave a feeling of mistrust and a policy of competitive purchasing can be one of the most deeply held business tenets. Involving suppliers in the design process implies a new contractual relationship and this aspect does need careful thought both over the choice of supplier and the form of the agreement; price provisions may have to be included as well as rights to the design if the supplier goes out of business or decides not to produce the item.

The semi-autonomous way in which the task force works makes it particularly well suited to the private sector where the application of SE has tended to be on product evolution or product improvement programmes. In part, the timescale benefits come from the fact that much of the advanced engineering is done in parallel with the concept study; the implication of this is that the product specification can only be defined some way into the project. This may be perfectly acceptable to a company that takes a flexible view and wishes to draw on the expertise of its task force to evolve a product specification that will secure it the best commercial advantage in terms of development time, quality and cost. It may not, however, be acceptable to an outside organization that has contracted for a product to be developed. Such organizations usually set their own specifications, and until these are fully defined and agreed, would be unwilling to release anything other than minimal funds for advanced engineering. Where really novel or breakthrough projects are attempted, there can be questions over the broad front approach; it often happens that a more evolutionary process takes place, and investment made in production engineering at an early stage could prove to be nugatory as the product evolves into something different from that originally envisaged. For example, the Concorde aircraft underwent a major re-design between the prototype and production aircraft, as did the Harrier V/STOL fighter that evolved from the earlier Kestrel.

Simultaneous engineering has much to offer as a managerial concept and it fits well with the management-by-projects approach; the emphasis on team working and involvement of all relevant disciplines at the start is a welcome change from some of the more proceduralized methods used in the past. Its application marks a cultural shift and anyone contemplating introducing it should recognize that fact and be prepared for the problems it can raise. Whereas it undoubtedly brings advantages, it should not be considered a panacea; its most suitable use is in projects where the outcome is reasonably well assured. Where the outcome is less certain, either because of the customer or the technology, a more cautious, step-by-step approach may be appropriate.

Quality by design

Mention has already been made of the fact that Japanese design techniques have resulted in products with a level of quality and reliability that is often superior to their Western counterparts. The team approach that accompanies SE ensures that quality management staff are involved in the design process throughout the project and are no longer seen in their traditional role of inspectors who simply pronounce judgement on other people's work. This new role places a responsibility on quality engineers to play a creative part in the design process; they can no longer assume the posture of critics, but should be looking to find ways that ensure quality, reliability and performance are a direct function of the design, not merely related to the number of defects that might lay undiscovered in any product.

Quality has its price and cost-effectiveness comes into the equation, one simple solution to many quality problems is to specify more exotic or stronger materials, improve the finishes and tighten up the manufacturing tolerances. This would certainly improve performance in some respects but it could lead to a product in the Rolls-Royce category, too expensive for the mass market. If the business strategy is to concentrate on niche markets, then this may be appropriate; but if the everyday market is the goal, a more subtle and sophisticated approach is needed. The Japanese have shown that high quality and reliability is a direct function both of the design concept and the detail of the engineering. Foremost among the techniques they have pioneered are the methods devised by Dr Genichi Taguchi. He introduced the concept of 'robustness' in design, by which he meant the ability of a design to tolerate deviations without its performance being affected. Robust designs have inherently high reliability but they do not necessarily need to cost more; in fact robust designs tend to have fewer parts and only require close tolerances where they can really contribute to performance.

Taguchi methods

Statistical process control has been a feature of quality assurance methods for many years but the application of statistical methods to the design process is a more recent innovation. Genichi Taguchi devised its methodology while working for the Japanese telecommunications company NTT and brought it to the USA in 1980, where it was quickly adopted by Ford followed by General Motors, Xerox, ITT and others. Taguchi's emphasis on the design stage being crucial to reliability as well as performance stems from studies that showed that no more than 20% of quality defects can be traced to the production line, the remaining 80% derive either from the inherent features of the design or from purchasing policies that value low price over the quality of purchased parts and materials.

The basis of Taguchi's methods lies in the branch of applied statistics that deals with the analysis of variance; it allows the relative contributions of various factors that contribute to an observed effect to be separated and measured. By careful experiment design, the important factors that combine to degrade product performance can be isolated and design effort may be applied to remove these factors. It will be realized from this that Taguchi methods are most suitable for use with products made in quantity; companies that tend to produce one-off, custom-built items will find less use for them unless their products are assembled largely from standard designs and parts.

Product design can be divided into three major areas:

1. System design.
2. Parameter design.
3. Tolerance design.

System design involves the creative processes of the designer to create the initial functional design; it may work but it is unlikely to be optimal in terms of either performance or cost. **Parameter design** is the process of optimizing the controllable design features such that the system is not merely functional, but maintains a high level of performance under a wide range of conditions. **Tolerance design** involves setting limits on product or process variability such that system performance can be maintained.

In many industries only steps 1 and 3 are performed. A design is created to meet a functional specification; if it functions as required, tests are conducted to determine reliability, etc., and where problems are seen, higher-quality, closer-tolerance parts are specified to cure the difficulty. The opportunity to test the design features for optimality is simply overlooked. Taguchi lays emphasis on assessing the features of the design that are under the designer's control (the parameters) and then proposes a system of experiments to identify those parameters that contribute most to performance and variability. The designer is thus guided towards applying effort to those areas of the design where the greatest benefits can be obtained. Whereas this may lead to tighter tolerances and higher specification materials in some areas, significant reductions in costs can be obtained in other areas where the contribution to performance or variability is small.

Taguchi proposes a technique for experiment design that allows products, systems or components to be tested to determine the effects of various internal and external factors on the performance of the item under study. Experiments are designed using orthogonal arrays of parameters and disturbing effects. The controllable parameters are inherent in the product or process performance. They arise directly from the design and must be identified, the expected levels of variability must also be defined. External factors that are outside the control of the designer also have a bearing on product performance, such effects are termed 'noises'. These also must be recognized and quantified, along with the levels of variability that can be expected. Using these

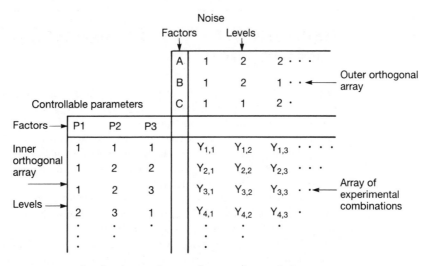

Figure 5.2 Example of orthogonal arrays for experiment design.

two sets of variables, a series of experiments can be designed that is precise in its results, yet economical in terms of the number of tests to be carried out, for several variables can be tested simultaneously. Controllable parameters and their levels of variability are defined in an **inner orthogonal array**; noises and their levels of variability are described in an **outer orthogonal array**. The matrix of experimental combinations is formed by the combination of the two orthogonal arrays; Figure 5.2 shows the format.

An experiment must be performed for each combination in the array. These could be in the form of laboratory tests or they may be simulated if the relationships between the parameters and noise variables can be defined mathematically. To measure the effect of each variation of a parameter on system performance, Taguchi uses the **signal-to-noise ratio** (S/N ratio). Over 40 S/N ratios are proposed depending on the experiment's objective. In general, S/N ratios relate the sample mean (average value) to the spread of results (standard deviation). If, for example, the objective is to minimize a particular characteristic (e.g. vibration, wear, friction, etc.), then the appropriate S/N to choose would be the one that selects the 'smallest-the-best' result; for this case it is:

$$S/N \text{ (smallest-the-best)} = -10 \times \log(\text{mean square deviation}) \qquad (5.1)$$
$$= -10 \times \log(1/n \times \Sigma Y_i^2)$$

Other particularly useful S/N ratios are '**nominal-the-best**' when closeness to a particular specification is preferred (e.g. oil viscosity) or '**largest-the-best**' where the highest value is preferable (e.g. component strength).

The S/N ratios for the matrix of controllable design parameters with respect to the levels at which they can be set forms a response table. This can be examined to determine the optimum level of each control variable to cope with the defined noise levels. The use of the orthogonal arrays and the S/N ratio to design a test sequence and interpret the result is illustrated by an example.

Example 5.1: Test for lowest fuel consumption

Suppose a new fuel additive for petrol engines became available that is claimed to reduce fuel burn and a designer wishes to test if (a) the claim is true, (b) what proportion of additive is best and (c) whether it is more effective than some other simple modifications that are also being considered. The modifications are: reducing the viscosity rating of the specified oil and increasing the thermostat operating temperature. The nominal fuel consumption at the rated power output is 12.51 per hour.

The oil is to be tested at levels between SAE 50 and 10, the fuel additive at concentrations between 2% and 10% and the temperature between 80°C and 90°C. As these parameters are all within the control of the designer, they will form the factors in the inner array. Noise effects must also be considered and two are felt to be significant: (a) the fuel may be either leaded or unleaded; and (b) the ambient temperature may be 15°C above the test nominal temperature. Thus the arrays of controllable parameters and noise factors are as given in Table 5.1.

For the experiment design, a standard Taguchi array has been selected for three variables at three levels for the controllable parameters. This is the inner orthogonal array at the left and the set of nine tests is much less than the total number of combinations possible. The full combination of possible tests is given for the outer noise array at the top. For each combination of variables a test is performed and the fuel consumption at rated power is noted. The results are given in Table 5.2.

The S/N ratio is the performance measure that accounts for both the mean and the variability; Taguchi proposes many different S/N ratios but the smallest-the-best S/N is appropriate as the best result will occur with the lowest consumption. The formula has already been quoted:

$$S/N = -10 \times \log(1/n \times \Sigma Y_i^2)$$

The S/N ratios have been computed and are inserted beside the results tabulation; for test series No. 1 the S/N ratio is:

$$-10 \times \log_{10}(1/4 \times (12.7^2 + 12.4^2 + 12.3^2 + 12.0^2)) = -21.835$$

It is necessary to determine the contribution of each control parameter and the level at which it will best meet the objective of low consumption. This is done by assessing the average S/N ratios for each combination of parameter and level. These are termed the responses and are shown in Table 5.3.

The response is calculated by taking the average S/N from the S/N ratios that were observed each time the variable and level were used in combination. Thus parameter F1 at level 1 was used in experiment sets 1, 2 and 3 and the response S/N ratio is the average of these three S/Ns:

$$\text{F1 at Level 1, S/N} = -1/3(21.835 + 21.788 + 21.974) = -21.869$$

Plotting the S/N ratios for each parameter against each level clearly shows the effects of each variable and the best choice of parameters for the best fuel consumption; this is shown in Figure 5.3.

Table 5.1 Experimental variables and levels

Controllable parameters

	F1 Oil viscosity	F2 Fuel additive	F3 Temperature
Level 1	SAE 50	2%	80°C
Level 2	SAE 30	5%	85°C
Level 3	SAE 10	10%	90°C

Noise factors

	A Fuel type	B Ambient temperature
Level 1	Leaded	Nominal
Level 2	Unleaded	+15°C

Table 5.2 Test results and computed S/N ratios

No.	F1	F2	F3	A	1	1	2	2	S/N ratio
				B	1	2	1	2	
		Levels				Results (l/h)			
1	1	1	1		12.7	12.4	12.3	12.0	−21.835
2	1	2	2		12.3	12.2	12.4	12.3	−21.798
3	1	3	3		12.2	12.7	12.8	12.5	−21.974
4	2	1	2		12.2	12.4	12.5	12.1	−21.799
5	2	2	3		12.1	12.4	12.6	12.3	−21.834
6	2	3	1		11.9	12.1	12.0	12.3	−21.638
7	3	1	3		12.4	12.6	12.9	12.4	−21.991
8	3	2	1		12.2	12.0	12.1	12.3	−21.692
9	3	3	2		11.9	12.0	11.6	11.9	−21.475

Table 5.3 S/N ratio, response table

		Parameters F1	F2	F3
Levels	1	−21.869	−21.875	−21.721
	2	−21.757	−21.774	−21.690
	3	−21.719	−21.695	−21.933

Variable F2, the fuel additive, is the most effective factor and level 3, a 10% concentration, would be the best parameter level. The oil viscosity has less effect, but the thinnest oil consistent with good engine lubrication would be the best choice, again level 3. Increasing the engine temperature shows a small increase in performance up to level 2 but then drops with increasing temperature. The optimum parameter settings for lowest fuel consumption happen to correspond to test No. 9 but this does not always occur. When an untested

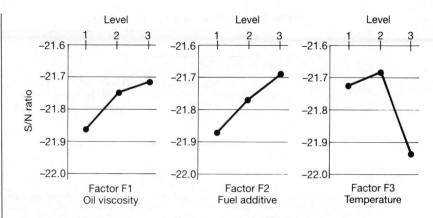

Figure 5.3 S/N ratios plotted against variable levels for each factor.

combination is suggested as being the best, a test should be run to confirm the result. The average fuel consumption over the four runs in test No. 9 was 11.851 per hour, this is a reduction of 5.2% over the nominal consumption figure.

The example shows just one aspect of Taguchi's approach to product design through experimentation. Any factor that one chooses to make a design objective could be the subject of the method; for example, choosing between low-cost alternative components could be done through Taguchi testing if low production cost for consistent performance is a principal objective. Market reaction to product changes could also be studied in a similar way. **Quality function deployment** takes this a step further, it is a technique that allows a firm to use the results of its market research to specify the engineering parameters of a product's design that will best meet its customers' needs. A principal feature of Taguchi's strategy is that the failure of a product to meet customer expectations, either through failure to perform as specified or producing undesirable side-effects, produces a measurable loss both to the producer and society as a whole. This loss is defined through a parameter termed the **quality loss function** (QLF); a high QLF affects the producer through excessive scrap, reduced output, high labour costs, etc. Target values may be set for the QLF against which both the performance of the design and the product can be measured (Taguchi, 1989). Its greatest use would appear to be in the area of process control during production. Taguchi suggests that the costs associated with poor quality are proportional to the square of the deviation of any parameter from its target value; thus:

$$L_y = K (y - m)^2 \tag{5.2}$$

where: L_y = the loss associated with the deviation of parameter y
K = a constant of proportionality
y = the target value of the parameter
m = the measured actual value of the parameter

This relationship yields a parabolic loss curve equally distributed about the target value. Taguchi lays emphasis on the achievement of the target value with as little deviation as possible rather than the traditional approach of simply accepting components or features that lie within the extremes of their tolerance. There is an obvious intellectual appeal in this proposition but it does raise some questions about both its realism and its practicality. There will clearly be cases where the loss associated with deviating from target in one direction will be much greater than the other. For example, in the case of the hardness of components from a batch after heat treatment, those that are under-hard will either be rejected and be a total loss or be re-hardened and incur an additional processing cost but those that are well above nominal hardness may still be acceptable and thus incur no loss at all. A half-parabola may be more appropriate in this case.

The concept of a continuously increasing loss associated with deviation from target also implies that the use of Go/No-Go gauges should be phased out in favour of direct measurement during the manufacturing process. The costs and practicality of doing this needs careful consideration in the context of any particular process or operation. As the Quality Loss Function is essentially an economic argument in favour of conformance with the nominal specification, determining exactly what losses are incurred due to small deviations needs to be done carefully as well as assessing the costs of more precise measurements. The practicalities of the production situation and human attitudes have also to be considered. For example, take the case of an operator grinding the bore of a cylinder to fine tolerances; if he had achieved a diameter that was just inside the lower limit, and thus technically acceptable, should he be encouraged to take another cut to bring the diameter closer to the target value when a) this would increase the time per piece thus putting up the product cost and possibly reduce his bonus earnings and b) run the risk of taking too deep a cut and scrapping the part?

Taguchi methods have proved themselves to be effective within the companies that have adopted them. They are not, however, a solution for all design and quality problems and they will not solve fundamental problems of design technology. The methods have not achieved complete acceptance amongst all quality practitioners and some have argued that in certain cases the results are no better than with earlier more conventional experimental methods and may even be misleading (Tribus and Szonyl, 1989; Hendrix, 1991). However, where the technology is well established but significant problems are encountered with performance, reliability and repeatability, then the methods can serve to identify ways in which these difficulties can be designed out. By concentrating effort in the areas at the root of the problems, the solutions that are evolved should be the most economical. Applications of Taguchi methods that have been published have tended to indicate that they have found their greatest use when applied to specific components or individual features of a design rather than to complex products as a whole. Instances of successful use of the methods include the following (Taguchi, 1989):

- Defect reduction in grey iron castings
  - 45% reduction achieved.
- Reduction in leaf-spring free height variability
  - variability reduced by 82%.
- Maximizing the integrity of spot welds
  - time per weld reduced by 33%.
- Improving the di-electric strength of high-tension ignition cables
  - improvement achieved within existing processes.
- Reducing tool costs and increasing productivity for nylon tube assemblies
  - tool cost reduced by 75%, productivity increased by 20%.
- Improving the durability of emission control harnesses
  - inspection savings of $100 000 per month.

This has been a brief description of a very comprehensive and complex methodology; readers wishing to study this subject in more detail are referred to Dr Taguchi's original texts listed in the Further reading section.

Design reviews

Mention has already been made of project reviews, but the design itself should be subject to review at points in the development process where significant commitments have to be made. In cases where the project is externally funded, the sponsor may demand that reviews are carried out in his presence prior to release of funds for the next stage. Whether externally funded or not, there is much to be said for at least one formalized design review during the development phase. Often two are carried out, one towards the end of the prototype phase, sometimes termed a 'preliminary design review', and a second one prior to commitment of money on the production phase, sometimes called a 'critical design review'.

The purpose of the **preliminary design review** will be to appraise the progress of the design in meeting all its objectives; in essence, the emerging design is assessed against its specification in all aspects: performance, cost, timescale, reliability, etc. Some of these factors will not have been fully explored at the time the review is carried out, but the Design Department should be in a position to make statements on all these issues, based on (a) the design that has been created, (b) test results obtained or (c) estimates based on studies already carried out. This review should take a close look at what has been achieved to date, and ask itself if the emerging product is likely to be satisfactory and the right one for the market. Beyond this review, the scope for changing the product will be much less as most of the development work will have been completed before the next review.

The **critical design review** serves to assess the product as it has been developed and, more important, the proposed production item. It also serves to ensure that the design has been carried out correctly and that no facets of the design process have been omitted. Where external sponsors are concerned, they will take a critical look at the product from the viewpoint of their specification and how well it meets it; they may also ask how much is the production item going to cost? Whereas the preliminary design review can generate guidance to the design team in terms of the way the design should evolve, the changes that should be made and any additional work that should be carried out, the critical design review is primarily a confirmatory exercise – a last chance to ensure that the design is right before money is committed to production.

Design reviews may be called by the sponsoring organization in an externally funded project, or by the Technical Director or Project Manager in a private project. They are normally carried out in front of a review panel who act as assessors. Sponsoring organizations or Technical Directors generally do not wish to act as chairman at the review (this is often delegated to the Project Manager), but they will normally expect to be involved in setting the agenda.

Depending on whether the project is internally or externally funded, the conduct of the review and the stances taken by the individuals can vary. For the most part, with internally funded projects the participants can be much more free with comments as all parties stand to gain from criticism that leads to constructive new ideas that will improve the competitive position of the product. Everyone in the review process has an interest in seeing the most commercially attractive product emerge. With externally funded projects, the position is rather different – the sponsor will be looking to see that the product meets his requirements in all respects. He may be eager to criticize small deviations if he can use this to negotiate price reductions on production items on the grounds of failure to meet the full specification. In this case, the design review can become something of a politically charged event, with the developing contractor seeking to show his product in the best possible light and avoiding difficult issues.

The composition of the review panel can very according to circumstances, but the most important thing is that the members should be completely independent of the project. For many projects a review panel of three consisting of representatives from the Design, Marketing and Production departments would be adequate; large, complex projects may demand a larger panel. A secretary is usually appointed to note all discussion and suggestions arising; because of the technical nature of much of the conversation, this person is usually an engineer. The agenda might typically consist of:

- A review of the objectives of the project.
- A description of the design features and performance characteristics.
- A review of progress to date and problems encountered.
- A review of outstanding areas of work and any concerns arising.
- An assessment of the design against a design review checklist.
- A summary of findings by the review panel.

Representatives from all departments who are actually working on the project will be expected to give a presentation and answer questions. The secretary's minutes will normally be circulated to attendees and include all recommendations and actions mentioned at the review. After the review, the panel may reconvene and compile a separate report on their findings and recommendations. Whether an internally or externally funded project is involved, the status of the review panel is generally an advisory one; it will be for the Project Manager and the Principal Designer to consider all recommendations and decide which should be implemented.

Design review checklists

Checklists are an important feature of the review process as they serve to stimulate enquiry and discussion, as well as ensuring that important issues are not forgotten. Each type of product will have its own special characteristics that demand attention, hence an all-purpose checklist would be impossible to compile, but general subject areas tend to be similar. Topics that would form the basis of a checklist are:

Specification
   Is the specification full and complete?
   Are there areas still to be defined or agreed with the customer?
   Is there scope for changing the specification?
   Are changes desirable?

Market
   Are all marketing studies complete?
   Do market studies indicate that the product as specified will sell?
   What competition exists and do their designs have significantly better features?

Have target selling price levels been established?

Have sales volume estimates been made and what confidence can be had in them?

Technical

Performance and specification

Are there areas where difficulties can be expected in meeting the specification?

Has sufficient testing been done to ensure that all areas of the specification can be met?

Will additional testing to that in the programme be needed?

Are any modifications proposed as a result of the tests?

Are there any areas where performance is significantly better than specified and can this be exploited?

Has product reliability been established?

Drawing status

How complete is the drawing set?

When will a set of production drawings be ready?

Are significant changes expected between the development and production standards?

Value engineering

Have design-to-cost principles been applied?

Have all VE studies been completed?

Have all recommendations been incorporated?

Will incorporation have any impact on or nullify tests already completed?

Are significant changes possible resulting from ongoing studies?

Product legislation

Does the product design comply with all relevant health and safety standards, codes of practice (British Standards or others) and environmental standards?

Have all certification and legally required approval or type tests been planned or carried out?

Will additional testing or product modifications be required to conform to overseas standards?

Intellectual property

Are any aspects of the design patentable?

Are any aspects of the design likely to infringe existing patents?

In either case, what action has been taken?

Production

Have all production engineering studies been completed?

Have any expensive, difficult to manufacture, short supply, sole-source or overseas-supplied items been identified?

Have any recommendations been made about these points?

Have requirements for special tools, fixtures and facilities been defined?

Have production costs been established?

Are these estimates or have firm quotations been received?

Quality Assurance

Has a quality plan been prepared?

Have any aspects of the design been identified where quality/repeatability problems can be foreseen?

Are adequate configuration control procedure in place to assure confidence in the production item conforming to specification?

Configuration management

In any complex project, keeping a tight control on changes to the design as the product evolves can be one of the greatest challenges to the project team. The increasing complexity of modern products that frequently involve interfaces between electrical, mechanical, hardware and software elements implies that the scope for discrepancies and mismatches between constituents is growing at a rate not seen previously. **Configuration management** has grown up as a discipline that provides a framework in which a product can be structured and changes can take place in a controlled fashion.

Its origins as a distinct technique lie in the early days of the 'space race' in the 1950s. Massively sophisticated systems were being evolved to launch and control space vehicles involving the most complex interfaces between individual elements that had ever been created. Large amounts of trial, test and modification work was done on what were essentially one-off vehicles. The problem came when the US Air Force wanted to order repeat versions of successful systems; no one could say exactly what had been built and matters really came to a head, in one instance, when the only way to find out what had been made was to examine the actual article – unfortunately, that was in orbit. It was clear that industry was not sufficiently well organized in the area of design, manufacture and quality control for customer organizations such as the Department of Defense and NASA to be confident that the products they were receiving conformed to the expected design standard. Determined to change the situation, and after much research and consultation with industry, the US Air Force, in 1962, issued AFSCM 375-1, 'Configuration Management in the Development and Acquisition Phases'. It set down the basic principles for design, modification and manufacture control and these remain good today.

Confusion over terms

The term **configuration management** is less well used in the UK where **configuration control** is currently more popular. This is somewhat confusing as, in the original US definition, a specific meaning was given to configuration control, and even though this term arose in aviation circles, it has also acquired other and somewhat different meanings within that same aviation context (Figure 5.4). However, the term configuration management seems to be gaining wider recognition, if not usage, and will be used here as the overall term for the subject. It was originally used in the context of electromechanical systems but it has now been taken up by the software developers. For the remainder of this discussion **configuration management** shall be defined as: *The discipline of identifying the constituent elements that make up a product, together with all that is necessary to define the manufacture and support of that product, and then systematically controlling changes to all of these items such that the traceability and integrity of the design in terms of form, fit and functional requirements is maintained throughout its life cycle.*

A similar but rather more elaborate definition can be found in BS 5750, section 8.8: 'Design change control'. It will be appreciated that we are considering an information system and a method of ensuring that when changes occur, the resulting product will be as the designer intended. Figure 5.5 shows the principal elements of

Configuration Control is used to describe a system within an aircraft that manages the external shape of the craft in flight and responds according to the flight conditions and control demands. Such a system would be used in an aircraft that, for example, combined thrust vectoring with a variable foreplane, both of which could be used in an interactive mode to generate unusual flying characteristics. Configuration in this context refers to the geometric arrangement of both the flying and control surfaces and the engine. Aircraft of this type are called Control Configured Vehicles (CCVs)

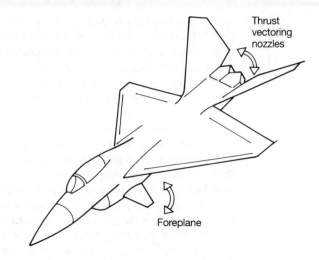

Hypothetical control-configured aircraft

Configuration Control in the context of aircraft construction is sometimes used to mean a system that ensures that the aircraft 'as drawn' and the aircraft 'as built' are the same. It arises from the difference between the way aircraft are designed and the way they are built. For example, the fuel system consists of tanks, pipes, etc., a set of drawings will be generated to define the system and it is from this that it will be approved as complying with the design requirements. However, the main tanks are also likely to be the wing structure as it is common practice to store the fuel between the spars. The tanks will, thus, not be built as tanks in their own right but as part of a wing. For ease of assembly, aircraft are built in sections with the various systems and fittings installed in them prior to join-up. Thus, the fuel system will not be built as a separate system and installed in the plane but will come as part of the major sections. When they are joined-up a fuel system will exist.

The problem is one of ensuring that all the parts that are called up on the system drawings (the 'as drawn' standard) are included in the parts listings in the assembly process sheets that define how any section of the plane is to be built and what is to be included (the 'as built' standard).

The 'as drawn' fuel system

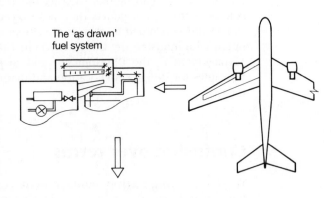

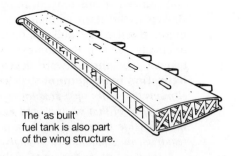

The 'as built' fuel tank is also part of the wing structure.

Configuration Control: Aircraft manufacture

Figure 5.4 Other uses of the term 'configuration control'.

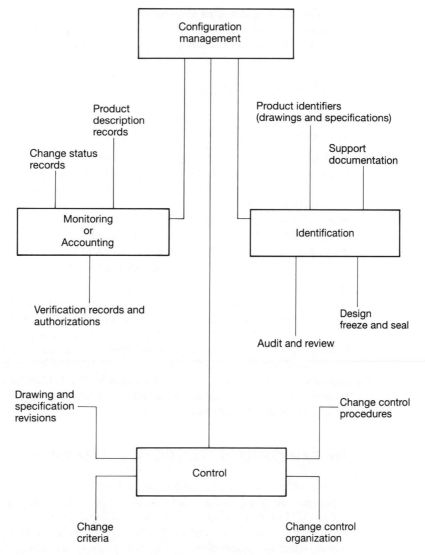

Figure 5.5 Functional relationships within configuration management.

configuration management, and they are defined below. Configuration management is the general term which describes the total discipline and has been defined above.

Configuration identification refers to: *the complete description of the physical and functional characteristics of a product. The term can also be applied in a wider context than just the product drawings and can include the technical descriptions to build, test, operate, enhance and maintain the product.*

Configuration control is: *the systematic evaluation, coordination and approval of proposed changes to the design of a product whose configuration has been formally approved.*

Configuration status accounting or **configuration monitoring** is: *the recording and reporting of product descriptions and all departures planned or made from the authorized design through comparison with the as-built standard of the item.*

An additional element was also identified in the original concept and that was

configuration audit and review, this involves formalized inspections and conformance checks at the output of the first item of each new or significant standard. It can, however, also be considered as part of configuration identification.

Project suitability

In general, projects that are most suitable for configuration management are ones that exhibit some or all of the following characteristics:

- There is a large and complex technical content.
- Extensive and sophisticated test programmes are involved.
- Support equipment, services and software are of a complexity comparable with the principal item.
- A high percentage of the work is subcontracted.
- Repeatable volume production is anticipated.
- A variety of production standards is anticipated.
- A high incidence of design or engineering change is characteristic.

This list characterizes the aerospace industry from which the technique originated but it is by no means the only business sector that can benefit from its application. Many of these factors apply to the development of software, hence the growing application of the technique to the creation of increasingly complex computer systems where the configuration aspects apply both to the hardware and software. In many cases, the last four factors, by themselves, make its use worthwhile. High incidences of engineering change often tend to result from technical complexity but it need not be the only cause, particularly if a large number of variants is created to specific customer requirements.

Design control during development

Configuration management will be considered in the context of a project to develop a product designed to be made in quantity; this implies a somewhat narrower definition, but it will illustrate all the principles. Control of the design is needed at each stage of a development project; certain elements have to be formalized at the outset, while for others this tight formality can be left until a later point. Figure 5.6 shows the basic elements of the configuration management process though the various stages of the project.

Where subcontract design authorities are concerned, the two most important elements of information that need to be controlled are the design specification and the interface definition. The **design specification** defines the performance requirements of the item to be created, together with any other criteria, such as environmental conditions, design standards that have to be complied with and, possibly, cost targets. The **interface definition** specifies the physical dimensions to which the item must conform if it is to work as part of a larger system. Other interface aspects will be covered, if necessary, such as electrical characteristics (input supply currents, bonding and screening requirements, etc.) or fluid flow requirements (mass flow rates, pressures, etc.). These two documents form the basis from which all design starts and must be brought under formal control at the beginning of the project; agreement to them should form part of the contract arrangements and any change carries the implication of a contract change. It is normal practice to set up specifi-

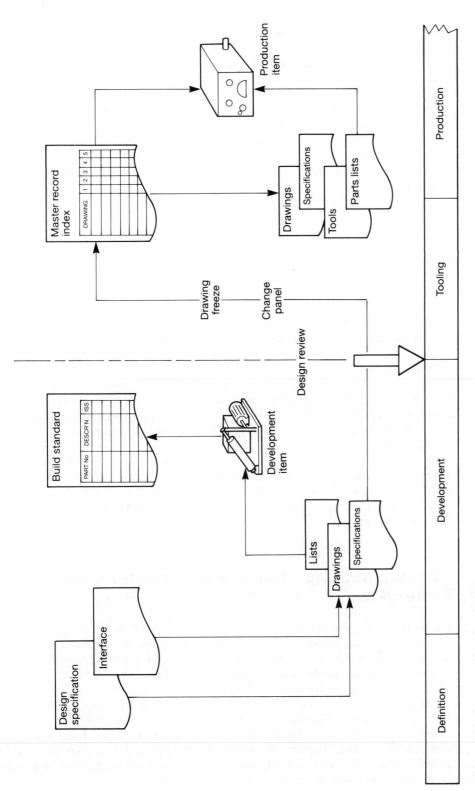

Figure 5.6 Configuration management through the project cycle.

cation and interface registers where a record of issue number, date, change details, circulation, etc. are kept.

During the development phase, design changes will be frequent as difficulties are experienced with manufacture, and testing produces adverse results. The customer may require alterations in the knowledge of the emerging product or the marketing department may suggest changes to improve sales potential. Whatever the reason, the systems used to control change during development must not be so cumbersome that change is inhibited as this could have an adverse effect on the development timescale and the end-product. For this reason, normal drawing office procedures are used for raising the issue of drawings and releasing them for manufacture. There will normally be one authorized signatory for passing off drawings and normal inspection procedures will be used to ensure that the item conforms to the standard required.

When testing is carried out, it is important to know exactly what standard of hardware has been used; this can often be difficult through direct reference to the drawing set as many changes may have been introduced, thus the issue status of the complete set with respect to any particular build may be impossible to define. This problem can reach a peak of complexity where a variety of standards for the product are needed, each of which is used to test a particular feature and which may have components deleted or added to aid testing. Under these conditions, test hardware is usually defined by a **'build standard'**; this is a retrospective compilation of the drawing issues that relate to the item as built, and it is normally compiled from the build record cards.

It becomes particularly important to be able to define the production item fully when the time comes to procure tools and machinery for volume production. Once tooling-up begins, the less formal controls that may have been applied during the development programme will need to be tightened. An endless stream of small modifications or uncontrolled changes after tools have been purchased can wreck production schedules, send costs soaring and lead to frustration. To avoid these problems the drawing set is normally brought under formal control. This process is often called **'freezing'** and from that point the design will come under the control of an Engineering Change Panel or Modifications Committee; it cannot be changed without their consent.

The Engineering Change Panel/Modifications Committee

As the design approaches the end of development it will be necessary to start the process of releasing drawings for production. During the development programme, expedience combined with good record-keeping is the main criterion for drawing control, but in the production situation repeatability, standardization, traceability and product assurance become the dominant issues. Entry into production is also a significant step from a cost point of view, and for these reasons, an Engineering Change Panel or Modifications Committee is often set up. The first task of the Change Panel will be to assess each drawing against known requirements, trials information, pending changes, etc. and to decide at what point either an individual drawing or a sub-system drawing set can be released for production. If sufficient confidence exists that the drawing is not likely to change, then the drawing will be deemed to be 'frozen' and release for production can occur. Freezing of a drawing is sometimes signalled by giving it a new part number at issue 1 or reissuing the drawing with a new issue number.

The reasons for this approach are:

(a) To ensure that full consideration is given to the design state of each item before production release.
(b) To ensure standardization of the production item.
(c) To stop the introduction of small variations on a random basis.
(d) To stop uncontrolled cost growth.
(e) To ensure traceability of modification action.

The Change Panel will usually be chaired by the Chief Engineer, Chief Designer or the Project Manager; it is most important that the chairman should have an appreciation of the whole design and production situation. The composition of the panel should encompass most of the departments: Design or Drawing Office, Production Engineering, Shop Management, Purchasing, Quality Control, Reliability Engineering and, possibly, Marketing who should be able to give an assessment of customer reaction.

The roles and responsibilities of the Change Panel are:

(a) To assess all drawings as to their fitness for production and apply the 'freezing' procedure.
(b) To vet all proposed modifications for feasibility, desirability and effect on cost, programme and market.
(c) To issue instructions on embodiment of modifications that are satisfactory, given the criteria in (b) and reject those that are not.
(d) To maintain control of the drawing set and build definition.

When the need for a modification arises, this is signalled by the raising of a **modification proposal** or **engineering change proposal** by a responsible member of the design organization. Items that need to be included on the proposal are:

(a) Originator.
(b) Description of change.
(c) Evidence in support of change.
(d) Drawings affected.
(e) Effect on prices and costs:
  – unit production price;
  – new tooling, gauging and test equipment;
  – scrap costs or cancellation costs;
  – design incorporation costs.
(f) Point of introduction of change in production.
(g) Effect on product performance, characteristics, qualification, safety or reliability.
(h) Manuals, handbooks or specifications affected.
(i) Any other companies involved who should be notified.
(j) Additional or repeat testing.
(k) Interchangeability.

An example of a modification proposal form is shown in Figure 5.7.

Formal change proposals should be submitted to a technical clerk or junior engineer, who should collate all proposals and present them to the Change Panel; he or she can also progress successful proposals to see that they are implemented and act as a secretary to the panel. He should maintain records of all panel meetings, taking and circulating minutes, as well as keeping a record of all proposals submitted, the decisions made and subsequent action taken.

ENGINEERING CHANGE PROPOSAL

Title: *New Plastic Cover* Originator: *P.L.P.* Date: *11/3/93* Mod No: *M137*

Product: *Control Unit* Drawing: *P 19·17* Type No: *P20*

DESIGN

Proposed Change	Reasons for Change
The current cover is an alloy casting. It is proposed to change it to a polycarbonate moulding. See sketch attached.	Value engineering study shows a worthwhile saving. See report VE/061 attached.

Performance Affected: No	Safety Affected: No
Reliability/Maintainability Affected: No	Support Equipment Affected: No
Interchangeability Affected: Yes. New fixings may be needed.	Certification/Qualification Affected: No

PRODUCTION

Applicable series of Production Items: From *3001* to *End*

Delay in Production: — weeks. Firms Affected: *Aldie Castings*
            No further orders beyond item 3000

Recall Required Y/N: No Items Affected:

Effect on Unit Production Cost: £ *12·50* per Unit *SAVING*

ESTIMATED COSTS OF EMBODIMENT

Design Incorporation:		Trials/Tests:	
Hrs. 52	Cost £ 1,620	Hrs. —	Cost £
Scrap: —	Cost £	Facilities: —	Cost £
Cancellation Cost: £		Production Equipment: Tools: *Mould tool*	Cost £ 3,500
Recall: —	Cost £	Gauges: —	Cost £
Rework: —	Cost: £	Test Gear: —	Cost £
Total Cost of Embodiment: £ 5,120			

CHANGE PANEL RECOMMENDATION

Implement as written. Recommend look at further use of polycarbonate.

Signed: *J. Davis* Date: *24/4/93* Circulation: *JFL, BW, RFL*
PANEL CHAIRMAN

ATTACH ADDITIONAL SUPPORTING MATERIAL FOR CIRCULATION

Figure 5.7 Example of an engineering change proposal form.

The Master Record Index

As modifications are approved they will be entered into the drawing set. The composition of the drawing set will thus be altering continuously and, consequently, the design standard of the deliverable item. A precise knowledge of the standard of all issues of components in the final item is vital to ensure:

- that components ordered into production will fit into their respective assemblies;
- that the end item is as the designer intended;
- that the correct standard of components can be produced if spares are needed.

As modifications are incorporated, all the drawings affected must be recorded against the modification number. If the drawing set is large, this may appear a laborious process but there really is no alternative.

The document that contains the drawing numbers, issues, modification numbers and points of embodiment is often referred to as a **Master Record Index** (MRI)

MASTER RECORD INDEX									
MODULE No. P19-18	DESCRIPTION Control Console					Sheet 1 of 4 Sheets			
DESCRIPTION	ITEM No.	ISSUE NUMBERS							REMARKS
Cabinet, Console	P19-18A001-D	1	2	3	4	5	4		
Panel, Front	P19-18C001-D	1	2		3	4*	3		
Cleat, Panel	P19-18D002-D	1	2						
Bracket, Panel	P19-18D004-D	1							
Hinge	P19-18D005-D	1				2*	1		* For P.M.I.
Stiffener	P19-18D007-D	1			2	3*			
Stiffener	P19-18D008-D	1		2	3				
Panel, Side	P19-18C009-D	1							
～～～									
Bracket, Rack	P19-18D037-D	1		2					
MAIN ASSEMBLY Total Power Unit	MODIFICATION NUMBER	FREEZE	M003	M017	M039	M077	M080		For any Mod. the correct issue is the last issue shown.
ASSEMBLY No. P19-10A003	PRODUCTION INCORPORATION	001 to 999	001 to 999	001 to 999	060 to 999	101 to 999	151 to 999		
MAIN MRI NUMBER P19	MRI ISSUE NUMBER	1	2	3	4	5	6		DATE: 20-6-92

Figure 5.8   Master Record Index format.

or **Design Record**. The format of an MRI is shown in Figure 5.8. In the example shown in the figure if, for instance, in the future it is necessary to supply parts for the Console Cabinet No. 079, it can be seen that the correct drawing issues are detailed in issue 4 of the MRI as this issue applies to all items numbered between 060 and 100. Here items whose numbers are 101 to 150 had special modifications that were not incorporated in later production and a special modification had to be created to allow the design to revert to an earlier standard for production of items numbered 151 onwards.

This method has certain advantages, particularly if allied to the production control system; by raising a modification even where it reverts the design to an earlier standard, Production Control knows that the correct standard to order is that defined by the latest issue of the MRI. The MRI need not be confined to the detail part drawings, but may be extended to cover manufacturing specifications, process sheets, tools, gauges, etc.

Where the drawing set is very large, the MRI can be changing continuously if the number of modifications to be incorporated is large. While this situation may be unavoidable, the amount of administrative effort can be reduced by constructing a series of MRIs controlled by a top-level MRI. Each MRI controls the drawing set of a major sub-assembly or a major element of the system, but each can relate to the top level directly rather than by the logic of the main assembly sequence. The top-level MRI contains only the modification states of the MRIs beneath.

Control of the drawing set

This activity is closely allied to control of the master record index. Incorporation of modifications into the drawing set needs control if the MRI is not to become an unworkable document and it must be linked to the production plan. This plan, if it is for an item with a long production run, should define the batch sizes in which the product will be ordered. Knowledge of this plan is vital for the Change Panel as they will need to specify the modification incorporation points. It may be that a modification cannot be incorporated into production immediately because: (a) the machine producing the part cannot be taken out of the line until a scheduled maintenance point, or (b) a large quantity of the particular part has already been ordered. In this case, it will not be wise to incorporate the modification into the drawing set until shortly before production of the modified part begins. If this procedure is not obeyed, it can lead to a situation where parts are required at issue 6 but not incorporating the modification introduced at issue 5, obviously an undesirable situation. To avoid this a series of modification embodiment points (or design freeze points) should be defined to conform with the batches in the production plan. Modifications that cannot be embodied until some point in the future can be approved by the Change Panel but must be held back from incorporation in the drawing set until the design freeze point immediately preceding the point of production implementation. Figure 5.9 shows the principle, while Figure 5.10 shows the effect on the MRI of failing to hold back changes and the confused situation that arises.

If the drawing set is large with hundreds of parts, and the number of modifications is also large, the MRI may be changing so rapidly that an easy interface with the production control system becomes difficult when the item is in volume production. To avoid problems in deciding what issue of any particular part to manufacture, a

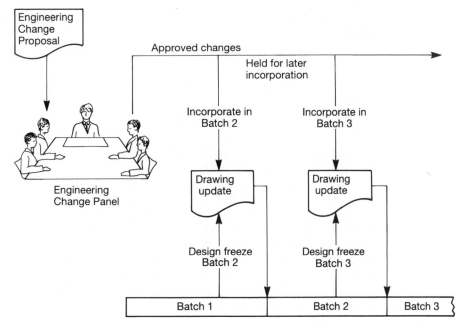

Figure 5.9 Updating the drawing set to conform with the production batches.

MASTER RECORD INDEX								
MODULE No. P19-18	DESCRIPTION Control Console					Sheet 1 of 4 Sheets		
DESCRIPTION	ITEM No.	ISSUE NUMBERS						REMARKS
Cabinet, Console	P19-18A001-D	1	2	3	4	5	6	
Panel, Front	P19-18C001-D	1	2		3	4		
Cleat, Panel	P19-18D002-D	1		2	3			
MAIN ASSEMBLY Total Power Unit	MODIFICATION NUMBER	FREEZE	M 0 0 3	M 0 1 7	M 0 3 9	M 0 7 7	M 0 8 0	For any Mod. the correct issue is the last issue shown.
ASSEMBLY No. P19-10A003	PRODUCTION INCORPORATION	001 to 999	001 to 999	251 to 350	101 to 150	060 to 999	351 to 999	
MAIN MRI NUMBER P19	MRI ISSUE NUMBER	1	2	3	4	5	6	DATE: 20-6-92

Figure 5.10 Illustration of difficulties with the MRI due to failure to incorporate changes in accordance with the production schedule. Confusion can arise if modifications are introduced into the drawing set in a way that is out of sequence with the production batches. It can result in theoretical standards that cannot be built. In the example, item No. 61 cannot be built to issue 5 of the MRI, even though it runs from item 60, as this contains modifications that apply from items 101 and 250, nor can item 101 be built to issue 4 as this does not contain a relevant modification at issue 5.

simple rule may be adopted. It is that the part number is changes if a modification introduces:

- a change to a part such that the part will no longer fit with either its neighbour or its assembly tooling; or
- it introduces a significant and specially required performance alteration or cost improvement.

To implement this system each part number must carry with it the series of items in the production sequence to which it is applicable. This procedure allows the production department to order parts for any item in the production run without reference to the drawing issue because the part number alone is sufficient information to indicate that it will fit with its assembly. This rule does not do away with the need for an MRI as a part may undergo many modifications which do not affect performance or interchangeability. Tolerance easements and revised surface treatments are typical of controllable changes that do not affect interchangeability.

For very complex projects, the above method may be the only way to effectively control the build as the definition contained in the drawing set and its MRI is too difficult to use. To make this work satisfactorily a separate build control system will be needed. Its primary function will be to generate the parts lists applicable to each standard of production hardware.

Control of the production item

Computerized **manufacturing resource planning** (MRP) systems have been developed over the past 30 years and all contain a facility for creating a build register that can relate detail parts to their sub-assemblies through to the final build. Quantities of parts per unit, lead-times, sources and destinations of parts, etc. can be contained within the register, hence such systems have much greater use than build control alone. Build and kit lists can be generated automatically and in the correct sequence. However, in order to arrive at a satisfactory definition of the assembly as finally built it will be necessary to note, on a history document, the issue numbers and, possible, batch numbers of the parts used. Here again, the computer can help as build records can be stored on a computer file.

Systems of this type are becoming increasingly common; not only do they aid shop loading, planning and build control, but the traceability of parts contained in the history files is increasingly being recognized for its contribution to quality control. In some industries traceability is mandatory for public safety reasons, but in other areas it is proving worthwhile when analysing defects and the frequency of failures that are reported by users of the product.

Very little software is available specifically designed for configuration management, but elements of the system can be found in contemporary MRP systems. These, however, tend to be full-scale production control systems but it is in this field that the reader should look for suitable software. One specifically designed system is 'Configuration Management Facility', marketed in the UK by GEC-Marconi Software Systems. It was developed by Expertware, Inc. of California and is intended for controlling the development of software. As such, it was designed around US DoD Standard 2167 that defines a means for establishing, evaluating and maintaining the quality of software and its associated documentation. The problems associated with software development have many parallels with that of hardware systems but the

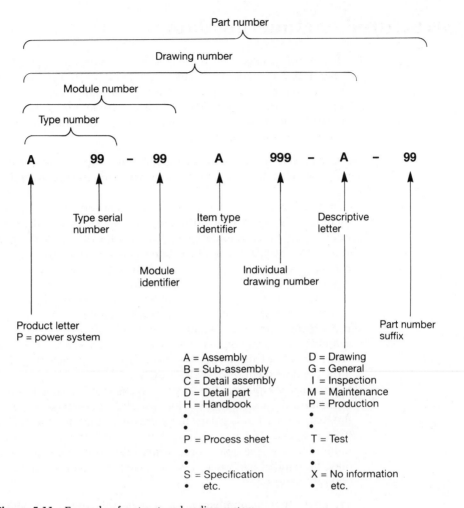

Figure 5.11 Example of a structured coding system.

scope for both errors and changes is many times greater. Parallels cannot be drawn in all areas, however, as the production phase of a project is not strictly analogous to software work.

In perspective

Configuration management can be viewed as an extension of good engineering management practice. Although there are costs to be incurred in operating the techniques, there are important benefits that stem from the formalized approach, in particular, production quality can be assured more easily and fewer errors should occur in the ordering process; both of these are beneficial to product cost; reliability and traceability are also improved. Project Managers responsible for developing new products will be aware that product quality is one more battleground on which the war of competition is being fought.

Structured engineering data

Configuration management is the process of controlling engineering data, it can be a complex task but it can be greatly simplified if a rational structure is applied to the dataset. Presented here is a numbering system that is applicable to a product that is designed as a series of discretely controlled modules but is also capable of being made in a variety of standards to the requirements of different customers. The coding structure is shown in Figure 5.11:

The *type number* is a three-character code made up of a letter indicating the product type followed by two digits taken out sequentially to indicate the particular product.

The *module identifier* is a two-digit number that indicates the particular module, the module indicator taken with the type number will give the module number. This number will be used to designate the MRI for the particular module.

The *item type identifier* is a single letter that indicates the nature of the item; for example, A = Assembly; B = Sub-assembly; C = Detail assembly; H = Handbook; P = Process sheet; S = Specification; etc.

The *individual item number* is a three-digit number taken out sequentially from a register, one register being kept for each module.

The *descriptive letter* is an additional item of information to aid identification; for example, D = Drawing; G = General; I = Inspection; P = Production; X = No information. All the characters taken up to and including the descriptive letter form the document or drawing number.

The *part number suffix* is defined by two digits that are added to the drawing number to indicate the part number. This is useful in a data structure as it indicates that the item referred to is a part, not a drawing; it allows one drawing to define more than one part and is thus useful in keeping the size of the drawing set to a minimum. For example, some firms draw only one item of a pair where an opposite handed equivalent is also needed, the part as-drawn is coded 01 and its opposite hand 02.

Examples of item numbers generated by this system are given in the drawings indicated in the MRI shown in Figure 5.9 and in the examples below:

- P19-18C009-D-01 and P19-18C0090-D-02

These are the console cabinet right- and left-hand side panels, P19-18C009-D-01 being the right hand, as drawn, item and 02 being the left hand. Both items are defined by the same drawing, P19-18C009-D, and the C character indicates that this is a detail assembly drawing; it must therefore also call for the assembly of some parts, the fitting of anchor nuts, for example.

- P19-00S003-T

This is the third test specification associated with the complete total power unit, S indicating specification and T indicating test.

- P19-18S002-P

This is a production specification relating to the console cabinet indicating, for example, the paint to be used.

- P19-19T001-X

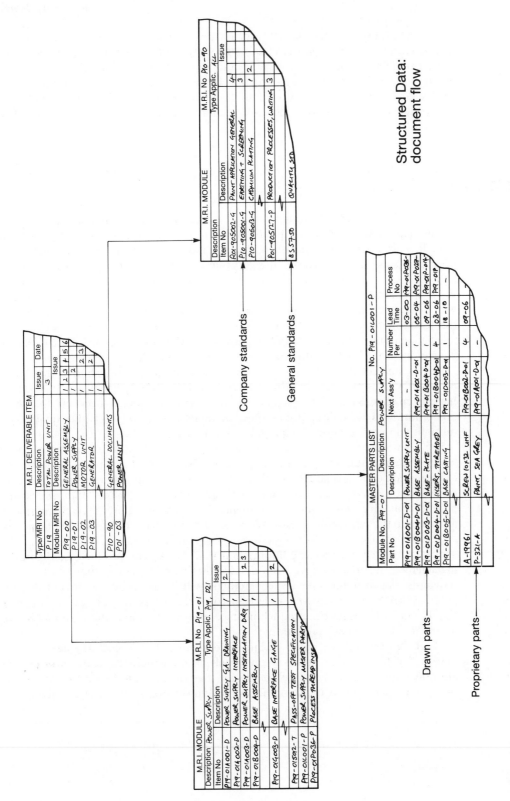

Figure 5.12 Document relationships in a structured data system.

This is a tool used in the manufacture of the console cabinet that is defined on a manufacturing process, and therefore controllable, but for which no drawing exists.

An example of the document flow and representative information is given in Figure 5.12; it shows the logical structure of the data and the way that information on one document leads to expanded information on the next. The numbering format always allows the reader to establish the item to which data relates and the MRI that controls it.

Summary

Good product design is fundamental to business success, but good design goes beyond excellence in technical performance. It must incorporate features that make a product attractive in the market-place and these include appearance, reliability and price. The success of innovative design projects is governed by a number of factors both internal and external but what is becoming clear is that the approach taken to the project can have a marked bearing on the outcome. The team-based approach as exemplified by simultaneous engineering has shown itself to be effective at reducing the lead-time for product development. A business culture that keeps the commercial objectives of the project uppermost in the minds of the design team is equally important; where this culture is absent, projects have been less successful.

Quality and reliability are increasingly recognized for the contribution they make to product sales through improved image in the market-place. Taguchi methods have been devised to aid designers in the search for robust concepts that have inherently high reliability. Use of these methods has shown that high quality and reliability do not necessarily imply high product costs.

The transition from the design phase to full-scale production marks the point where experimentation ends and repeatability becomes all-important. Review procedures should be instigated to ensure that all the design and test work has been carried out in a way that complies with all legal requirements and results in a product that conforms to the requirements of the maket before large commitments are made to the production phase. With complex products, the scope for change that exists, particularly in the early days of the production programme, is such that careful control is needed over all the information that defines the product. Configuration management techniques have been devised that allow precise definition of product standards and introduction of such methods will be aided by the advent of computerized MRP systems. However, decisions over configuration management methods should not be left until the production stage, instead the foundations should be laid during the development programme.

All of the above issues come within the domain of the Project Manager; it is for him to decide how any or all of them will be implemented on the projects that are under his control. It is thus important that each should be given proper consideration when structuring the programme and controlling the design activities.

6

The cost and value of products

- Value for money in product design
- Design-to-cost
- Value analysis
- Value engineering

Value for money

Value for money is a concept that each of us will readily understand, we apply it in our daily lives to the things that we purchase; if we don't think something is good value, we probably won't buy it. It follows that value and sales potential are closely related. No matter what the product, obtaining the best value from every component should be a project goal. Project Managers may think that they are keeping costs firmly in mind but how many can be sure that better-value designs cannot be created?

'Prices aren't set by costs, they're set by competition.' Every businessman will understand this well enough but, surprisingly, this simple truth is not always recognized by managers who have the ultimate responsibility for the costs incurred in making a product. Designers may feel that their responsibility ends with achieving the specified performance and appearance; Production Engineers may know what the production costs are but are not involved with the selling price as that is a matter for the Marketing Department. As industry is shifting towards a project-based approach to the development of new products, the Project Manager is finding himself in a unique position to influence both the design and cost of the product that eventually emerges.

In the period since the Second World War, manufacturing sectors in which the UK was self-sufficient, such as motors, white goods and consumer electronics, have been decimated by an influx of foreign goods that, in simple terms, offer consumers better value for the money they are paying. Price alone was not the only factor: design quality in terms of function, reliability and appearance were equally important. In some cases, imported items became synonymous with affluence and good taste; there can be no better example of this than the status attached to the smart and efficient single-lens reflex cameras when they were introduced by Canon and Pentax. It is no longer possible to look at locally produced goods to assess the price or quality of anything we may choose to purchase, for we now live in an international market and our perception of what anything is worth is set by international standards. Every company that seeks its fortune through making and selling goods must adapt its way of working, so that the value of the goods for the price paid is as good or better than that found elsewhere.

Where product cost is of prime importance, the producer should always be looking at ways in which cost can be lowered without a reduction in performance or quality. A number of ways are possible:

1. Start with a basic design aimed at low product cost.
2. Analyse existing designs to create lower-cost solutions.
3. Improve production techniques.
4. Subcontract to lower cost suppliers.

Of the four methods, by far the greatest potential for low cost lies with method 1 as the greatest savings in product cost are made on the drawing-board. A simply designed item that is easy to make from the outset will always be capable of being made more cheaply than a complex item, no matter how sophisticated the tooling or how competitive the purchasing. Having recognized this fact and with a very clear view of both the target production cost and the selling price, many companies are adopting 'design-to-cost' as a part of their design and drawing office procedures.

Design-to-cost

The technique of **design-to-cost** goes back a long way and, if not a formalized method, was endemic to some industries from their earliest days. It appeared in the products of the volume car makers during the intense sales battles that took place in the lean interwar years. Price competition was fierce and designs were created with specific selling prices in mind and aimed at well-defined market sectors. This tradition remains at the heart of product design in the highly competitive consumer durables industries such as motors, white goods and consumer electronics. It has yet to be adopted so fully in the capital goods and defence sectors which tend to be more orientated towards design to meet very exacting specifications. Obviously compliance with the fundamental aspects of the specification is very important; however, there are often elements in the specification where strict compliance can be very expensive but also where some relaxation would not result in a significant reduction in product usefulness. With this in mind, the US Department of Defense in 1975 introduced Directive no. 5000.28 for the application of design-to-cost principles to major development projects.

Design-to-cost is not solely a design activity, but should also be thought of as a management concept that permeates the whole development process. In the case of consumer goods, purchase price will be the primary element of cost to be considered. Where capital goods or defence equipment are concerned, the total costs over the whole life of the item may be the major consideration. Besides the initial purchase price, running costs, repair and maintenance costs, and even disposal costs, may be considered in the formulation of the product design. Whether it is initial purchase or life-cycle cost that are to be the target of a design-to-cost exercise, the important point is that precise cost targets are set at the start of the development phase.

Throughout the development programme, progress in meeting the cost targets will be measured. In assessing overall progress cost is ranked equally with performance and schedule. Unit cost is not automatically sacrificed in an attempt to meet the ultimate in performance or to preserve a tight development timescale. When difficulties arise, the effect on cost of meeting an awkward performance parameter is assessed and, if need be, the parameter is downgraded in importance to ensure that costs are not allowed to rise. Of course difficult decisions have to be taken, and if some expensive features of the design are deemed essential, then other features that may only be considered desirable may have to be lost. This sometimes comes as a shock to designers who have been taught to aim for the best technical solution. Something that can do 95% of the specified jor for 80% of the anticipated cost may be far more attractive to customers and therefore a better solution commercially. There may also be additional benefits that arise from adopting a simpler design solution, including a reduced development timescale and lower technical risk.

The design-to-cost procedure

Figure 6.1 shows in schematic form the job plan and procedure for implementing design-to-cost principles. It presupposes a company of sufficient size to have discrete Engineering, Marketing and Corporate Planning (or Business Management) departments. This is not essential for design-to-cost, but it does make the division of responsibility easier to define.

The product that the company chooses to develop should form part of a corporate plan aimed at satisfying well-understood business objectives. The strategy may be product led if the company has particular design and product strengths, or it may be market led where analysis reveals the need for a product that can be developed using existing design strengths and product knowledge. Analysis may also indicate that new expertise or technologies may have to be acquired to enter or remain in the market. With any new product that will require an investment in development effort, a rigorous assessment must be made of the concept and price that will be required to gain the anticipated market share. The Engineering Department will be required to carry out a feasibility study that should aim to generate an outline specification and a product cost estimate. The project management organization should also be required to look at the product concept, specification and unit cost estimates and generate a project cost estimate, together with a feasible timescale for development. With these inputs, a decision can be made regarding the launch of the project and whether the project is to incorporate design-to-cost procedures; if so, the cost goals should be set at the start.

Responsibility for achieving the goals will rest with the Project Manager. He will be required to generate a plan and procedure that will state how the goals will be defined, monitored and achieved and how this work will integrate into the project

Design-to-cost – job plan and procedure

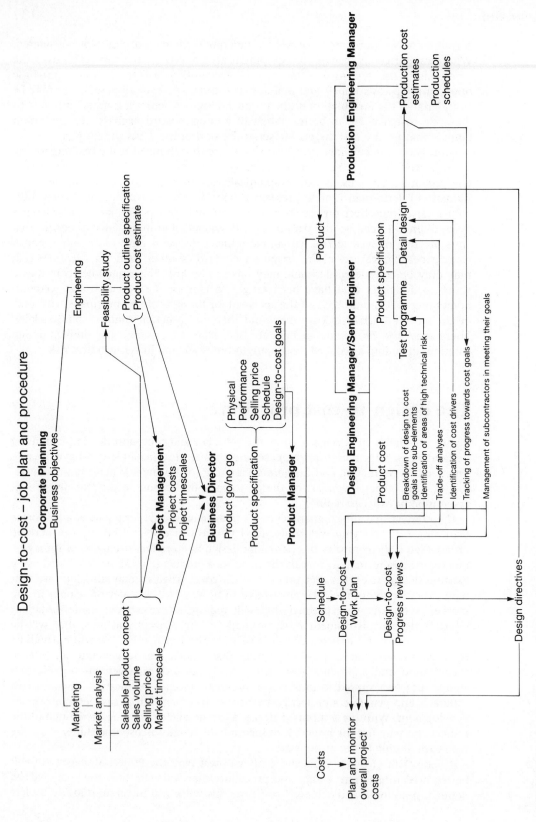

Figure 6.1 Design-to-cost job plan and procedure.

development plan as a whole. The plan should be approved by a director with sufficient authority to ensure that goals, once set, cannot be breached without the implications being fully considered. The plan should contain at least the following elements:

- How design-to-cost will fit into the overall project plan, its scope and definition.
- Responsibilities for specific actions or areas of interest within the plan.
- The timescale by which specific actions will be required to be completed.
- The schedule of design-to-cost progress reviews and the composition of the review panel.
- The format for design-to-cost reporting and updating.
- The procedures to be applied when design-to-cost goals look likely to be breached.

Design-to-cost should be seen as a continuous process which has its greatest impact at the initial design stage when it is easiest to revise the specification as the costs of the emerging design become apparent. The further the project proceeds, the more expensive in cost and schedule any change will become. However, costs must be monitored throughout the development programme to ensure that minor changes and design improvements do not creep in and drive costs up.

The scope of the design-to-cost exercise also needs to be defined, in some cases cost goals may themselves be the subject of contractual guarantees; this is particularly true of military contracts where the total cost of ownership over the whole life of the product can be a design goal. Here the initial purchase price of the item is only one element of the total cost and operational costs must also be considered. If life-cycle costs are part of the cost goal, then studies such as failure modes and effects analysis and reliability modelling will have to be included in the scope of the design-to-cost plan.

As the heart of design-to-cost is the concept that costs are largely determined by the product as it is designed, it follows that much of the responsibility for implementing the procedure must lie with the most senior designer assigned to the project. He or she should ensure that the following activities are performed:

1. The major goals must be broken down into smaller sub-goals and responsibility assigned to individual engineers.
2. Those features of the specification which result in potentially high-cost elements of the design must be identified, they are often called 'cost drivers'.
3. Formalized trade-off analysis must be carried out, particularly in respect of cost drivers. Design options for sub-elements should be viewed and their costs versus other benefits assessed. It is possible at the early stage that some revision of the cost goals associated with each sub-system is desirable as analysis may show that higher costs in one area may lead to a reduction in another. These early trade-off studies are very important as they will define the concept in detail for the whole programme. Evaluation of design options must be rigorous and objective; as much as possible, those human qualities of bias ('this is my very own idea') and wishful thinking ('wouldn't it be good to have a go at . . .') should be left out.
4. Areas of high technical risk should be identified. Trade-off studies may show that there are significant savings to be made if, for example: a new technology is employed, the design uses a novel production technique or a single supplier with special skills is involved in the design and supply of a critical item. Each of these may represent a benefit to the product cost but there is also a risk. The new technology may take longer to develop and cost more than anticipated, the novel

DESIGN-TO-COST STATUS REPORT

BUSINESS AREA	PROJECT TITLE	ISSUE	DATE

SUBSYSTEM TITLE	DRAWING REF.	RESPONSIBLE MANAGER	PROJECT MANAGER

REFERENCE DATE M Y	INDEX AT REF. DATE	REVIEW DATE	REVIEW POINT N°	INDEX AT REVIEW DATE	INDEX SERIES	COST REFERENCE FACTOR	RESPONSIBLE ENGINEER

ANALYSIS OF CURRENT VARIANCES	PLANNED CORRECTIVE ACTIONS, RECOMMENDATIONS
CURRENT ESTIMATE	% OF ESTIMATE BASED ON FIRM DESIGN %
PREVIOUS ESTIMATE	% ACCURACY OF ESTIMATE %
CURRENT GOAL	ESTIMATE METHOD
ORIGINAL GOAL	
CURRENT ESTIMATE AT REFERENCE DATE	THRESHOLD % VARIANCE FROM GOAL %
VARIANCE FROM CURRENT GOAL	VARIANCE AS % OF CURRENT GOAL %

SUMMARY OF PREVIOUS ACTIONS, DECISIONS, ALTERATIONS

REVIEW POINT	DATE	ACTION

% CHANGE

+40
+30
+20
+10
GOAL
−10
−20
−30
−40

REVIEW POINT 1 2 3 4 5 6 7 8 9 10 11 12

COMPILED BY:	CIRCULATE TO:

Figure 6.2(a) Design-to-cost status report.

DESIGN-TO-COST STATUS REPORT

		ISSUE 2	DATE 17/6/88

BUSINESS AREA Heating Systems

PROJECT TITLE TOTAL HEAT MODULE

PROJECT MANAGER P. M. JONES

SUBSYSTEM TITLE CENTRAL CONTROL UNIT

RESPONSIBLE MANAGER K. JARVIS

RESPONSIBLE ENGINEER S. PAULSON

DRAWING REF. A1.002.01

INDEX SERIES ELEC. IND. 138·2

COST REFERENCE FACTOR 121·4 / 138·2 = 0·88

REFERENCE DATE M 5 Y 88	**REVIEW DATE** 121·4	**INDEX AT REF. DATE** 3/2/89	**INDEX AT REVIEW DATE** A1.002.01

REVIEW POINT N° 6 **REVIEW DATE** 3/2/89 **INDEX AT REVIEW DATE** 138·2

CURRENT ESTIMATE 1320

% OF ESTIMATE BASED ON FIRM DESIGN 75 %

PREVIOUS ESTIMATE 1287

% ACCURACY OF ESTIMATE ±10 %

CURRENT GOAL 1200

ESTIMATE METHOD INTERNAL PLUS SAMPLE QUOTES

ORIGINAL GOAL 900

CURRENT ESTIMATE AT REFERENCE DATE 1158

THRESHOLD % VARIANCE FROM GOAL 15 %

VARIANCE FROM CURRENT GOAL -42

VARIANCE AS % OF CURRENT GOAL -3·5 %

ANALYSIS OF CURRENT VARIANCES
COST OF DISPLAY UNIT £21 HIGHER THAN ESTIMATE,
CONSOLE CASING, PRICE NOW REDUCED BY £64·50 FROM QUOTE

PLANNED CORRECTIVE ACTIONS, RECOMMENDATIONS
NONE IDENTIFIED

SUMMARY OF PREVIOUS ACTIONS, DECISIONS, ALTERATIONS

REVIEW POINT	DATE	ACTION
1	9/88	CONNECTOR COST HIGH, REASSESS
2	12/88	DITTO ABOVE
3	3/89	ADDITIONAL REDUNDANCY IDENTIFIED CONNECTOR, REQUIREMENT REVISED, COST STUDY OF CONSOLE CASING
4	6/89	REDEFINITION RECOMMENDED AT DESIGN REVIEW 3/5/89
5	9/89	SPEC S.002/T/KS REVISED 21/8/89, NEW COST GOAL OF £1200
6	12/89	SAMPLE QUOTES CONFIRM ESTIMATE

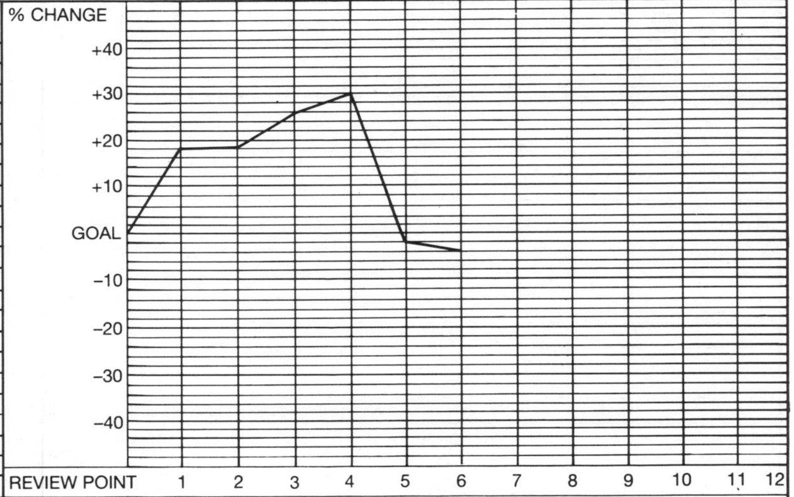

% CHANGE

+40
+30
+20
+10
GOAL
-10
-20
-30
-40

REVIEW POINT 1 2 3 4 5 6 7 8 9 10 11 12

COMPILED BY: P. MARTIN

CIRCULATE TO: JP, T.F.B., A.P.L., P.M.S., K.J., S.P., LIBRARY FILE

Figure 6.2(b) Example of a design-to-cost status report in use.

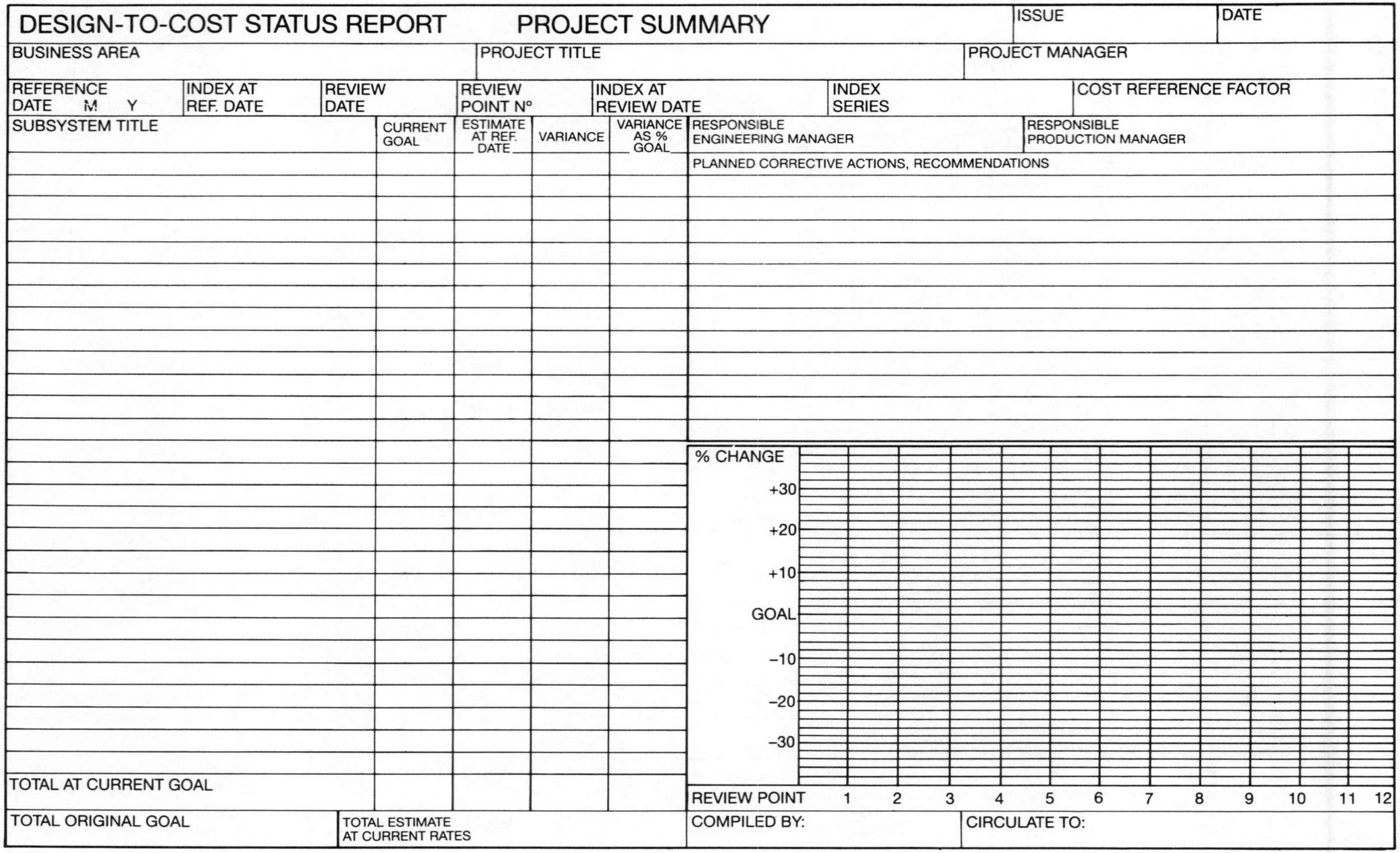

DESIGN-TO-COST STATUS REPORT — PROJECT SUMMARY

BUSINESS AREA | PROJECT TITLE | ISSUE | DATE

PROJECT MANAGER

REFERENCE DATE M Y | INDEX AT REF. DATE | REVIEW DATE | REVIEW POINT N° | INDEX AT REVIEW DATE | INDEX SERIES | COST REFERENCE FACTOR

SUBSYSTEM TITLE | CURRENT GOAL | ESTIMATE AT REF. DATE | VARIANCE | VARIANCE AS % GOAL | RESPONSIBLE ENGINEERING MANAGER | RESPONSIBLE PRODUCTION MANAGER

PLANNED CORRECTIVE ACTIONS, RECOMMENDATIONS

% CHANGE
+30
+20
+10
GOAL
−10
−20
−30

REVIEW POINT 1 2 3 4 5 6 7 8 9 10 11 12

TOTAL AT CURRENT GOAL

TOTAL ORIGINAL GOAL | TOTAL ESTIMATE AT CURRENT RATES

COMPILED BY: | CIRCULATE TO:

Figure 6.3(a) Design-to-cost status report format, project summary.

DESIGN-TO-COST STATUS REPORT — PROJECT SUMMARY

ISSUE 1   DATE 17/6/89

BUSINESS AREA: HEATING SYSTEMS

PROJECT TITLE: TOTAL HEAT. MODULE   PROJECT MANAGER: P.M. JONES

PROJECT N°: 4

REFERENCE DATE: M 5 Y 88	
INDEX AT REF. DATE: 121.4	
REVIEW DATE: 5/6/89	
REVIEW POINT N°: 4	
INDEX AT REVIEW DATE: 132.2	INDEX SERIES: ELEC. IND.
COST REFERENCE FACTOR: $\frac{121.4}{132.2} = 0.92$	
RESPONSIBLE ENGINEERING MANAGER: K. JARVIS	RESPONSIBLE PRODUCTION MANAGER: J. PERCIVAL

SUBSYSTEM TITLE	CURRENT GOAL	ESTIMATE AT REF. DATE	VARIANCE	VARIANCE AS % GOAL	PLANNED CORRECTIVE ACTIONS, RECOMMENDATIONS
BOILER UNIT	620	703	83	+13.4	1) SAFETY STUDY SHOWS REDUNDANCY REQUIREMENT, REF D.R.
HEAT EXCHANGER	520	532	12	+2.3	3/5/89 SPEC TO BE REVISED, NEW COST GOAL TO BE SET
PUMP AND FLOW CONTROLLER	350	312	-38	-10.9	2) ALTERNATIVE SOURCE OF SUITABLE MOTOR TO BE INVESTIGATED
MOTOR AND FUEL SYSTEM	1700	1900	200	+11.8	3) DELETE EMISSION MONITOR; THIS FEATURE TO BE EXTRA TO
EMISSION MONITOR	250	370	120	+48.0	CUSTOMER REQUIREMENTS.
SENSORS AND THERMOSTATS	95	90	-5	-5.3	4) INVESTIGATE REDUCTION IN NUMBER OF THERMOSTATS
CENTRAL CONTROL UNIT	900	1160	260	+29.0	5) ALL GOALS WHERE CURRENT ESTIMATES ARE BELOW GOAL
PIPE CONNECTIONS AND VALVES	300	282	-18	-6.2	TO BE REVISED DOWNWARD BY MAXIMUM 10%.
CHASSIS + COVERS	155	175	20	+12.9	
PUBLICATIONS	12	12	0	0	

TOTAL AT CURRENT GOAL	4902	5536	634	12.9

TOTAL ORIGINAL GOAL	4902	TOTAL ESTIMATE AT CURRENT RATES	6017

% CHANGE: +30 +20 +10 GOAL -10 -20 -30

REVIEW POINT: 1 2 3 4 5 6 7 8 9 10 11 12

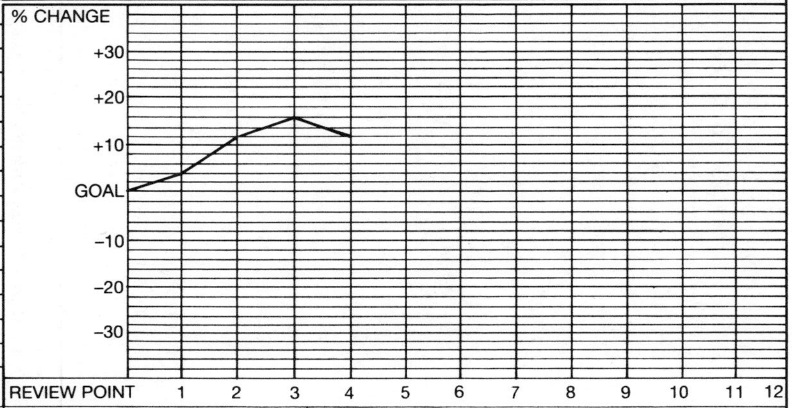

COMPILED BY: P. MARTIN

CIRCULATE TO: T.F.B., J.P., AR., P.M.J., K.J., P.B., L.S.V.S.P., FILM

Figure 6.3(b) Example of design-to-cost status report project summary in use.

production method may have hidden difficulties and the single supplier may prove unreliable. These are three examples of technically induced risks; the impact on the project due to a failure resulting from a technical risk must be considered against the potential for cost saving.

5. Progress towards cost goals must be monitored. Regular assessment of the cost of the emerging design is needed to ensure: (a) that all responsible staff are aware of the costs; (b) that attention is paid to keeping costs under control; and (c) that progress is actually made towards achieving the goal. Design-to-cost status reports of the type shown in Figures 6.2 and 6.3 are useful for summarizing the position. Figure 6.2 shows a form that provides detailed information about a particular sub-system. The report has sections in which variances between the current goal and the current estimate are analysed and the planned corrective actions are stated. An index number series is used to revise the current estimated prices to the economic date at which the goal was set. A graph is included to give a visual indication of the variance between estimate and goal throughout the project and there is a section for the history of recommendations and actions. A threshold variance is stated; if this is exceeded, formal reporting to the business area director is required. Figure 6.3 shows a summary report which gathers together the estimates and variances for all the sub-systems in the project and gives the overall position.

6. Subcontractors may be employed to design some elements of the product and they must be brought into the design-to-cost discipline. It may be possible to do this on a contractual basis but many companies are unwilling to accept, as guarantees, price limitations on production items still in the development stage. Design-to-cost allows the subcontractor more freedom to meet the cost target as it allows scope for specification changes. However, changes to the specification cannot take place in isolation and must be considered for their impact on the product as a whole. The Design or Engineering Manager will thus be required to monitor progress of subcontractors in the same way as his own staff and ensure that they report their progress honestly and in line with the schedule.

Individual engineers should be assigned sub-systems whose design will be under their direct control. They should be responsible for designing their element to meet the cost goal and maintain up-to-date status information to record their progress. They must provide design descriptive data in the form of drawings, sketches, parts lists, etc. in a form suitable for estimating purposes. Engineers considering alternative designs or design changes that are likely to have a significant impact on the cost estimate for their element will be responsible for assessing the cost of these alternatives before any change decision can be made. Should the assessment result in a breach of a threshold value of a cost goal, the responsible engineer must initiate a review meeting with both the senior designer and the Project Manager to assess what corrective action should be taken.

The Production Engineering Department will also have a role to play, often the cost-estimating section of a company is located in this department. Production Engineering using assessments from the Marketing Department must set out basic assumptions on production schedules, output rates, batch sizes, in-house or bought-out manufacturing and work breakdown. These will be key elements in the process of cost estimating and should not be varied without agreement from the business area director.

As design schemes and details emerge they should be passed to the estimating section for formal estimates and quotations on bought-out items. Production Engineering should also provide a feedback of suggestions for ways in which items can be designed for easier and cheaper production. In some industries the cooperation between Design and Production Engineering takes place naturally but in others, notably in the aerospace world, there has historically been a significant gulf between the two. Formalized design-to-cost helps to build an effective bridge across that divide.

The design-to-cost plan will be circulated to the relevant section heads and the Project Manager must ensure that it is adhered to. Two ways are open to him:

1. He can ensure that status reports are completed on time and distributed to all relevant senior management. If potential breaches of overall cost goals are indicated, then he must set up a meeting with his business or other director to define a corrective course of action. Before initiating such a meeting, the Project Manager should meet the responsible engineer, together with his manager, to review the reasons for their inability to meet the cost goal and to suggest options for corrective action. This must include any implications for other sub-systems that may be affected or even implications for the concept of the product as a whole.

2. He can call design-to-cost reviews at regular intervals. At the review meeting the entire design and production team will be present. Each will have to account for progress, though not in an atmosphere of criticism if difficulties are being met. With the whole team present, ideas may be generated whereby costs can be contained by looking across the range of interacting sub-systems, something that may not be easy for engineers to do while working alone. Suggestions may include changes to the specification, but may also indicate further studies of new technologies or more experimentation. Implications for the project cost and schedule could flow from such suggestions and they must be carefully evaluated. At the end of each review, the project manager must assess the progress of the project and whether or not the product is likely to meet its cost goal. All suggestions presented must be reviewed for their impact on the product specification and schedule. In consultation with the senior design engineer a revised work plan should be devised and issued.

Design-to-Cost is a cyclical process and it must continue until a satisfactory production design can be defined. Whereas design-to-cost can never guarantee that a product will meet its cost goal if performance or timescale demands take a higher priority, a far better chance of achieving it will follow from its application throughout the development programme.

Value engineering

Whether the project is to design and erect a building or to create an item for mass production, maximizing the value obtained from each constituent item is a goal that should never be overlooked. If the project is to develop something that will go into full-scale production, then the production programme could have a value that is many times that of the development project. All companies wish to increase their competitiveness and profitability through reductions in production costs but the problem comes in identifying where and how savings can be made without lowering quality and performance or making the product less attractive in the market-place.

Value engineering is a solution to this, and it now finds a place in the development and production strategies of many companies. It has evolved as a technique, distinct from design-to-cost, that aims not only to generate items of low cost, but more important, of high value for the price that is paid. This is an important distinction as design-to-cost starts with the premiss that features can be traded to achieve a set manufacturing cost which can be decided at the start. Value engineering begins by questioning the worth of each and any feature, then attempts to use creative techniques to generate the same worth but at lower cost.

The procedure was originally developed in the USA as a formalized approach to cost reduction by the General Electric Company (GEC). It arose from a systematic study of the alternative materials and processes that were substituted in their products in order to maintain the required output during the Second World War. The studies showed that, in most cases, the substitute materials performed just as well as the original; sometimes they actually performed better but, in many cases, the more plentiful substitutes were significantly cheaper. Using this experience, GEC set out to create a programme that would ensure that all possibilities for alternative materials and parts were considered when developing a new product. Product '**value**' emerged as the conceptual yardstick against which all alternatives could be assessed. Since then value engineering has become recognized as a discipline in its own right.

Value, as a concept, does not merely relate to purchase price although that may have a very strong influence. If asked to define 'value', many would state price as being the sole determinant, but that would be a wrong view. A more searching assessment of what is termed 'value' shows it to be divisible into four different economic measures:

1. The use value: the cost to the purchaser associated with the properties and qualities of an article which allow it to perform its required function or service.
2. The cost value: the sum of all the materials, labour and overhead costs that are required to produce the article.
3. The esteem value: that extra cost that the purchaser is willing to pay to acquire the article due to its special qualities, attractiveness, exclusivity, etc.
4. The exchange value: those properties or qualities of an article that enable it to be exchanged for something else.

These values need not be constant and may vary over the life of an article. Products of a similar nature may also vary greatly in terms of their costs and value to the purchaser: consider three examples of the familiar wristwatch, as shown in Figure 6.4.

As all three watches do the same job, their use value is always the same, but their costs, prices and value to the owner can all be very different. The term '**use value**' is also termed the '**functional worth**' as it defines how much it is worth for any function to be achieved. With the gold watch, neither the design and marketing concept nor the person who buys it could have been influenced by a functional worth of only £10. The cost and selling price of any product must be based on the market perception of the product and its projection within that market. If the market is well served with a variety of products all providing a similar function but little else to distinguish between them, selling price will be very sensitive and have a direct bearing on total sales. In a market such as watches where fashion and esteem can be the significant factors, market image can be much more important and price can be part of that image, high price indicating exclusivity and craftsmanship. Whatever the project, the marketing objective must be borne in mind throughout the design and

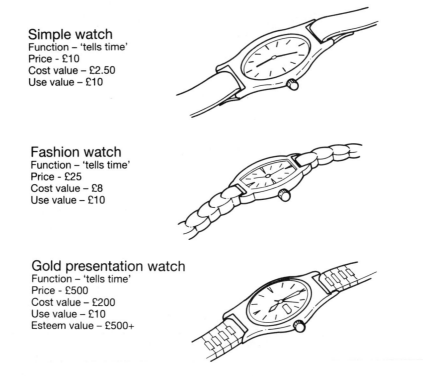

Simple watch
Function – 'tells time'
Price - £10
Cost value – £2.50
Use value – £10

Fashion watch
Function – 'tells time'
Price - £25
Cost value – £8
Use value – £10

Gold presentation watch
Function – 'tells time'
Price - £500
Cost value – £200
Use value – £10
Esteem value – £500+

Figure 6.4   The wristwatch: same function, different value.

development phase, particularly if the product is to compete in a price-sensitive market.

The value engineering process can be broken into two major segments:

1. An analytical phase in which the product is examined for the functions that it fulfils and the worth attached to each is established.
2. A creative phase in which new designs are generated and change is implemented.

Value engineering is the term currently applied to the total process but the expression **'value management'** now seems to be coming into use to describe all activities associated with generating better-value products.

When to apply value engineering

Value engineering provides a systematized method for establishing the design that gives the best value for any product. Any object that is under design, development or production can be the subject of value engineering but there is an optimum time to do it and it is generally as early as practical in the product life cycle. An item that is designed for low-cost manufacture at the outset will always show an overall cost advantage over an item that is changed to reduce cost at some point in the production programme. The Project Manager must decide if his product is to be the subject of value engineering and when that work will take place. Figure 6.5 shows the

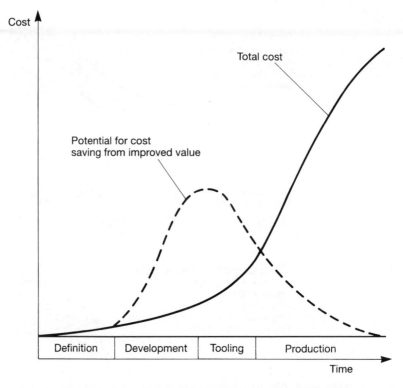

Figure 6.5   Total project cost and potential for cost saving from improved value.

relationship between the potential for cost saving from improved value and the total programme cost. Whereas Figure 6.5 indicates that the potential for making a reduction in overall project costs can be obtained by analysis at the development stage, it should not be construed that it is not worth doing during the production phase. Continued emphasis on value improvement throughout the product's life can increase competitiveness and sales, as shown in Figure 6.6.

Organization for value engineering

Value engineering challenges fundamental precepts of design and production and seeks improvements. Change, however, is not brought about easily, for resistance can and will exist at any level in an organization. Most people have some vested interest in maintaining the status quo and if change is not properly handled it will, undoubtedly, meet resistance. It may be seen by some as implied criticism of their work and unnecessary obstacles can be put in the way of suggested improvements. Staff in the Design Department may feel most vulnerable as it was they who created the item in the first place; Production Engineering and Purchasing personnel may also feel exposed when changes are suggested in production methods or bought-out materials. It is important therefore that it is seen as a creative process, not a

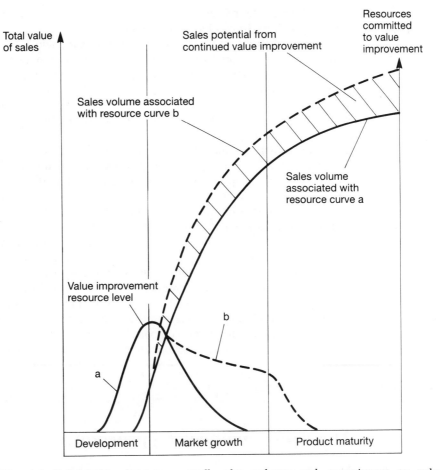

Figure 6.6 Relationship between overall sales volume and commitment to value improvement.

destructive one, and also that obstacles are not allowed to defeat the object of the work. This can be achieved in two ways:

1. By creating a Value Engineering team that incorporates as equals, members from the Design, Production and Purchasing departments.
2. By setting up a Value Engineering Committee having sufficient authority to ensure that proposals approved by the Committee are implemented.

Support and commitment from senior management is vital, without it the whole process can grind to a halt in an air of apathy and frustration. One further element is necessary, namely a properly trained Value Engineer to lead the study.

As the method starts by challenging features of the design, it is primarily a design function and all changes will require design approval; it can be expected that the Value Engineer would come from the Design Department. However, in companies that practice value engineering the Value Engineer often comes from the Production Department as production engineers are often the people that compile the production costs and are thus familiar with the elements of the design that contribute most to cost. It may also indicate a lack of understanding of the economics of production that is sometimes shown by design engineers.

Members of the team should be drawn from the main functional disciplines that have a bearing on product cost, typically Design, Production Engineering, Purchasing, Quality Control, Marketing and Project Management. This is an ideal combination: if the team is too small the full benefit of the diversity of input may not be achieved, while too large a team might inhibit its own operation. The Value Engineer will lead the study making use of the particular contribution that each member can bring.

The team will evaluate the design under study and propose improved value solutions. At this point, the whole process can fail unless people with sufficient authority in the company are convinced of the value of the proposed changes and ensure that the proposals are implemented. The Value Engineering Committee, mentioned earlier, fulfils this role as all proposals must be referred to the Committee and it must decide whether or not they should be put into effect. The Committee should consist of: the Project Manager, the project Chief Designer, the Technical Director, the Production Director, a senior marketing person and a secretary. This may seem a heavyweight team to be considering value changes; in some large companies the Technical and Production directors may find themselves too busy to attend, but they should remember that the profitability of companies depends on the maintenance of both market share and margins and neither can escape responsibility for the cost and value of the company's products. Thus, if they cannot attend in person, they should ensure that one of their directly reporting staff attends on their behalf.

The value engineering procedure

The technique of value engineering can be divided into a number of major phases which should be carried out in the order laid down:

Phase 1: orientation;
Phase 2: information and analysis;
Phase 3: speculation;
Phase 4: evaluation;
Phase 5: implementation and follow-up.

These phases are set out in Figure 6.7.

Phase 1: Orientation

This is a preliminary phase that sets the general scope, restrictions and aims of the study. It should be initiated by the Project Manager at a time when the benefits of such work can be identified. The team members should be selected and a timetable for the study with a schedule of meetings fixed. A preliminary assessment of the product should be made to divide it into broad areas of study and establish the current costs; it may also be worthwhile to set cost targets for each area. These targets must be agreed among the team; they can prove a yardstick against which

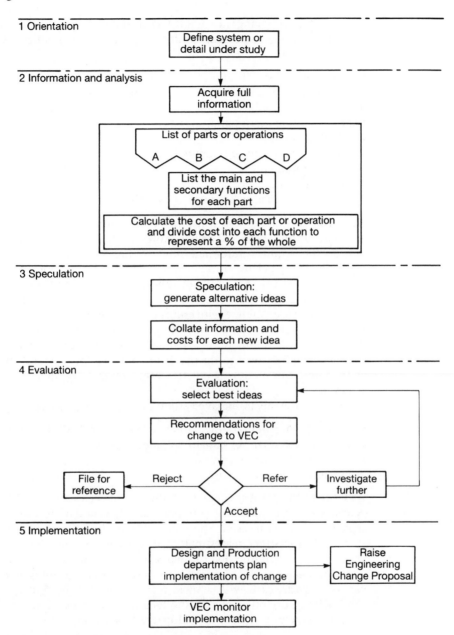

Figure 6.7 Value engineering job plan.

future progress can be measured and they will help in directing the study into the areas where most benefit can be obtained.

Phase 2: Information and analysis

The orientation phase will produce a plan for the study and set out broad targets; although these may be subjective, basic intuition often indicates where the best opportunities for savings are and the team should begin here. Under the direction of the Value Engineer, all essential information about the product needs to be obtained; it will include:

- Drawings and specifications.
- Current or estimated costs of parts, materials and labour.
- Weights of parts.
- Production quantities and rates.
- Details of suppliers.
- Current manufacturing methods.
- User requirements.
- Market trends.
- Details of competing products, if available.

Value engineering is a task which involves dealing directly with people and challenging some of their ideas and beliefs. However, these same people will be necessary to provide the required information. It is thus important that the Value Engineer maintains the goodwill of all the staff that he comes into contact with and the appointed engineer should have sufficient maturity, both in human and technical terms, to be able to gain the confidence of others even when enquiring into their areas of expertise. Value engineering activities can easily annoy the more sensitive as it may imply criticism of the way things have been done or be seen as snooping into their business. It is important when gathering information that these suspicions are dispelled: the best way to do this is to convince the sceptical that everyone has a vested interest in producing a better-value job and, by cooperating, that aim can be achieved.

Selection of items for detailed study can be done in several ways:

- By identifying and ranking parts in a **pareto (A,B,C) analysis** according to cost.
- By a cost-to-weight or cost-to-volume analysis.
- By a cost-to-function analysis.
- By an historical comparison.

With the pareto (or A,B,C) analysis, the cost of each part is established, as well as its percentage of the total cost; the parts are then ranked in order of increasing percentage cost. Typical results show that 20% of the parts account for 80% of the cost – this 20% offers the greatest potential for saving or value improvement and should be studied first. This method can work well where the product can be divided into a relatively small number of major parts or sub-systems. It still applies where a product has many parts, each with a small relative contribution, but it is sometimes more convenient to use other methods to focus on the items worthy of study.

Cost-to-weight or **cost-to-volume analyses** highlight items with high cost for relatively small size or weight. Selecting items on the basis of high cost-to-weight alone may give a misleading view; these tend to be the lightest and often smallest parts. Although the potential for a large reduction in cost-to-weight may exist, the actual saving in money terms could be low. High-cost items with low cost-to-weight ratios could also be a poor choice as the low ratio indicates that the potential for further cost reduction may be limited. A better measure for ranking parts using weight as a parameter is: $cost^2/kg$. This gives more weighting to the higher-cost items where the greatest potential for cost reduction must lie but reduces in importance those items which already have a low cost per kilogram. Care should be taken in interpreting any of these types of analysis, particularly if the product has

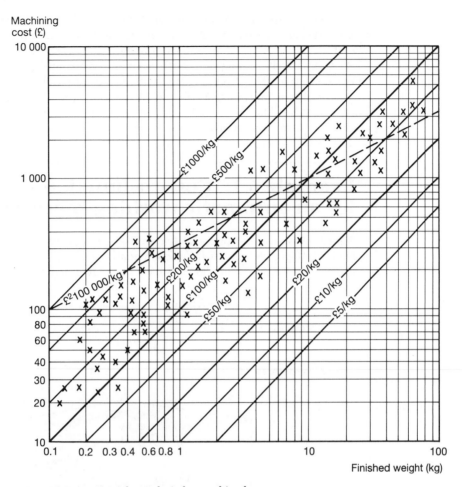

Figure 6.8 Cost-to-weight analysis for machined parts.

many parts with differing densities – e.g. metals and plastics. Figure 6.8 shows a
cost-to-weight analysis for machined parts in aluminium using the criterion of
$cost^2/kg$ for selection. The figure of $£^2 100\,000/kg$ has been chosen as the lower limit
for study; items showing a greater figure being worthy of attention. If instead cost
per kilogram had been used as the criterion and the figure of £100/kg taken, then
some low-weight but relatively low-cost items would have been included, while
some heavy and relatively expensive items would have been ignored, even though
likely to offer a good potential for savings.

Cost-to-function analysis is a technique that looks beyond the simple parameters
of cost and weight and aims to discover what it is costing to accomplish any function
that the product or its constituent parts and systems must perform. It is a far more
challenging assessment and thus has a greater potential for value improvements. It
will demonstrate where money is being spent to perform a particular function, each
can then be assessed for its contribution to the overall product function. Parts and
systems that appear to cost a disproportionately high figure to perform a relatively
trivial function would be worthy of study. It could also reveal the opposite, that too

little is being spent on functions of significance and that if more was spent it could improve the product overall. Perhaps the amount spent on finish, appearance and ease of use is too low and an improved image with easier handling would improve sales. Alternatively, it may be worth spending more on better-quality key components if that benefits reliability and reduces warranty claims.

The concept of functional worth was introduced earlier, cost-to-function analysis aims to discover the functional costs. It begins by defining the functions that a product performs and at what price. An illustrative example of a cost-to-function analysis is given for a familiar product.

Example 6.1: Cost-to-function analysis for an automatic washing-machine

Figure 6.9 shows the principal features of a typical washing-machine, while Figure 6.10 shows the cost-to-function analysis set out on a standard form. For this assessment 14 major elements have been identified as making up the unit,

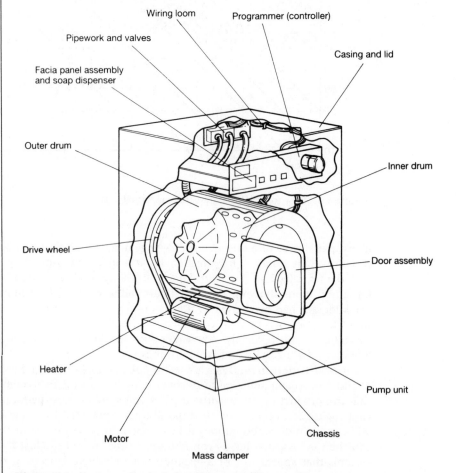

Figure 6.9   Features of a typical automatic washing-machine.

VALUE ENGINEERING: FUNCTIONAL ANALYSIS, ASSEMBLIES AND SYSTEMS

Title: WASHING MACHINE
Part Nos: Issue:
Used On:
Ref No: Date:

FUNCTION → / PART or OPERATION	PROVIDE PROTECTION Cost	%	POSITION PARTS Cost	%	RETAIN WATER Cost	%	CONTROL OPERATIONS Cost	%	PROVIDE OR RESTRAIN MOTION Cost	%	DISTRIBUTE WATER Cost	%	HEAT WATER Cost	%	LOOK ATTRACTIVE Cost	%	Total Cost of Ass'y / Cost of Part or Operation
CASING, TOP + CHASSIS	12·90	60	5·38	25											3·22	15	21·50
DOOR ASSEMBLY	1·50	15			7·50	75									1·00	10	10·00
WATER HEATER AND THERMOSTAT							0·94	10					8·41	90			9·35
ELECTRONIC PROGRAMMER							30·50	100									30·50
WIRING LOOM							7·20	100									7·20
FACIA PANEL ASSEMBLY							9·15	75							3·05	25	12·20
MOTOR									32·00	100							32·00
OUTER DRUM	3·06	25	1·22	10	7·94	65											12·22
INNER DRUM AND DRIVE WHEEL									18·15	85					3·20	15	21·35
PIPEWORK AND VALVES					1·98	15					11·22	85					13·20
PUMP											10·50	100					10·50
MASS DAMPER			6·44	70					4·10	100							4·10
SUNDRIES, FASTENERS, ETC.									1·38	15					1·38	15	9·20
PACKAGE	2·25	90													·25	10	2·50
Target Cost of Function (Total)																	
Actual Cost of Function (Total)	19·71		13·04		17·42		47·79		55·63		21·72		8·41		12·10		195·82
% Cost — Target % of Target / % of Actual Cost	10·07		6·66		8·89		24·41		28·4		11·09		4·29		6·18		100

Figure 6.10 Value engineering, functional analysis, assemblis and systems.

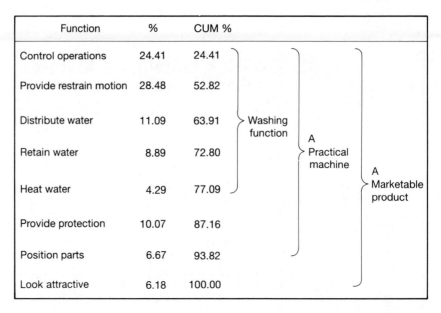

Function	%	CUM %
Control operations	24.41	24.41
Provide restrain motion	28.48	52.82
Distribute water	11.09	63.91
Retain water	8.89	72.80
Heat water	4.29	77.09
Provide protection	10.07	87.16
Position parts	6.67	93.82
Look attractive	6.18	100.00

Washing function
A Practical machine
A Marketable product

Figure 6.11 Functional build-up of the washing-machine.

these are listed in the left-hand column. Along the top, eight functions have been defined. Each major element has been assessed for its contribution, expressed as a percentage, to each function. For the casing, top cover and chassis, it was felt that 60% of its function was providing protection, 25% positioning parts and 15% presenting an attractive external appearance. Breaking down the £21.50 cost of this element by the percentages gives the cost contribution of each function. By considering each element in this way, the picture of the whole product in terms of its functional contributions can be built up.

Taking the results of the study and rearranging them reveals the relative build-up of the machine in terms of what it costs to accomplish its basic function, the costs needed to make it into a practical machine and the costs involved in providing an appearance that will cause customers to be pleased to own it, this is shown in Figure 6.11.

As a utilitarian product it is not surprising that 77.09% of its cost is associated with achieving its basic function of washing clothes through piping in water, heating it, providing a mechanical washing action, piping the water away and providing a spinning action. As the machine is automatic, over a quarter of the washing function cost is taken up by controlling the sequence of operations. The remainder of the cost is associated with creating a practical machine and making it look attractive. Both the external finish, including the design of the facia panel, and the internal finish of the washing-drum contribute to its appearance. Whether these percentage contributions seem reasonable is a matter for the team to decide; the form shown in Figure 6.10 has boxes which can be used to define target percentages and cost values that may be set as goals for a re-engineered product.

The final analytical method is a comparative assessment with examples of items with similar functions that have been made for earlier products. Where these designs appear simpler or cheaper, then a case for a re-assessment becomes clear. Comparisons with competitor products, if they can be obtained, can be similarly instructive.

The information and analysis phase should end with a clearly defined series of components or areas of the design which appear to have high costs for the contribution that they make to the product. The value engineering team should also set targets for the savings they hope can be made, and these should be compared with any overall targets that may have been set at the orientation phase. Any or all the methods outlined can be used in analysing value – it is surprising what a dispassionate look at a product can reveal, particularly where products have been evolved through a series of design upgrades.

Phase 3: Speculation

The objective of this phase is to generate alternative solutions to the areas of the product that have been identified in phase 2. At this point, the whole of the team must become involved as their interaction is vital to generating fresh ideas and breaking out of the mould of the product as currently conceived. Two steps are necessary:

1. A clear identification of the function of the item under study.
2. A free-thinking speculation on alternative ways to achieve the same function culminating in recommendations for change.

All items have a primary or basic function which, if it cannot be performed, would make the item useless. Additionally, many items have secondary functions which compliment the primary one; they are not essential to the item's purpose but they may contribute to its value in other ways. How much it is worth paying for these secondary functions is a matter of judgement. To take the example of the wrist watch, its primary function is 'tells time', but as most people are proud of their watch and wear it as ornamentation, it has a secondary function of 'looks attractive'. In the case of the presentation watch, a further secondary function might be 'bears inscription' – some might consider that to be its primary function, although no one would be pleased to be presented with a watch that did not work. It is thus important to decide what the primary function of any item really is and what, if any, are its secondary functions. It does not follow that when deciding how to apportion cost to function, most of the cost should be allocated to the primary function, although in many cases it will be. In the case of the fashion watch, far more will be spent on the appearance than on the mechanism, for it is its look that will attract the customer to buy one watch rather than another.

Having established the functions of the item under study, the first question to be asked is: 'Does the function need to be performed at all?' If an item performs several functions, each should be considered in turn to see if any can be eliminated. Objective assessment is needed, for it is sometimes found that components in existing designs offer no real value to the customer but have been inherited from earlier designs. In some cases, the function may result from an external or operator requirement; this should be challenged if its real worth appears to be minimal. If the function is essential, then one must ask if it can be done by some other part that already exists elsewhere in the design. Once the team is satisfied that the function and the need for the item really does exist, ideas for alternatives must be generated. The most popular way of doing this is by **brainstorming** and here all the members of the team can participate.

Generating original ideas to order can be one of the more difficult tasks that faces us. We have all experienced the occasions when problems we encounter seem intractable, then suddenly inspiration comes along and a new solution to the problem appears. Fortuitous though this may be, inspiration through casual discovery cannot be relied upon to produce the right answers at the right time. What is needed is a method that will make the process of inspiration and discovery function when we most need it; a number of methods have been suggested and by far the most popular is brainstorming. It was developed as a formalized technique in the 1930s by Alex F. Osborn, of the New York advertising agency Batten Barton Durstine and Osborn. He defined brainstorming as: *a means of getting a large number of ideas from a group of people in a very short time*. The definition contains three important facets:

1. That the number of ideas should be large, the larger the better.
2. That brainstorming is a group activity.
3. That the time in which the ideas are generated is strictly limited.

Brainstorming sessions need a leader, without him the process will not function correctly; the leader is there to stimulate the creative processes in the team, keep order and generally control the process, he can put in ideas of his own and is expected to do so. The project Value Engineer is a prime candidate for this role. The composition of the team is important as the participants should be of roughly equal seniority; if there is too great a gap, free speculation can be inhibited as the more junior, and sometimes the more senior, members may fear making a foolish suggestion. The session can be divided into four stages:

1. Stating the problem.
2. Restating the problem.
3. Speculating on possible solutions.
4. Assessing the ideas produced.

The leader begins by taking the item under study and either states its basic and secondary functions as he sees them or asks the team to give their opinions. It is important that everyone should reach agreement on the functions, primary and secondary, and understand them clearly. Stage 2 allows the team to see if there are other ways in which the same functions can be described – this is important as it can throw the problem into a wider perspective and ensures that the perceived functions are viewed from every angle. For example, the watch may have a primary function that is stated as 'tells time' but it could also be stated as 'marks the passage of the hours'. Many restatements will be little more than semantic changes, but occasionally a restatement will reveal the function in a new light. On other occasions, the function is so basic or fundamental that no restatements are possible but time devoted to this activity will not have been wasted as the discussion will have enlightened everyone.

Stage 3 consists of free speculation as to all the ways that can be thought of to perform the required functions. Here the emphasis will be on quantity and it is important that nothing should inhibit the free flow of ideas. The leader should stimulate the team with a few ideas of his own and encourage others to generate as many as they can. No criticism is allowed, no matter how wild, humorous or facetious the ideas may be. The wildest ideas, while often being impractical in

AW VALUE ENGINEERING: CHECKLIST	Yes	No
Use the questions to speculate on improvements.		
Can the function be achieved in another way?		
Can the part or function be eliminated?		
Can some secondary functions of the part be eliminated?		
Can the part be combined with another?		
Is there a cheaper alternative part?		
Can cheaper or novel material be used?		
Can the part be redesigned for cheaper material?		
Are all features of the part needed?		
Can the part be made from standard section material?		
Is material received in the most economical shape and size?		
Can a standard part be substituted?		
Can the part be made common with existing parts?		
Is the part stronger than necessary?		
Can minor changes reduce material waste?		
Can tolerances be relaxed to ease manufacture?		
Are finish requirements essential?		
Could alternative finishes be used?		
Can machining be replaced by forgings, pressings or castings?		
Would improved tooling reduce costs?		
Are all screws, rivets and other fasteners standard?		
Can labour content be reduced by design changes?		
Have high-volume production methods been considered?		
Have alternative, novel processes been considered?		
Could the part be procured more cheaply outside?		
Could an externally supplied part be made cheaper in house?		

Figure 6.12 Example of a value engineering checklist.

themselves, can lead to practical suggestions that are truly original and may be among the most valuable. Writing all the ideas down and displaying them as they are suggested will lead to more ideas being triggered. If ideas seem to be drying up, the leader can call for a minute of silent meditation when no ideas are suggested. When the minute is up, the leader starts the session again. Eventually the flow of ideas will start to become exhausted – only when the leader recognizes this point has been reached should he bring the session to a close.

The fourth stage, assessing the ideas, can either be done straight after the speculation or after a suitable period to allow the mind to clear; it might be arranged that the lunch-break forms a natural gap. Evaluation will take much longer than speculation, perhaps a whole afternoon. It needs to be controlled by the leader and, before looking at each idea, criteria should be established by the group against which each suggestion can be tested. The ideas can either be taken in the order they were put forward or they can be given a cursory ranking from the most likely to be a winner to barely feasible. Examination against the criteria will quickly eliminate many of the ideas, perhaps 60–70%, but before any idea is finally discarded, the leader should ask the group if they can think of any way that such an idea could be made to work; sometimes a really novel idea can emerge that has not appeared in the original session. Finally, the group should agree on a best half-dozen ideas that appear to meet the criteria most closely and these should be the subject of study outside the team.

Other methods of creative thinking can be used, in particular, checklists are very good when it comes to essential components of a system where the scope for improvement is strictly limited by the surrounding design. An example of such a checklist is given in Figure 6.12, and it invites the team to consider each of the areas in which an improvement can be made. Listing the attributes or properties of an item can also lead to suggestions for ways in which each of these could be improved or even eliminated if it is felt that their contribution is negative.

Phase 4: Evaluation

The final selection of ideas will be put forward for a full evaluation. This work will normally be done by the Value Engineer, who will take all the ideas generated and interpret them in the form of design sketches. These will have to be taken to the Manufacturing and Purchasing departments for their comments and estimates of cost. Cost data may not be forthcoming immediately and approaches with sketches may have to be made to potential suppliers. Cost alone may not be the only factor to consider, design comments may be needed on such topics as weight, volume, durability, reliability, etc. The Marketing Department may also have to be consulted if customer acceptance could be a problem. All the Value Engineer's sketches should be circulated to the team members, so that they have time to consider each proposal from the point of view of their own specialist discipline. About three or four weeks after the speculation session, a full evaluation session is held. Here each member will be asked to look critically at each idea for both good and bad features. The Value Engineer should provide the cost estimates he has received and any comments on the proposal that were made during his studies. The proposals, features and costs can be recorded on an evaluation sheet, as shown in Figure 6.13. In this example, data has been obtained on alternatives to a machined link. Weight has been identified as an adverse property, some value is therefore attached to producing a light component, and low technical risk is also a desirable feature. While these are not strictly functions of the part, they are properties that contribute to value and, in the final evaluation, should be taken into account. Figure 6.14 shows a value analysis sheet in which a '**measure of value**' has been established for each alternative. The five functions and properties identified by the team are listed along the top and each has been given a weighting to signify the importance attached to it. Starting with the existing item, each alternative solution is considered to assess how its performance

AW	VALUE ENGINEERING: FUNCTION AND EVALUATION SHEET			

Title:	Part No:	Issue:	Used on:	Ref. No.: 196
TOGGLE LINK	A96-531086	2A	CONTROL ACTUATOR	Date 15-12-93

FUNCTION(S): Define by VERB and NOUN:

PRIMARY FUNCTION: ......TRANSMITS....MOTION.............

SECONDARY FUNCTIONS

1 TRANSMITS SPRING FORCE 4 LOW TECHNICAL RISK
2 RESTRAINS MOTION   5 ....
3 BE LIGHT IN WEIGHT   6 ....

	List possible solutions below and comments opposite. Begin with the existing design.	Good Features	Bad Features	Estimated Unit Cost
1	EXISTING LINK : MACHINED FROM SOLID	STRONG	HEAVY, EXPENSIVE	£ 23.00
2	CAST LINK: MACHINED ENDS	LOW COST	HEAVY, STRENGTH	£ 8.20 + TOOLS
3	FORGED LINK: MACHINED ENDS	STRONG, LIGHTER THAN CASTING	HEAVY	£12.50 + TOOLS
4	PRESS FORMED HALVES, WELDED, NO MACHINING	LOW COST, STRONG	HEAVIER THAN FORGING	£6.50 + TOOLS
5	G.R.P. MOULDED LINK, STEEL INSERTS	LIGHT	TECHNICAL RISK STRENGTH, QUALITY CONTROL	£13.25 + TOOLS

Figure 6.13 Example of a function and evaluation sheet.

AW VALUE ENGINEERING: VALUE ANALYSIS SHEET

Title: TOGGLE LINK	Part No: A96-53/086	Issue: 2A	Used on: CONTROL ACTUATOR	Ref. No. 196	Date: 16-12-93

FUNCTIONS AND PROPERTIES		Primary		Secondary			% Performed	Unit Cost	Measure of Value
		Transmits motion	Transmits spring force	Restrains motion	Light in weight	Low risk	a	b	a / b
WEIGHTING FACTOR		0.7	0.1	0.05	0.1	0.05			
EXISTING LINK	% Satisfied	100	100	100	50	100			
	% Performed	70	10	5	5	5	95	£23.00	4.13
CAST LINK	% Satisfied	100	100	100	25	50			
	% Performed	70	10	5	2.5	2.5	90	£8.20	10.97
FORGED LINK	% Satisfied	100	100	100	40	100			
	% Performed	70	10	5	4	5	94	£12.50	7.52
PRESS FORMED + WELDED LINK	% Satisfied	100	100	100	30	80			
	% Performed	70	10	5	3	4	92	£6.25	14.72
G.R.P. MOULDED LINK	% Satisfied	100	70	100	80	20			
	% Performed	70	7	5	8	1	91	£13.25	6.87
	% Satisfied								
	% Performed								

Figure 6.14 Example of a value analysis sheet.

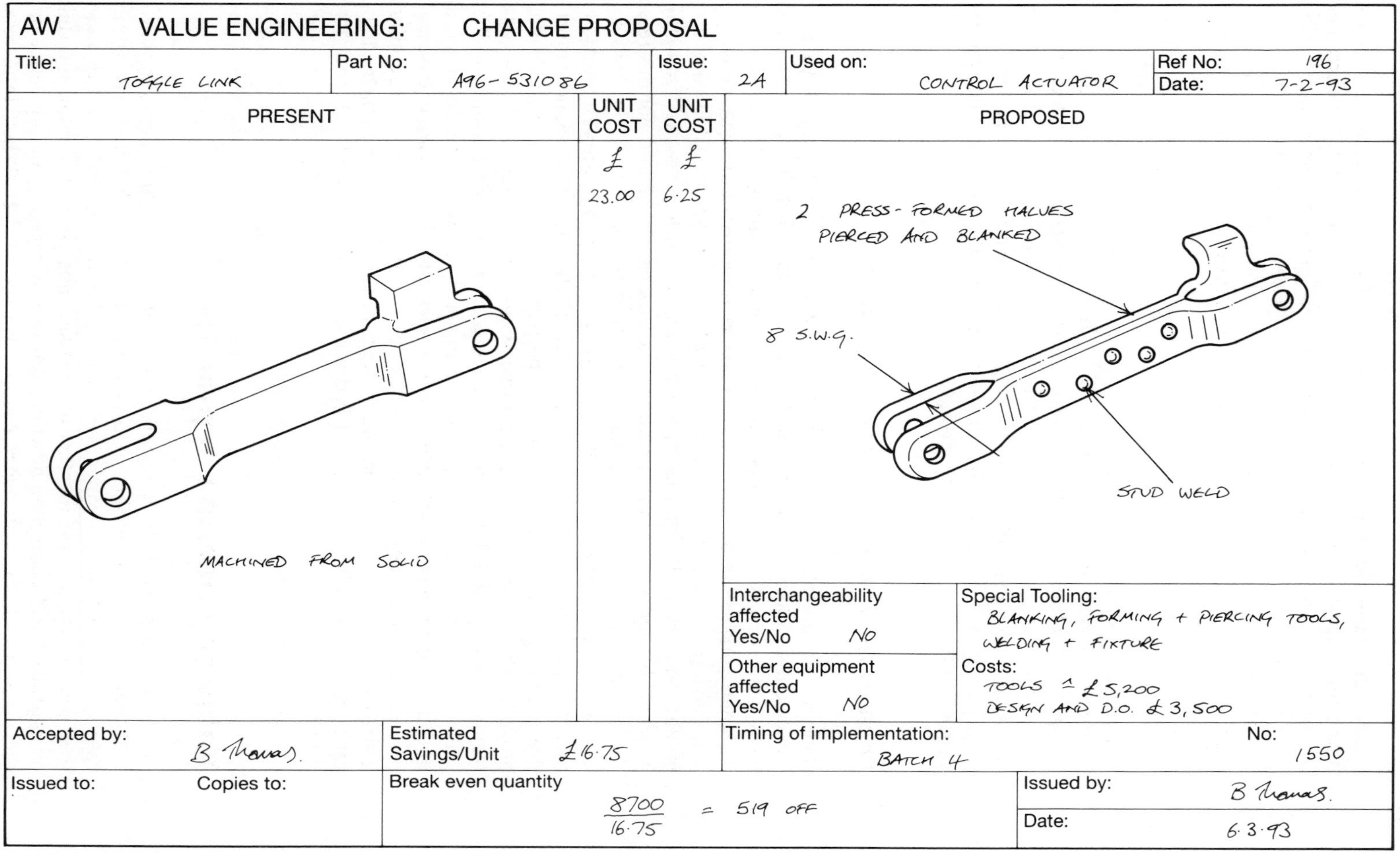

AW **VALUE ENGINEERING:** **CHANGE PROPOSAL**

Title: TOGGLE LINK	Part No: A16-531086	Issue: 24	Used on:	Ref No: 196

CONTROL ACTUATOR Date: 7-2-93

PRESENT

MACHINED FROM SOLID

UNIT COST £ 23.00

PROPOSED

2 PRESS-FORMED HALVES PIERCED AND BLANKED

STUD WELD

8 S.W.G.

UNIT COST £ 6.25

Special Tooling: BLANKING, FORMING + PIERCING TOOLS, WELDING + FIXTURE

Costs: TOOLS ≈ £5,200 DESIGN AND D.O. £3,500

Interchangeability affected Yes/No No

Other equipment affected Yes/No No

Timing of implementation: BATCH 4

No: 1550

Estimated Savings/Unit £16.75

Break even quantity 8700 / 16.75 = 519 OFF

Accepted by: B Nana

Issued to:

Copies to:

Issued by: B Nana

Date: 6-3-93

Figure 6.15 Example of a change proposal form.

satisfies the particular function or property and a score is given as a percentage. When these satisfaction values are multiplied by the weighting, a percentage performance figure is generated – the sum of these gives the percentage performance for the item as a whole. Dividing the percentage performance figure by the unit cost gives a 'measure of value' and this is shown at the right. In the example in the figure, the existing design scores highest on performance; only its weight counts against it, but its high cost gives it the lowest measure of value. The press-formed and welded solution has the highest measure of value and is thus the preferred choice.

A change proposal showing details of the new design is prepared by the Value Engineer and will be presented to the Value Engineering Committee (VEC). A change proposal form is shown in Figure 6.15, together with the details of the new design, the tooling cost and the break-even quantity. All supporting information, including the analysis by the Value Engineering Team, should be available to the VEC. Acceptance of the change proposal by the VEC will represent an executive instruction to proceed with the change.

Phase 5: Implementation and follow-up

None of the potential savings will come about unless the proposed changes are implemented, and effort may still be needed to ensure that the approved changes are really made. Pressure of work in the design or drawing offices may cause the required work to slip down the queue and be forgotten. Prototype or sample items may have to be obtained for evaluation and testing before a full commitment to production is made. Unless the appropriate degree of priority is attached to the work, it can fall behind and the momentum of the process will be lost. For this reason, the Value Engineer must generate a plan of action that will cover all the tasks necessary for the implementation phase and state those persons who are responsible for each task. A copy of this plan should be approved by the VEC. The engineer must ensure that each responsible person is aware of his part in the plan and must also follow up progress. The Committee too should review progress on approved changes at their regular meetings and the Value Engineer report on the tasks currently in hand.

Finally, when the change has been completed, a check is made to see that the intended savings have in fact been made. Checks should be made to ensure that the performance and quality of the product has not deteriorated. All the information gathered during the study, and the findings at the end of the implementation, are gathered up and filed as they can become a useful source of reference for future studies.

Value engineering in practice

The process described above may seem obvious to some and many firms will claim that they do it as part of their normal design function. This, however, is rarely the case as, by its nature, it involves people from different disciplines taking time out of their normal day to come together to speculate, analyse and recommend. Unless it is an organized and controlled function, centrally directed, it simply won't happen – the pressures of the daily work routine will see to that. When formalized value engineering is done, it is surprising what suggestions can arise and how companies can discover that they do not know their products and costs as well as they might have supposed.

Value engineering should not, however, become just another routine, its effect comes from the fresh approach that the team members bring to the task. Make it an institution and the freshness dries up, taking with it the essential element of creativity. It is best tackled on a project-by-project basis with a Value Engineer and a team specifically assembled for the job. Once the objectives have be achieved, the team should be disbanded. The Value Engineer should, however, continue with the work as implementation may go on for some time beyond the finalization of all recommendations.

The importance of senior management involvement has already been stressed; the Project Manager alone cannot overcome all the obstacles to generating an improved value product if he is not seen to be backed from the highest level. The creation of a VEC is one way of achieving this, particularly where it has Board-level members. In most cases, money will have to be committed to achieving a better product either through design and development work or new tools and processes; senior management needs to be convinced of the value of making the changes as it is they who will sanction the expenditure. The Project Manager can institute as many value engineering studies as he likes, but if money is not approved to make the recommended changes, then it is all a waste (yet practicioners of value engineering say that this is often what happens). It would seem that some firms do not see the benefit of spending money early to ensure benefits in production cost later on.

It is difficult to say in advance what degree of saving is likely to result from a value engineering study. It depends on many factors, including the maturity of the design, the level of cost consciousness applied at the design stage and the extent to which scope for change exists. For items that have progressed to the production stage and investment already made in tooling and development testing, the scope may be limited and savings in the region of 5–10% of total cost should be achievable. In the development phase when the design is less mature and little has been committed to tooling, the scope is much greater and savings as high as 30% are possible. It should not be expected that the same level of savings can be made in all areas, and it may be the case that even with a value engineering exercise, costs in some areas may rise above their estimates or targets. This author has known the situation where development testing has revealed deficiencies that could only be cured by a significantly more complex and costly design than was originally proposed. This does not mean that the value engineering was pointless, but rather it underlines the cost and, ultimately, the worth to the customer of having a design that meets the requirements in all respects.

Summary

In the face of worldwide competition for the sale of manufactured goods, generating products with low costs but high value is a significant factor in business success. Project Managers with the responsibility for product development projects have a unique opportunity to influence the cost and value of the end-product by the approach taken. They can either let the design process take its course or they can actively structure the project programme to promote ways that lead to low-cost or high-value solutions. The two principal methods are design-to-cost and value engineering, each is a well-established technique but approaches the problem from different perspectives. Design-to-cost lays emphasis on cost as a project parameter that is ranked equally with performance and schedule, it implies a willingness to trade among these parameters to achieve the best overall project solution. Value engineering can be considered as an improvement process aimed at increasing the value to the user of each element of a product. It can be applied at any stage in the product life cycle, but the earlier it is done the more beneficial it is. Value engineering can challenge deeply held ideas about a firm's products, and it can also reveal that firms do not know as much about their products as they thought.

7

Managing the flow of materials

- Build sequences
- Feasible output capacity calculation
- Line-of-balance techniques
- Computerized materials management

Whereas few would disagree that good management of the flow of materials and parts is a vital element in the success of a production programme, it may be less obvious that the same degree of management can be just as important to the outcome of the development phase. Shortages of parts lead to delay; as a result, tests may not be completed on time and important results may not be available when significant decisions have to be made. Parts shortages at shopfloor level may cause work to stop, workers to be put on idle time or transferred to other activities. Whichever occurs, disruption will result, impetus will be lost and each delay adds to the overall cost. Even more serious can be the effect of not having the product in the market at a time that maximizes the benefits of its innovative qualities; a delay of one month can be disastrous for orders if sales are highly seasonal.

It is too frequently found that parts shortages and other manufacturing delays are among the root-causes of project slippage. It would, however, be impossible to imagine a complex programme in which no shortages occurred; in reality, there will always be unforeseen problems, design errors, mistakes by operators, process difficulties and unreliable suppliers, that ensure vital parts are not available when wanted. Although unforeseen difficulties will arise, the project team is not exempt from contributing to the problem if it has not planned the acquisition of parts in a satisfactory way. It is necessary to recognize that delays are likely and to appreciate the capacity limitations of both in-house manufacturing shops and external suppliers. Knowledge of the lead-times for parts and understanding the order in which parts go together is vital in planning an achievable manufacturing, purchasing and subcontracting programme.

However, all to often, over-optimistic estimates are made, suppliers' promises, however well-meaning, are taken at face-value and allowances for return and re-work action are not included. When final assembly starts, sub-assemblies cannot be put together due to shortages, panic action is instituted to make urgently needed parts or chase suppliers. Work-around plans are hastily generated to try to preserve the timescale and further confusion results as the work is done out of order; it may even result in abortive work. The result is frustration at every level and in the eyes of the shopfloor it will be seen as another example of poor management.

Planning the acquisition process

The depressing scenario, outlined above, is a common one but much of this could be avoided if more attention and greater understanding was applied to the planning. An acceptance of realities, including building in contingencies, is essential for the manufacturing programme must be both realistic and achievable. These criteria lie entirely within the hands of the Project Manager; if they are not met, then rational control will be lost, firefighting, panic expediting and 'who shouts loudest wins' will result. However, developments in production planning and control techniques and the application of computers has led to a more disciplined and logical approach. In particular, the 'line-of-balance' method for stock-level reporting became popular during the 1950s but it is now being replaced by more elaborate **manufacturing resource planning** (MRP) systems.

These systems are mostly put into companies for managing the day-to-day production work and control of them may lie outside of the sphere of influence of the Project Manager. Essential differences between production and development work may mean that MRP systems do not conform quite so easily with the less certain and more reactive demands of development and some modification or accommodation may have to be made if they are to be used successfully. Nevertheless, the logic and discipline that is inherent in computer-based scheduling can force managers and planners to make realistic appraisals; when unrealistic demands are entered, the output reports show that the objectives cannot be met as projected delivery dates lie well beyond the requirement dates. Some Project Managers find this particularly uncomfortable if the project has high visibility within their own organization or with outside customers. Some may even feel that if they cannot indicate that all objectives can be met at the next project review, their own future as a manager may be at stake. This feeling can result in the temptation to reject the output, but that is unwise: to be forewarned is to be given a chance to do something about the difficulties before the reality becomes irreversible.

Build sequences

Planning for material and parts acquisition starts with a breakdown of the final assembly into its component parts. The level to which the assembly should be broken down will normally be that level at which items enter the company. Thus items to be made completely in house will need to be taken down to each piece part

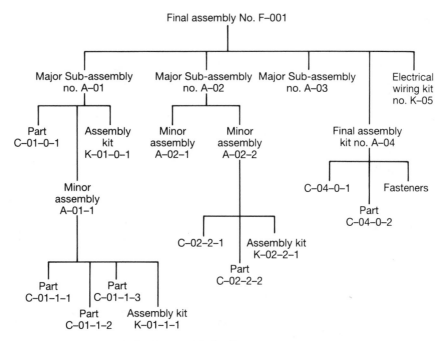

Figure 7.1 Component and sub-assembly family tree.

or to the level of the material if non-stock material is needed. Subcontracted assemblies or standard parts that are bought as complete assemblies will not be broken down further, but their lead-times must be known. The logic of the build up of components must be established, as must be the lead-times for completing the work at each stage and the quantity of each part in each sub-assembly; this is most easily expressed in diagramatic form. For very large and complex products, a full diagrammatic breakdown may not be worthwhile or practical, even so it is worth doing for the main elements of the final assembly.

Figure 7.1 shows the build up of parts in a typical product, the diagram is often called a 'parts family tree'. When lead-times and quantities are incorporated, the chart can be redrawn to form a **build sequence diagram**; Figure 7.2 shows a part of the build sequence diagram for the product shown in Figure 7.1. Besides the assembly logic, the diagram has been drawn on a scale that indicates the time taken by each activity. In this way, the order in which the work must be done and the time at which each activity must take place can be appreciated.

A standardized notation has been used which is both simple and explicit (Figure 7.3). When assessing the lead-times for each part, inter-machine movement and queuing time, set-up time and inspection time should be added to the basic operation time to form the elapsed time. In batch-working shops it is not untypical for a machined part with nine operations on six machines with two inspections and a total working time of 15 hours to take six to eight weeks to go from material to finished part. Movements between shops in the figure have been drawn with thin arrows and include an allowance of at least one week. These times take into account the losses in time that tend to occur when parts travel between shops and also form

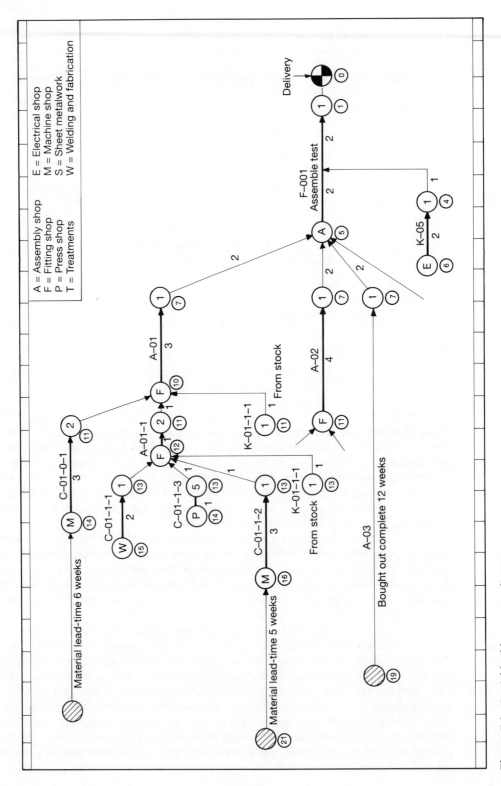

Figure 7.2 Partial build sequence diagram.

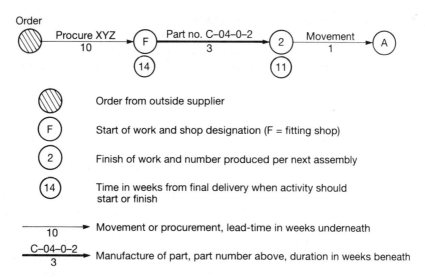

Figure 7.3 Standardized sequence notation.

an additional float in the build sequence that allows a small amount of lateness to occur without jeopardizing the whole build programme. Using the method outlined, a realistic view can be generated of the order of work and the time it is likely to take; it will form the basis for ordering materials and for setting priorities in the Design Department.

The notation also allows the quantity of parts in the assembly to be calculated by working forward through each level of part and sub-assembly, multiplying together the quantity figures in each terminal node. Thus, in Figure 7.2, there is one part A-01 in the final item but this contains two parts A-01-1, each of which has five parts C-01-1-3, making ten in all. This form of notation, making use of multiplication rather than total numbers in the final item, allows sub-assemblies to be considered as individual build sequences in isolation; it is the most convenient method with large or complex assemblies and it also has the advantage that suits the operational logic of MRP systems. These create parts requirements by a 'backward explosion' where quantities are calculated by working downwards from the final assembly through all the sub-assembly levels, multiplying together the quantities until the numbers of individual parts are found.

Where only one or two prototypes are required, build sequences of the type shown may be sufficient for planning and controlling manufacture. In this case, they take on a role similar to a project network and the layout makes it easy to translate them into network activities. The activities can be entered into a suitable project management computer system but it will not have the ability to calculate parts requirements, only time-based progress monitoring will be possible. Control of activities and parts movements will normally be the responsibility of a progress chaser (or expeditor) acting on behalf of the Project Manager. In smaller projects the expediting function may be included in the overall scope of work of an engineer dedicated to ensuring satisfactory production and resolving design and manufacturing problems.

Control and coordination

Unlike the simple project involving only one or two prototypes, many development projects require a large number of examples of the item under test; this may be because:

- statistically representative samples are needed;
- testing tends to be destructive;
- many specially configured or instrumented examples are needed, each to test some specific aspect;
- many small design variations each need to be tested.

With projects to develop munitions (bombs, missiles, etc.), where the object under development is destroyed in the course of the test, the numbers required can become so large as to warrant small-scale production runs lasting for a year or more. When this occurs, additional steps must be taken to ensure satisfactory control as the work takes on more of the aspects of production control than would be the case with the more usual planning and progressing functions. This point should not be over-looked as network analysis techniques are not suitable for controlling complex manufacturing activities which involve both large numbers of parts and capacity limitations.

Contemporary development projects are tending towards the creation of complex products that are themselves systems of specially designed components or sub-systems, each of which requires highly specialized technology, particularly in the military sphere. The contractor responsible for the development of the end-product may not have the necessary capabilities to develop all the elements of the system. When this occurs, the development and manufacture of the specialized parts has to be put out to subcontractors with the required skills. Managing materials and parts then becomes a matter of managing subcontractors, as well as operations within the parent company. If the project is sufficiently large and complex, a specialist group of staff will be required for this role; their primary functions will be to:

- translate trials and test programmes into hardware requirements;
- ensure that an adequate design definition exists for all required items;
- assess the capabilities of each contractor or manufacturing shop to do the required work;
- generate procurement schedules that meet the demands of the test programme and lie within the contractor's capability;
- communicate the procurement schedules to each contractor;
- where conflicts between the demands of the test programme and the contractors' capacity exist, report this to the project manager and suggest solutions;
- monitor performance and liaise with all parties to ensure timely progress.

The common desire to compress the project timescale frequently produces problems when hardware demands exceed capacity. Careful planning and supplies management becomes essential and a continuous feedback approach is necessary. Figure 7.4 shows the control system; it will be seen that the supplies and manufacturing control group exists as a unit that interfaces with the various sections within the project group, the supplying subcontractors and the manufacturing shops. The role of the group will be one of planning monitoring and liaison and the reports on progress and possible future delays must be taken seriously by the Project Manager.

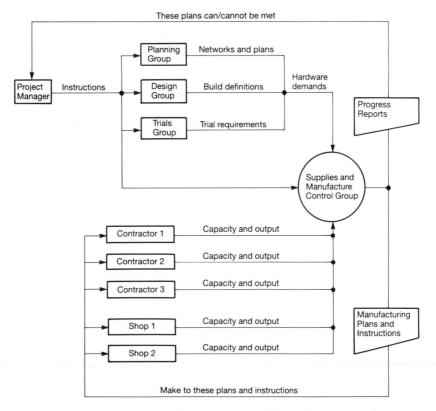

Figure 7.4 Functional relationships for the supplies and manufacture control group.

Feasible output programmes

It is quite likely that when the test programme is first set out, no consideration will be given to the ability of any shop or contractor to supply the hardware in the quantities needed. Although this may sound perverse, there are good reasons why this happens. At the start, the test programme will be laid out as the shortest or most economical way to achieve all the tests necessary to prove the design. This may generate a requirement for hardware which, when drawn on a timescale, produces marked peaks and troughs in the demand level, often with a large number of items being required in a very short timespan either at the beginning or end of the programme. This may be far from ideal from a manufacturing point of view, particularly if large numbers are needed that demand significant resources for their production. Few companies would be willing to go above the normal peak output capability of their development shop or turn over the whole or part of their production organization for a few months' activity making development hardware.

When these factors are taken into account, some re-planning of the test activities will almost certainly be necessary, but this is better done at the planning stage than having trials laboratory facilities booked and engineers standing by only to find out that hardware is not going to be available for another month.

Where subcontractors or special facilities are involved, each will have its own level of capacity and earliest starting point. When a number of subcontractors are involved, the overall output programme will be governed by the slowest and/or the latest starting contractor; to establish a feasible trials programme the overall output capacity needs to be found.

Example 7.1: Feasible output calculation

Consider a product whose build sequence is as shown in Figure 7.5. The product to be manufactured consists of five major items and is dependent on assembly tooling. The output rate for each of these items and the calendar week number in which the first delivery can be made is given in Table 7.1. The question is what output rate can be expected for item A01, and will there be a delay in reaching the planned peak output of 20 units per week?

Table 7.1 Output rates and first delivery dates for components and assemblies

Item no.	Start week no.	Output per week from start											
		1	2	3	4	5	6	7	8	9	10	11	12
A01	21	2	4	6	10	12	15	17	19	20	20	20	20
C02-1	12	2	4	4	6	10	12	16	18	20	20	20	20
A03	13	4	6	8	10	12	16	20	22	24	25	25	25
C03-1	10	4	8	10	15	20	20	25	25	25	25	25	25
C03-2	12	5	7	8	9	10	12	13	15	16	17	18	20

It is necessary to find the achievable output programme for the final assembly: item A01, and this is done by working forwards from the earliest deliverable item taking each assembly in turn. A table is constructed showing the output of each assembly as it would be possible if each component of the assembly is the only constraint on output. The position for item A03 is given in Table 7.2; it shows that if item C03-1 is the limiting factor on output, the first

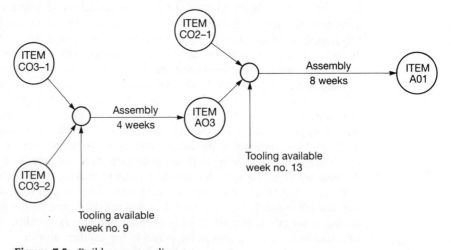

Figure 7.5 Build sequence diagram.

Table 7.2 Calculation of feasible output for item A03

Item no.	Earliest start week for A03	13	14	15	16	17	18	19	20	21	22	23	24	25	26	27
									Calendar week no.							
C03-1	14		4	8	10	15	20	20	25	25	25	25	25	25	25	25
Cumulative			4	12	22	37	57	77	102	127	152	177	202	227	252	277
C03-2	16				5	7	8	9	10	12	13	15	16	17	18	20
Cumulative					5	12	20	29	39	51	64	79	95	112	130	150
A03	13	4	6	8	10	12	16	20	22	24	25	25	25	25	25	25
Cumulative		4	10	18	28	40	56	76	98	122	147	172	197	222	247	272
A03 shifted to week 16					4	6	8	10	12	16	20	22	24	25	25	25
Cumulative					4	10	18	28	40	56	76	98	122	147	172	197
Feasible output for item A03					4	6	8	10	11	12	13	15	16	17	18	20
Cumulative					4	10	18	28	39	51	64	79	95	112	130	150

Table 7.3 Calculation of feasible output for item A01

Item no.	Earliest start week for A01	20	21	22	23	24	25	26	27	28	29	30	31	32	33	34	35
												Calendar week no.					
C02-1	20	2	4	4	6	10	12	16	18	20	20	20	20	20	20	20	20
Cum.		2	6	10	16	26	38	54	72	92	112	132	142	152	172	192	212
A03	24					4	6	8	10	11	12	13	15	16	17	18	20
Cum.						4	10	18	28	39	51	64	79	95	112	130	150
A01	21		2	4	6	10	12	15	17	19	20	20	20	20	20	20	20
Cum.			2	6	12	22	34	49	66	85	105	125	145	165	185	205	225
A01 shifted to week 24						2	4	6	10	12	15	17	19	20	20	20	20
Cum.						2	6	12	22	34	49	66	85	105	125	145	165
Feasible output for item A01						2	4	6	10	12	15	15	15	16	17	18	20
Cum.						2	6	12	22	34	49	64	79	95	112	130	150

example of assembly A03 could appear four weeks after the first item C03-1 arrives (i.e. week 10 + 4 = week 14) and four units should be available as four C03-1s will arrive and can be assembled.

The table shows that although the first example of item A03 could be produced by week 13, if all the parts are available, it is not possible because item C03-2 dictates that the earliest time it can be done is week 16. The output of item A03 has to be shifted to start in week 16; by comparing the possible output rate of A03 with the supply of items C03-1 and C03-2, the feasible output can be established. Whenever the supply of parts is less than the possible output of the end-item, the lower figure is taken; thus from week 21 onwards the supply of A03 is dependent entirely on the deliveries of C03-2. During weeks 16 and 17, the possible output of A03 is less by two than the supply of C03-2, and these two items can be used to maximize output in weeks 19 and 20. Using this result and the possible output for item C02-1, the feasible output programme for item A01 can be established and this is given in Table 7.3.

It will be seen that the peak output rate of 20 items per week will not be achieved until week 35, largely due to the slow output build-up of item C03-2. If Item A01 alone had been considered, 20 per week should have been reached by week 29, by which time a cumulative output of 105 might have been expected; in fact only 49 can be produced.

Only a calculation of the above type reveals the feasible capacity but, in many cases, it is not done – only the final output figure, simply stated, is taken in the assumption that all incoming supplies will be adequate. This may contribute some of the cause of much frustration on the part of Project Managers when output from shops and subcontractors does not match expectations. Tedious though it may seem, a

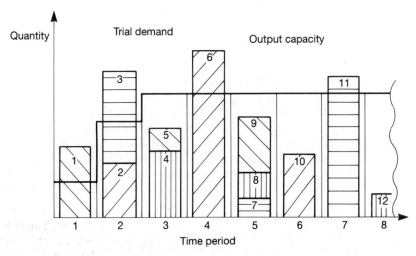

Figure 7.6 Comparison of output capacity with trial demand shows that demand exceeds capacity at times.

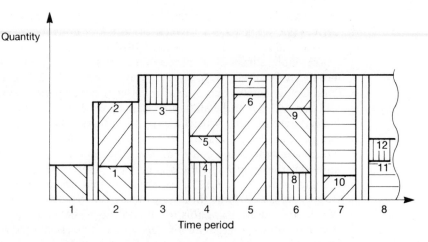

Figure 7.7 Scheduling trials demands within the output capacity reveals the earliest time at which trials can take place.

feasibility calculation is worth doing. Every item in a complex assembly need not be considered as many detail parts will be made in a single large batch and output growth will not be a factor. There will generally be a few, easily identifiable parts that will have both a definable start date and a known build-up rate to peak output. These are the items that should be studied in the way shown and even large and complex systems can be reduced to some 10–20 critical items.

When the feasible output programme has been established, it can be compared with the hardware required by the test programme followed by whatever rescheduling is necessary. In the example in Figure 7.6 it will be seen that the earliest trials cannot take place at the required time as the test hardware will not be available. The earliest point at which trials can take place can be found by scheduling within the feasible capacity curve and this is shown in Figure 7.7.

Monitoring progress

The **line-of-balance** technique became popular in the 1950s after its application to US Navy projects as a method of monitoring supply situations and is still used for some simple projects. The advent of computerized systems has seen the graphical method virtually disappear, although the principles still remain valid. The purpose of the method is to define at any point in time, the quantities of any or all the items required by the manufacturing programme and compare the requirements with the actual deliveries and stock balances.

Before the line-of-balance method can be used, a build sequence must be drawn to show all the items worth monitoring. Stock parts and materials that can be bought in bulk at short notice will not normally be considered. The output schedule for the final item must also be defined, for this is the objective against which supply performance will be assessed.

Example 7.2: Construction of a line-of-balance chart

A product with a build sequence as shown in Figure 7.8 is to be built in the following quantities:

- 10 units are to be produced in the first 8 weeks of production;
- 20 units are to be made in the following 10 weeks;
- production is to continue thereafter at 10 units every 3 weeks.

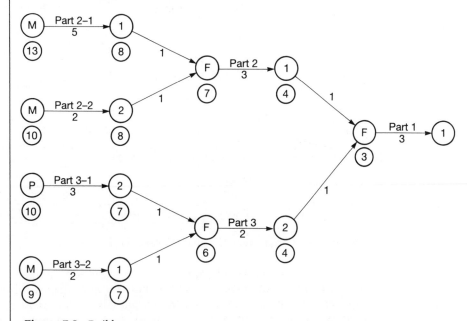

Figure 7.8 Build sequence.

At the eighth week of production the following quantities of all the parts in the build-sequence have been delivered:

Part no.	Deliveries at week 8
1	9
2	17
2-1	33
2-2	60
3	32
3-1	70
3-2	60

We wish to know which, if any, of the deliveries are running late and by how much.

A line-of-balance chart for this situation is shown in Figure 7.9. The graphical method, although somewhat dated, illustrates the method very clearly. The chart is essentially two diagrams drawn side by side with a common vertical

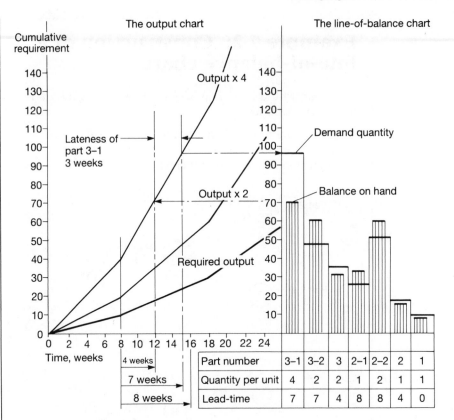

Figure 7.9 Construction of a line-of-balance chart.

axis that shows cumulative requirements for parts and assemblies. In the left-hand part the cumulative required output is drawn against a horizontal axis showing the time in weeks from the output date of the first item. The right-hand part is divided into columns, one for each item to be monitored. Under each column, the part number is written, together with the quantity of each part in the final product and its lead-time to completion. Where parts are required in multiples for each end-product, multiple quantity lines are drawn above the required output line. In this form, before the balance quantities are drawn, the chart can be copied, one copy being required for each occasion on which monitoring is to be done.

The line-of-balance can now be drawn; as we are interested in the position at week 8, a vertical line is drawn at that point on the output chart. The lead-times to completion are now drawn projecting forward from week 8; in this case, three lead-times are involved: 4, 7 and 8 weeks. For part number 3-1, there is a 7-week lead-time and four are required in each end-item; by projecting up from the 7-week lead-time point (i.e. week 15) onto the 'Output × 4 line', it can be seen that 95 of these parts should have been delivered. An open column can then be drawn above part 3-1 in the table. The actual balance of deliveries on hand is then drawn as a shaded column above each part number. For part 3-1, a comparison with the 70 items supplied shows that this part is running three weeks late in terms of deliveries. Items 1, 2 and 3 are also slightly behind schedule.

The example illustrates both the strength and the weakness of the graphical method. The visual impact and the ability to calculate actual (and potential) lateness makes it ideal for project management meetings, allowing discussion to focus on only items that are late. The weakness of the method lies in the fact that, if the product is complex, many charts may have to be drawn, and if many different multiples are involved, the chart can become confusing. Difficulties can also arise over the choice of a suitable vertical scale; where large numbers are involved, a logarithmic scale may be more appropriate. Furthermore, a new chart has to be constructed each time that reporting is done. However, the basic simplicity of the calculation lends itself to spreadsheet computer methods which overcome all the problems.

One other drawback, and it is the most serious, is that line-of-balance is primarily a monitoring method that is designed to say how well or how badly the suppliers are doing at any point in time; of itself, it does not generate a schedule of requirements. To overcome this difficulty computerized material requirements planning systems have been developed that do all that line-of-balance can do and much more.

Computerized materials management

The application of computers to the problems of manufacture control has a long history. In the early 1960s stores record-keeping and inventory control were among the first areas to receive attention from the computer technologists, workshop scheduling was another. Stores recording was a relatively simple computer application, but scheduling work through a series of machines and workshops in an efficient way was recognized from the start as a particularly difficult problem as the requirements for efficiency and optimality frequently conflict. Typically the objectives are to reduce job lateness to a minimum and increase machine utilization to a maximum, while reducing work-in-progress to a minimum. The process of scheduling involves assigning work to areas of capability such that the capacity is not exceeded, the work is done in the correct sequence and the jobs that are required earliest are planned to finish earliest. Simple though this objective may seem, achieving it has practical difficulties when combined with the criteria for efficiency; the greatest problems stem from the huge number of possible schedules that can be devised for any situation, including relatively simple ones, and then finding the best one.

Thoughts of scheduling efficiency were very much in the background when the first shop scheduling systems were devised; they worked by:

(a) backward scheduling from the output programme to find requirement dates through a parts explosion;
(b) comparing demands with stocks to generate net requirements;
(c) backward scheduling through the manufacturing processes;
(d) assigning process demands to a capability at the times indicated by the backward scheduling.

No account was taken of the real capacity limits of any capability, section or department to do the work, hence this arrangement is termed **infinite capacity scheduling** and its simplicity made it popular. It was to be some time before the more logical but more complex **finite capacity scheduling** came into use; with this arrangement, the capacity of each section to do the work at the time required is taken into account and the schedule adjusted accordingly.

By the mid-1970s, the whole field of production control had begun to develop a language and methodology of its own and this was first embodied in the principles of **material requirements planning** (MRP), promoted in the USA by Oliver White. It is a production-control technique based on the computerized scheduling methods outlined and aimed at generating plans for the acquisition of materials and parts in a logical and timely way. Early programs were designed to operate as stand-alone systems, but production control cannot remain aloof from all the other functions that go on in a factory – it is intimately linked to purchasing, accounting, store-keeping, etc. The demands of greater integration of data within companies has led to the creation of computerized systems that link together all these functions and which also include such features as shopfloor data collection, automatic order gen-eration and master production scheduling. They are referred to as MRP II systems, now referring to **manufacturing resource planning** and indicating a second gen-eration of production control systems.

The network analysis method dealt with in Chapter 4 might, at first glance, seem a suitable computerized approach to materials management in development projects, particularly as build sequence diagrams have similar characteristics to networks; if all items were made singly, or the project consisted of building just one item such as a ship, this would indeed be the case. Where many similar items have to be made over a long period with a limited capacity to do the work and routed to a variety of different final products, the network approach runs into serious difficulties. The problem with Network Analysis is that it is a tool for evaluating networks in terms of their properties such as float, criticality, latest finish date, etc., and for this to be done, the entire project has to be shown on the network. Where a great number of parts are concerned, the network can soon become impossibly large for convenient use if all the parts have to be shown. Even more serious, however, is the fact that a network is a hand-created plan in which all the logic has to be correct before the analysis is run. In order to make the logic of the network correct it is necessary to make sure that all the material supplies activities are correctly scheduled, but this has to be done before the network is analysed. The most awkward part is generating the correct schedule in the first place, and this is why networks have not proved a success with complex materials management – they simply do not help with the most difficult part of the problem.

MRP II systems contain the scheduling routines necessary to generate the supplies requirements that are a vital part of the project plan. However, these systems have, for the most part, been devised to deal with production situations where items are made to order or for stock and then despatched to a customer. With development work, there are a number of differences that should be noted, particularly when it comes to choosing a system as some modifications may have to be made if it is to work satisfactorily. When a test is defined and included in the programme, the hardware to be tested will be defined as far as the quantities and the functional characteristics are concerned. What may not be known are the part numbers of the items as at the time that test is defined the items will almost certainly not have been designed. This is quite different to a production situation as products are usually specified in precise detail at the time the production plan is created. One might ask why it is necessary to know all the hardware details in a development project before they have been designed, but without precise knowledge of the hardware types and quantities, the project cannot be costed in total. This may not matter greatly if the quantities are small and the project is of low overall value but it is highly relevant if the hardware is a significant element of the total cost. It can become of supreme importance if the project is being funded by an outside customer or if subcontractors are asked to quote for the supply of items at fixed prices. Knowing when the hardware will be supplied and paid for is also necessary for cash-flow planning.

A demand for hardware by a test can be likened to an order for a production item. However, a production order can only be fulfilled by making an item and supplying it to the customer, but a trial demand can be satisfied in several ways:

- by making a new item for test;
- by taking an item that has been used for a previous test;
- by modifying an item that has been used for a previous test to create a new item.

Only the first condition is typical of a production situation, the other two conditions may not be easily handled in a conventional MRP system without modification. The case study given below describes the features of a computerized system that was specifically designed for managing manufacturing in development projects that involve large amounts of hardware. Its features overcome the difficulties that have been mentioned above.

Case study 7.1: A computerized materials management system

The subject of this case study is a materials management system that was designed from the outset for development work, where the projects require a long series of proving trials each needing large quantities of hardware in a variety of standards, and made by a number of subcontractors. It can be considered as an 'ideal' system and its principal elements are shown in Figure 7.10.

Four main files hold all the data; their functions are as follows:

Capacity and delivery file: this carries details of all the suppliers' output capacities on a month by month basis over the whole manufacturing programme. It also carries the running totals of all items delivered.

Build sequence file: this carries details of all build sequences with part numbers, descriptions, origins and destinations, lead-times and quantities.

Trial requirements file: this carries details of all the items of hardware that are needed to carry out a trial, including those items that will be supplied from a previous trial. Hardware can include complete end-products or components which may be supplied as spares or are the subject of a trial in their own right.

Trial data file: this carries the details of the trial including its purpose, programmed date, venue, assembly point, preparation time, special facilities, name of the person responsible for the conduct of the trial, etc.

Hardware is classified as either an end-item, called a **prime item**, or a **component** – i.e. a part called into a prime item. The system output is divided into three main groups: schedules, status reports and data reports; their functions are:

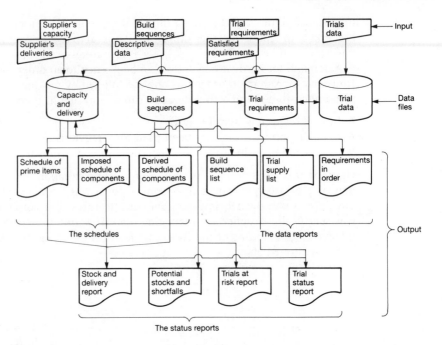

Figure 7.10   Computerized material management system.

Schedules

Three types are produced:

(a) Schedules of all Prime Item Delivery Requirements, these are scheduled within the output capacity limit specified. An example of this report is shown in Figure 7.11.
(b) Derived Component Schedules, these are created by back-scheduling through the lead-times of the build sequences and grouping together all like items in required date order. An example of this report is shown in Figure 7.12.
(c) Imposed Component Schedules, these are produced where there are known limits on the capacity to supply component parts; in this case, the derived schedules, which are at infinite capacity, are further re-scheduled within the limiting capacity.

Data reports

Three types are produced, their function is to show basic data about the project:

(a) Build Sequence Report, this shows the build sequences as they are input.
(b) Trial Supply List, this gives all the prime hardware required for each trial and the breakdown into component parts and quantities. This report is useful for agreeing the hardware standards with the trials manager before manufacturing instructions are issued.
(c) Requirements in Requirements Order Report, this lists all requirements in trial date order by hardware type; it is the basic unsmoothed demand.

```
AJT 0110                SUPPLIES MANAGEMENT SYSTEM   DATE 18/06/90 PAGE 21

                        SUPPLY SCHEDULE (SUMMARY)

TRIAL REQUIREMENT: 67SR   DESCRIPTION: Motor, Prototype R

         SCHED DATE  JAN FEB MAR APL MAY JUN JUL AUG SEP OCT NOV DEC   YEAR

             0890     0   2   3   6   8   0   0  15  15  20  25  20   1990

                     20   0   0   0   0   0   0   0   0   0   0   0   1991

-------------------------------------------------------------------------
TRIAL/ITEM   SUPPLY TRIAL No. ---HARDWARE--- QTY CUM NETT  -SUPPLIER- MON ALL
REQUIREMENT  DATE                                    TOTAL            QTY QTY
   67SR                  2705A                                 MAC. Ltd      1
   67SR                  2706A                                 MAC. Ltd      4
   67SR/1                5003                                  MAC. Ltd      8
   67SR                  2079                                  MAC. Ltd      6

   67SR      01/08/90    2705A               1   1   1        MAC. Ltd
   67SR/1    01/08/90    2032                3   3   3        MAC. Ltd
   67SR/2    01/08/90    3137                2   2   2        MAC. Ltd
   67SR      01/08/90    3140                2   2   2        MAC. Ltd
   67SR      01/08/90    2569A               7   7  30        MAC. Ltd   15

   67SR      01/09/90    2569A              15  22  30        MAC. Ltd   15

   67SR      01/10/90    2569A               8  30  30        MAC. Ltd
   67SR      01/10/90    2705A              12  12  14        MAC. Ltd   20

   67SR      01/11/90    2705A               2   2  14        MAC. Ltd
```

Figure 7.11 Prime item supply schedule (note items in top part of schedule already supplied and allocated to trials).

```
AJT 0111                SUPPLIES MANAGEMENT SYSTEM    DATE 18/06/90 PAGE 165

              DERIVED COMPONENT SUPPLIES SCHEDULE (SUMMARY)

COMPONENT CODE: BR04         DESCRIPTION: Control Valve for Motor type R
-------------------------------------------------------------------------
COMPONENT  SUPPLY  QTY   --PRIME ITEM-- TRIAL NO NEXT ASSEMBLY -SUPPLIER- QTY
           DATE    REQD                          AREA                     ALLOC
BRO4/15   02/06/90  3    67S/AC/S        2604    Imex Ltd     MB & A
BRO4/16   02/06/90  5    67S/AR          2604    Imex Ltd     MB & A
BRO4      09/06/90  1    67SR            2705A   MAC Ltd      MB & A
BRO4      09/06/90  3    67SR            2032    MAC Ltd      MB & A
BRO4      09/06/90  2    67SR            3137    MAC Ltd      MB & A
BRO4      09/06/90  2    67SR            3140    MAC Ltd      MB & A
BRO4      09/06/90  7    67SR            2569A   MAC Ltd      MB & A

BRO4      11/07/90 15    67SR            2569A   MAC Ltd      MB & A

BRO4/2    21/07/90 25    DIRECT TO TRIAL 2460                 MB & A

BRO4/2    04/08/90  2    DIRECT TO TRIAL 2402                 MB & A
```

Figure 7.12 Derived component schedule (note relationship of components to prime items in Figure 7.11).

```
AJT 0115                 SUPPLIES MANAGEMENT SYSTEM   DATE 18/06/90 PAGE 255
                              TRIAL STATUS REPORT

TRIAL No: 3140  DESCRIPTION: Low Temperature Running CONTROLLER: S. Marshall

TRIAL DATE: 06/10/90 (4190) VENUE: MAC Ltd        VENUE LEAD TIME: 0 WKS

REQ = REQUIRED                    ASSEMBLY AREA: MAC. Ltd   AREA LEAD TIME: 4 WKS
ALL = ALLOCATED
PRE = FROM PREVIOUS TRIAL  REMARKS: Test to be completed by 30th September
NNQR = NET NEW QUANTITY
------------------------------------------------------------------------

--TRIAL/ITEM--  ----QUANTITIES----  --------DATES-------- -SUPPLIER- PREVIOUS
REQUIREMENTS    REQ  ALL  PRE  NNQR REQUIRED   MAN SCHED             TRIAL
67SR             2    0    0    2   08/09/90   01/08/90  MAC. Ltd
Motor, Type R

34SR            10   10    0   10   08/09/90   07/07/90  BenCo
Relay Unit
67SEN/R          4    0    0    4   08/09/90   14/07/90  MAC. Ltd
Temp. Sensor
67ICE/R/1        4    0    2    2   08/09/90   29/09/90  MAC. Ltd   3905
Ice Detector
```

Figure 7.13 Trial status report.

```
AJT 0121              SUPPLIES MANAGEMENT SYSTEM   DATE 18/06/90    PAGE 3
                          STOCK AND DELIVERY REPORT

PROJECT: Project 67 Power Supply        REMARKS:
------------------------------------------------------------------------

PART No. ----DESCRIPTION----  -SUPPLIER- TOTAL TOTAL DIFF NOTIONAL WEEKS BALANCE
                                         REQ'D DEL'D       STOCK   AWAY  OF DEL
67PY     Orifice             Remex Ltd   25    19   -6     9      -2     42
67RT/4   Harness Loom        Remex Ltd   42    46    4    28      +1    168
67ST/4   Metering Unit       Remex Ltd   17     6  -11     2      -4     65
67PR     Instrumented Valve  Remex Ltd    4     4    0     2       0     34
------------------------------------------------------------------------
34ST/1   Gasket Set          S & L Co   135   200   65   157     +12      0
67ST/2   Seal                S & L Co   157   200   43   104      +8      0
```

Figure 7.14 Stock and delivery report (note potential problem with the supply of the metering unit).

```
AJT 0119                 SUPPLIES MANAGEMENT SYSTEM   DATE 18/06/90 PAGE 2
                              TRIALS AT RISK REPORT

PROJECT: Project 67 Power Supply                REMARKS:
------------------------------------------------------------------------
TRIAL No: 2851 Fuel Consumption PLANNED DATE 04/02/91 EARLIEST DATE 02/03/91
----ITEM---- ---DESCRIPTION---  REQ QTY REQUIRED SCHEDULED SLIP WKS  SUPPLIER
67ST/4       Metering Unit         1    06/01/91 02/02/91     4    Remex Ltd
67PR         Instrumented Valve    2    06/01/91 20/01/91     2    BenCo
------------------------------------------------------------------------
TRIAL No: 3140 Low Temp Running PLANNED DATE 06/10/90 EARLIEST DATE 28/10/90
----ITEM---- ---DESCRIPTION---  REQ QTY REQUIRED SCHEDULED SLIP WKS  SUPPLIER
67ICE/R/1    Ice Detector          2    08/09/90 29/09/90     3     MAC. Ltd
------------------------------------------------------------------------
```

Figure 7.15 Trials at risk report (note potential delay for part 67ICE/R/1 and its effect on the data of trial 3140).

Status reports
Four are produced:

(a) Trial Status Report, this shows the position of all hardware requirements for each trial with the scheduled dates for supply and the quantities actually delivered. An example of this report is shown in Figure 7.13.
(b) Stock and Delivery Report, this shows the cumulative delivery of all parts and compares this with the requirement at the date on which the report is compiled. One report is produced for each supplier or manufacturing shop listing all the parts that have been supplied. In this form it is similar to a line-of-balance report, an example is shown in Figure 7.14.
(c) Potential Stock and Shortfall Report, this is a comparison between the unsmoothed demand for prime hardware and the available capacity. It indicates where potential shortfalls will occur or stocks are likely to build up.
(d) Trials at Risk Report, this shows all the trials where their dates cannot be met due to the scheduled hardware dates from the available capacity falling after the programme date for the trial. It also lists all the hardware causing the delay with the projected slip on the trial date given in weeks. An example of this report is given the Figure 7.15.

The reports form a complete statement of the material supply position, both in terms of projected output and the current situation. Collectively they satisfy all the requirements for the control loop shown in Figure 7.4. The Schedules of Requirements are distributed to each supplying shop or subcontractor. The Stock and Delivery reports and the Trial Status reports give the current project position and are essential documents for the Project Manager's regular progress meetings. The Trials at Risk report indicates potential programme problems and is passed to the Trials Manager and the project planning group.

A particular difficulty that sometimes occurs with development work is the large numbers of variants which may be required by the trials programme, each variant being specially configured to test some particular aspect of the design. All these variants can draw on the same manufacturing capacity, and it is also a common feature that at the time the planning and scheduling is done, the variant part numbers are not known as the parts have not yet been drawn. To overcome these problems an item coding system was employed rather than attempting to use the part numbers. The coding system was:

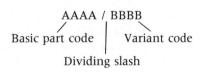

The dividing slash (/) character has special significance as it marks the point at which the variant departs from the basic part. All basic parts are assumed to draw on the same manufacturing capacity irrespective of the particular variant. Both prime items and components use the same part coding system; but it is of greater significance for prime items as each variant of a prime item has its own build sequence calling up its own unique combination of components. The system reads the code as far as the slash character and schedules together all requirements with the same basic part codes, fixing priorities from the pro-grammed trial dates. The actual part numbers, when they are issued, can be held in a descriptive field along with the part description, but they take no part in the logic of the system's operation.

The component schedules are derived by examining the scheduled dates for each prime item but taking note of the variant code and back-scheduling through the lead-times in the build sequence for each component called up. Should there be a restriction on component output, then the derived com-ponent schedules can be further scheduled within the available capacity, again taking note of the basic part of the code number.

In operation, the system described was extremely effective. By generating the supplies requirements by an automatic process, most of the drudgery of creating the manufacturing plan was removed. Furthermore, all manufacturing activities were removed from the overall project network, thus reducing its size and making it much more manageable. It allowed the integration of costs and plans received from supplying contractors to proceed much more rapidly than previously as they were all logically tied together and conformed to their stated supply capacities. Finally, the improvement in overall project control, the speed with which manufacturing plans could be created and the reduction in the size of the overall network led to a reduction in project staff levels with a beneficial effect on total cost.

The strength of the computerized approach lies in its logic and the discipline it imposes upon the whole project. Providing honesty and realism are used when establishing the lead-times and capacities, the resulting reports and schedules will show a feasible material supply programme as it is constructed entirely through logic. Of course it will not resolve fundamental problems if they exist but they will, at least, be clearly highlighted. Additional benefits come from the fact that the project network does not have to include a mass of supplies detail. If it is known in advance that some trials cannot take place as planned because hardware is not going to be available until later, sensible re-planning can take place.

Leading the materials management group

A specialist team may need to be set up to manage the supplies and materials programme; because of the pivotal nature of such a group, a specialist may need to be appointed to lead it. If he is required to devise, implement and control the supplies management system, including the use of computerized techniques, he should at least be a person with some higher training and experience in the methods of production control. A mature outlook is needed; as he will have to interface with so many parts of the project organization – internally and with external suppliers – he can also expect to become involved in the 'politics' of the situation. This stems largely from the personalities involved, including that of the Project Manager, and he may come under pressure to accommodate illogical views or unrealistic pro-grammes. It is therefore important that the individual has sufficient strength of character and discipline of thought that he can always present a realistic and achiev-able viewpoint. If the project suffers timescale slippages or regular programme revisions, he will also need a degree of skill in manipulating the data to reflect the project's intentions, and he must exhibit sufficient authority and control to ensure that data on progress is gathered regularly and in an accurate and timely fashion.

A computerized system can help him in this respect as it takes much of the routine effort out of materials-control work, leaving the more junior members of the team free to concentrate on those aspects of the job where human qualities count. Increased job satisfaction should result from knowing that if each team member keeps his area of responsibility under tight control and puts into the system the most up-to-date information, a very accurate picture of the present will result and valuable insight should be gained into what the future may hold.

Summary

Satisfactory management of the supply of parts and materials is essential to the timely completion of the project. For simple projects, planning the acquisition of parts may be a staightforward process, but with complex projects involving many suppliers and a wide variety of parts, special techniques are necessary. Hardware demands derived simply from the requirements of the trials programme are not enough, the suppliers' lead-time and capacity limitations have to be considered when devising a manufacturing programme that is both realistic and achievable. Failure to recognize this point is to ensure trouble from the start.

For efficient control of the material supply situation, a special group may have to be set up that will devise the manufacturing plan, liaise with subcontractors and monitor their activities. Their role is more akin to that of a production control unit and the techniques that they will need to use owe more to that discipline than those normally associated with project management. In the past, mistakes have been made by trying to implement network analysis methods for solving complex supply problems. The materials requirements planning approach is more suitable and Project Managers with projects that have large manufacturing elements should look to this area when defining systems for managing the flow of materials and parts.

8

Progress, performance and control

- Project control cycle
- Slip diagrams
- Cost−performance measurement
- Work breakdown structures
- Performance measurement in practice
- Progress reporting, meetings and reviews

The project control cycle

If we start with the idea that a project is any set of tasks that we define as leading from 'state A' to 'state B', then implicit in the concept of 'state B' is that it is discrete and definable. Tasks or groups of tasks that do not have discrete and definable end-conditions cannot be called a 'project' in our terms. For example, installing a new production line in a factory can be deemed a project as the end-objective is the line installed and operational. Operating the line is not a project, in our sense, as it will continue until such time as the need for the product ceases, which may not be known at the outset. If we assume that a clearly defined end-objective exists, then all the planning and control activities in the project will be directed to achieving that goal. The objective may be simply stated (e.g. to create a saleable product), but the programme that is devised to meet that objective may be complex in terms of what is required and constrained in terms of how it can be achieved.

The principal constraints are resources, time and money, and it is the job of the Project Manager to control the project such that the objective is achieved within the imposed constraints. Even if the resource limitations prove difficult to evade, it frequently happens that the objectives cannot be met within the time and cost limitations. If the Project Manager is not aware of a pending situation in which the limitations are likely to be breached, then the project can be said to be out of control as it implies that the impact of events as they occur is not recognized and understood, thus no controlling or corrective action can be taken.

A view frequently held by senior management is that projects that exceed their budgets must have been out of control. But senior staff may only see a project in financial terms and be ignorant of its workings. In some cases, this view may be correct, but on other occasions it can be quite mistaken. A project can exceed both its budget and planned duration and yet be under perfect control throughout. The important point is that for proper control, events are interpreted correctly as they occur, appropriate responses to deviations are implemented and when changes are necessary they are introduced in a rational, conscious way. None of this implies – in any way – that the initial view of the project as contained in the original plan and budget will hold good until the end. Innovative projects, by their nature, contain an element of something that has not been done before; in that situation, no one can have complete knowledge of what the future may bring. A plan only says what should happen, not what will happen; and a budget only says what costs are expected, not what the costs will be. One thing is certain, changes and deviations will arise. In this situation, it is vital that the Project Manager sets up channels of communication and methods of reporting that allow him to see all that is relevant in terms of what is happening and also implement methods that will aid interpretation and allow changes to take place in a controlled fashion.

Figure 8.1 shows the principal elements of a system to control any project. It starts with a well-defined objective, that is something that can be clearly stated and communicated to all the members of the project team and against which progress can be measured and changes be assessed. The objective must be translated into a plan (i.e. a statement of all the tasks necessary to meet the objective) and it needs to be agreed with all the parties that are going to participate in the project. Before it can be put into operation, it needs to be authorized, that is it must be endorsed by those in authority. This may be the senior management or the customer's representative, for it is they who will be responsible for providing the money and, in the case of the company's own senior management, the resources as well. Once authorized, the first formal issue of the plan and budget is normally termed the **project Baseline**; it is also sometimes called a **development cost plan** (DCP). From this baseline all future progress will be measured until such time as a new position for the project is formalized and agreed, in which case this becomes the new baseline.

From the moment the plan is put into operation, variations will begin to occur. They can come about in two ways: 'changes' (i.e. alterations to the circumstances in which the project is carried out) and 'deviations' (i.e differences between what was planned and what actually occurred). Changes are essentially external to the project domain, while deviations are internal. Greater opportunity exists for control of internal deviations; external changes, in general, cannot be controlled, all that can be done is to react to them in a way that aims to maintain the objective.

Changes in the circumstances of the project may stem from actions internal to the company or from outside. Internally induced changes may arise through a new view of the project being taken by senior staff that are responsible for it but take no part in its running. It can result in alterations to (a) the priority attached to the project, (b) the scope of work to be undertaken or (c) the funding and resources made available. If the project is being performed on behalf of a customer organization, then similar changes may also be introduced if a different view is taken. Where there is no

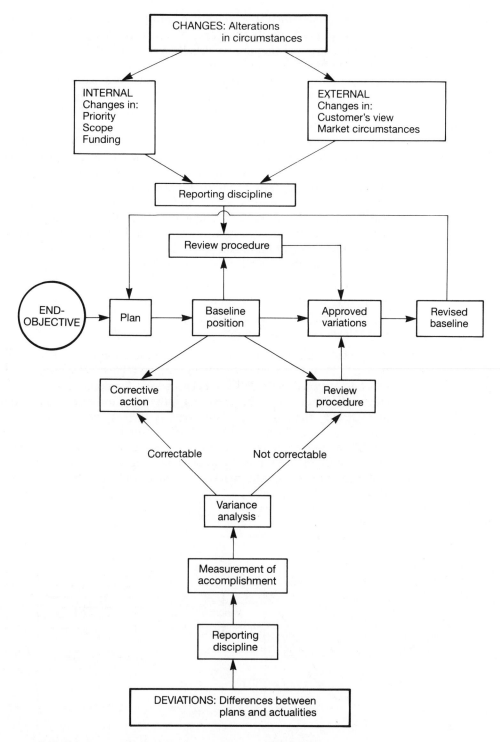

Figure 8.1   Principal elements of the project control cycle.

specific customer for the development project, changes in the market in terms of timescale, product specification or cost may force changes upon the project.

Whereas external changes are usually well signalled and result from relatively few causes, internal deviations can come about in many ways. Poor communication of plans, loosely defined objectives, poorly conceived plans, loose controls on staff, unauthorized work, conflicts of priority, uncommitted team members and unforeseen technical problems are all sources of deviations. With the exception of unforeseen technical problems, all the other factors come within the Project Manager's scope of control. However, some of these factors will not be recognized as significant at the start, for example, no Project Manager would accept poorly conceived plans if he had the alternative of well-conceived ones; the deficiencies only come to light as the project proceeds. The conceptual weaknesses within the plan may derive from a number of other factors such as: the newness of the task leading to a lack of realization of what is required; undue optimism that stems from enthusiasm among staff; and pressure to keep costs down that leads to important but peripheral activities being ignored until it is realized that they are necessary.

When deviations occur, it is important that:

- they should be detected as early as possible;
- the reasons for them should be ascertained;
- their impact should be assessed;
- whatever corrective action is necessary is instigated.

The project control system must provide timely information on both progress and costs in a form that is meaningful and can be related directly to the project baseline position. Various methods have been devised for doing this, the most popular are graphical as they display progress in a way that allows the position to be appreciated more readily than with tabulated reports. Typical presentations are 'S-curves' of planned and actual expenditure and marked-up bar charts, shown in Figure 8.2.

Whereas both these methods give some information on the progress of the project, they do not provide some key information and in the case of the S-curve it can be positively misleading. The marked up bar chart is useful for focusing attention on

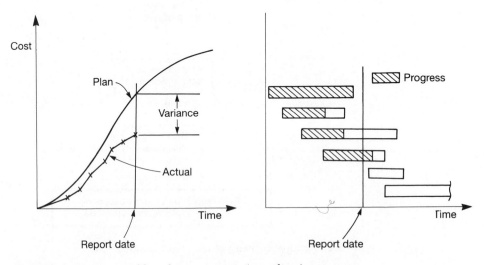

Figure 8.2 'S-curve' and bar chart representations of project progress.

activities where the expected progress is not being made; but neither method gives any clear view as to where the project is likely to end, either in cost or time terms. However, methods have been devised to address both points.

The slip diagram

Predicting where the project will end is a game that all can indulge in and there will be as many predictions as there are staff engaged on the project. For many this will be a whimsical exercise that is part of the everyday banter, but for the Project Manager and his backers this can be a very serious issue and something that requires attention. One predictive method that can be surprisingly effective but at the same time very simple is the **slip diagram**, an empirical method based on a quirk of human nature. We all tend to be optimists when it comes to predicting the future as it would not be rewarding either in our personal or professional lives to take a pessimistic view.

That optimism may stem from a mixture of subconscious wishful thinking and a genuine misperception of the way things are proceeding. If a project were to proceed at a rate where all activities happen exactly as planned, then at any point one could reasonably predict that the project would be completed on time. Other projects, however, show deviations from plan; in particular, they exhibit lateness. Once lateness begins to occur, the project is subject to slippage and thereafter the end-date is in doubt. The curious thing is that once a project begins to slip behind schedule, and this becomes recognized, our perception of the amount by which the end-date will move with respect to the current position tends to remain constant as the project proceeds. An example will illustrate this point.

Example 8.1: Completion of a set of drawings

A drawing office supervisor was asked to give an estimate of the time to produce a set of drawings; the answer given was 'ten weeks' and this was entered into the project plan. The work started and after five weeks he was asked to estimate how long it would take to finish the task; the answer given was, 'it should be complete in seven weeks' (i.e. a total duration of 12 weeks). At the eighth week another forecast was made by the supervisor and then it was 'five weeks to go' (i.e. week 13). At week 11 the forecast was 'three weeks' (i.e. week 14) and at week 14: 'it'll be finished next week, just some final checking to do.' We can probably believe this final statement and we can be reasonably sure it will finish between weeks 15 and 16. This task over-ran its original duration by 50% but nowhere was this degree of over-run indicated in any of the increases – all were small increases over the previous forecast and the amount of increase as a percentage of the task outstanding tended to remain fairly constant. This point can be seen if a slip diagram is drawn (Figure 8.3).

Care needs to be taken in constructing a slip diagram. Conventionally they are drawn with the vertical axis reversed; when this is done an equal number

---

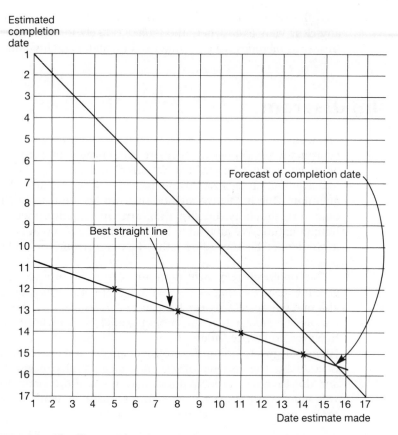

Figure 8.3 Slip diagram for the completion of a set of drawings based on the supervisor's estimates.

of divisions must appear on each axis and there is no time = zero/zero origin. The vertical axis shows the estimated completion date, and the horizontal axis shows the date at which the estimate was made. A line at 45° joins the extremities of both axes and links all points that are the same in time, this is the completion line. A point is plotted each time a new forecast is made and the best straight line is drawn through the points; when this is extended to cut the completion line, a forecast is obtained of the likely completion date. (If required, slip diagrams can be drawn with conventional axes in which case there will be a time = zero/zero origin. The completion line will then be a line linking common points in time and will be at 45° through the origin. Use of the diagram is the same in both cases.)

It might seem surprising that such a simple technique could be of worth in a complex project environment, yet slip diagrams have shown themselves to be re-markably accurate predictors. It does seem that trends, once established, tend to remain constant throughout a project; it is very difficult to move a project off its path once it has been set on it. Some researchers into project progress have noted that trends can be detected at a point as early as 15% of the way through the project duration that remain more or less the same until its end.

While there is no restriction on the tasks that can be monitored using slip diagrams, the picture can become confusing if too many low-level activities are monitored by this method. They are best employed for monitoring progress on very significant events that encompass the whole project activity such as the first flight date of a new aircraft or the date of commissioning of a new plant.

The example in Figure 8.3 shows a clear trend that has consistently indicated a completion date. Occasionally, however, a trend may emerge that places the completion date well beyond any acceptable date, or worse still, does not indicate any foreseeable conclusion. Should this trend become apparent, then the whole project is questionable, termination may be the only reasonable option left open – and the sooner this is recognized, the less that will be wasted in pursuing an unattainable goal. The project detailed in the case example shown in Figure 8.4 is one such instance.

The slip diagram can be a powerful tool for assessing the progress of the whole project and predicting the final position which might even include the prospect of termination; however, care must be taken with the result. The whole basis of the technique is that the error in perception of the remaining work remains constant, and part of that perception is the required end-date. If that date is changed on the basis of a prediction which is based on a slip diagram, it could do more than become a self-fulfilling prophecy, it could do worse. In the case of the drawing office supervisor, all his estimates of the completion date were made against a background of a requirement to complete the work by week 10. If by week 8 an estimate of completion at week 15 had been made and the supervisor informed, it may have altered his perception both of the amount of work and when it was required, which may have caused him to alter the priority given to the work and leading to a further slippage.

Case example 8.1: Slip diagram for the BAe/GEC Nimrod AEW 3 project

Throughout the period of almost ten years when it was under-way the Nimrod AEW 3 early-warning aircraft development programme attracted considerable public debate; it was one of the most expensive and ambitious airborne projects undertaken in the UK. Having started as a programme that employed British technology and used 11 'spare' Nimrod airframes, it finally ended as a failure after more than £900 million had been spent. It is beyond this text to look at the ills of that project but the changes that were announced to the date when the aircraft was expected to enter service are instructive. Figure 8.4 shows a slip diagram for the expected in-service date based on both official statements and press reports made during the life of the project.

The programme went through many changes, some of which were induced by the customer who asked for a radar system that was originally designed to

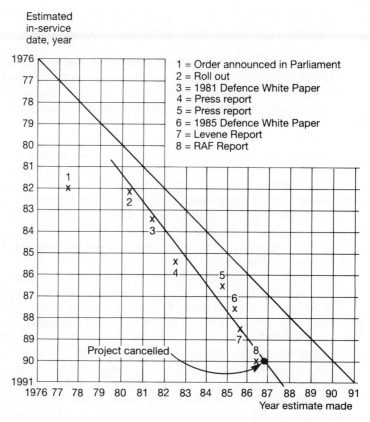

Figure 8.4 Slip diagram for the in-service date of the Nimrod AEW 3 Aircraft.

work over water to be made to work over land as well; this, in turn, led to major changes to the computer system. From the time that the project entered the testing phase slippage was apparent, and by 1982 a clear trend was emerging that indicated no end was in sight. The project continued for another four years, each new assessment of progress putting the in-service date further away. With a trend line such as that shown, it is clear that the prospect of a technical success within an acceptable timeframe was looking increasingly unlikely. Cancellation was the outcome and the trend line had indicated this likelihood several years before it came about.

Slip diagrams work well for assessing the total project position but where more detailed assessments are required, both of individual elements of work and of the project's costs, more sophisticated techniques have been developed.

The origins of formalized cost and schedule control

The technique of **cost and schedule performance measurement** – also known as **earned value costing** or **C-spec application** has been in existence for almost a quarter of a century, yet little use seems to be made of it in British industry and many Project Managers are still ignorant of the method and its true worth. That situation is about to change due to two independent factors: first, competitive and economic pressure will force more companies to look closely at the value they are obtaining from every element of the workforce, including the project staff and the work they are doing; and secondly, the arrival of software that will ease its introduction and application. At the heart of the technique lies a simple principle known to all managers, that of accountability for achievement. Historically many managers and section heads have hidden behind the inefficiencies of the cost reporting systems in their own companies to the detriment of the overall profitability of their firms. This may be a very human reaction, particularly where innovative projects are concerned, but the long-term effects can only weaken their position.

The origins of cost–performance measurement lay in the realization at the time that the PERT system was invented that if cost rates can be added to the hours and durations that are attached to project activities, a powerful system will exist for predicting and, ultimately, controlling the costs of projects. The US Department of Defense (DoD), as the largest instigator of projects involving the highest technical risks, saw the immediate application of the idea and sought to impose the system on its major contractors under the title PERT/Cost. The application was, however, very heavy-handed as it specified the total costing system that was to be used throughout the project. The result was a complete rejection by an industry that had already made large investments in its accounting systems and was not about to change to a new and untried method.

However, the problems of cost control and cost prediction came to a head with a number of aircraft development projects that ran into massive cost over-runs that seemed not to have been foreseen. Determined that this would not happen again, and taking note of the failure of PERT/Cost, the DoD issued in 1967 a new Directive that specified only the reporting criteria that contractors would have to comply with, and leaving the choice of system open to each individually. Central to the system would be the objective of complete visibility of cost and achievement throughout the life of the project.

Such an apparently powerful technique must have an obvious appeal, yet it has not found great acceptance outside of defence circles. A number of reasons can be identified for this situation:

- As set out, the technique is a set of reporting criteria and a project methodology. Unlike PERT, it is not a product that can be easily marketed in its own right; the marketing drive of the major software vendors has not, until recently, been behind it.
- The technique involves the integration of both the planning and the costing of the project; traditionally these have been the domains of separate departments within the project structure. Without a suitable method of integrating both the costs and the plan, it is difficult to use and expensive in terms of clerical effort.
- As it places emphasis on the measurement of achievement, resistance to the method may have been encountered from those who may feel most exposed by it.
- There seems to be a general lack of awareness of the method outside of defence industry circles.

With the recent arrival of software specifically designed to integrate both the planning and costing, and provide cost–performance reports, one of the major obstacles has been removed and an upsurge of interest is to be expected.

Terms and methodology

At the outset, a fundamental point was recognized, that simply measuring cost differences, or variances, between expenditure and plan would not be sufficient to define the true position of a project. Cost variances come about because activities are done either earlier or later than planned or because they cost either more or less than was originally estimated. If an accurate picture of progress is to emerge, any variance would have to be subdivided into that element which is due to things being done at a different time and that which is due to things being done for a different cost. Furthermore, once this fundamental split has been made, it is not difficult to gauge the real value of what has been achieved and from there make a projection of the likely outcome of the project in terms of both time and cost.

The cost–performance measurement terminology that has come to be accepted is based on the US DoD **Cost/Schedule Control Systems Criteria**. It defines the difference between the cost of a task, as set out in the budget, and the actual cost incurred, by subdividing the difference into that part due to variations in price for the work done (i.e. the '**cost variance**'), and that part due to work being done at a different time from that scheduled (i.e. the '**schedule variance**'). Three distinct measurements of cost have to be made at each reporting point and are given the following titles:

1. **BCWS** – Basic or Budgeted Cost of Work Scheduled. This is the sum of all the costs in the project, or any given part of the project, up to the reporting date.
2. **BCWP** – Basic or Budgeted Cost of Work Performed. This is the cost of all the progress achieved in the project, or part of the project, up to the reporting date and expressed in terms of the costs originally set out in the initial estimate; it is also termed the '**earned value**' as it represents what has been earned, not simply what has been spent.
3. **ACWP** – Actual Cost of Work Performed. This is the total of all expenditure on the project, or part of the project, up to the reporting date.

The relationship between the BCWS, BCWP, ACWP, cost variance and schedule variance is illustrated in Figure 8.5, which shows a project at the mid-point of its life and in which there has been a significant deviation between the budget and the costs incurred. It will be seen that the actual cost is below the budgeted spend, while the earned value, the BCWP, is below the actual spend. In this case, it can be assumed that the project is likely to finish late because of the adverse schedule variance and be overspent because of the adverse cost variance.

Two useful index numbers can be calculated that give an instant measure of performance: the Cost Performance Index (CPI), and the Schedule Performance Index (SPI). They are defined as:

$$CPI = \frac{BCWP}{ACWP}$$

and:

$$SPI = \frac{BCWP}{BCWS}$$

Index values greater than 1 indicate performance either in cost or schedule terms that is better than planned, values lower than 1 indicate a worse position. The CPI is,

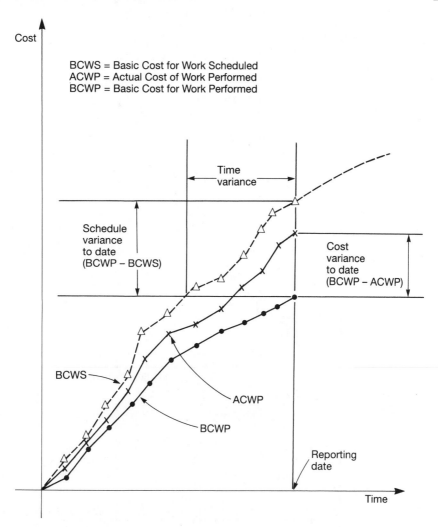

Figure 8.5   BCWS, BCWP and ACWP relationships.

perhaps, the more useful of the two: it shows the real worth that is being created by the project, thus a CPI value of 0.85 indicates that for every pound spent, only 85p worth of value is being created on the basis of the original budget. The behaviour of these two indices can be plotted as the project proceeds and they give a good indication of the real progress and what the future may hold. Figure 8.6 shows a typical situation in terms of the ACWP, BCWP and BCWS, the indices have been derived and are plotted. Using the indices gives a clearer view of the position than reading the relative ACWP, BCWP and BCWS values. Figure 8.7 shows the behaviour of the CPI and SPI under various conditions.

The two index numbers can also be used to generate an estimate of the position of the project at completion, in terms of cost and schedule, based on the situation when the indices were calculated and assuming the indicated trends continue. For the cost at completion, the formula is made up of two parts: the cost already expended plus the estimate of future cost:

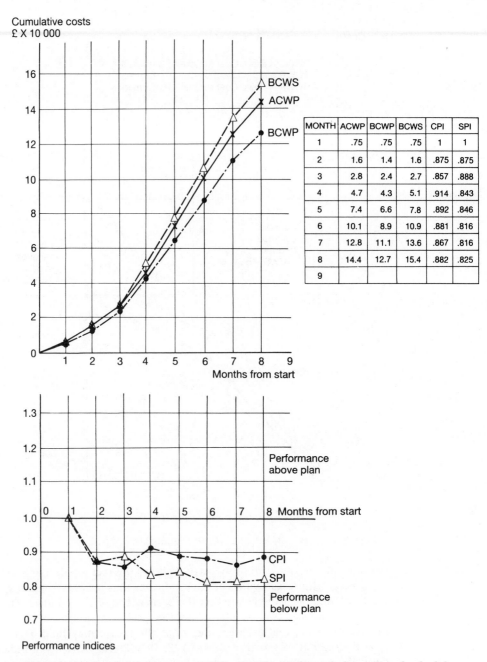

Figure 8.6 Relationship between BCWS, BCWP, ACWP and the cost and schedule performance indices.

$$EAC = ACWP + \frac{BAC - BCWP}{CPI}$$

where: *EAC* is the Estimate at Completion
         BAC is the Basic or Budgeted Cost at Completion.

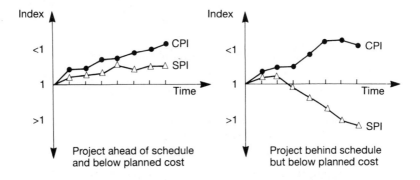

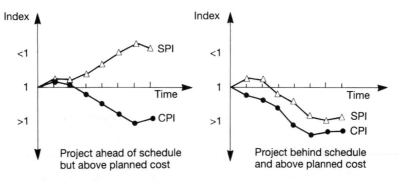

Figure 8.7 Alternative positions indicated by the movement of the CPI and API.

This expression can be reduced:

To simplify the working, let

$$ACWP = A$$
$$BAC = B$$
$$BCWP = P$$
$$CPI = C.$$

now:

$$EAC = A + \frac{B - P}{C} \tag{8.1}$$

but

$$C = \frac{P}{A} \tag{8.2}$$

Looking back at expression (8.1):

$$EAC = A + \frac{B - P}{C} = A + \frac{A(B - P)}{P}$$

Bringing to a common denominator:

$$\frac{PA}{P} + \frac{BA - PA}{P} = \frac{PA + BA - PA}{P} = \frac{BA}{P}$$

and from expression (8.2):

$$EAC = \frac{B}{C} = \frac{BAC}{CPI} \tag{8.3}$$

For the Estimated Time to Completion the formula is:

$$ETC = ATE + \frac{OD - (ATE \times SPI)}{SPI} \tag{8.4}$$

where: *BAC* is the Basic or Budgeted Cost at Completion;
ATE is the Actual Time Expended;
OD is the Original Duration.

Again, the expression is made up of two parts, ATE being the actual time elapsed and the additional part being an estimate of future time based on the current SPI.

Let
$$ATE = T$$
$$OD = D$$
$$SPI = S$$
$$BCWS = W$$

now:
$$ETC = T + \frac{D - (T \times S)}{S} \tag{8.5}$$

Looking back at expression (8.5) and bringing to a common denominator:

$$ETC = \frac{TS}{S} + \frac{(D - (T \times S))}{S} \tag{8.6}$$

$$ETC = \frac{TS + D - TS}{S} = \frac{D}{S} = \frac{OD}{SPI} \tag{8.7}$$

The relationship between these terms is shown in the following situation.

Example 8.2: Estimate of the outcome of a project at the mid-point of its life

A project set to last seven months contains the major tasks with costs and timings as shown in Table 8.1. Assuming an even spend rate, in each task, the expenditure plan is as shown in Table 8.2.

At the end of month 3 the position of the project in terms of assessed progress and actual expenditure is given in Table 8.3. Note that in this case the Actual Cost of Work Performed is above the Budgeted Cost for Work Scheduled. A simple variance between the two figures might indicate that if spend, alone, is the measure of progress, the project is progressing well; this, however, is far from the case.

To calculate the BCWP, each of the percentage completion figures must be multiplied by the original budgets; this is set out in Table 8.4:

The $CPI = \dfrac{BCWP}{ACWP} = \dfrac{£17\,750}{£24\,300} = 0.730$

Table 8.1 Task durations and timings

Months task no.	1	2	3	4	5	6	7	Cost (£)
1								10 000
2								12 000
3								2 500
4								6 000
5								6 000
6								9 000
7								2 000
8								3 000

Table 8.2 Expenditure plan

Task	1	2	3	4	5	6	7
1	5000	5 000					
2	1500	3 000	3 000	3 000	1 500		
3			1 000	1 000	500		
4			4 000	2 000			
5			1 000	2 000	2 000	1 000	
6				3 000	6 000		
7					500	1 000	500
8						1 500	1 500
Total £	6500	8 000	9 000	11 000	10 500	3 500	2 000
Cum. £	6500	14 500	23 500	34 500	45 000	48 500	50 500

Table 8.3 Position at the end of month 3

Task no.	ACWP (£)	Percentage complete
1	9 500	100
2	9 800	45
3	1 200	10
4	1 700	15
5	2 100	20
Total ACWP	24 300	49

Table 8.4 BCWP calculation at month 3

Task no.	Percentage complete	Budget (£)	BCWP (£)
1	100	10 000	10 000
2	45	12 000	5 400
3	10	2 500	250
4	15	6 000	900
5	20	6 000	1 200
Total BCWP	49	36 500	17 750

The $SPI = \dfrac{BCWP}{BCWS} = \dfrac{£17\,750}{£23\,500} = 0.755$

The $EAC = ACWP + \dfrac{BAC - BCWP}{CPI} = £24\,300 + \dfrac{£50\,500 - £17\,750}{0.730} = \underline{£69\,163}$

The $ETC = ATE + \dfrac{OD - (ATE \times SPI)}{SPI} = 3 + \dfrac{7 - (3 \times 0.755)}{0.755}$

$\qquad = \underline{9.272 \text{ months from start}}$

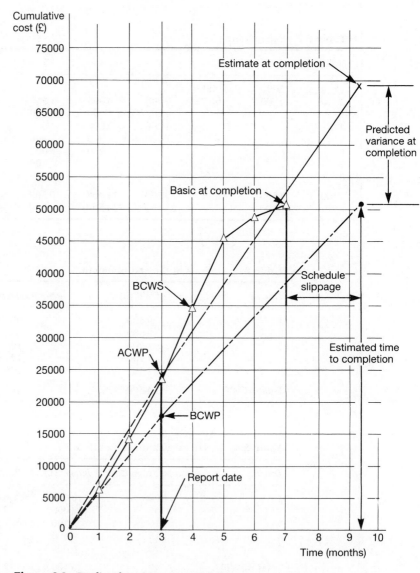

Figure 8.8 Predicted position at completion.

> Figure 8.8 shows the position graphically, and it illustrates both the potential overspend and slippage that will occur on the basis of the trends to date. The calculation only indicates the end-condition, the path that the actual cost curve will take is not indicated.

Difficulties with the predictive formulae

Despite the straightforward nature of the predictive formulae, they can lead to difficulties under some circumstances. In some cases, the simplified formulae (8.3) and (8.7) are quoted without reference to the original, more fundamental, expressions from which they derive. Whereas the algebra may indicate that this is acceptable, it has a hidden pitfall that particularly affects the calculation of the ETC. Expression (8.7) states that dividing the OD by the SPI is a correct way to calculate the estimated time to completion, the algebra seems to indicate it but that conclusion would be misleading. This may not appear obvious, given the working shown above, but the explanation lies partly in both a quirk of algebra and in the nature of what is being done. In essence, cost and time cannot be treated in the same way; when no work is done, costs stand still but that is not true of time, that goes on whatever the work situation may be. Furthermore, the cost that a project incurs is the sum of all the costs in the project, that is not true of time because the time that a project takes is governed by the time taken by just a few activities – i.e. the critical ones. Because of the additive nature of the costs and the fact that the CPI is calculated from the cumulative costs, the EAC expression holds good in its reduced form.

If we look at the SPI, calculated from BCWP/BCWS, we find that it has some rather unusual properties because it is using cost as the analogue of time, which is not strictly true; it works well until the original planned duration is exceeded after which it changes its character. The schedule aspect of Cost/Schedule Control Systems Criteria always has been a problem and there was a debate in the early days as to whether or not the term 'schedule' should even be included in the title.

The problem is best illustrated with a worked example of a project with two major activities, with costs and times as shown in Table 8.5.

Although the EAC shows a steadily increasing prediction in line with the actual costs, there is clearly a problem with calculating the ETC using the simplified formula as the predicted duration starts to diminish after the planned duration (three periods) has been exceeded. Furthermore, there is an apparent improvement in the SPI from 0.75 at period 3 to 0.875 at period 4, even though there is no actual improvement in the rate of schedule progress on activity B, which is the only activity current between 3 and 4. The same applies between periods 4 and 5. This anomaly stems directly from using cost relationships to determine progress through time; in fact, once the planned duration of any activity or project has been exceeded, the SPI becomes a measure of percentage completion, not schedule progress.

That does not fully explain the reason for the diminishing value for the ETC, and to find it one has to look back at the original expression (8.4). The problem stems from the fact that the algebra says nothing about the relative values of the terms in the expression. Once the duration (D) is exceeded, the whole expression $(D - (T \times S))/S$ in expression (8.5) will eventually become a negative value; this is obviously a nonsense as it has the effect of subtracting a sum from the elapsed time and time never goes backwards!

Table 8.5 Example of the possible error in calculating the estimated time to completion (ETC)

	1	2	Period 3	4	5
The Plan (BCWS)					
Planned cost, Cumulative £					
Activity A	1000	2000			
Activity B		1000	2000		
Cum. total (W)	1000	3000	4000		
The Actual Costs Incurred (ACWP)					
Activity A	1000	2000			
Activity B		1000	2000	3000	4000
Cum. total (A)	1000	3000	4000	5000	6000
The Earned Value (BCWP)					
Activity A	1000	2000			
Activity B		500	1000	1500	2000
Cum. total (P)	1000	2500	3000	3500	4000
Performance Indices					
CPI (C = P/A)	1.0	0.833	0.75	0.70	0.667
SPI (S = P/W)	1.0	0.833	0.75	0.875	1.000
Estimates at Completion					
EAC (B/C)	4000	4802	5333	5714	6000
ETC (D/S)	3.0	3.6	4.0	3.4	3.0

However it can be corrected if it is noted that:

$$ETC = T + \frac{D - (T \times S)}{S}$$

This can be used for all cases where the planned duration is not exceeded – i.e. $T < D$. Once the originally estimated duration D is exceeded, $T > D$, the formula is changed to:

$$ETC = T + \frac{T - (T \times S)}{S} \tag{8.8}$$

i.e. the elapsed time is substituted for the original duration.

This can be simplified to:

$$ETC = \frac{T}{S} \tag{8.9}$$

If this change is made and we look at the situation at period 4, we now get an ETC of $4/0.875 = 4.57$ periods; an improvement on the original and obviously incorrect prediction of 3.4 periods. However, the result could be further improved if the calculation is based solely on the performance of the activity, or activities, that actually govern the schedule progress of the project. In this case, the reduced form cannot be used and the expression should be modified to:

$$ETC = T + \frac{D_1 - (T_1 \times S_1)}{S_1} \qquad (8.10)$$

For $T_1 < D_1$ or $D_1 = T_1$. For $T_1 > D_1$. D_1, T_1, S_1 are the values relevant to the critical activity.

In this example, activity B is clearly critical to progress so it may be decided to generate the ETC at, say, period 3, using the factors that come from activity B alone. In this case, it will be necessary to calculate the SPI for activity B at period 3 and it is $1000/2000 = 0.5$.

Substituting in expression (8.8):

$$ETC = 3 + \frac{2 - (2 \times 0.5)}{0.5} = 3 + \frac{1}{0.5} = 5 \text{ periods}$$

Using the same formula at period 4 also gives the correct prediction. In fact the same procedure of dividing the formula into its component parts could have been applied to the EAC to generate a more precise estimate, although this is less important than with the ETC.

The reader is thus left with the choice of using either the simplified formulae, if he or she is happy with the CPI and SPI generated by the aggregate of all costs in the project, or the fundamental formulae, if it is wished to base predictions on the performance of those current activities which are seen to be critical.

The organizational impact of cost–performance measurement

For cost–performance measurement to work successfully in any project organization, certain major elements must exist:

Systems elements
- A time-based plan.
- A work breakdown structure.
- A cost collection system.
- A method of assessing progress.

Managerial elements
- A responsibility/authority matrix.
- The right culture (i.e. management backing).

A network forms the ideal medium for the time-based plan and is well understood as a project technique. The work breakdown structure may be less familiar but it exists in one form or another in most companies and projects; what may be absent is the formality needed by cost–performance measurement. The cost collection system, again, is present in most companies through the time bookings and purchase accounting systems. The method of assessing progress will be new and must be linked to the responsibility matrix. Finally, the whole system must have backing at the most senior level if it is to succeed.

Work breakdown structures

The **work breakdown structure** (WBS) needs special consideration as it plays an essential part in the process. It is an hierarchical structure of project work elements in which costs associated with the lowest-level elements can be aggregated upwards into related higher-level sections of the project; three types are possible:

1. organization based;
2. product based;
3. task based.

Figure 8.9 shows the three alternatives.

With an organizational structure (Figure 8.9(a)), work is defined according to the department within the company that does the work. When costs are collected

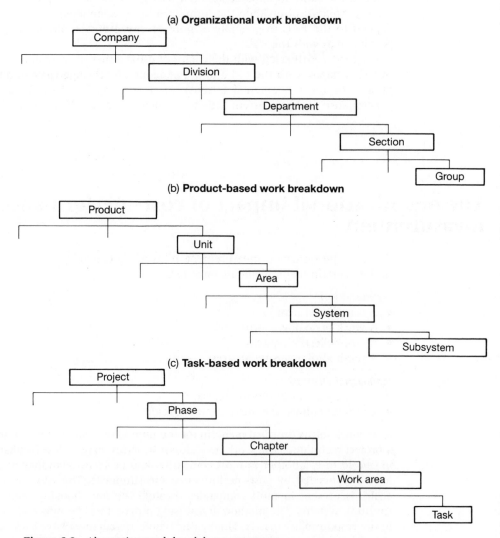

Figure 8.9 Alternative work breakdown structures.

through the time sheet or bookings system, cost reports will show which departments or divisions in the company have been working on the project and how much has been spent.

The product or physical structure (Figure 8.9(b)) gives a cost system that relates costs to the physical elements of the product. Here, when costs are collected, they will show what parts of the product have been worked on and how much has been spent on designing or making each element; what it may not tell is who (i.e. what department) has been doing the work.

The task or functionally based structure (Figure 8.9(c)) relates costs to the tasks that are expected to be performed. Cost reporting in this arrangement shows what work people have been performing in terms of the tasks they normally carry out. This system might seem to offer less than the other two in terms of control, but it has much more to recommend it in the context of performance measurement than either of the others. The reason is that in order to assess progress it is necessary to refer to the project plan and this is normally structured around the activities or tasks that are expected to be performed. Because the other structures lay their emphasis on either (a) who does the work or (b) what part of the product it relates to, it is often difficult to construct a satisfactory plan in those formats that fully describes the planner's intentions, for planners think in terms of tasks rather than components or departments.

When companies in the UK first began applying cost–performance measurement, little thought was given to the relationship between plan and work breakdown structure and, in consequence, the technique proved to be awkward to apply. It was not impossible, though, as the plan was in the hands of the planners who could make an assessment of progress, while the costs were in the domain of the accountants who can normally provide the up-to-date expenditure. By some means, progress was agreed between the two parties and some measure of performance derived. What was lacking was a means of automatically linking the two, this is now available through software specifically designed for both planning and costing but throws into focus another problem.

Work breakdown structures used in the past have tended to be product based, and this was encouraged by the US Department of Defense (DoD) as its contracts define a work breakdown structure as a 'product-oriented family tree'. This arrangement helped the DoD's own Project Managers to account for what the money was being spent on; that is, they could relate expenditure to items of procured hardware. It also helped them to estimate and compare the costs associated with developing various items of defence equipment and, from their point of view, this made considerable sense. The WBS that was imposed under this arrangement is called the **contract work breakdown structure** as it is specifically designed for reporting against the contract statement-of-work which is normally written in terms of the hardware to be acquired. However, the implementation guide to the DoD's C/SCSC procedure goes on to define a relationship between the organization structure and the work breakdown structure; where these two structures meet, a **cost account** is created. The significance of the cost account as the principal means of cost collection has not really been appreciated in the UK and the term is little used; much more stress is laid on the WBS as the principal means of cost collection. As for the project plan, this was normally contained within a network but, due to the failure of PERT/Cost, the DoD did not insist on the use of networks for project planning and some contractors avoided using them.

However, given the abundance of cheap and effective project management software, that approach is now antiquated as all contemporary software makes use of a network as the principal data model for the project. The difficulty comes in integrating the plan and the costs; in many companies the WBS coding is used for cost reporting as staff use it on their time sheets, Purchasing put it on requisitions, etc., but often this coding has no relationship to the activity coding used on the project network. Before the days of software that could perform both network analysis and cost–performance calculations, this did not greatly matter, provided progress could be agreed between the cost accountants and the planners. However, the relationship between the plan and the WBS becomes vitally important once it is decided to integrate the two in a computerized environment.

The best and most direct method of updating the project plan is from the data that is captured by the time-bookings and purchasing systems as it is the most accurate and up-to-date information, but as has been said, it is often coded according to the WBS rather than the plan. Some contemporary software will allow WBS codes to be attached to activities in the project network but they can only be used as a method of summarizing costs associated with related groups of activities; they cannot be used as a means of directly updating any activity because several activities can all have the same WBS code and the software can have no way of distinguishing between them.

Relating the work breakdown structure to the project plan

Both the WBS and the project plan represent two sets of structured knowledge but any system that forges a link between two sets of data demands a discipline of its own that must be recognized and understood. If that discipline is built in at the outset, then the process of control will be much easier; try to put it in when the project is under way and things may become awkward. By creating a WBS that allows the network to be coded directly from it, a way can be found to structure both the network and the WBS such that they are precisely related and mutually compatible. The most convenient way of doing this is to use the WBS coding as the key code for activity numbering in the network. This appears to run contrary to the network coding systems that are currently fashionable as mentioned in Chapter 4, but this is the basis of the new discipline. It will be realized that this is a fundamental decision; it will affect the whole project data structure and has to be taken at the start. Furthermore, it imposes a discipline of thought upon the project planners that they will not have been used to previously.

For complete cost control, any WBS must satisfy the criteria that the work packages are (a) mutually exclusive and (b) collectively exhaustive – i.e. no work should appear twice and all work must be covered. This principle must not be violated and applies equally to the network. In this respect, a matrix type of work breakdown is particularly useful as it lends itself to generating all the required packages and can also be used to draw the top-level network directly from the matrix. Figure 8.10 shows a sample of a WBS based on a matrix.

The most significant feature of Figure 8.10 is that the WBS is expanded by including the principal tasks that the staff normally perform, as well as the main subdivisions of the project and the responsible sections of the organization. This

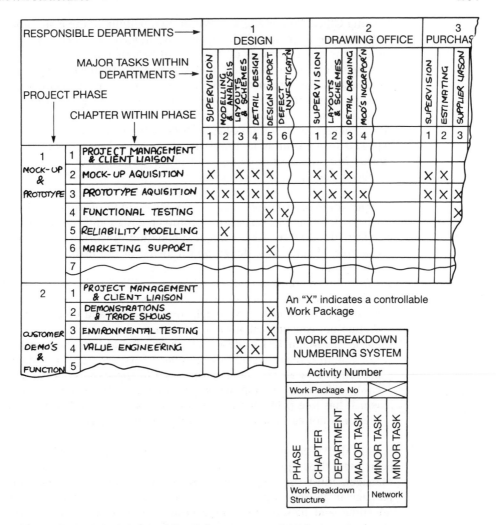

Figure 8.10 Functional work breakdown structure based on a matrix.

feature takes the WBS one step further towards the project plan than is normally the case. The principal tasks that any department of a company can perform are termed 'major tasks' and they are the lowest level in the WBS. A major task is thus the point at which the project plan and the WBS meet. To define the major tasks a careful look will be needed at what each department actually does as discrete, identifiable and controllable functions. Examination can often reveal that seven or eight functions can be used to completely define the scope of tasks that a department undertakes. The arrangement of these major tasks, on the basis of the order in which they are performed, will be the starting-point for the project plan.

In Figure 8.10 it will be seen that a formatted sheet has been used to create the WBS. Along the top the major responsible departments have been defined: Design,

Drawing Office, Purchasing, etc. Within that definition, the main functions that they perform have been specified: supervising, modelling, scheming, designing, etc. At the side the main elements of the work to be undertaken can be inserted; these can be subdivided into two: Phase and Chapter, alternatively they can be subdivided according to the product structure if cost reporting is required in that format. Inserting a cross in a box in the matrix will indicate the identification of a package of work that has to be performed and one worthy of control in its own right. This arrangement produces a task-based WBS as it has the tasks that each department is expected to perform as its lowest level. A Work Package Number can be derived directly from the position of the cross in the matrix. In this example, it is a four-digit number made up from the elements:

1st digit: the Project Phase – i.e. a major subdivision of work within the project as a whole (for example, phase one, prototype design and construction).
2nd digit: the Chapter – i.e. a major subdivision of work within a project phase (for example, chapter two, design and drawing of the main item of development in phase one).
3rd digit: the Work Area Code – i.e. the area of the company in which the particular skill is to be found (for example, work area code 3 is the Drawing Office). Work area code 9 is reserved for bought-out materials and other items of expenditure that do not consume labour but incur costs.
4th digit: the Major Task Code – i.e. the particular activity that is required to be done (for example, major task 5 in work area 1 is Design Support). Major tasks 9 and 0 are left free in all cases and can be used to specify any special tasks that are not easily defined by the pre-designated numbers. There is also a work area code 0 which has free fields that can be used to specify any other miscellaneous activity that does not easily fall into any of the other categories.

Once the WBS has been established, all the work packages in the project will have been identified. The Project Planning Engineer, in conjunction with the Project Manager, must use judgement in selecting an item to be the subject of a work package in its own right. For example, a major task in the design area may be 'meetings and liaison'; in a large project with regular liaison meetings with the client, this may be a significant item of both time and cost and worthy of special control. In a smaller project, even though there will be meetings, these may be considered as part of the normal design process and not singled out. The greater the number of identified work packages, the greater will be the detail contained within the reporting, but this must be set against the extra complexity of ensuring that times and costs are correctly booked to a multiplicity of task codes.

A basic network should be constructed using the work packages or major tasks to lay out the main logic and establish overall timescales. The major tasks themselves will be too large and general for both control and precise logic definition, hence they will have to be broken down into minor tasks or activities. These activities will specify a definable amount of work to the same level as would be expected in a normal network but they must all emanate from, and be contained within, their own work package; activities which cross work package boundaries are not allowed. The activities are numbered by adding an extra digit, or digits, onto the work package number from which they arise. This approach will be seen by some planning engineers as robbing them of some of the freedom of thought that they had

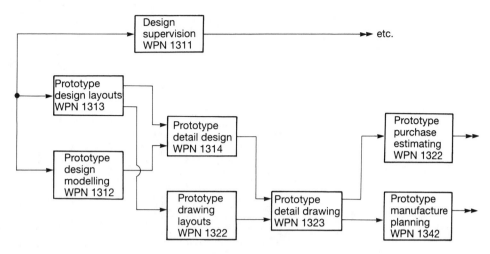

Figure 8.11   Basic task logic derived from work breakdown structure.

previously enjoyed and resistance to using it may be encountered. However, this resistance must be overcome; the point to make is that planners should no longer think of planning for activities alone, but planning for the total project control process which includes the costs.

The major advantage of this approach is that just one number is used throughout, there is never any need to transpose data from one coding system to another in order to update the network with progress or generate the costs associated with work packages. It means that the network can be updated with progress directly from the data generated by the time-bookings and accounting systems as the codes in both systems are identical. There is no need to employ 'data capture sheets' which require staff to record their working hours against both the cost code (work package number) and the activity number; when such methods are tried, either staff do not bother to fill them in, or when they do, half the time they are filled in incorrectly. The benefits of using a single code number throughout cannot be overstressed; an arrangement that involves independently maintaining two sets of data in parallel while keeping a strict relationship between the two but using different codes can be one of the biggest sources of errors and confusion, particularly if the project is large and the plan subject to frequent changes.

Figure 8.11 shows the basic logic in precedence form drawn from the matrix of Figure 8.10, while Figure 8.12 shows the expansion to form the detailed network. Figure 8.12 gives further information as the activity boxes contain details of the grade of labour to be used, along with the estimated hours and the activity duration in days.

In the example in the figure, a standard system of labour coding has been used; this is to be recommended where it is wished to plan company-wide across a range of projects all calling on the same resources. In this example, the labour coding system is made up of two letters and a digit. The two letters indicate the job, the first letter indicates the discipline:

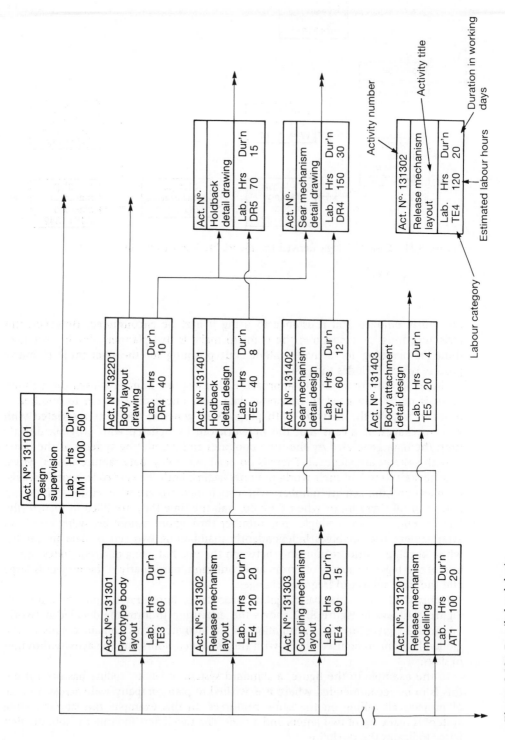

Figure 8.12 Detailed task logic.

$$T = \text{Technical (Design Engineering)}$$
$$D = \text{Draughting, etc.}$$

The second letter indicates the role within that discipline:

$$M = \text{Manager}$$
$$E = \text{Engineer, etc.}$$

The digit at the end indicates the hourly charge rate for costing purposes.

Thus activity no. 131101 (Design Supervision of the Prototype) requires 1000 hours of technical management time over a 500-day period at charge rate 1. With the project plan expressed in this form, it can be loaded into a project management computer system.

Organization for cost–performance measurement

Figure 8.13 shows the data structure and organizational relationships, together with the principal data flows, for a performance measurement system to work. It will be seen that the WBS forms the bridge between the organization structure that defines who is responsible for each task and the network which holds the plan of what is to be done and when. A suitable project management software package is essential to perform all the necessary calculations. Besides the normal start dates, criticalities, etc., it will generate, first, the costed schedules of work which form both the budgets and the instructions as to what each section manager is expected to perform, and secondly, the performance reports. The budgets must be agreed with each section manager before the system is put into operation as no manager is going to be held responsible for budgets to which he has not agreed. Budgets and targets can be set but they have no meaning unless those with authority take responsibility for achievement. Section managers who are sufficiently close to the task and have enough authority must be appointed to take responsibility for performance against their budgets. It is these managers who will receive the cost–performance reports and will be expected to take action according to whatever is indicated.

At the end of the planning and costing process, a plan defining all the activities and their associated budgets will be generated for Board approval, but it is at the Board approval stage that things can start to go wrong. The plan may look reasonable and the project is desirable but in the eyes of the Board the costs are seen to be too great. Perhaps there is a fear that the competition may be offering something cheaper, that the customer may reject the proposal or that there is not enough money in the development budget for the given year. All too often, it is concluded by senior management that the estimate itself must be wrong. Clearly, they reason, the planners and managers have put in excessive contingencies and made pessimistic assumptions, and this time there will not be the problems that occurred on the last project. As most of the estimates represent the judgement of the individuals they can usually be 'persuaded' to modify that judgement. After downward revisions, contingencies are usually the next thing to go; they may be seen as a luxury provision for something that may never happen and if they are included they will be spent whether needed or not. Finally, arbitrary cuts may be applied to bring the budget down to an 'acceptable' level. This depressing story will be only too familiar to many Project Managers.

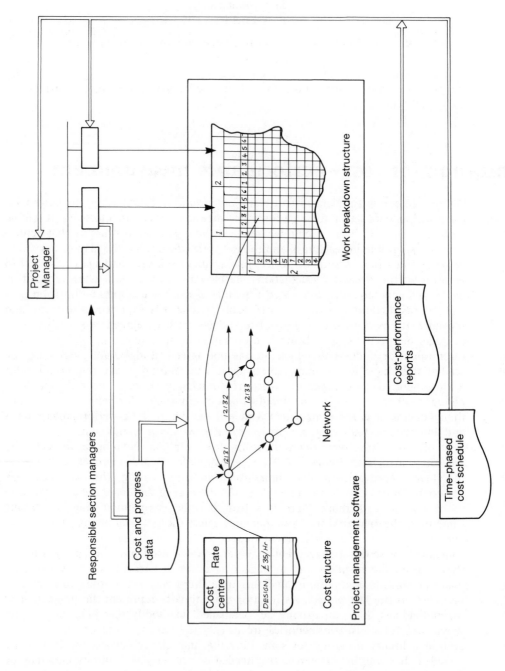

Figure 8.13 Organization and information relationships for cost–performance measurement.

Of course estimates should always be scrutinized and things challenged if they seem unreasonable, but one should be careful that scrutiny combined with wishful thinking does not lead to distorted judgement. History shows that the 'savings' made on paper are likely to be illusory and will disappear as the project proceeds. Few development projects are completed within their budgets – most over-run their targets, sometimes by quite considerable amounts. This may not necessarily imply a lack of control, simply the impossibility of foreseeing all that will happen in the future and the problems that may be encountered. Project Managers should guard against applying wishful thinking and undue pressure for low estimates in an attempt to get their project selected and be wary if they observe the process in other more senior individuals. An over-optimistic view at the beginning with budgets below their real needs can sow the seeds from which thorny problems later grow.

Measuring project progress

Once the system is in operation, each responsible section manager will be required to participate in the control process through his own assessment of the degree of progress. Inevitably, there is a subjective element in this but it is necessary in order to establish the BCWP. A number of methods are possible, each has drawbacks, but all are worthy of consideration for different circumstances:

(a) At regular intervals, perhaps once a fortnight, the section managers are asked to estimate the percentage completion of each of their activities that are currently authorized to be in progress.
(b) At regular intervals the managers are asked to estimate the remaining number of weeks that they expect to elapse before each of their current activities is complete.
(c) At each reporting point an amount of progress is credited to each current activity according to an agreed method of scoring.

Provided that the responsible managers can be trusted to make a reasoned assessment, method (a) can work well. It might seem easy to hoodwink the system, and in the early stages of each activity this is so, but as time passes and the assessed progress is not in fact being made, it soon begins to show and the manager cannot disguise it.

With method (b), one needs to assume a uniform rate of spend in each activity. This may not be a valid assumption in all cases, but it is reasonably accurate if the work packages are small enough. Using the estimated duration of the remaining work, the BCWP is:

$$BCWP = \frac{\text{Budgeted Duration of the Work Package} \times BCWS}{\text{Predicted Duration of the Work Package}}$$

The predicted duration is found by adding the expected remaining duration to the time elapsed since the activity first started; the BCWS is found from the current schedule as generated by the computer or by a simple calculation based on a uniform spend rate. Should the budgeted duration be exceeded, the actual duration to date is substituted in the above formula.

Method (c) requires an assessment to be made of the likely rate of spend and the identification of well-defined milestones against which progress can be credited. At its simplest, a rule for crediting progress might be: give 50% of budgeted cost when the activity starts and 50% when it ends; for very short and simple activities this can be satisfactory. More complex activities with a longer duration need a more sophisticated method of scoring progress. For example, if in the drawing office there is a package of work that covers the output of a set of drawings for a certain item, the rule for assessing the BCWP could be: credit 10% of budgeted cost when the activity starts, give another 50% when 25% of drawings have been issued, give another 25% when 75% of drawings have been issued and give the final 15% when all work is complete. Each of the above methods has its place; method (c) is particularly useful where milestones are easily definable or quantifiable output can be measured but this is not always the case. For service types of activity such as quality control, milestones do not apply, hence methods (a) or (b) are more appropriate. (Method (a) was used in the earlier example in this chapter.)

Contemporary software

The majority of the more generalized project management software packages now offer cost−performance measurement features, this innovation has come about in the past few years. One of the first to offer comprehensive reporting features as a standard part of the program was PRESTIGE, now marketed as Artemis-Prestige for Windows. Computer Associates' SuperProject V2 also contains these features as part of the package; as does Project Manager Workbench from Hoskyns in Version 3.1. Other packages offer add-on modules which enhance the basic system; examples of this are CORoNET, introduced by Computerline to accompany PLANTRAC and Parade which accompanies Primavera Project Planner from Primavera Systems. Output report formats from both Parade and CORoNET are similar and reflect their intended compliance with the US DoD specification DOD 7000 for cost reporting. Cascade, from Mantix Systems, is possibly the first system designed from the outset to make cost−performance measurement its central concept and is thus a very comprehensive tool; its appearance marks the realization that cost−performance will become the principal management method in the years to come. Figures 8.14 and 8.15 show sample outputs from some of the above-mentioned systems. More details of current software can be found in Chapter 13.

Cost−performance measurement in practice

For many staff working in the development field, performance measurement will come as something of a shock. There can be little doubt that upon its introduction there will be resistance from some quarters, most probably from the Design and Trials groups. It may also come from Project Managers who may feel that a technique that exposes potential cost or schedule over-runs to demanding or unsympathetic senior management at an early point in the project could be damaging to their own prospects. This resistance is understandable; with innovative work, there is always an element of the unknown and people cannot be expected to meet and solve unknown problems within fixed time and cost parameters. However reasonable this proposition may seem, the business world in general does not take that view and there is a growing insistance on the part of customer organizations for

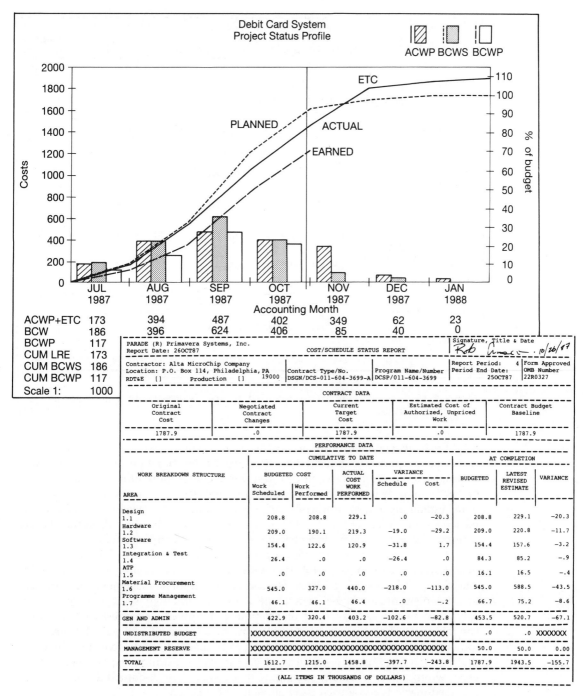

Figure 8.14 Histogram and cost/schedule status report from Primavera-Parade (note predictive cost profile similar to that shown in Figure 8.8).

Prestige PC	Earned value – variances and indices	Page number :	1
		Run date :	12Apr90
		Time now :	31Mar90
		Forecast end :	06Dec90
		Required end :	31Aug90

PROJECT: PROJECT DEFINITION STUDY   REPORT AC03

VERSION 00

DRAWING OFFICE: PHASE 1

Activity ident.	Description	Acutal to date	Earned value	Budget scheduled	Schedule variance	Cost variance	Schedule perf. index	Cost perf. index
12310	D.O MANAGEMENT	.00	.00	1490.40	–1490.40	.00	0.00	
12320	D.O.–SCHEME CONTROL PANEL	247.77	275.30	275.30	.00	27.53	1.00	1.11
12321	D.O.–SCHEME LOOM LAYOUT	1624.27	1569.21	1569.21	.00	–55.06	1.00	.97
12322	D.O.–SCHEME NEW CASING	853.43	853.43	853.43	.00	0.00	1.00	1.00
12327	D.O.–SCHEME FINAL DESIGN	.00	.00	00.0	.00	.00		
TOTALS		4157.03	4074.00	8070.07	–3995.63	–82.59	.50	.98

Figure 8.15 Variances and indices reported by Artemis-Prestige now marketed as Artemis ProjectView.

fixed-price development contracts with closely defined technical objectives. The traditional response to uncertainty, in a fixed-price situation, is to put in large contingencies, both in time and cost, but this becomes more difficult in the context of competition. It is therefore imperative that industry pay closer attention to both initial estimating and control while the project is under way. Departmental managers must become more responsible for the value generated by their departments and performance measurement is probably the only way it can be done.

It thus becomes important to ensure the full cooperation of all concerned. A 'hearts and minds' campaign, together with education and training, will be necessary and it must be seen to be effectively backed by senior management. Performance measurement must not be seen to be a threat (although some will see it that way), but rather as a method of promoting improved awareness and increased commitment. The majority of people want to do a good and valuable job, performance measurement actually allows the worth of their efforts, to be seen in a way that has not previously been clear. It also provides warning signals about things going wrong; there is usually something that can be done about a difficult situation, provided that it is recognized early enough.

These are positive benefits but they need to be sold to the staff, commitment is all-important. It must be pointed out that every member of a company is a stake-holder in its future, for it is the company's future that holds the key to their own prosperity. The continued presence of any company in the market-place is totally dependant on providing the customer with what he or she wants at a price they can afford, and that implies giving value for money. The earned value concept contained within performance measurement is aimed directly at the 'value for money' objective.

If performance measurement is to be implemented, the decision should ideally be taken at the outset of the project and incorporated in the planning and control arrangements. It can be implemented at a mid-point in a project but that can be difficult and time-consuming. Managers submitting estimates must be persuaded to thoroughly scrutinize the project plan and the technical specification to ensure a full understanding of what is expected and its implications. Undue pressure for low estimates should not be applied. Planning engineers should also ensure that adequate time is allowed for each activity. Resource demands should be approved by senior management, for it is they who will be tasked with ensuring that the resources in terms of staff, materials and money will be made available when required. In simple terms, a new and more formalized arrangement will exist between all the parties. Departmental managers must be made responsible for their budgets and this must be clearly understood in their relationship with the Project Manager.

Reporting systems must be set up to gather the cost and progress data. The time-booking system will usually prove convenient for gathering labour cost data and Purchasing or Accounts will have data on orders and payments. The relationship to the master plan must be quite clear and the WBS matrix and activity numbering system will help. A dedicated software system with the cost−performance features must be acquired and project management staff need to become familiar with its use and accept the disciplines it brings with it; some changes to company procedures may be necessary. Work must proceed through a system of task authorizations; unauthorized work must not be allowed to start. Here the project management software can help as the better-quality packages allow the generation of customized reports, and this feature can be used to create authorizations at the appropriate time directly from the plan.

The generation of regular performance reports is vital, responsible managers require to see how they are doing at regular and well-defined points. It must be made clear that progress assessments will be required for each work package and the responsible manager is required to submit his report on time. Resistance may be encountered here but knowing that senior management will be interested in the results can be a great incentive. Project management staff responsible for operating the system must set up a regular routine for themselves and ensure that authorizations go out on time and that managers know when progress assessments are needed.

Once a system of performance measurement has been established, its value will be recognized by all; they may not like it for sometimes they, as individuals, will be in the spotlight but they can learn to live with it and, hopefully, profit from the experience. Cost−performance measurement cannot alone guarantee that projects will be concluded within their cost and schedule targets, but where performance measurement is employed managers are more aware of costs and that must increase the chances of a profitable outcome.

Progress reports

Today's Project Manager has never been better served for numerical data about the state of his project, computerized project management packages can generate a host of reports at the touch of a button that only a few years ago would have needed an army of clerks to compile. Whereas computerized status reports that show completed activities, cost and schedule performance indices and forecasts to completion may reveal part of the story, they certainly do not show the whole picture. They have nothing to say about such issues as staff competence or technical performance, yet it is in these areas that the causes of a project's problems may lie. The Project Manager must ensure that these non-quantitative issues are reported with as much attention and detail as the purely numerical measures. Regular status reports are a convenient method of gathering information of all current activities.

Meaningful reports take time and effort to compile, hence the frequency of reporting has to be tailored to the circumstances. If the frequency is too great, effort may be wasted and the degree of cooperation that is so important may be lost, but if the period between them is too long, the impact of developing trends may not be realized before it is too late to do anything about it. For many projects, a monthly frequency is ideal as it often fits in with the monthly cost figures released by the Accounts Department. The reports can also form a basis for the Project Manager's monthly team meeting. Team meetings can of course be held on a more or less frequent basis if the situation demands but it can waste individual's time if they are required to attend too many meetings at which their contribution is small.

Formal status reports should be compiled for each open work package; a typical report format is shown in Figure 8.16. The upper section contains numerical information regarding costs, progress and forecasts to completion, while the lower section contains narrative fields that invite descriptive material to give meaning to the numerical data; the fields covered are:

- General progress.
- Costs.
- Staffing.
- Technical performance.
- Problems encountered or foreseen.
- Tasks or actions to be undertaken in the next period.
- Comments by the section head.

Reports such as this should be compiled by a Project Engineer or Progress Engineer; often such staff are attached to the project planning section as they are the group most closely in touch with overall progress. The Project Engineer will need to assess the situation on each work package within his domain by reference to current plans, accounts data and face-to-face interviews with staff engaged on each activity. He should aim to report the position as honestly as possible, drawing attention to any problems that have been met or are likely to arise. A degree of personal maturity is needed in individuals that take on this role; for very human reasons, some people in responsible positions are not always willing to disclose the real position or only wish favourable situations to be reported. The Project Engineer must have the insight to see behind this without alienating or losing the cooperation of the person involved. This arrangement is preferable to that used on some projects where the responsible section managers are required to compile a monthly report on activities under their control; for the reasons mentioned, this can lead to biased reporting or even deliberate concealment of awkward situations.

Every work package should have a manager or section head nominated to be responsible for its satisfactory completion. Before the status report is issued, he should see it; unless there is a factual error, he should not be allowed to change it

AW	PROJECT STATUS REPORT		

Project Ref. No	Project title	Issue	Date
PA - 03	**POWER UNIT DEVELOPMENT**	**9**	**16/2/93**

Work Package No	Work Package Title	Section Head
2614	**LIFE CYCLE TESTING**	**J ROBBINS**

Original Baseline Budget	£ **20,500**	Current Baseline Budget	£ **25,350**

Original Completion Date	**4/9/92**	Current Completion Date	**25/9/92**

Issue No. **1**	Date **1/3/91**	Issue No. **4**	Date **12/6/92**

BCWS (Current Budget)	ACWP (Current Budget)	BCWP (Current Budget)
£ **15,650**	£ **17,394**	£ **16,050**

Estimated Cost at Completion	£ **27,464**	Cost Variance at Completion £ **2114 (+)** (+/–)

Variance as a % of Budget	Original Baseline **33.97%+**	CPI	This Period **0.923**
	Current Baseline **8.34%+**		Last Period **0.930**

Estimated Date at Completion	**23/9/92**	Variance **0.4 (–)** Weeks (+/–)

Variance as a % of Schedule	Original Baseline **27% +**	SPI	This Period **1.026**
	Current Baseline **1% –**		Last Period **0.985**

Summary of Current Position		
Progress	Costs	Staffing
SATISFACTORY AT PRESENT	*SLIGHT UPWARD TREND SINCE LAST REVISION*	*SATISFACTORY*

Technical	Facilities
TWO SPEED GOVERNOR FAILURES NOTED. EXCESSIVE VIBRATION AT 200 HRS PROBLEM TRACED TO DRY BEARING, NEW SEALS NEEDED.	*TEST INTERRUPTED BY REQUEST TO 'BORROW' VARIOUS ITEMS.*

Problems encountered or foreseen
TESTS MAY BE HELD UP WAITING FOR NEW DESIGN OF OIL SEAL. GOVERNOR 'STICKING' STILL BEING INVESTIGATED BUT SHOULD NOT HOLD-UP TEST.

Tasks/Actions to be undertaken in the next period
COMPLETION OF LOW TEMPERATURE RUNNING, STRIP & INSPECT, INSTALL NEW OIL SEALS START HIGH TEMPERATURE RUNNING.

Comments by Section Head
So far so good, high temperature test may be more severe test than previous.

Compiled by	Circulate to	Signed	Signed
L.K. TURNER	*JKR. PL, RFG & FILE*	PROGRESS ENGINEER	SECTION HEAD

Figure 8.16 Example of a project status report.

but there is field in which he can comment on what is stated above. By filling in and signing the status report, the section head is acknowledging that he has read the report and accepts responsibility. When all status reports have been compiled, they should be collated, a summary written by the Project Engineer and the set deposited with the Project Manager.

Lines of communication

Good communications between all members of the project is a vital ingredient in the success of the venture. Communication means letting people know what is going on and listening to what people have to say: it is a two-way process. Clearly everyone cannot be communicating with everyone else all of the time because that would be totally unproductive, but people must be made aware of things that affect them and have the means to let others know of issues that have a bearing on their work. It is up to the Project Manager to ensure that good channels of communication exist and the form that they take. Communication may be verbal or written and the choice between them says much about how the communication is expected to be received and interpreted.

In general, written communication is suitable or preferable in cases where:

(a) it needs to be recorded for later reference;
(b) the content is too involved for it to be remembered from verbal communication;
(c) no response is required or a delayed response is acceptable;
(d) the message needs to be repeated many times;
(e) verbal communication is difficult or impossible (e.g. where translation from one language to another is needed).

Verbal communication is more suitable in situations where:

(a) both parties agree that no record is required of the information that passes (e.g. when confidentiality is important);
(b) the information conveyed affects individuals directly and personally;
(c) an immediate response is required;
(d) the information is trivial or simple and does not need repeating.

Both forms of communication can co-exist in any situation. For example, letting an employee know that he has been promoted is best done by face-to-face discussion as it affects him personally, it is a straightforward message and is not likely to be forgotten. It will need to be followed up by a letter as the change of status needs to be recorded for reference. To send the employee a letter without the preceding discussion might be perceived as indicating that the supervisor is not interested in the employee personally. Similar situations apply between organizations that have contractual arrangements; issues that affect them both may be discussed as immediate responses to suggestions are needed in a negotiation. Once the negotiation is complete, it can be recorded for reference in letters, minutes and contract changes. Without such a formal record, there is always the danger that one or other party will misunderstand, ignore or forget about what was agreed.

Besides the form of communication, the channels by which information spreads throughout the project organization are another matter for the Project Manager. Classical organization structures emphasize formal lines of communication; these generally result in arrangements whereby junior staff in different departments have to communicate formally by sending the message to their department head, who then sends it to the corresponding department head to transmit it down to the junior levels. This approach was designed to emphasize the position of the department head at the centre of communications and it stemmed from military thinking on matters of command and control. Military problems can be solved, in part, by good order and a disciplined approach, but they are not the same type of problem as that faced by people engaged in what are essentially creative processes involving a mix of different skills.

The classical communications structure has shown itself to be deficient when it comes to innovative work as it tends to stifle the spontaneity that is vital to creative problem-solving. This has been recognized by the increasing use of 'team working'; here the formal communication barrier between more junior members of staff has been removed as all members are integrated into a 'team'. Within the team members from different departments are free to communicate at all levels, but the team must communicate with the rest of the organization through the its leader; teams can be considered as a microcosm of the project structure itself. It has to be recognized that, as far as the higher levels of the project organization are concerned, some measure of day-to-day control is lost by the team working approach. The compensating benefit is that teams have shown themselves to be effective at problem-solving but control is still needed and it can be exercised in two ways: first, by clear goal-setting, and secondly, by formalized reporting. At the formation of the team, the reason for its existence must be clearly understood by all the members and the goal that is to be attained must be precisely set out; each member should be aware of the role that he is to play and what is expected of him. The team goal cannot be changed without agreement from the Project Manager. While the team performs its function, there are no barriers to the exchange of ideas but progress must be reported accurately and in a timely fashion. It is up to the Project Manager to define the reporting criteria and insist that they are adhered to; the cost–performance measurement approach can be particularly useful in this respect. The team should not be allowed to become a self-perpetuating group that indulges in its own goal-setting.

When considering the management style to be adopted, the Project Manager generally has a choice. As projects can be run in a number of ways, he has the option to use a classical, formalized communication structure or he may prefer the team approach. He may choose to communicate with his team only through his section managers or he can adopt an 'open door' policy expecting all team members with an issue to discuss to have free access to him. All these methods have been adopted successfully in differing circumstances but success may depend on the suitability of the approach taken with respect to several criteria, in particular: the nature of the project, the personalities involved and the prevailing organizational culture. Whatever choice is made, it should be a conscious one; it can have a fundamental bearing on how well the project performs, yet many Project Managers never give this issue much thought – for the most part, they either do what suits their own personalty or what they have seen done before.

Meetings

The value of regular progress meetings cannot be overstated; by bringing the senior members of the project organization together on a regular basis, the Project Manager reinforces their identity as a team. Meetings provide a forum at which all the responsible staff can discuss their part in the project, the problems that they have and their view of the future. These meetings can be among the most valuable form of communication as all present can hear what is said and each has the chance to respond; they are an opportunity to use the creative power of the team approach to solve problems. The Project Manager should chair the meeting and all decisions taken and actions decided upon should be minuted with responsible personnel nominated for each action. Ideally, minutes should be approved and circulated within three days of the meeting. Minutes should be filed and retained; along with the status reports, they provide a history of the project and this may prove valuable when it comes to estimating and assessing future projects.

Reviews

From time to time, project reviews may be required. For the most part, reviews are not the prerogative of the Project Manager, they are called by the sponsoring organization. That organization may be a customer or it may be the Board of the company if the project is a private venture. Reviews are called for one of a number of reasons:

- An important decision has to be taken involving the commitment of significant funds.
- The circumstances of the project have changed necessitating a rethink of the project strategy.
- There is a significant technical problem, the solution to which may be in doubt.
- A review is required as part of the annual budgeting process.

Reviews are an opportunity for the sponsor to assess the progress of the project and its future prospects but they can be a worrying experience for the Project Manager. If the review shows the project in an unfavourable light, the sponsor may instigate changes that he sees as necessary. This could involve a change of key personnel which could include the Project Manager himself, at worst it could result in the project being cancelled. Such things are commonplace and those engaged in project management must learn to take them in their stride. It cannot be said that every project that is started ends as a success. However unpleasant it may be for those involved, if its prospects of success look poor, then it is better to stop the project than to keep investing in something that is unlikely to make a satisfactory return.

Reviews normally take the form of a meeting; the sponsor may choose to take the role of chairman or he may delegate that to the Project Manager and take the position of an investigator and jury. Whichever approach is taken, the sponsor will normally set the agenda, possibly in conjunction with the Project Manager. To allow adequate time for preparation, the date and agenda are often set a month or more before the meeting takes place. After the introductory formalities, the agenda for the review could take the form of answering four basic questions:

1. Is there still a need for the product, if so what form should it take and what is the preferable cost and timescale?

    This should be supported with:

    Estimates of future sales figures with dates

      Assessments of competitor companies and products

      Selling price to sales volume curves

      Alternative product specifications.

2. What has been achieved so far?

    This should be supported by:

      A review of design progress

      Areas in which success has been demonstrated

      Areas in which tests have yet to be conducted

      Current or foreseeable technical problems

      Estimates of unit production costs

      Potential for product enhancement.

3. What more has to be done and at what cost?

    This should be supported by:

      Cost and schedule performance figures

      Estimates to completion

      Review of outstanding work

      Estimates of the cost of setting up the production facility

      The plan for sourcing production items.

4. If we continue to invest in the project what return is likely and what confidence can we have in the forecast?

    This should be supported by:

      Project cash-flow and profit forecasts

      Internal rate-of-return forecasts

      Risk analyses.

Many actions and directives may result from a project review, they should be minuted and circulated to all attendees. Project reviews have their part to play in the control cycle; they can cause the 'project' to look at itself, as well as having the benefit of an outside opinion. However, one thing must be remembered: it is that no one is ever un-biased at a project review, everyone in the project team together with the sponsor has a vested interest of some sort in the outcome of the project.

Summary

Without proper control, the project will not proceed in an orderly fashion towards its goal. It is the responsibility of the Project Manager to ensure that adequate controls exist within the project. The chief method will be through a communications structure that informs those responsible of the goals they are expected to attain and demands a report of progress. Today's Project Manager has the choice of package software that offers extensive planning and reporting facilities and the latest software includes some new techniques. Cost–performance measurement allows the progress of the project to be seen with a clarity that has not been possible before and it also aids prediction of the project outcome. It cannot be seen, however, as just another software tool, for it has implications for the organization in terms of the project data structures and the reporting responsibilities of individuals; here resistance may be encountered as it can amount to a cultural change. Change is in the air, however, and a growth in the use of performance measurement techniques can be expected over the coming years.

Besides the purely numerical data generated by software systems, the Project Manager must ensure that all the surrounding technical, personnel and financial issues are reported regularly and honestly. Regular project team meetings and occasional project reviews will aid this process.

In today's competitive conditions, Project Managers must ensure that they are using the most appropriate methods to control projects that are becoming increasingly complex and demanding.

9

Planning and implementing the production programme

- Production programmes
- Simultaneous engineering
- Economic aspects of tooling
- Learning curves
- Production progress
- Production readiness

Where projects are intended to lead to products that are to be made in volume, the production phase should be planned at the very beginning. Senior management frequently express surprise and disappointment when the production phase fails to start on time and the build-up to peak output takes longer than exected. The implications for the firm may be serious as markets and customers can be lost, costs in the first year may exceed budget and even a cash crisis may result. Yet much of this could be avoided if more attention was paid to planning for production in the development phase and a better understanding existed of the nature and difficulties of starting production with a technologically new product. All too often, the assumption is made that within a few weeks of the first item being produced the plant will be running at peak capacity, but the reality turns out to be very different as problem after problem is encountered, each needing time and effort to resolve.

The phases of a typical production programme are shown diagrammatically in Figure 9.1. It will be seen that in order to achieve production within a reasonably short time from the end of development there must be a high degree of overlap between the development and the production procurement phases, particularly if there is need for capital plant and new or modified buildings. Throughout the initial

225

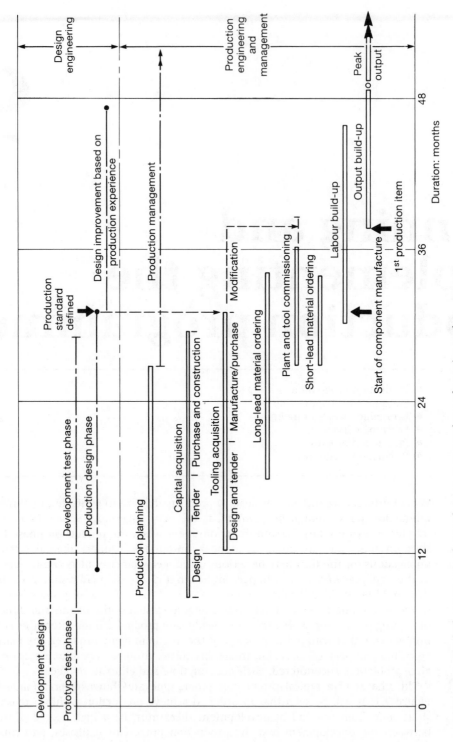

Figure 9.1 Typical activities in the production start-up phase of a major project.

design period, production engineers should be on hand to advise on likely production techniques and ensure that all production aspects are considered. This will pay immense dividends later on as trying to productionize a design after it has gone through its development process, particularly if qualification testing has been done, could be both time-consuming and introduce a new range of problems that were not present in the original design. At the end of the prototype design phase, when design of the far more representative development standard is started, the serious work of production planning should begin. The basic production processes should be established, important policy decisions regarding whether some items will be sub-contracted or made in house must also be made. The impact of these decisions may mean modifications to the existing buildings or even the construction of a new one. If this is likely to be the case, the necessary planning applications should be submitted at the earliest possible time. If there are likely to be planning objections, it is as well to know them and deal with them before they have a chance to make a serious impact on the production costs or timescale, which could of course happen if things are left too late.

The successful conclusion of the prototype test phase should mark the start of the process of defining and acquiring the production plant, facilities and tools. If prototype testing is not going well and serious performance problems still have to be resolved, then it would not be wise to put in hand the expensive process of plant and tool design only to have it changed later. Furthermore, if the problems thrown up in these early tests look likely to be time-consuming to resolve, then the whole project may have to be reviewed for its viability. Under these circumstances, few companies would wish to commit much in the way of resources to production procurement. At the end of prototype testing, sufficiently good results must be obtained to give a high degree of confidence in eventual success – this is an important milestone, for the next stage will see the commitment of significant resources, both human and financial.

Capital acquisition starts with the design of the basic plant and buildings and when drawings are complete they can be put out to tender. As the design of the development standard item comes to an end, the designers and production engineers must work together to create the definitive production design. At the same time, tooling engineers will start drawing the special tools or writing specifications for tools, equipment or software to be procured externally. Throughout the production design phase detail changes are to be expected as the results of development testing and suggestions from potential customers or the Marketing Department are fed into the evolving design. Some of the tool design work will probably be nugatory or need modification, this has to be accepted as the price to be paid to reduce the time between the end of development and full production. As the profits come from sales, shortening the time to get the product to the market is always a worthwhile aim.

When the development and test phases are complete, the design must have proved itself in all important respects and the chief designer must be able to fully underwrite all the performance requirements. If this cannot be done, the company could find itself with a large amount of money committed and spent on the production equipment and, in consequence, could face cash difficulties. In this event, crash action is appropriate; whatever resources are required will have to be committed to curing the problems, revising the specification, altering the market strategy or whatever else may be felt appropriate. The aim should always be to have the production standard item defined as quickly as possible after the end of the development testing, for by this time most of the capital and tooling will have been purchased and plant commissioning well under way. It is also possible that some production labour will have been already hired and under training on the new line. From this point onwards, events must be phased to ensure that commissioning of plant and tools proceeds smoothly and in step with the planned build-up of labour with the aim of achieving the first production item by the target date.

Obvious as this process may seem, it is not always practised and there are sometimes boundaries, both organizational and cultural, that exist within companies that prevent a satisfactory phasing between development and production. Often the demarcations are fundamental to the way in which the company is run; for many companies, the design engineering function, incorporating all development work, comes under one division headed by the Technical or Engineering Director, while all production activities including production engineering belong to another under the Production or Manufacturing Director. Marketing activities often belong to yet another division headed by the Sales or Marketing Director. With organizational boundaries such as these, the Project Manager can find difficulties in gaining the degree of commitment needed from all the parties at the required time in the project. There may also be cultural differences between individuals in the various departments based on different educational experiences and the way in which they perceive both their roles and professional goals. At its worst, the Technical Director may have a PhD degree in an area of complex mathematical engineering theory and regard design as a largely intellectual exercise directed at creating the perfect solution, while the Production Director may have worked his way up through every level from an apprentice turner and fitter. It is hardly surprising that these two individuals may have very different views on the appropriateness of any design; they may be barely understandable to one another. Cultural and perceptual differences of this kind have led to the process of **over-the-fence engineering**, where 'fences' (i.e. artificial boundaries) are erected between departments, each pursuing its own ends in a way that is largely independent of the others. It is easy to see how this can happen; design engineers may take as their goal the ultimate in performance: 'let's design a world beater.' There is nothing wrong in that but world beaters are few and far between and often rely on some radical new innovation, for the majority of products a good competitive position is the best that can be hoped for. Being competitive relies on more than just excellence in performance; attractiveness in the market also implies that the product is available when customer demand is high and it can be sold at a price that people are willing to pay for it. Designers cannot therefore divorce themselves from production, cost and programme aspects in their search for the ultimate but sometimes they choose to think that production costs and market strategy belong to someone else: 'it's up to Production and Marketing to find ways to make it cheaply and sell it, that's what they're there for.' Production engineers may also feel that it is not worth getting involved in design work too early: 'why waste time on sketches and ideas that are only going to change later on? When they've got a firm set of drawings we'll look at them.' Understandable as these sentiments may be, they lead to the view that product design has to take place in a serial fashion with each department passing its work 'over the fence' to the next. Competitive pressures from Far Eastern producers that are able to achieve significantly reduced times from product concept to market launch have begun to change that view.

Simultaneous engineering is a newly coined phrase to describe the process of reducing the time from product concept to its arrival in the market by a high degree of overlapping of the various project phases (see Chapter 5). The justification for this approach is the apparent success of Japanese companies in shortening their lead-times with new products. Comparative studies between Western and Japanese projects would seem to indicate that the Japanese achieve lead-times that are three-quarters to two-thirds that of their European equivalents. Comparisons of this type are always suspect as the amount of applied effort in terms of money and manpower, the degree of product innovation, the amount of investment already existing in auto-mated equipment, CAD, etc. is not always taken into account, but the overall result cannot be ignored. The principal feature of the simultaneous engineering method is the concept of the multi-disciplinary team, sometimes called the task force, set up at the start of the project. Boundaries are abolished, representatives from all contributing disciplines, Design, Testing, Production, Procurement, Quality Assurance, Marketing, etc., are brought together as equals into one unit where each participates in the process of product evolution from the very start of the project. Thus Production Engineering and Marketing have their input and can get started on their tasks as early as possible. A greater degree of autonomy is afforded the team than would otherwise be usual, only strategic or policy decisions are referred upwards through the organization structure. Team members are expected to meet problems and deal with them quickly and on a consensus basis. If this all sounds familiar, one should not be surprised as it would seem to be the 'project'-based approach to engineering development that is the basis of this entire text. The principal difference seems to be that of the degree of commitment involved. Within many companies that claim to practise the 'project' approach to product development, Project Managers are appointed to plan and control projects but they have to negotiate the use of staff on their projects with the relevant departmental heads and it is here that all the old prejudices, boundaries and perceived priorities come in to play. There is nothing magic in the concept of simultaneous engineering, its success may be simply due to the degree of commitment involved, first, on the part of the company by dedicating staff to the project, and secondly, on the part of the individuals as they all feel that they have an equal contribution to make and an equal stake in the project outcome. The team need not simply be confined to members of the company, for if there are key suppliers or business partners involved, they too can be included.

Companies that have adopted the simultaneous engineering method claim to have had considerable success with it. The Perkins Group, manufacturers of diesel engines, recently implemented the approach on a major project to improve their 'Phaser' engines when stringent new emission standards were introduced in the USA. It was a project against the clock and a dedicated team with representatives from all relevant departments was created with a high degree of delegated authority. From Perkins' point of view it was an outstanding success as the programme was completed six months ahead of schedule; it was made possible by the degree of increased motivation through personal commitment combined with the close working relationships of the team members which allowed activities to be carefully planned and run in parallel. Team working methods are slowly gaining acceptance but many organizations are still resistant; in some cases, it results from prejudice or apparent loss of authority on the part of some senior staff, or often it is claimed there are not enough staff for people to be spared from their day-to-day work to form part of a dedicated team. In very small companies where the numbers of staff in each department are in single figures this can be a real obstacle but it is for the company to decide if it can afford not to have its products on the market at the earliest possible time. Where staff shortages are a real factor, subcontract designers and draughtsmen can always be brought in to supplement a dedicated team.

Types of production

The amount of design and development effort that is put into any product will depend on a number of factors but one will be the expected sales volume and the type of production that is envisaged. Obviously, there is more to be gained through extensive engineering aimed at low-cost production where the sales potential is vast and price competition is severe than there would be in a less competitive but low-volume market. In general, production processes can be divided into three categories, each with their own special characteristics:

1. *Flow Production (Production Line)*: this is repetitious manufacture on a specially built production facility. It is typical of the automobile and consumer durables industries. This type of production is characterized by:
   - A small number of different products on offer.
   - High output rates with long production runs.
   - A large investment in special tooling and equipment.
   - The production machinery laid out in the order of the production processes.
   - A large use of semi-skilled labour.
   - Short operation cycle times.
   - The effect of operator learning is very measurable.
   - Group incentive or measured daywork payment schemes.
2. *Batch Production*: in this case, items are made in discrete batches, there is repetitious work within each batch but at the end of a batch the machinery is reset for different work; it is typical of the aerospace industry and many general engineering companies. This type of production shows the following characteristics:
   - A larger range of products on offer or a large number of different components.
   - Lower output rates.
   - Some investment in special tooling for individual batches.
   - Many general-purpose machines.
   - Some machines may be arranged in the order of their use on products, while others may be grouped in cells offering a specific capability or function.
   - A mix of skilled and semi-skilled labour.
   - The effect of operator learning is less marked but still measurable.
   - A variety of payment schemes may be in use: piecework, daywork, group schemes, etc.
3. *Jobbing Production*: this is the manufacture of bespoke, one-off items or manufacture in very small batches on an infrequent basis; it is typically found in tool and die makers, specialist instrument makers, shipbuilders and many small engineering firms that offer of fast turnaround and a general machining capability. Its characteristics are:
   - A diversity of products made specially to individual customer orders.
   - Little or no investment in special-purpose machinery.
   - Mostly general-purpose machinery employed.
   - Machines grouped by function.
   - Many skilled operators employed.
   - Little opportunity for learning to apply.
   - Payment by daywork or sometimes piecework.

Batch working is a somewhat vague term: very large batch manufacture may have some of the characteristics of flow line work, whereas small batch work may be akin to jobbing. In many industries all three types of production can be found within the same organization; for example:

- Assembly of finished products may be done on a production line.
- Detail parts and sub-assemblies may be made in batch production machine shops, press shops and fitting shops.
- Special tooling may be made in a jobbing tool-room or prototypes made in an experimental shop.

Whichever type of production is envisaged, it will have a significant bearing on the amount invested in tools and machinery for the production phase.

Economic aspects of tooling

When any design is selected for production, a primary consideration will be selling price. Competitive market forces will ensure that price is uppermost in the mind of both the marketing executive and the production engineer. It should also be fundamental to the designer but a lack of understanding of the economics of production or its processes sometimes means that price is a secondary factor and performance, which is often more easily established in engineering terms, is the all-important goal. It then becomes the task of the production and tooling engineers to 'do for a quid what would cost anyone else a fiver'. Obviously, the earlier in the design process that production engineers can be brought into the design process, the more valuable will be their eventual contribution and much redesign between prototype and final production standard may be avoided.

In general, market prices are determined by competitive pressures rather than production costs and it is the case that some companies may feel such an overriding need to preserve a minimum presence in the market by offering a full range of competitively priced products that they are prepared to sell some lines at prices below their actual costs. Whereas selling below cost can never be advocated as a general policy (unless subsidies are involved) it can, in some instances, make sense when a total marketing concept is involved, particularly in penetrating a new field.

From value analysis or studies of competitor products, the production engineering department should have a precise guide to the target price breakdown of the whole product structure; this may not apply to every detail part, but it should be established for each major element. From marketing projections there should be a clear indication of the intended peak production rate, the period of run-up and the expected duration of the whole production programme. Without such data, it is not possible to make a detailed economic evaluation of alternative production methods and decide whether or not special production tooling should be acquired. However, there may be occasions, even if production quantities are low, when special jigs and fixtures may be essential simply to allow manufacture to proceed (e.g. the production of aircraft); in this case, economic considerations may rest on choices between alternative forms of tooling, whether to put in two parallel production lines or run one line night and day.

Calculation of break-even quantities for tooling

The cost of acquiring special equipment needs to be considered at an early stage in the production planning process. If long production runs are expected, special-to-purpose tooling or machinery should show a cost saving when compared to using standard machine tools. For establishing approximate quantities, the simple formula below can be used:

$$Q = \frac{C}{E - S} \qquad (9.1)$$

where: Q = the break-even quantity of items to be produced
   C = the cost of the special tooling or equipment
   E = the manufacturing cost of the product using existing equipment
   S = the projected cost of the item using special-to-purpose equipment.

Note that S does not include the cost of depreciation or capital recovery associated with the new equipment, the projected cost is thus made up of the basic labour cost plus the general factory overhead. At the break-even quantity the actual cost of making the item will equal the cost of the product using existing equipment; beyond that quantity the actual manufacturing cost will drop to the projected figure, S. Alternatively, the formula can be rearranged for establishing the tooling budget for making a part for a given basic price over an assumed production run, as given in expression (9.2):

$$C = Q \times (E - S) \qquad (9.2)$$

Example 9.1: Acquisition of a special machine, simple analysis

An item can be produced in 82 s by a standard, existing machine tool at a cost, excluding material, of £0.61; production studies have shown that a time of 25 s ought to be possible with special-to-purpose automated equipment. If the production run is estimated at a minimum of 400 000 units, the break-even price for the equipment can be calculated:

Assuming the general factory labour and overhead rates apply, the basic manufacturing cost per unit with the automated equipment is

$$\frac{0.61}{82} \times 0.25 = £0.1860$$

and the maximum cost of equipment is

$$400\,000 \times (0.61 - 0.1860) = £169\,600$$

The figure sets a maximum value for tooling based on the minimum production run providing the time per piece can be reduced to 25 s and no additional standard machinery has to be purchased. Any proposed equipment that either costs more than £169 600 or cannot meet the 25 s time should be examined on its merits as there still may be a saving when other factors also have a bearing on the issue. If the future shop load indicates that the existing machine capacity could be overloaded with the proposed new job, to the extent that more machines would have to be purchased, then a more productive special-to-purpose machine could be more economical in terms of floor space, operator time, capital costs, etc. In the above example, if a productive running time of

6.0 h per day, 225 days per year is assumed, then the special-to-purpose machine can make:

$$\frac{6 \times 60 \times 60 \times 225}{25} = 194\,400 \text{ items each year.}$$

If, for example, the 400 000 items were to be made over a four-year period: 50 000 in the first and last years and 150 000 in the second and third, then the machine would be run at three-quarters of its capacity over half of its working life but it would have plenty of spare capacity if greater output was needed. At 82 s per item the standard machine could make only:

$$\frac{6 \times 60 \times 60 \times 225}{82} = 59\,268 \text{ items Per year.}$$

If two standard machines are available but one is already committed to future work throughout the foreseeable future, it is clear that for an output of 150 000 items per year, either an extra new machine will have to be purchased and arrangements will have to be made for double shifting or two extra machines will be needed. The purchase of new machinery is likely to increase the general overhead rate, thus making the item produced on standard equipment more expensive. Shift premiums will also tend to push costs up and if two machines are purchased, more floor space will be needed. When the price of a special-to-purpose machine is received, a decision can be made.

The above example illustrates a situation where a choice exists between either a high expenditure and high productivity option or a lower expenditure and low productivity solution, either way money will have to be spent. Similar options can also exist with simple or complex fixtures that may be needed to adapt existing plant. Where such choices exist, the best solution may not be immediately obvious; where this occurs, a decision can be made by calculating the total annual cost for each option. This can be considered to be made up from the annual machine cost, the annual tool cost and the annual labour cost. Taking the terms individually:

$$\text{The annual machine cost} = \frac{M}{N} \times \frac{P \times R}{Y}$$

where: M = the total cost of the machine including installation;
N = the number of years allowed for machine depreciation;
P = the time per piece in hours;
R = the number of pieces to be made each year;
Y = the number of machine running hours per year on all work.

$$\text{The annual tool cost} = \frac{C}{B} + D$$

where: C = the initial cost of the tool;
B = the number of years allowed for tool depreciation;
D = the annual tool refurbishment cost.

$$\text{The annual direct labour cost} = P \times R \times W$$

where: W = the hourly wage rate.

Thus the total annual cost, A, is:

$$A = \frac{M}{N} \times \frac{P \times R}{Y} + \frac{C}{B} + D + (P \times R \times W)$$

Rearranging gives the simplified expression:

$$A = \frac{C}{B} + D + \left[P \times R\left(W + \frac{M}{N \times Y} \right) \right] \qquad (9.3)$$

If it is wished to include the fixed overheads associated with the machine based on the floor area it occupies, the expression for the annual machine cost can be expanded to:

$$\left[\frac{M}{N} + (F \times S) \right] \times \frac{P \times R}{Y}$$

where: S = the fixed cost per square meter per year;
F = the floor area occupied by the machine.

The final expression for the total annual cost then becomes:

$$A = \frac{C}{B} + D + \left[P \times R \times \left(W + \frac{M + (N \times S \times F)}{N \times Y} \right) \right] \qquad (9.4)$$

To see if a reduction in price really will come about if a special-purpose machine or a special tool is acquired, it will be necessary to calculate the total annual costs for both the existing and proposed methods.

Example 9.2: Acquisition of a special machine, total annual cost analysis

We shall continue the previous example by comparing the total annual costs of the standard machine with the special-to-purpose machine using the additional data provided in Table 9.1. In this case, the quoted price of a special machine is £135 000 and the price of a standard machine is £55 000; it is further assumed that a special fixture, costing £3500, will be needed for use with the standard machine.

Table 9.1 Comparative data on standard and special-to-purpose machines

Feature	Standard Machine	Special Machine
Cost of machine, M	£55 000	£135 000
Number of years for depreciation, N	10	4
Time per piece in hours, P	0.0228 (82 s)	0.0069 (25 s)
Machine running hours per year, Y	1350	1350
Number of pieces per year, R	59 268	194 400
Initial cost of tools, C	£3 500	0
Years for tool depreciation, B	4	0
Annual refurbishment cost, D	£1000	£1500
Wage rate plus variable overhead per hour, W	£16.00	£16.00
Cost per square meter per year, S	£300	£300
Floor area of machine (m^2), A	24	24

Considering the standard machine:

$$A = \frac{3500}{4} + 1000 + \left[0.0228 \times 59\,268 \times \left(16 + \frac{55\,000 + (10 \times 300 \times 24)}{10 \times 13\,50} \right) \right]$$

$$= £36\,208 \text{ per annum for } 59\,268 \text{ items.}$$

In order to make the comparison, the cost, A, will have to be brought to that necessary to make 150 000 units per year as that is the demanded peak output.

On the assumption that shift working is not employed, the total annual cost will be:

$$£36\,208 \times \frac{150\,000}{59\,286} = £91\,610$$

and the cost per unit will be:

$$\frac{£91\,610}{150\,000} = £0.61$$

Considering the special-to-purpose machine at an output rate of 150 000 units per year:

$$A = 0 + 1500 + \left[0.0069 \times 150\,000 \times \left(16 + \frac{135\,000 + (4 \times 300 \times 24)}{4 \times 1350} \right) \right]$$

$$= £49\,455$$

and the cost per unit is £0.33.

The case for choosing the special machine becomes very clear as the annual cost is substantially less than with the standard one and there is a cost benefit to the product. Two standard machines would need to be bought. Had the decision been taken to opt for double shifting the standard machines, only one would be needed and the total annual cost would be approximately half the £91 610 figure; in practice, it would be higher than half because of the effect of shift premiums on wages and generally lower overall availability usually results from double shifting as the machines are worked harder and cannot be maintained during the night without disrupting output. This would then bring the unit costs for the two options to an approximately similar figure, in this respect the standard machine benefits from the 10-year period allowed for depreciation on the assumption that it can be used for work other than just the product in question. However, it must be borne in mind that there may be little or no surplus capacity if increased output is required, whereas the special machine has ample capacity to double the output.

Decisions such as that outlined in the example have to be made regularly during the production planning phase, not all will require as rigorous a treatment as that shown as the tooling costs may be relatively small or the annual output rates relatively low and thus expensive fixtures can never be justified. However, where high outputs or large expenditures are necessary, a comparactive analysis of the type shown should be undertaken. In neither case were any discounting factors applied as it was assumed that the costs and profits would all arise in an identical period and thus would not affect the result.

The learning process

Human processes that need acquired skills are subject to reductions in the time taken to carry out the process the more often it is repeated. From personal experience few would disagree with this simple statement, and everyone can appreciate that practice is necessary in order to achieve a good performance. This improvement in performance is described as industrial learning as distinct from the intellectual process of acquiring pure knowledge. This distinction may be more one of convenience than reality as learning improvements have been noticed on the part of whole organizations as well as individuals, and in this situation the acquisition of pure knowledge must have played some part.

During the early years of this century, it was believed that after a suitable period of practice manufacturing operatives would reach a time for each operation that was an absolute minimum. By the 1930s, however, observations made on long production runs indicated that there might be no lower limit as very small time reductions were still being noticed after very many repetitions. The rate at which learning takes place also came into foucs when it was observed by manufacturers of aircraft in Germany during the First World War that each time the number of airframes built was doubled, the time to produce one went down by 15%. Work done by industrial and production engineers in the aircraft industry in the 1930s and during the Second World War confirmed this result and gave more substance to the understanding of industrial learning.

Learning curves

Learning curves have been developed as an empirical, mathematical attempt to describe the rate at which improvements in performance occur but their effect is neither simple nor straightforward. As individuals vary greatly in their abilities, any formula must always be treated as both a generalization and an approximation. Observations made on individual operatives show that improvements in performance tend to follow the pattern shown in Figure 9.2. When first introduced to a job, there may be an initial stage of discouragement when getting to understand the job may appear difficult. After a small amount of practice, confidence and ability grow rapidly and there is a steep rise in output performance. However, this rise may not be maintained and there may be a period of consolidation during which no improvements are made, this pause in learning is termed a '**plateau**'. This will not last as, after some time, a further improvement will be made but with a smaller increment than the initial one. After this, there will be more plateaux and further improvements, each one smaller than the previous.

In industrial applications, a knowledge of the effect of learning is important for establishing:

(a) labour costs of individual batches of work in a long run;
(b) the optimum labour force for a production run;

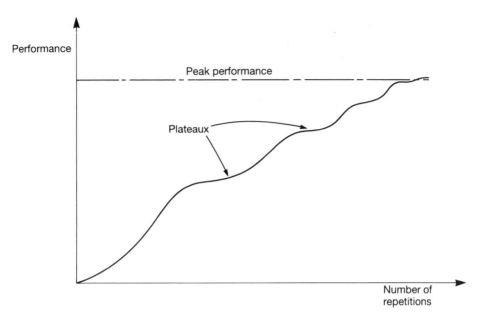

Performance

Peak performance

Plateaux

Number of repetitions

Figure 9.2 The learning process.

(c) the likely output build-up rate;
(d) the period required for training.

The mathematically expressed learning curve is used for convenience but it ignores the plateaux which are a somewhat unpredictable effect. A number of formulae have been devised to describe the learning effect and they fall into two broad categories: those that predict the rate at which the time to perform a task decreases, and those that describe the number of repetitions needed to come up to a given level of performance. These are respectively termed 'linear unit' and 'time-constant' types, and of the two, the linear unit curve is probably the more commonly used.

Linear unit learning curves

With the **linear unit** method, the time taken to perform any individual operation in a repeated sequence is given by:

$$T = FN^a \tag{9.5}$$

where: T = the time for the particular item;
F = the time for the first item made;
N = the cumulative number of items made, (number of repetitions);
a = an exponent that defines the rate of learning.

This expression is most commonly handled as its logarithmic transform:

$$\log_e T = \log_e F + (a \times \log_e N) \tag{9.6}$$

In this form it can be used simply on log/log graph paper as it produces a straight-

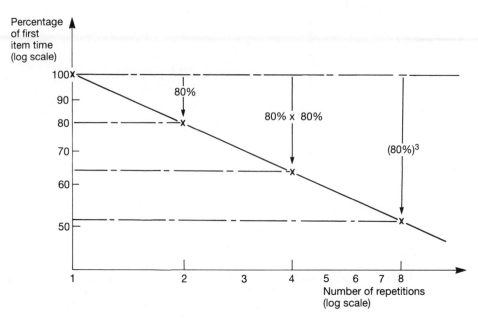

Figure 9.3   Construction of an 80% learing curve on log/log paper.

line graph. The exponent, a, is the slope of the straight line; it takes a negative value, thus generating a decreasing value of T.

The slope of the curve is normally expressed as a percentage value less than 100 or as a factor less than one, and it defines the rate at which the time for each repetition decays. Plotting the curve on logarithmic scales is shown in Figure. 9.3.

It will be seen that the learning curve drawn in Figure 9.3 exhibits the property that each time the number of repetitions is doubled, the time for the operation is reduced by a constant factor; as was observed by the German aircraft makers. In this example, the second item takes 80% of the time of the first one, the fourth item takes 80% of the time for the second and the eighth unit 80% of the time for the fourth, etc. This is an example of an **80% learning curve** and the basic relationship holds true for all percentage values less than 100. Despite its simplicity, it is not always the most convenient way in which to use the curve, particularly when it is reguired to estimate the time to complete a series of items or to estimate the learning rate from actual data. For this situation, it is more useful to express the curve in its cumulative average form. This is given by the expression:

$$C = \frac{\sum_{0}^{N} T}{N} \tag{9.7}$$

where: C = the Cumulative Average Operator Time over the run of N repetitions.

This can be expressed analytically as:

$$C = \frac{\int_{0}^{N} F N^{a} \, dN}{N}$$

which yields:

$$C = \frac{FN^a}{a + 1} \tag{9.8}$$

As the learning curve is an integer function, the analytically derived expression, which assumes a continuous variable, tends to overestimate the result, particularly over the first few repetitions. However, this error reduces to become negligible as the total increases to 2000 and beyond. The cumulative average curve does not plot as a straight line on logarithmic scales; a set of linear unit curves and their resulting cumulative average curves is given in Figures 9.4 and 9.5. They have been plotted on a log/linear scale as this is easier to read than a log/log plot. Learning calculations can be done directly from expressions (9.5) and (9.8), but using the curves may be more accurate particularly with the cumulative average values; the exponent a can be calculated from the learning factor value by the expression:

$$a = \frac{\log_e(LF)}{0.693145} \tag{9.9}$$

An 80% learning curve has a learning factor of 0.8, thus:

$$a = \frac{\log_e 0.8}{0.693145} = \frac{-0.2231}{0.693145} = -0.3219$$

The time-constant learning curve

This learning model relates the reduction in operator time to the amount of time spent in repeating the process by looking at the improvements in output rate over time. The **time-constant learning curve** is given by the expression:

$$R_t = R_c + (R_m - R_c)(1 - e^{-t/k}) \tag{9.10}$$

where: R_t = the output rate at any time;
   R_c = the output rate at start-up;
   R_m = the maximum ouptut rate;
   t = the time from start-up;
   k = a time-constant that describes the rate of improvement.

This model is particularly suitable for short, repetitive production process in continuous flow industries and is less applicable to industries where the unit of production is very large such as one aircraft. It also allows for the fact that there may be a maximum production rate that cannot be exceeded and is definable at the outset; this is often the case as there are many occasions where a production process contains some incompressible fixed-cycle elements. The weakness of the linear unit curve in its simplest form is that it does not allow for these incompressible elements.

Figure 9.6 shows a plot of the rate of output growth based on an initial ouptut rate of 5 units per day rising to a peak of 25 per day; the time-constant has a value of 9.3. It will be seen that it shows a shallow curve that approaches the peak output at an ever decreasing rate. The number of units output up to any time, t, is given by:

$$\int_0^t R_t \, dt = [R_c t + (R_m - R_c)(t + ke^{-t/k})]_0^t \tag{9.11}$$

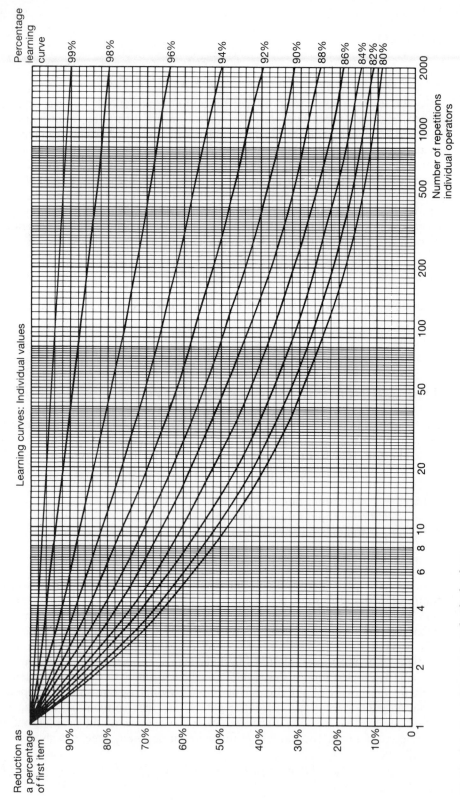

Figure 9.4 Learning curves: individual values.

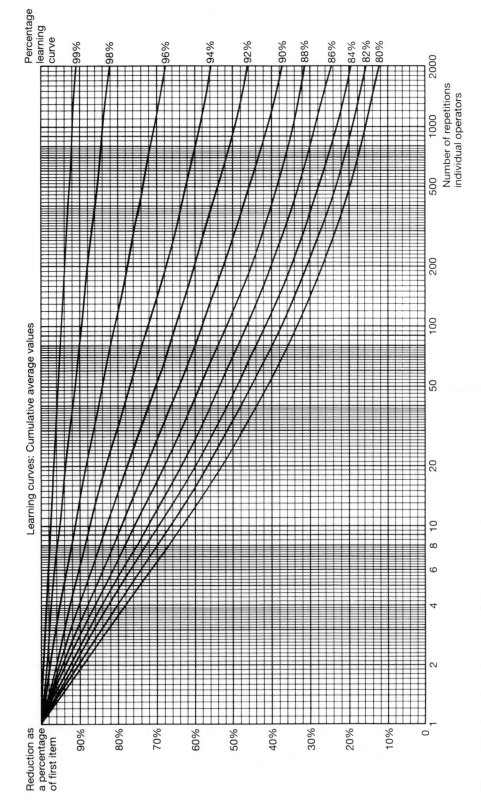

Figure 9.5 Learning curves: cumulative average values.

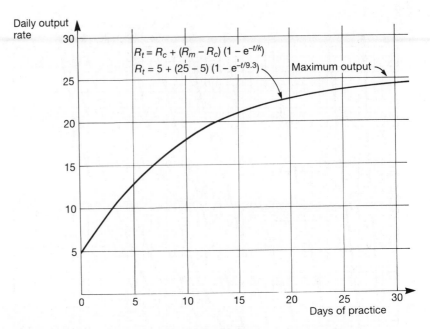

Figure 9.6 Example of a time-constant learning curve.

Note that this integral is given between limits; when evaluating it, one must re-member to calculate the value at time t = zero.

The practical application of learning curves

Different types of work and the conditions under which it is done attract different rates of learning. Obviously, reductions in time due to learning can only take place on those operations that are entirely under human control. Operations under machine control may have fixed-cycle times and learning cannot apply there; thus basic job design including the degree of automation can have a bearing on the rate of time reduction. It is therefore important to separate out any fixed elements when considering a particular operation and the likely reductions in time. Typical learning rates are given below:

(a) Fabrication and mechanical fitting have learning reductions in the region of 80% to 92%.
(b) Light manual assembly (typically female assembly work) has learning reductions in the region of 90% to 96%.
    There are several reasons for the learning appearing slower than fabrication:
    – job and tool design for high output may reduce the scope for learning;
    – the work is sometimes done in batches with gaps in between while other work is done;
    – training periods are often given to new operators on a separate facility, hence all subsequent learning appears slower.
(c) Machine shop work is likely to produce learning reductions of 95% to 99% as

there are often fixed-cycle elements where learning is not possible and in a batch working environment there is no guarantee that subsequent batches will go to the same operator.

The conditions under which the work is done will also have an effect on the rate of learning; factors which could affect things are:

- Payment by incentive schemes: this tends to accelerate learning.
- Restrictive practices: this may decelerate learning.
- Basic level of operator skill: less skilled staff may show higher rates of learning, although from a longer unit time for the first item.
- Number of modifications introduced: many modifications will interrupt and reduce learning.
- Degree of labour turnover: if turnover is excessive, the benefits of learning will be reduced.

Use of the learning curve

The application and use of learning curves is a subject that is frequently misunderstood but a full appreciation is essential for success. If the Project Manager is required to make use of learning theory in formulating the production strategy or estimating the production cost, then it is as well to be acquainted with the method and its application. The first problem likely to be faced is what rate of learning to use and here the first source of information is likely to be historic production records. If these are available from the Production Control or Estimating departments and show accurate times taken on the production of similar items in the past, then a simple analysis should indicate an appropriate rate of learning.

Case example 9.1: Time reductions for fabricated aircraft panels

The data in Table 9.2 shows the times taken to build the first 20 aircraft structural panels; these were fabricated items made with a single jig. This data can be used in conjunction with a set of learning curves to determine the observed rate of learning.

Columns 1 and 2 show the raw data, while column 3 shows each successive time taken as a reduction from the time for the first item made. This data can be plotted directly onto the linear unit curves and it will be seen in Figure 9.7 that the data shows considerable scatter; this is typical. It does, however, reveal a clear decreasing trend that is tending towards a value of 88%. Much of the scatter can be removed by taking the cumulative average reductions; this method is to be recommended and the values are calculated in the three right-hand columns. When plotted onto a set of cumulative average curves as shown in Figure 9.8, it reveals much more clearly that the underlying rate of learning is tending towards 89%. In estimating future work of a similar nature done under similar conditions, this figure could be used with some confidence.

Table 9.2 Assembly times for the first 20 aircraft panels

Panel no. n	Recorded time T	Reduction as a factor of 1st time T_n/T_1	Cum. time (h) T_n	Cum. average time $T_n/N = C_n$	Cum. average reduction from 1st C_n/T_1
1	90	1.000	90	90	1.000
2	89	0.989	179	89.5	0.989
3	81	0.900	260	86.66	0.963
4	80	0.888	340	85.00	0.944
5	75	0.833	415	83.00	0.922
6	70	0.777	485	80.83	0.898
7	69	0.766	554	79.14	0.879
8	72	0.800	625	78.13	0.868
9	65	0.722	691	76.77	0.853
10	50	0.555	741	74.10	0.823
11	53	0.588	794	72.18	0.802
12	50	0.555	844	70.33	0.781
13	55	0.611	899	69.15	0.768
14	59	0.655	958	68.42	0.760
15	51	0.566	1009	67.26	0.747
16	54	0.600	1063	66.44	0.738
17	53	0.588	1116	65.64	0.729
18	50	0.555	1166	64.78	0.722
19	54	0.600	1220	64.21	0.713
20	51	0.567	1271	63.55	0.706

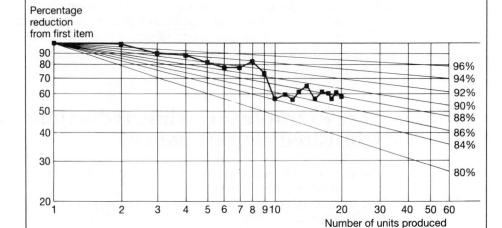

Figure 9.7 Data plotted on unit learning curves on a log/log scale.

The example above shows the importance of the time for the first item produced as it is the starting-point from which all subsequent times are derived. Estimators are not, however, always used to thinking in terms of first item times; they tend to think of standard times and these assume a motivated operator who has learned the job fully. This is something of a contradiction as it is fundamental to learning theory that reductions in time are always possible and learning never ceases. For practical purposes, however, jobs do have to be considered as fully learned and for convenience various definitions have been

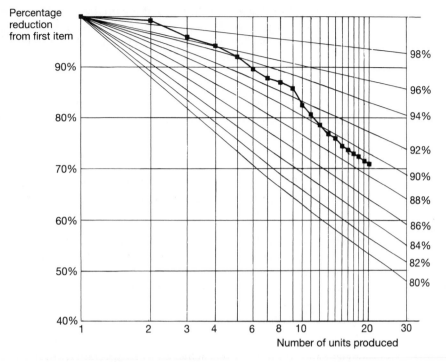

Figure 9.8 Data plotted as cumulative average values on a log/natural scale.

tried – e.g. when the month-on-month decrease in time is less than 1%, learning can be considered complete. Without previous production records, there is no simple answer to predicting the learning period; it is easy to be optimistic, many Project Managers are disappointed by the length of time it takes to run up a new production line to its full rate.

Example 9.3: Batch costs for vehicle chassis

A production order for 200 vehicle chassis has been negotiated as a two-stage contract consisting of an initial order for 40 followed directly by a batch of 160; separate tender prices are required for the two batches. There is a large manual labour content in assembling the chassis, and the question is how many labour hours should be allowed for each batch if time reductions due to learning are considered significant?

Previous production records indicate that the estimator's standard time tends to be achieved by the 50th unit and a 90% learning rate is normally observed. In this case, the standard time is 50h per unit. The curves given in Figures 9.4 and 9.5 can be used to generate the estimates by the following method. The time for the first unit is found by establishing the reduction factor for the 50th item on the individual unit curve for a 90% reduction. By inspection, this is found to be 55%; the time for the first item is found by dividing the standard time by 0.55 to give 90.91 h. Using the cumulative average curves the reduction factor for the first 40 items on the 90% curve is 66.0%. The average time per unit over the first 40 items is found by multiplying the times for the first item by 0.66 and it is 60.0 h; the total time for the first 40 units is thus:

$$40 \times 60.0 = 2400\,h$$

For the remaining 160 units, the average over the whole 200 must be found from the curves and the cumulative average reduction over 200 is 53%. The whole batch of 200 will take:

$$200 \times 90.91 \times 0.53 = 9636\,h$$

and the time taken for the final 160 units will be:

$$9636 - 2400 = 7236\,h$$

These figures can then be used for pricing the labour content on the assumption, to be stated in the contract, that the second batch follows directly from the first. Should a significant gap occur between the two batches, it can be assumed that there will be some loss of learning and this can be reflected in a clause that allows for the tendering of a new price in the event of a customer-induced delay.

In the above examples, learning was taken on the basis of individual operators or single teams. If production is achieved using several identical production lines run in parallel or by a day- and night-shift, the rate of time reduction against total output will appear slower. This is because it is the individual operators that do the learning and it is the number of repetitions that each individual performs that produces the time reductions. Operators on the night-shift cannot learn from the work done on the day-shift, nor can operators on one production line gain repetitive experience from others on a line running in parallel. When two shifts or several lines are employed, the base of the learning curve must be adjusted to predict the overall rate of learning.

Example 9.4: Learning rates with two shifts

With the vehicle chassis order, it is decided that to meet the delivery schedule it will be necessary to run both a night- and a day-shift from the very beginning; we wish to know what the reductions at the 40th and 200th units will be and what effect double shifting will have on the expected rate of learning.

With the single-shift case the learning rate to be expected is 90%, but with double shifting the base of the learning curve must be reduced by a factor of two. The learning achieved by the 40th unit will be that expected at the 20th unit on the individual curve, this is 63% of the first item time. The time taken at the 200th will be that for the 100th and a 43% reduction. It will be seen that double shifting has reduced the overall learning rate to close to 91.5%. Although this reduction may seem small, its effect can become large over a long production run; had a factor of 91.5% been used in the previous example, the total time for the 200 bodies would have been:

$$200 \times 90.91 \times 0.59 = 10\,727\,\text{h}$$

This is over 1000 h more and would have a significant effect on the tender price, which would tend to be made even higher by the effect of shift premiums.

Cost reductions attributable to learning

The reduction in unit manufacturing times has important implications for unit costs and it is the expectation of cost reduction that is often taken into account in justifying projects well before detailed consideration is given to unit production times. The price structure and estimated level of profitability may be based on a minimum assumed production run and cost reductions due to learning will be anticipated in order to achieve the target manufacturing cost. The learning curve can be used for estimating reductions in unit cost, but two factors must be borne in mind:

1. the element of the manufacturing time which is governed by fixed-cycle working and thus not subject to learning;
2. the uplift in real wage costs if operators are subject to an output-related incentive scheme.

Both factors tend to reduce the rate of cost reduction compared to a simple learning situation where the observed rate of learning is applied to the total direct operator time.

Example 9.5: Cost reductions where an incentive scheme is in operation

An operator is paid under a bonus scheme which provides a basic hourly rate of £5.00 per hour and a piecework element of £0.40 per piece produced. The job has been timed at 6 min of fixed-cycle working and, when fully learned, a standard time of 4 min under operator control. An 86% learning curve is typical for the job under consideration and it is considered to be fully learned when the 500th item is made. The problem is to find the rate of cost reduction and the uplift to be applied to the 86% figure.

From the individual unit learning curves the reduction factor for the 500th item is 0.258, hence the uplift on the labour time for the 500th item is a factor of $1/0.258 = 3.876$; thus the estimated time for the first item is:

$$4 \times 3.876 = 15.50\,\text{min}$$

The total time for the first piece is $6 + 15.50 = 21.50\,\text{min}$

This is equivalent to an output rate of $\dfrac{60}{21.5} = 2.79$ items per hour

At the start, the operator's hourly earnings are:

$$£5.00 + £(2.79 \times 0.40) = £6.12$$

The earnings per piece are:

$$\frac{£6.12}{2.79} = £2.19$$

The fixed-cycle element is worth:

$$\frac{6 \times £6.12}{60} = £0.61$$

The price per piece for operator controlled time is:

$$£2.19 - £0.61 = £1.58.$$

The operator earns £5.00 per hour plus the piecework bonus; at the peak rate, six pieces can be made; this is worth £2.40 making total hourly earnings of £7.40.

The earnings per piece are:

$$\frac{£7.40}{6} = £1.23$$

The fixed-cycle element is worth:

$$\frac{6 \times £7.40}{60} = £0.74 \text{ per piece}$$

and the price per piece for operator controlled time is:

$$£1.23 - £0.74 = £0.49$$

The reduction factor from the first to the 500th item is:

$$\frac{0.49}{1.58} = 0.31.$$

Inspection of the learning curves shows this to be equivalent to an 88% learning curve. To obtain the rate of cost decay for the element of the job time that is subject to learning a figure of 2% must be added to the learning rate to compensate for the effect of wage growth under this incentive scheme. Due to the fixed-cycle element, the overall reduction in cost per piece is much less as no reduction is possible on the greater part of the job time. The price per piece for the first item is £2.19 and for the 500th item it is £1.23; this gives a reduction factor of 0.56 which equates to a 94% cost reduction curve.

For any real situation, to obtain the cost reduction curve a calculation similar to that shown in the example, above, must be done using the actual payment system in use; there is no quick or rule-of-thumb method. Under pure piecework, with no bonus or guaranteed minimum, there would be no cost reductions per piece as the cost is fixed although some benefit will be derived from reduced overheads per piece as output goes up (this may not be immediately obvious under some accounting systems). With pure day-work the cost reduction for operator controlled time should equal the learning rate. However, under this condition there may be less time and cost reduction than there would be if an incentive scheme is applied.

At the project estimating stage, it is neither necessary nor practical to know the product in all its detailed elements, but the basic breakdown into items likely to be machine made and those parts largely made by operator controlled effort should be established if an accurate estimate is to be made of cost reduction as output proceeds.

The rate of production progress

The production programme during the first year or the 'learning period' will normally be a compromise between the desire to increase output as quickly as possible and the rate at which labour can be absorbed onto the production line. In achieving this balance advantage can be taken of the learning curve, in particular the time-constant method. The learning curve drawn on the basis of output per unit time is recognized by industry for its usefulness, particularly when the horizontal axis is drawn on a basis of elapsed time rather than number output. It has important properties which need to be considered when setting out the plan for the start-up phase of production. Where operators are taken on progressively during start-up, an idealized profile for the growth in output is as shown in Figure 9.9.

This curve, with a shallow 'S' shape, is found to be a good fit with the growth in output actually achieved, even when the labour is not taken on in the idealized way shown. The reason behind this statement is that as new production facilities are commissioned and production lines are run up to their peak rate there is also learning on the part of the shop management, maintenance engineers, production engineers and their learning also contributes to and influences the rate of output growth. Idealized output curves and their equivalent labour curves are shown in Figure 9.10.

The figure shows that the profiles in (a) and (b) are ideal and the choice may depend on confidence in the plant and tooling, the speed at which labour can be taken on and trained, confidence in subcontractor's ability to supply and the planned time to achieve the peak output. A growth curve that accelerates towards the peak, as shown in (c), may be more difficult to achieve, yet management often expect that output will increase in the way shown. This is to ignore the true nature of learning

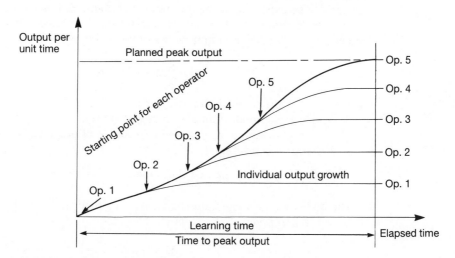

Figure 9.9 Growth in output as operators are progressively started.

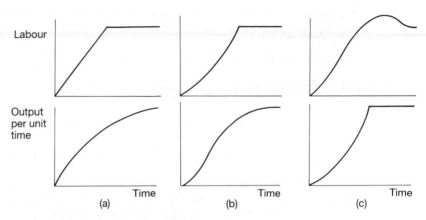

Figure 9.10   Labour growth curves for various output curves.

as the better one gets, the more difficult it is to make improvements. Unless additional operators can be made available to meet the 'hump' in the labour curve, excessive overtime is worked or subcontract staff are used, the desired output will not be met and the resulting curve will tend towards that shown in (b). Of course there are occasions when output does accelerate without additional labour but this is often due to an outside effect that has artificially held output growth down such as when a troublesome piece of equipment is finally made to work properly or when the intermittent supply of good-quality parts from a subcontractor turns into a steady, reliable supply.

The measurement of production progress

Studies conducted during and after the Second World War on the output growth on aircraft production lines led to the formulation of a general law that describes the progress to be expected during the start-up period. This has subsequently been found to fit a wide range of industrial manufacturing situations, often far removed from aircraft work. The law is simply stated in the formula:

$$\sum_{i=1}^{n} t_i + C = t_1 n^m \tag{9.12}$$

where: t_1 = the time for the first item;
n = the total number of items produced;
m = an exponent that defines the rate of progress;
C = a constant;
$\sum_{i=1}^{n} t_i$ = the total elapsed time from t_1 to the nth item.

The terms t and n are interchangeable, in that either could represent time or quantity. When reversed the equation becomes:

$$\sum_{i=1}^{t} n_i + C = n_1 t^m \tag{9.13}$$

In this case, n_1 is the number of items output from the first unit time, and m is a different exponent from that in equation (9.12).

The constant, C, normally has a value of zero and when this is the case expression (9.12) becomes:

$$\sum_{i=1}^{n} t_i = t_1 n^m \tag{9.14}$$

The cumulative average cycle time, t_a, to any item is:

$$\frac{\sum_{i=1}^{n} t_i}{n}$$

and from expression (9.13) we have:

$$t_a = t_1 n^{m-1} \tag{9.15}$$

Both equations (9.14) and (9.15) yield a straight line when plotted on log/log paper. In practice, real data does not always produce a convenient straight line, but this can be generated for forecasting purposes by the addition of the constant, C, as in equations (9.12) and (9.13). This property makes the model both accurate and simple to use. It might seem unlikely that such a simple law should be applicable to many and varying manufacturing industries but measurements in a number of industries have shown this to be the case; furthermore, it has been shown to describe the progress that individual operators make when learning new skills, as well as the progress of whole organizations. The similarity that exists between the progress functions detailed above and the learning curve functions indicates that these functions are directly related and probably fundamental. An understanding of the characteristics of the start-up phase of a production programme as expressed by equations (9.12)–(9.15) is essential for planning and control purposes, and for convenience a graphical treatment will be used.

Equation (9.12) can be transformed to:

$$\log_e(t + C) = \log_e t_1 + (m \times \log_e n)$$

and is represented graphically on log/log scales in Figure 9.11; it is important that the scales are of equal pitch on both axes.

Figure 9.11 shows a construction that will allow the prediction of the point at which the planned peak output rate will be achieved and the number of items that will be produced by that time. To obtain this points are plotted of the cumulative output against elapsed time as shown and a straight line drawn through them. Next a point on the output axis which equals the planned peak is marked. It is now necessary to construct a line at 45° from the cumulative output axis but set back from the peak output point by an amount equal to the actual dimension on the graph from the origin (output = 1) to the value of the tangent of the angle that the observed output line makes with the vertical axis. Transferring this dimension and drawing the line will show an intersection point with the observed output line; this point marks the time at which the planned peak output will be reached and the number of items made at that time. Beyond that point, further improvements may take place to reach a new peak, provided that the production programme allows it and restrictive practices are not applied.

Occasionally when the cumulative output vs time data are plotted on log/log paper, the points will not lie on a straight line but form a curve. For forecasting

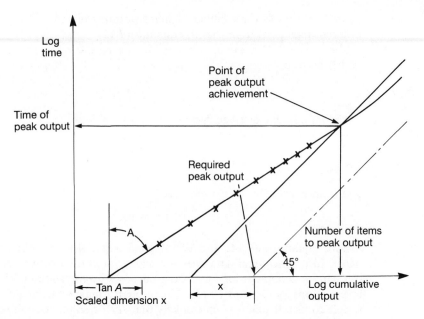

Figure 9.11 Construction of a progress function forecast of the point at which the planned peak output rate will be achieved.

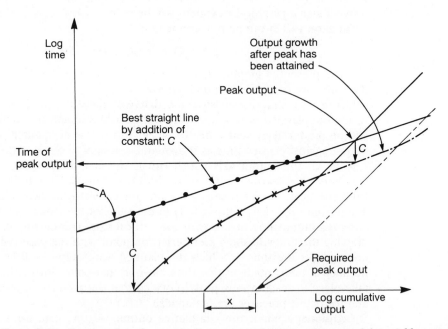

Figure 9.12 Construction of a straight-line progress function when actual data yields a curve.

purposes, a straight line is needed and this can be generated by giving the constant, C, in equation (9.12) a positive value and adding it to the time element: this is shown in Figure 9.12. Trial and error will have to be used, changing C in small increments, to find a straight line. Once a satisfactory line has been obtained, the same construction as before can be used to predict the point of achievement of the peak output, but it must be remembered to subtract the value of C to find the correct time.

Example 9.6: The build up of production output

The output target for a new production line is given in Table 9.3 and the line was planned to produce 100 units per week by the tenth week from start-up. The actual results for the first eight weeks have been recorded; management wish to know if the planned target will be reached by the tenth week and if not what will be the lost production by the time the planned peak is reached.

The actual data is plotted in Figure 9.13 and it will be seen that a straight line cannot be drawn through the resulting points. In this case, the constant C is not zero; to make a forecast a straight line must be generated by successive trials of values for C, and here a straight line results when C is set at two weeks. The angle formed by this line and the vertical is 66° and its tangent is 2.264. The planned peak of 100 units per week is marked in and the dimension from 1 to 2.264 is transferred to give the starting-point for the achievement line. The

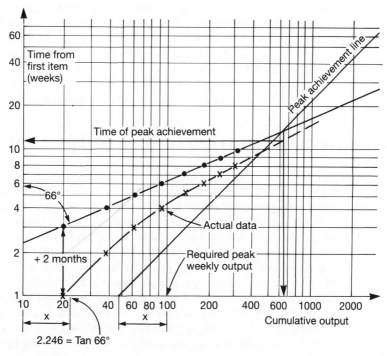

Figure 9.13 Prediction of point of peak achievement from first eight weeks' performance.

intersection occurs at an output figure of 650 units and projecting down by two weeks gives the time of achievement as the week 12. The target number of items to be made by week 12 is 750 but as the output is likely to be 650, the lost production will be 100 units.

Table 9.3 Planned and actual output levels during the start-up of a new production line

Week no.	Planned output	Cumulative planned output	Actual output	Cumulative actual output
1	15	15	20	20
2	20	35	18	38
3	25	60	24	62
4	40	100	33	95
5	50	150	39	134
6	60	210	46	180
7	70	280	62	242
8	80	360	60	302
9	90	450		
10	100	550		
11	100	650		
12, etc.	100	750		

In practice, adjustment may have to be made to the model where lost capacity or equipment failure has distorted the basic pattern of progress. Besides electrical and mechanical work, the progress function has been found to apply to the start-up period for process plants. It cannot be used where production, even in great numbers, is done in large, discrete batches separated in time; output under those circumstances may be dictated more by capacity and scheduling constraints. It may also prove difficult to use in cases where management take extraordinary action to force up the output rate; the sudden introduction of a second shift can distort the progress curve, so that forecasting becomes awkward.

Management responses to low output rates

Example 9.6 illustrates the use of a simple model for predicting the point at which learning will be complete, at least as far as the planned maximum in concerned. Of particular significance would be a forecast that showed the point of peak achievement well past the planned target or even lying beyond the duration of the production run. Either case could be serious in terms of the sales forecast, effect on market share and the price of each item through non-recovery of fixed overheads due to reduced output in the year. The early warning given by this method is one of the principal uses and these signals should not be ignored. There is normally something that can be done to improve matters and prompt attention to the situation will be needed. Initially, all reasons for low performance should be established, whether it is tooling and equipment problems, lack of component parts or human factors.

Difficulties with tooling and equipment can be among the most insidious as they can have an effect on operator morale, as well as the loss of output that they cause in their own right. Where operators are paid through an incentive scheme, inability to earn the expected bonus causes frustration and can also lead to a loss in operator learning as the group of workers may subconsciously set a 'shop norm' for themselves at less than their potential peak capacity. In this case, learning is effectively curtailed, and even when the troublesome equipment is cured, output may not rise in the way hoped for. Options open to management in the case of equipment problems (besides the obvious one of getting it fixed) lie in (a) providing quick-reaction, on-the-spot maintenance, (b) providing a duplicate item if one can be obtained quickly or even (c) installing a new and different piece of equipment. A further option may be to run a second shift with the equipment thus doubling its effective output albeit in a costly way; however, the cost of this action may be considerably less than the costs due to lost production from a complete assembly line. The choice among these options will depend on how appropriate each is to the situation; with special-to-purpose machinery or expensive capital plant, there may be little alternative to improved maintenance and an adequate stock of spare parts. Where equipment suppliers are at fault, then they should be required to send a working party to rectify any demonstrable shortcomings in performance or compensation may be sought. In the latter case, where possible, equipment purchasers should include clauses in the purchase contract that specify performance guarantees or liquidated damages for poor performance. Occasionally, rather than any equipment malfunction, the processes themselves exhibit poor consistency leading to higher than expected reject levels. These are among the most awkward problems and a satisfactory solution may only come from experimentation with the process to determine what parameters or settings have the most critical bearing on the output quality; Taguchi methods may prove useful here. Once these have been discovered, a change of operating procedures must be implemented immediately.

Component supplies, if they do not meet the planned input rate, can clearly affect the final output rate. It is always wise to ensure that a good stock of component parts exists before production begins and, to this effect, ordering lead-times for the first few batches of parts should be extended over that which may be normal for steady state output. Once confidence in the supply of parts is gained, the 'just-in-time' philosophy can be applied but not before. Where subcontractors are responsible for supplying parts, logarithmic plots, as shown, can be used for assessing their performance. Taking on additional subcontractors is an obvious solution although there may be extra costs to be borne by the purchaser, particularly if the new subcontractors need to procure their own sets of tools.

Even where equipment is functional and supplies of parts are satisfactory, human problems can still arise. Poorly designed equipment or tooling, lack of proper training and supervision, lack of cooperation or misunderstandings with trade unions can all lead to poor operator performance and restrictive practices. If human factors appear to be the problem, their causes should be established as soon as possible. Low performance due to poor working practices or low motivation should not be allowed to become the norm, good management to worker communication is essential. When operators have genuine complaints or suggestions for improvements, they should be investigated immediately, so that bottlenecks can be cleared and efficient working established.

To summarize, actions that management should consider at both the planning and implementation stages are:

• Ensure good management to employee communications exist from the very beginning. The introduction of a new product means change; new skills and working practices will have to be learned and this will cause anxiety for some. As soon as plans are formulated, trade unions or employee representatives should be informed, for not only does it foster a sense of belonging to a team with a common purpose, but the workers often have something to say that could be beneficial if incorporated at the planning stage.

- Where operator controlled tooling or equipment is used, ensure that proper attention is paid to the ergonomics at the design stage – waiting until it is put into operation to discover that it is tiring or awkward to use helps no one.
- Ensure that working conditions are appropriate with adequate space, lighting and suitable temperature and humidity controls.
- Where new skills are needed, a programme for training should be instituted. The performance of individuals can be monitored using logarithmic plots, it soon becomes clear which personnel are likely to achieve a satisfactory performance and those which will find it more difficult. For those with difficulties, careful supervision and extra or remedial training should be applied; it may also become obvious that one or two trainees are unlikely to meet the required target, and once identified, they should be re-deployed before they have a chance to affect the performance of the whole team.
- Introducing incentive schemes can also have a beneficial effect on output. Schemes can be related to the individual but over the past 25 years it has become increasingly popular to recognize the benefits of the team working approach, hence the development of group incentive schemes. The chosen scheme does need some consideration, it should provide a sufficient proportion of the weekly pay to make a worthwhile incentive while not forming so large a percentage of the employee's wage that bonus earnings become a major issue and source of trouble in themselves.

It is possible that the required output cannot be achieved because the original estimates were too optimistic. Those elements of the job which cannot be done in the allotted time must be identified; increasing the size of the operator team may be the quickest solution to bottleneck areas. If the problem is really severe, then the addition of a second shift may be the only solution. Should this be necessary, the whole costing of the job may be in error as the labour element is greater than planned. The option to employ a second shift needs to be examined for its effect on costs and profits, but if the market demands it, it may have to be taken.

Production readiness

Before making the decision to commit large sums of money to the start of the production phase, a readiness review may be carried out. In some cases, particularly defence programmes in the USA where government money is concerned, the review is a contractual requirement and representatives of the customer will be present. Where such formal requirements are not mandatory, such as on private venture commercial projects, the extent to which a thorough assessment is made of the design and production situation varies greatly from company to company. In some firms, once the budget for the whole development and production programme is approved, production activities may start in a piecemeal fashion as drawings are released. Where the sums of investment money for each product are relatively small, production runs are short or subject to frequent model changes, this approach can be effective, provided that good project and production management controls are applied. However, some products demand a much greater investment in money and effort in order to achieve both a satisfactory output rate and a product that is acceptable in terms of functionality and cost. Where these conditions apply, a readiness review is worthwhile, for it can expose risks that may lie unnoticed. The best way to handle risks is to recognize them for what they are and deal with them before they have a chance to pose a threat to the programme.

The timing of the readiness review will depend on a number of factors, including: the anticipated degree of overlap between the development and production programmes, the timing of design reviews and the lead-times for major plant, tools or materials. All these conditions must be considered by the Project Manager when deciding on the appropriate time for the review: too early and there may be insufficient data from the development programme to make meaningful decisions, too late and the start of the acquisition of long-lead tools may be delayed and thus hold up the start of production. The readiness review may be timed to coincide with, or follow shortly after, the final design review and the composition of the review panel is similar. However, the aims of a production readiness review are somewhat different to the design review. In general, design reviews deal with functionality and performance and serve as a check that all the proper procedures associated with good design practice have been observed. A production readiness review aims to look at the total state of the project in terms of its fitness to proceed to the next stage and its significance lies in the amount of financial commitment that the production stage implies.

Because of the financial implications of the decision to proceed with production, the composition of the readiness review panel may be of a higher level than is the case for a design review; ideally panel members should be directors or departmental heads. There is no need for an independent assessor as it is not the aim to check on the rightness of what has been done, but to make decisions as to how to proceed in the future. Representatives from the following departments should be present:

- Design and Engineering
- Manufacturing and Production Engineering
- Production Planning and Control
- Purchasing
- Trials and Testing
- Quality Assurance
- Personnel
- Finance.

The basis of the review is a checklist designed to cover all the areas of design, production, costing, testing and quality assurance where risks may lie. It will be for the review panel to assure themselves that sufficient progress has been made in all areas and that the risks that remain are reasonable and do not contain the seeds of major problems. A review checklist is given in Figure 9.14; individual companies will find it useful to devise checklists of their own reflecting the particular features of their organization and products.

Prior to the review meeting, a review working team should be set up; this should be led by a senior production engineer, who should be able to call on the services of nominated staff from all relevant departments. They will be required to assist him in answering all the questions that appear on the checklist. The team of nominated individuals should be set up about a month before the meeting date and, under the direction of the leader, each should be given responsibility for dealing with questions specific to their department. Where questions cannot be answered with a simple,

AW	PRODUCTION READINESS CHECKLIST		Sheet 1 of 2
PROJECT TITLE:		Ref:	Date:
SUBJECT		YES/NO	REMARKS REF:

1 DESIGN AND ENGINEERING
  Design Status
  Is the drawing package complete?
  Does the design contain highly critical components?
  Are all drawings frozen?
  If not what drawings remain un-frozen?
  Are there risks associated with the un-frozen drawings?
 	
Value Engineering
  Have all VE studies been completed?
  Have all VE recommendations been incorporated in the
  drawings?
 	
Approval Testing
  Are all development tests complete?
  If not what tests remain?
  What risks are associated with tests yet to be done?
  Have tests revealed any shortcomings?
  Are there plans to introduce changes to
  overcome any shortcomings?
  If so, when is implementation planned?
  Has the cost impact of changes been assessed?			

2 PRODUCTION PLANNING
  Plans
  Has a production plan been formulated?
  Are all lead-times and milestones indicated?
  Does the plan minimize financial commitments
  until all design problems are resolved?
 	
Facilities and Plant
  Has a need for new facilities been identified?
  Has subcontracting as an alternative been considered?
  Have facilities costs been established?
  Are there any restrictions on facilities development?
  If so how with they be overcome?
  When must the order for new facilities be
  given and when will they be ready?
 	
Subcontractors and Suppliers
  Has a make or buy policy been established?
  Have all subcontractors and suppliers been identified and
  vendor rated?
  Are there any items of single source supply?
  Are there any items of overseas supply?
  If so, will there be import difficulties?			

Figure 9.14   Example of a production readiness checklist.

AW	PRODUCTION READINESS CHECKLIST	Sheet 2 of 2

SUBJECT	YES/NO	REMARKS REF:

PRODUCTION PLANNING Cont.
Tooling and Test Equipment
    Have all production test requirements been
    identified?
    Have all tools and equipment been identified?
    Have all potential suppliers been identified?
    Have lead-times and costs been established?
 	
Contingencies
    What plans exist for difficulties with suppliers,
    tooling, equipment, facilities or labour?		

3 PRODUCTION ENGINEERING AND MANUFACTURE
    Were any manufacturing problems seen in
    development?
    If so how will these be overcome in production?
    Have all production methods been tested in
    development?
    Have risks of untested processes been assessed?
    Do any processes need further development?
    Are they critical to function or progress?
    Are there any exotic or critical materials?
    If so can alternatives be specified?
    Will any processes involve safety hazards?		

4 LABOUR
    Have all grades and skills been identified?
    Will special training be necessary?
    Will it be necessary to take on more labour?
    If so, when and are they available locally?
    Will shift working be necessary?
    Will new working practices affect existing
    trade union agreements?		

5 PRODUCT COSTS
    Has a complete product costing been done?
    If not, have all cost-drivers been identified?
    Will cheaper substitutes be possible?
    Are costs commensurate with selling price?
    Are any parts/materials liable to cost swings?
    Have costs of shift working and training been
    included in the cost estimates?		

6 QUALITY ASSURANCE
    Has a product quality plan been prepared?
    Have critical features lists been prepared?
    Are workmanship standards defined?
    Have all gauges been identified/designed/costed?
    Has configuration control been applied?
    Have QA procedures been agreed with subcontractors?		

positive statement, a full written explanation of the situation must be prepared and cleared with the department head concerned. These responses will be gathered and collated by the leader and given a reference number which will be entered on the checklist. The list, with all supporting reports, should be distributed to all the review team members two or three days before the meeting.

The review meeting may be chaired by the managing director, the production director or a divisional director with sufficient authority to make a positive recommendation to start production. All issues raised by the checklist must be addressed and presentations may be called for; these may be given by the team members that compiled specific reports. Subcontractors with a significant input may also be asked to make a contribution. While the checklist shown in the figure deals with readiness to go into production from a technical standpoint, the sales and marketing situation should not be overlooked, it would be normal to expect a report and presentation from the Marketing Department on their view of the market and the sales forecast. Their expectation of timing at market entry, build-up rate and peak output will have a bearing on the planning and the scale of the facilities. The outcome of the review will normally be an instruction to proceed together with a list of actions resulting from the discussion. Sometimes, however, a positive recommendation cannot be given, there may be too many unknowns for the required degree of confidence and more work will be needed; a further meeting of the review panel will be required.

There is one other possibility that should always be borne in mind. It is that the product should not go into production at all; the reasons for this can be many, but if this is the case and it has been accurately identified, then the review panel will have done its job. It may be more sensible not to start than become committed to a loss-making production programme when resources could be better used elsewhere.

Summary

The production phase of any project aimed at creating a reproducible product must be considered during the development phase. Production engineering aspects need to be included in the initial design process, not left until the end; practices such as simultaneous engineering, which place a strong emphasis on the team approach at all stages, have shown benefits for the firms that have used them. Economic aspects including make-or-buy decisions, the amount to be spent on tooling and the effects of operator learning should also be addressed during the development programme. Specific mathematical techniques have been developed to aid the decision-making process but the factors to be considered are often complex with subtle interrelationships. To use the techniques successfully requires both insight and understanding, as well as a good database complied from previous production programmes.

Entering production brings with it some of the largest speculative expenditure on such things as tools, machines, plant and training. Before commitments are made, the readiness of both the product design and the company to enter the production phase should be assessed; review procedures can help. Once production has started, it is important both to measure progress and resolve any problems that may be holding the rate of production increase down. Analytical techniques can help in assessing output growth and alerting management to possible shortfalls. Prompt action must be taken to ensure that good working practices are adopted and that production rates do not settle at a level that is below the best that could be achieved.

10

The economics of projects

- Estimates of project costs
- Traditional estimating methods
- Parametric estimating methods
- Economic justification of projects
- Profit potential of new products

Estimating the project cost

Estimating the cost of innovative development projects has proved to be a notoriously difficult area. It can be argued that the very nature of innovation makes accurate prediction impossible, and it is probably true to say that cost over-runs are the cause of more worries, heartache and anguish for Project Managers than any other factor. Over-runs are the rule rather than the exception and these cost excesses result from a variety of causes, some of which are:

- initial low estimates;
- unforeseen technical difficulties;
- lack of task definition at the start;
- changes in scope and specification;
- economic and other external factors.

Initial low estimates stem from the perception of the task to be undertaken. We all have a natural tendency to assume at the outset that things will be easier than they actually turn out to be. The reason is simple, when asked to consider performing a task and how long it will take, most of us consider the task in isolation and further assume that things will go as planned. We do not tend to look for problems that we cannot be sure exist, nor do we consider all the surrounding activities, some of which will have an effect on our task. As we may often take this approach to the things that we plan in our daily lives, it is not surprising that it should influence our attitude to the things we undertake at work. However much of a rationale is applied to the estimates for development work, attitudes that influence our perception of things we undertake tend to creep in. Low estimates can also stem from other causes that lie in corporate attitudes to either internal expenditure or the generation of business.

Unforeseen technical difficulties, while having some origin in the problem of perception, can also have separate causes that stem from an inability to correctly predict how things will perform. The root of this problem lies in our competence as engineers, designers and managers but it should not be construed that failures necessarily imply incompetent design. Often it is the case that testing generates new insight into the performance of an item that could never be gained by examining a set of drawings or even extensive computer simulation. Failures are often revealed at the extremes of the performance or environmental specifications, the places where all designs are most vulnerable. What can be said is that the greater the degree of innovation, the more likely it is that unforeseen technical difficulties will arise.

Lack of definition results from either an unclear view of the task ahead or insufficient attention to planning the project. Lack of a clear view may stem from the fact that the product cannot be specified in detail at the start, or it may have novel features of which little experience exists. Lack of initial planning is more easily curable but it is sometimes seen as a costly exercise, likely to be negated by subsequent changes. This attitude is dangerous though understandable: failure to appreciate the true nature of the tasks ahead can lead to the start of projects on a basis which would be unjustifiable if a more thorough study was carried out.

Changes in scope and specification may be internally generated but mostly they are a result of some external stimulus. Market trends may alter during the development process, demanding changes to the product to meet the newly perceived requirements. Product legislation may alter and dictate that changes are necessary. Individual customers may require changes to meet their particular needs. Whatever the reason, changes imply that some earlier work will be negated and further time and money will have to be spent in pursuit of the objective.

External factors, such as inflation, will inevitably push costs upwards in real money terms and this effect will be compounded if technical and other difficulties lead to increased timescales. Increasingly environmental issues are seen as significant and, in some cases, have had serious consequences for some construction projects; public enquiries over the siting of nuclear power stations or railway lines have dragged on for years, upsetting timescales and sending costs soaring. Multinational public sector projects, such as new military aircraft, have also been subject to significant delays due to the national politics involved. Other factors, such as currency exchange rate fluctuation and changes in company overheads, may also cause costs to rise but their effect is unpredictable; if trading conditions improve over the project duration, it could be beneficial. However, where project delays are compounded with adverse interest rate movements, the effect may be disastrous, and this has been identified as one of the prime causes of cost over-runs on prestigious projects.

Research in the UK and USA into the relationship between the initial estimate of project cost and the final actual cost has shown that over-runs of 100% of the original figure are quite common and much higher figures have been recorded. A study in the early 1960s of 12 US weapon development projects showed an average cost increase of 220% on top of the original estimate. Things have not improved in the meantime; more recent, highly innovative aircraft projects such as Concorde and Nimrod AEW are cases in point. The latter aircraft was expected to cost a little over £300 million at the time of its launch in 1977, but by the time of its cancellation in 1986 the figure had climbed to £1500 million and was expected to rise even further. However lamentable this may be, the experience is not infrequent; civil engineering projects, while sometimes less technically innovative, have just as poor a record. The Humber Bridge had a planned cost of £19 million and a final cost of £120 million; and costs on the Thames Barrier rose from a planned £100 million to a final figure of £461 million and was more than five years late. Defence projects are among those with the worst record and, despite the use of sophisticated management controls, the situation is not improving; note the following from the *Los Angeles Times* of 29 March 1987:

'Arms systems running far over budget
'The Pentagon is seeking large funding increases for 20 major weapons programs, many of which have had technical problems and huge cost over-runs, according to the draft of a General Accounting Office report.
'...The report, which was leaked to the news media, indicates that overall the 20 weapons systems have experienced cost increases of $20 billion. Thirteen of the 20 programs are behind schedule, nine have posted cost increases...'

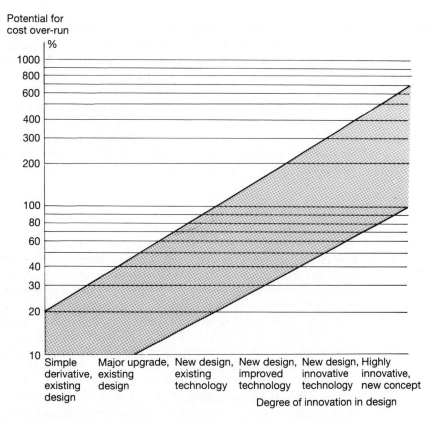

Figure 10.1 Potential for cost over-runs in development vs degree of innovation.

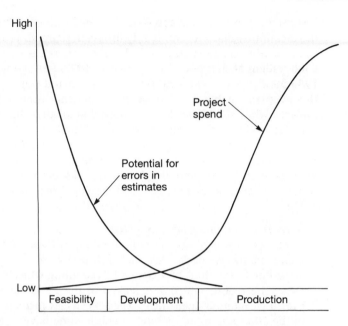

Figure 10.2 Potential for errors in estimates as the project proceeds.

What is clear is that innovative projects, in general, are subject to cost over-runs; and the more innovative the project, the greater the over-run is likely to be. Figure 10.1 is presented as a purely subjective guide to the broad potential for cost increases, according to the degree of innovation involved.

The potential for inaccuracy and underestimation at the start can have repercussions for the company if the profitability of the project becomes questionable due to cost increases. Fortunately, the greatest errors occur at the point when least has been spent. As the project proceeds estimates become progressively more accurate and by the time that major investment decisions have to be taken on such things as setting up a production line, the cost estimates can be very precise, as shown in Figure 10.2.

Estimating methods

Although evidence suggests that the accuracy of estimates for highly innovative projects is not good, projects still have to have a budget and an estimate has somehow to be made. A number of alternative methods are available, each has its place but two basic approaches are possible. The first, and most traditional, method is to consider all the elements described in the project plan and then by a process of experience, judgement or use of historic data, determine a quantity of resources in terms of man-hours, skills, materials and purchases against each element. Using current labour rates and material prices, a cost is derived for each element and the results are summed. Additional factors may be added to give a total figure for the project. The second group of methods relies on the idea that costs are related to certain physical characteristics of the product or there exists some fixed mathematical relationship between the cost of various elements of the project, this process is called **parametric estimating**.

The traditional estimating methods

Historically a number of estimating methods have been used; terms that have been coined to describe them are: subjective estimating, comparative estimating and synthetic estimating. **Subjective estimating** relies on the skill and experience of the estimator and does not place much reliance on data accumulated from past projects. **Comparative estimating** is made by considering the project or tasks in the light of previous projects and, with due allowance for differences in scope and technology, extrapolating the historic data to reflect the new proposal. The **synthetic estimating** method consists of breaking the project into a series of very small and discrete blocks of work which can then use historically proven relationships to generate an estimate. Synthetic estimating, in its true sense, needs a very detailed knowledge of the tasks and is most often applied to relatively small operations such as planning the production of a component where all the operations can be estimated using speeds, feeds and human factors data. Broader synthetics can also be derived for larger-scale estimating such as numbers of drawings per kilogram of product and numbers of man-hours per drawing.

In practice, a combination of all methods is likely to be used. For example, from basic information about the product, such as size and weight, the total number of drawings may be estimated and from historical records as it may be known that there is a well-established average number of man-hours per drawing. The amount of test work may, however, be a purely subjective estimate at the start, while the project management costs may be estimated by taking a known historic figure such as 12% of the total project labour hours.

The advent of computerized project management systems has placed a greater emphasis on detailed planning, and it has changed the style of estimating over the past ten years from a broad brush approach to a more reasoned and detailed one. This change has reinforced the traditional methods rather than the parametric as it has tended to focus on a more considered appreciation of each task in the plan. The approach has great appeal from the point of view of the faith that is often placed in it; the argument is that as each element of the project is looked at in detail, the full implications of the task are considered and the resulting figure is likely to be accurate as it is backed by the skill and judgement of the estimator. Established ratios and historic data may also be used, thus adding to the accuracy. The majority of current project management software packages are capable of building a project estimate from data of this type; the software will produce a time-phased estimate based on the schedule within the system.

From the point of view of project control, everything is in favour of such a method as a project work plan that has a cost plan precisely matched to it is a big advance over previous methods. However, certain drawbacks do exist; they are:

- the plan has to be known in sufficient detail to enter it into the computer system;
- the estimates of man-hours, skills and purchases may still be subjective judgements, even of previously known ratios are used.

Often, however, estimates are required early in the project's life and there may be little time to prepare a detailed plan. It commonly occurs when tenders are required for newly designed items that have to meet a specification and with a limited time in which to quote. In such a case, estimating normally cannot begin before a certain amount of basic design work has been done to define the product. Product maturity and the familiarity of the company with the intended design have a significant effect on the accuracy of the initial design concept. If the new product is an upgrading of existing items, its characteristics can be accurately predicted, but sometimes a novel product is required, and here the product concept may be poorly perceived at the start. The resulting estimate is at risk from two sources: (a) poor initial perception on the part of the designer (this need not imply any incompetence), and (b) errors of judgement on the part of the estimators and planners. Frequently the creation of the outline project plan will be under the direct control of the Project Manager, who may well be its chief architect, and as such he will be expected to have an insight into the whole development process. It is important that he fully understands precisely what the designer has in mind and reflects that in a plan adequately describing all the tasks that are needed to turn an idea into a product. This can be a heavy burden and few are so gifted as to foresee all that will be needed. However, there will still be an inclination towards underestimation because of inability to foresee all that may happen, and frequently also because of pressures emanating either subtly or more forcibly from within the company.

Attitudes to estimates and contingencies

Company pressures leading to underestimation may be considerable. Whether it is an in-house project or the subject of competitive tendering, there may appear to be advantages in a low initial estimate. All Project Managers know that a low cost figure is more likely to gain Board-level approval to start and, in general, is more likely to win in a competitive situation. Another view often taken is that, if a low initial budget is set, a lower overall project cost will result than if a higher and more reasonable figure had been fixed. Some managers adopt a hard line on estimates, saying they should all be based on success first time and contingencies should never be included, for once known, they will be used, whether needed or not. This attitude may stem from:

- wishful thinking – 'If I say it will happen, it *will* happen';
- a mistrust of human nature – possibly based on experience or a more general attitude to life.

Neither of these attitudes is an enlightened one, contingencies represent a reserve to cover the unknown and unforeseen: to refuse to admit contingencies is to assume perfect knowledge of the future.

Of course there may be good reasons for tendering with a low price, and if it is done in the full knowledge that costs may rise and a loss may be incurred, it is a rational decision aimed at generating business. This is quite a different situation to a low price generated through internal company pressure that distorts judgement.

Some organizations adopt a more reasoned view of contingencies and include a structured build-up within the project budget; Figure 10.3 shows the principle. Individual task budgets are set at a level that, in the view of the estimator and the manager responsible for the task, is reasonable for the defined work. This will be the budget issued to the personnel required to perform the task. Several minor tasks can come together to form a major task or work package, and either by rule-of-thumb or risk assessment a contingency is added to the budget to cover underestimates due to unforeseen difficulties in all minor tasks. The work package manager may, in theory, control the use of contingency to accommodate any over-runs.

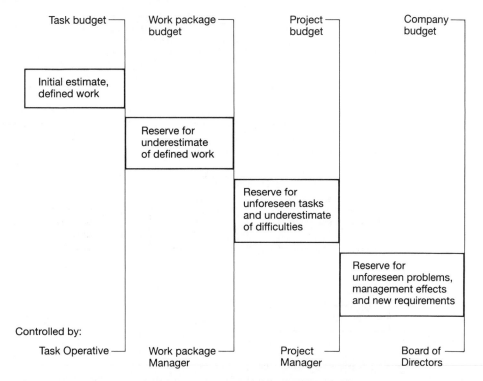

Figure 10.3   Build-up and allocation of contingency to various budgets.

All work package budgets including their contingencies can be summed to give a total budget, to this can be added an overall project contingency which is under the direct control of the Project Manager and can be released to the work package managers as needed. The company directors can determine the company budget by adding another contingency which can only be released on application by the Project Manager.

Just how easy it is to 'manage' a contingency fund must be questionable; once a task starts overspending due to a significant problem, money may have to be spent until it is cured whatever the size of the contingency. Despite this drawback, there are merits in this approach:

- it recognizes that the future contains unknowns and if problems arise they are likely to cause project costs to rise;
- provision is made in the overall company plans for increases in project cost;
- application to the contingency fund gives early warning of potential overspends.

The build-up of cost estimates

The traditional method of estimating is described by the diagram in Figure 10.4; the process needs little further explanation. It can be done by entirely manual means and this is still the practice in many organizations. However, the advent of package software means that much of the calculation can now be mechanized. The original

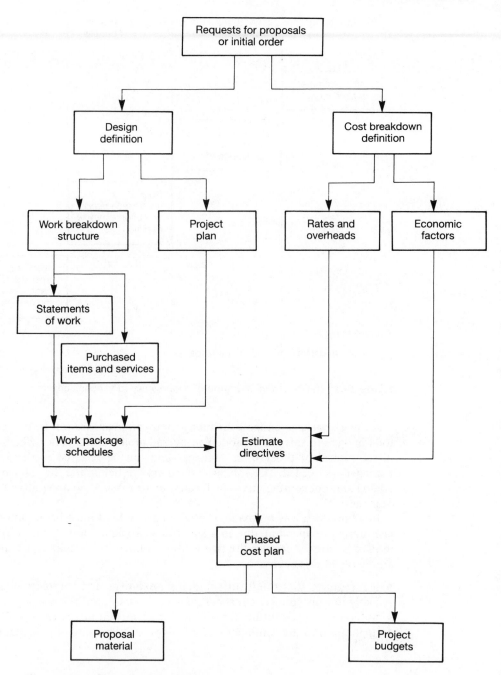

Figure 10.4 The estimating process.

estimates of resources, hours and purchases still have to be made by the estimator but the application of rates, overheads and other factors, such as inflation and contingency, can be done automatically. Estimates of individual work packages can be gathered together to form complete proposal documents or separated out and

ESTIMATE AND QUOTATION SHEET				

Project No. 27	Description DEFENSIVE AID	Type No. P04-2

Work Package No. 1364	Task No. 1364-07	Estimate No. 126

Work Package Description PHASE 2 ENVIRONMENTAL	Task Description VIBRATION TEST & REPORT.

Internal Labour

Skill	Category	Rate	Hours	Cost
SENIOR TEST ENGINEER	TE 3	10·80	40	432·00
TEST ENGINEER	TE 4	9:10	95	864·50
FITTER	PF 5	8·20	30	246·00
DRAUGHTSMAN (FIXTURE MOD)	DR 4	9:10	15	136·50
DRAWING CHECKER	DR 3	10:80	2	21·60
Sub-Total, Hours and Costs			182	1700·60
Labour Contingency ....10....%			18	170·00
Total Labour (bare), Hours and Costs			200	1870·60
Overhead ...320.... %				5985·92
Gross Labour Cost				7856·52

Bought-Out Costs

B/O Materials Specify BOLTS PLUS CLEAT MATERIAL	20·00
B/O Finished Goods Specify —	—
B/O Services and Facilities Specify HIRE OF TEST HOUSE PLUS INSTRUMENTATION PLUS RPT.	12300·00
B/O Sub-Contract Manufacture Specify FIXTURE & BOLT MODIFICATION	250·00
Sub-Total	12570·00
B/O Contingency ....15...... %	1885·50
Total Bought-Out	14455·50

Expenses

Specify ON SITE ACCOMODATION PLUS TRAVELLING	340·00
Total Costs	22652·02
Profit ....N/A.... %	—
Total Quoted Sum (ex VAT)	22652·00

Compiled: .....P.J.M......... Approved: .... Date: ..1/.11./.90.

Figure 10.5 Example of an estimation sheet.

summarized to form departmental budgets. 'Marshal', from Highbrook Services, is an example of a contemporary PC-based system for cost estimating and preparation of bids and proposals.

Where computer systems are not available, or where basic information has to be compiled, standardized cost estimating sheets may be used; an example is shown in Figure 10.5. Besides the heading details, it is divided into three main areas. The topmost covers details of the labour content, the middle section covers bought-out expenditure and the bottom covers expenses. It is important, in some companies, that these three categories of cost are kept separate due to the accounting conventions in use. Besides the basic costs, the two main areas have provision for a contingency element. The expenses section is used to cover such things as travelling, accommodation, special insurance, freight charges, entertainment, etc. With this document, all costs are compiled at current rates; economic factors such as cost revisions to reflect a different economic date are not normally taken into account at the initial estimating stage. The data may, however, be used in a system such as 'Marshal' to look forward in time, in order to produce a figure that takes into account the effects of assumed inflation.

Parametric methods

Although the traditional method of estimating is not likely to be displaced for many applications, the advent of computer modelling techniques has generated an alternative method of estimating project costs that may go some way towards removing the bias towards underestimation. The method is termed **parametric estimating** and it has been in existence for some time. However, while the technique is not generally well known or understood, it could be a useful tool for the Project Manager in the early days of a project, particularly when it comes to costing alternative design concepts or preparing bids. The concept behind parametric estimating is that all products and projects bear some similarity to products that have gone before, and similar products have similar costs. This concept is taken one step further in stating that the similarity, or conversely the uniqueness, is described by just a few simple characteristics that are easily defined, termed 'parameters'.

An example that will be readily understood is that of house prices, where two parameters, namely post code and number of bedrooms, can be used as a simple method of estimating. The post code will spot the precise location of a property and the number of bedrooms will give a good clue as to its size. If the relationship between size and price can be defined with respect to each housing area, a reasonable estimate can be made of the value of the house. For many applications, such an estimate would be deemed too loose; greater accuracy can be obtained, however, by taking more parameters. If the total number of rooms and plot size are also taken into account, a more accurate estimate can be obtained, provided that we have the data that relates these additional parameters to the cost of properties in general. Two things become apparent from this example: (a) the actual design of the house is not taken into account, only certain characteristics, and (b) rules that define the relationship between the characteristics and the cost must be established.

An example of a relationship between a physical parameter and the cost of development, in terms of man-effort, is that for design effort and airliner cruising speed, as shown graphically in Figure 10.6. All the aircraft identified embodied significant advances at the time they were designed; to make the figures constant with regard to increasing aircraft size, the man-effort has been divided by the number of passengers. It will be seen that the trend has been largely consistent from the dawn of commercial flying to Concorde, notwithstanding the considerable changes in technology.

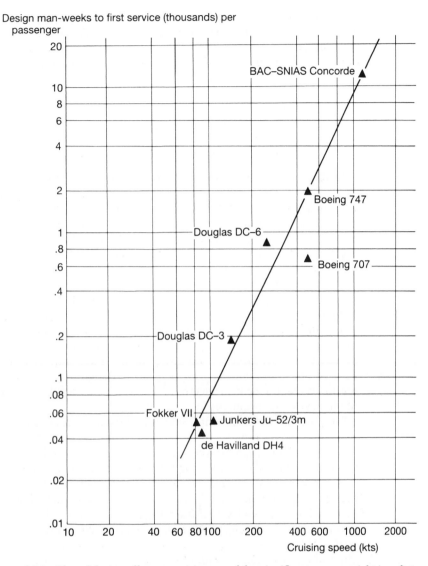

Design man-weeks to first service (thousands) per passenger

Figure 10.6 Plot of design effort vs cruising speed for significant commercial aircraft types.

The essence of the parametric method is of identifying the characteristics that define the product with such precision that a direct relationship to its cost can be established, and then defining the mathematical nature of that relationship. With this information, greater insight into the cost of a product can be obtained without defining all its detail. Parametric estimating belongs to that loosely defined category of systems called **knowledge-based or expert systems**, and the technique is a computer-based one. There is no fundamental reason for this, but in practical terms, for all but the simplest cases, the nature of the mathematics is such that hand calculation is hopelessly tedious.

The parameters chosen must relate directly to the particular product; they may be physical: weight, size, etc., or performance related: speed, thrust, output rate, etc., or some combination of both. External factors such as economic conditions and maturity of the technology may also be parameters to be taken into account. To illustrate a performance-related parametirc model the following formula has been suggested for estimating the design engineering cost for developing a rocket motor:

$$C = L(aT^{0.4} + KM^c)$$

where: C = cost;
L = design labour, current cost rate;
T = motor thrust;
M = mass flow; and a, K and c are constants.

In this example, the two performance parameters are T and M, thrust and mass flow, while L, the current labour rate, represents an economic parameter. The three constants are not parameters in themselves, but calibration factors that must be established empirically from historic data. This raises an important point, equations alone are not enough; all models have to be tuned or calibrated to their particular application and accurate historic data is necessary. The use of historic information, even where it results from projects that have known problems, assists in removing the bias that can affect conventional estimates.

In terms of application of the technique, the PRICE system, developed to a US Navy requirement by RCA, is the best known. It was created in the early 1960s for estimating the cost of electromechanical avionics and space systems, in particular, radar applications. Since 1975 it has been available to other users and has been acquired by many large corporations. Particular applications in which the system can be used are estimating the cost of: (a) the design, development and production of mechanical and electrical/electronic items; (b) the development of software; and (c) the life cycle of equipment.

The software development aspect is particularly refined as it contains: (a) a model that can estimate number of lines of code from functional descriptions; (b) a development cost model; and (c) a cost of ownership model. There is also a model specifically tailored to estimating the cost of developing microcircuitry.

The relatively high cost of PRICE may have been a deterrent to some firms acquiring the system but PC-based versions were launched in 1992. An alternative PC-based system is MATCH, from Highbrook Services; both systems are similar in general concept, although PRICE is best considered as a suite of systems. Using either system involves an initial calibration phase in which the user is invited to enter physical and cost data obtained from previous projects. By an iterative process, the model can establish **cost estimating relationships** that relate the parameters to the particular product cost; this is similar to evaluating the constants in the rocket model. Once this has been done, new products or projects can be assessed by inserting their particular parameters. The parameters that may be input are not wholly deterministic in physical terms as estimates of system complexity are also required; here the model user may exercise his own judgement in deciding just how much more or less complex the new item is than previous ones. Both systems are capable of assessing these complexity factors if no user input is provided.

Example 10.1: 'MATCH' parametric software

```
ITEM XBAA

                    MODEL RECORD INPUT SCREEN

DESCRIPTION     Forward Fuselage
DEV. START      01JAN91   DEV. END                  UNITS       I pounds 000
PROD START                PROD END                  DEV. TYPE A
QUANTITY(nha)   1         total qty/sys   1         CODE1
RUN SIZE                  YEAR TECH       1988       CODE2
PROTOTYPES      1.00      ENG. FACTOR     1.00       CODE3
PLATFORM        1.80      PROD. PROFILE   1          CODE4
                          DEV. PROFILE    1
==ELECTRONIC DATA=====  % =FUNC=TECH===  ==STRUCTURE DATA ======  % =MATL=TOL===

WEIGHT                                    WEIGHT    2200.00
DENSITY            []                     DENSITY    145.89  []
L/CURVE           []                      L/CURVE     87    []
NEW %                                     NEW %       60
INT FACTOR                                INT FACTOR  20
P.FACTOR          []                      P.FACTOR    7.75  [F]
D.FACTOR                                  D.FACTOR    7.75
- - - - - - - - - - - - - - - - - - - -  - - - - - - - - - - - - - - - - - - - -
P UPC          D.COST                     P UPC    1199.14 D.COST  10406.20


   last changed 07MAR90      results current Y

F1 exit   F2 help   F3 print screen   F4 delete          F5 quick look cost
PGup      PGdn      F6 calibrate      F8 input from file  F9 view output
```

Figure 10.7 'MATCH' input screen.

Figure 10.7 shows the input format required by 'MATCH' for a mechanical item. The example is the forward fuselage of a military aircraft; items that need to be specified include:

- the quantity of prototypes;
- the production quantity if applicable;
- the structure weight and density;
- the percentage of the product which is new in terms of detail design;
- the engineering factor – i.e. the relative novelty of the item;
- the 'platform'.

The last item is a complexity factor which defines the type of application – i.e. 1 = Ground, 1.4 = Mobile, 1.7 = Commercial Airborne, 1.8 = Military Airborne, etc. Additional complexity factors peculiar to this item are the integration factor and the production and development factors; these can be established by the model or there is a look-up table on a help screen to assist the modeller if he is making his own assessment.

Sample outputs from this particular example are given in Figures 10.8–10.10. Figure 10.8 shows the predicted hours and costs for the forward fuselage design and development, including the split of costs between functional skills.

```
Report 008: Cost breakdown by functional areas (000s pounds and 000s hours)

                             Total   Material  Labour  Labour  Start    Finish   Labour
                             Pounds  Pounds    Pounds  Hours   Date     Date     Per Hr

XBAA   Forward Fuselage
       Design & Drawing Office   5553            5553    185   01JAN91  26DEC92    30
       Systems Integration        669             669     22   01JAN91  26DEC92    30
       Project Management         585             585     20   01JAN91  26DEC92    30
       Documentation              226             226      9   06AUG91  26DEC92    25
       Prototype Manufacture     3188    1275    1913     48   11MAR92  03AUG92    40
       Tool & Test                184     184                   11MAR92  03AUG92    na
       Production              119914   36180   83734   2093   27DEC92  29JAN99    40
```

Figure 10.8 Cost estimate for forward fuselage development and production.

ITEM	DESCRIPTION*	DEVELOPMENT			UNIT........ PRODUCTION			
		TOTAL FOR ITEM	SUB-ASSEMBLY COSTS	INTEGRATION OF SUB-ASSEMBLIES	TOTAL FOR ITEM	QTY IN N.H.A.	SUB-ASSEMBLY COSTS	INTE-GRATION OF SUB-ASSEMBLIES
X	Aircraft	54646.90	54646.90	0	6819.76	1	6819.76	0
XA	Comms/Navigation	10976.70	10976.70	0	516.28	1	516.28	0
XAA	Communications	6833.70			172.64	2		
XAB	Navigation	4143.00			85.50	2		
XB	Airframe	43670.20	43410.00	260.20	6303.48	1	6234.58	68.90
XBA	Fuselage	28210.40	28018.70	191.70	3600.08	1	3578.00	22.08
XBAA	Forward Fuselage	10406.20			1199.14	1		
XBAB	Main Fuselage	17612.50			2378.86	1		
XBB	Wings	15199.60	15124.90	74.70	1317.25	2	1306.06	11.19
XBBA	Wing Structure	9992.70			907.50	1		
XBBB	Elevators	5132.20			199.28	2		

report 007: integration rollup

Figure 10.9 Overall product costing.

The production cost is also included based on a nominal run of 100 aircraft. The whole aircraft can be considered in the same way, Figure 10.9 shows a combined output of cost estimates for more of the aircraft, and the model will also predict the development timescale and produce a schedule bar chart, as shown in Figure 10.10.

REPORT 005: SCHEDULE BARCHART

ITEM	DESCRIPTION		START	FINISH
X	Aircraft	devt	01JAN90	30NOV96
		prodn	17MAR92	24FEB01
XA	Comms/Navigation	devt	01JAN90	30NOV96
		prodn	17MAR92	16NOV00
XAA	Communications	devt	01JAN90	16MAR92
		prodn	17MAR92	08JUN96
XAB	Navigation	devt	01JAN91	30NOV96
		prodn	01DEC96	16NOV00
XB	Airframe	devt	01JAN91	16MAY96
		prodn	27DEC92	24FEB01
XBA	Fuselage	devt	01JAN91	30MAR93
		prodn	27DEC92	11AUG99
XBAA	Forward Fuselage	devt	01JAN91	26DEC92
		prodn	27DEC92	29JAN99
XBAB	Main Fuselage	devt	01JAN91	30MAR93
		prodn	31MAR93	11AUG99
XBB	Wings	devt	01JAN91	16MAY96
		prodn	14OCT95	24FEB01
XBBA	Wing Structure	devt	01JAN91	13OCT95
		prodn	14OCT95	24FEB01
XBBB	Elevators	devt	01JAN91	16MAY96
		prodn	17MAY96	26OCT00

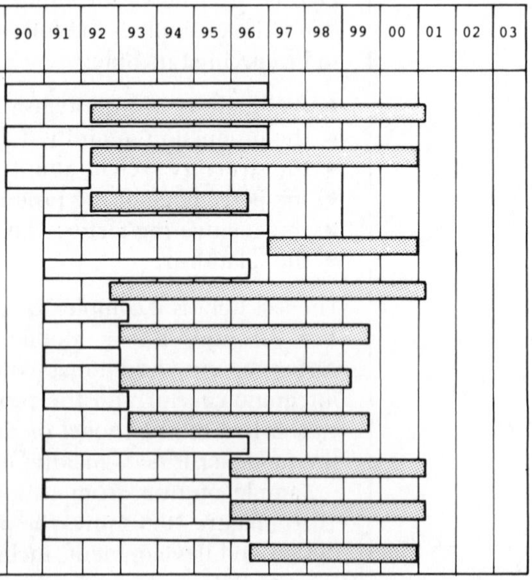

Figure 10.10 Overall development and production schedule bar chart.

In terms of the total development process, it should be noted that although a considerable amount of detail is generated about the cost of developing the item, it need not be complete. In particular, if the development programme calls for a significant amount of trial and test work this may not be shown. There can be a real difficulty in establishing any valid cost estimating relationships that can reflect the amount of testing that will be needed with any new design. It can depend on many factors, some of which may not become apparent until the detail design is done; for example, it may be decided that the introduction of a new material to reduce product cost in one area will demand the introduction into the test programme of a destructive strength test, whereas introduction of new materials into the design in other areas will not generate such a requirement. Some projects may involve a large amount of destructive testing, for example, munitions development, but the amount that is required may be hard to determine at the outset and may be influenced by factors that are nothing to do with the product itself, such as the number of customer demonstrations, which is obviously related to the number of customers and may change as the project proceeds.

It is of course possible for any company to construct its own parametric model specific to the requirements of its products or projects. The following case study shows something of the principles and the mathematics involved in creating a simple model that, in this case, was used for assessing the likely prototype unit cost and the production unit cost for an item of airborne equipment.

Case study 10.1: Product cost estimate, airborne equipment

At the start of the project to develop the model, it was recognized that the item specification and interface requirements alone were insufficient to define the product parameters as it was usually possible for the designer to generate at least two alternative schemes that could meet the specification. Further, from the physical dimensions and a comparison with previous products in the same general category, it was relatively easy for the designer to assess the product weight and the likely number of parts. Two products each performing a similar function – although in different aircraft and with no actual commonality – were assessed and it was found that weight and part frequency, when expressed on a percentage basis, were similar in both cases, even though one product was more complex than the other. Four types of material were also identified: steel, aluminium, composite and electrical. Figure 10.11 shows the frequency distribution for steel components, by weight, and the equation that gave the best fit between the two distributions. Similar results were obtained with aluminium and composites but the electrical parts were few in number, fulfilled different requirements in the two items and could not be made to fit a truly satisfactory equation.

Cost data was also obtained and fits were made with component weight. Data on production costs was relatively easy to obtain as prices had been established with suppliers, but costs for prototype manufacture were more difficult. Figure 10.12 shows the cost-to-weight relationship for production quantities of steel parts and the fitted equation.

The model could be run in two ways: either a total weight and number of

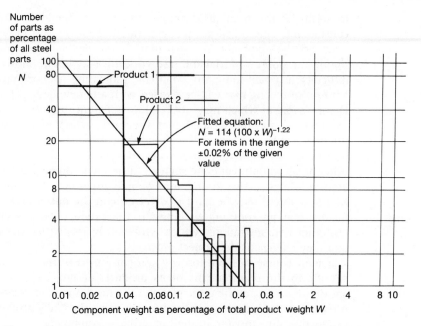

Figure 10.11 Frequency distribution for steel parts, by weight and fitted equation.

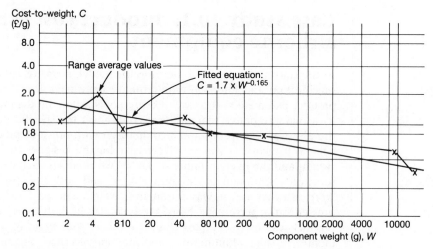

Figure 10.12 Cost-to-weight relationship and fitted equation for steel parts (production costs).

parts could be entered, in which case the model assumed a standard split between the four material types, or the weight and number of parts could be entered against each material type. The model first calculated the frequency distribution of parts by weight; Figure 10.13 shows the results for steel, aluminium and composite parts. It also shows that, in all cases, there are likely to be a small number of heavy parts that lie outside the general weight range and the number and average weight of these is also displayed. Fitting the cost

Range	Number of parts		
g	Steel	Aluminium	Composite
0.000– 14.000	39	7	10
14.001– 28.000	10	2	2
28.001– 42.000	6	2	2
42.001– 56.000	3	1	1
56.001– 70.000	3	0	0
70.001– 84.000	2	1	1
84.001– 98.000	2	0	–
98.001–112.000	1	1	–
112.001–126.000	2	0	–
126.001–140.000	1	1	
434.001–448.000	–	1	–
448.001–462.000	–	0	–
REMAINING PARTS	3	2	2
TOTAL No of PARTS	80	21	18

```
Number of STEEL parts remaining              = 3
Average weight of remaining STEEL parts      = 7697.667 g

Number of ALUMINIUM parts remaining          = 2
Average weight of remaining ALUMINIUM parts  = 2292.500 g

Number of COMPOSITE parts remaining          = 2
Average weight of remaining COMPOSITE parts  = 338.5000 g
```

Figure 10.13 Predicted frequency distribution of parts by weight for a product of total weight 35 kg and 120 parts.

equation to the frequency distribution gives an estimated unit cost both for a prototype quantity and a production run of about 250 units. Figure 10.14 (overleaf) shows the results for steel parts for products of two different configurations.

Parametrics is applicable across the whole spectrum of engineering, computing and construction. It is an effective tool for establishing the likely costs of products or projects before a full-scale design exercise takes place. This can be very useful at the start of projects when choices have to be made between alternative schemes but there is no time to do a detailed design of each concept and cost them by the conventional methods. It can also be useful for bid generation where limited time may be available to put in a fully costed proposal. In these circumstances, it has the advantage of being very complete in terms of what it calculates; if the model is correctly calibrated, nothing is left out when the estimate is made. Other uses include setting design-to-cost targets, evaluating the cost of changes to existing products and assessing the effects of new technology on product development and pricing. With the advent of PC-based systems, many more organizations will find it advantageous to use this technique as it has the potential to improve the speed and accuracy both of the initial estimating and design evaluation process.

AVERAGE WEIGHT OF PARTS (g)	No of PARTS	PRODUCTION COST of PARTS	DEVELOPMENT COST of PARTS
7.000	39	336.64	2642.68
21.000	10	216.02	543.95
35.000	6	198.56	294.67
49.000	3	131.49	137.75
63.000	3	162.19	

| 329.000 | 1 | 214.94 | 359.93 |
| 7697.667 | 3 | 8967.68 | 25262.02 |

TOTAL COST OF STEEL PARTS   11903.77   31664.14

TOTAL NUMBER OF STEEL PARTS = 80   WEIGHT = 26.740 kgs
1987/88 PRICES

AVERAGE WEIGHT OF PARTS (g)	No of PARTS	PRODUCTION COST of PARTS	DEVELOPMENT COST of PARTS
9.574	107	1199.63	6810.28
28.772	28	785.63	1430.59
47.870	16	687.74	738.09
67.018	10	569.27	431.28
86.166	7	491.53	

| 430.830 | 1 | 269.21 | 471.33 |
| 2359.033 | 10 | 11134.78 | 25809.02 |

TOTAL COST OF STEEL PARTS   21164.64   45478.05

TOTAL NUMBER OF STEEL PARTS = 220   WEIGHT = 36.573 kgs
1987/88 PRICES

Figure 10.14 Production and development price estimates for products of alternative configurations (note that in the case of the second item the weight has gone up by some 37% compared to the first but the large number of parts generates an estimate of production price that is almost twice that of the first item).

Function point analysis

Mention has been made of PRICE's ability to apply parametric methods to estimating the cost of developing software, but it should be noted that another method has also evolved for that purpose, known as **function point analysis**, introduced by A. J. Albrecht in 1979; and the technique in principle is gaining acceptance as a standard in the information technology world. Albrecht's method (called FPA Mk 1) looks at the functions a system is required to perform from the point of view of the user, this can be expressed in physical terms that describe the operation and environment such as expected numbers of transactions, transaction rates, numbers of external inter-faces, and also more subjective factors such as processing complexity. The result is a dimensionless score given in 'function points' which reflects the sum of all the factors, and it can then be converted into such things as man-effort or expected numbers of defects based on measured quantities per function point. A modified version, called FPA Mk 2, is now coming into use and has been adopted by the UK government as a standard. To use it, research will be necessary into the relationship between the function point results and the actual observations in the given environment; this is equivalent to the calibration phase in parametric estimating. Because it employs the user's view of the product, it tends to be more successful with systems that involve a high degree of user interaction; it has been less successful, however, with systems whose principal complexity is internal due to the complicated and sophisticated nature of the mathematics.

Justifying the project

'If there isn't a dime in it, it isn't worth a dollar' is a point that should always be borne in mind, but it sometimes gets forgotten. Development and production estimates form the basis on which any decision to proceed with the project is made. For the most part, projects have a cash-flow curve that resembles Figure 10.15; certainly this is true for private venture programmes where product development precedes production and sales. (The cost curve may be different for some public sector projects where the development is financed by the customer.) In general, there will be a period in which the company must fund the development from its own resources until profit from sales can be used to offset that outlay. A point will eventually be reached where the profit from sales equals the cost of development; this is the break-even point. Beyond that, further sales should generate an overall profit.

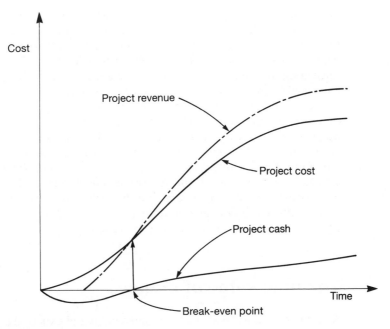

Figure 10.15   Project cost, revenue and cash vs time.

Project investment decisions

The greatest risks associated with undertaking a project lie in the initial decision as to whether or not to proceed with the project. If the decision is made to go ahead, then resources will be committed but the return cannot be guaranteed. If we put aside the question of the risks inherent in any forecast where the outcome cannot be stated with certainty, the question remains: how does one decide if a project is worth the investment? Ultimately, the criteria that is taken is the expected benefit with respect to the expected cost but what are the benefits and the costs?

A number of different methods have been devised to answer this question; unfortunately, they are not all guaranteed to give the same answer when put to the same problem. For the most part, the methods are most applicable to questions of choice between projects, whether to accept one and reject the other, or for setting some hurdle criterion if projects are considered singly. They fall into three broad types, payback, return-on-capital-employed and discounted cash-flow methods.

The **payback method** is the simplest and has the longest history. If the project cost curve in Figure 10.15 is taken, the break-even point is easily identified and can be calculated directly from the figures for cash outflows at the start and inflows once sales begin; working capital tied up in the project is not considered. All the cash figures are taken at present-day values and the time at which the inflows exactly cancel the initial investment is found, this is termed the 'payback period'. In general, projects with shorter payback periods are to be preferred to those with a longer period; given a choice between two projects that are equal in all other respects, the one with the shorter payback period would be chosen. Companies may also set a maximum payback period as a decision criterion, any project that has a payback period longer than, say, five years being rejected at the outset.

The simplicity of the payback calculation makes it popular where only elementary comparisons are required; perhaps, where the projects are of low value and short duration. What it does not take into account is the relative size in money terms of the project or the size of the expected benefit. To counter the objection of ignoring the size of the benefit the **return-on-capital-employed method** also became popular. Many variations have been devised for this technique, in particular, for calculating the capital employed. In essence, the approach is to calculate the capital employed from the initial project outlay, less any residual scrap value that may be left at the end, plus the annual operating cost of the project in the production phase multiplied by the number of years of production. This figure is divided by the total number of years for the project to give the average capital employed. The total estimated profit for the whole project is next taken and divided by the total project duration to give the average annual profit. When this figure is divided by the average capital employed, the return-on-capital-employed is obtained; it is usually expressed as a percentage figure, and the higher the figure, the more desirable is the project. This method is now declining in popularity; readers wishing to know more about it should consult specialist accounting texts.

The time value of money

A simple analysis to find the break-even point and expected profits may be all that is necessary if the undertaking is a very short-term one, perhaps over two or three years, and either of the above methods can be used to make a decision. However, where longer-term projects are involved the time at which profits arise can also become a concern that neither method takes into account. Where such projects are contemplated, it has become the normal practice to consider the **time value of money** by applying a 'discount rate' to future cash flows. In effect, it says that money earned now is worth more than money earned at some time in the future because of the additional return that could have been obtained if the money had been invested in the intervening period. The high interest rates of the 1970s and 1980s have focused the minds of accountants on this point. Applying discounting rates tends to show that projects that generate a profit early in their life cycle are to be preferred to projects where profits are obtained further downstream. Besides the purely financial appeal of this argument, there is merit in it as the further forward one looks in time, the less one can be certain of. Profits to be obtained many years away are thus more vulnerable to changed circumstances than profits to be generated in the near future. The technique of **discounted cash flow** (DCF) has become common in the financial evaluation of both capital and developmental projects as it takes into account the timing at which expenditure and profits arise. It shows the effective rate of return on the total investment over the whole life of the project. In evaluating the worth of the project this rate of return can be set at some boundary level which, if not met at the initial evaluation, will indicate that the returns are likely to be too low for the project to be worth pursuing, this may be 4% or 5% above the long-term view of interest rates.

Example 10.2: Project investment decision

Table 10.1 Project expenditure, revenue and cash flow at current rates

Year	Expenditure (£m.)			Revenue	Cum. revenue	Cash flow	Cum. cash flow
	Development	Production	Cum.				
1	0.5	0	0.5	0	0	−0.5	−0.5
2	1.5	0.1	2.1	0	0	−1.6	−2.1
3	2.0	0.2	4.3	0	0	−2.2	−4.3
4	0.7	2.5	7.5	0	0	−3.2	−7.5
5	0	5.2	12.7	3.8	3.8	−1.4	−8.9
6	0	7.1	19.8	10.6	14.4	3.5	−5.4
7	0	6.8	26.6	12.2	26.6	5.4	0
8	0	6.4	33.0	11.6	38.2	5.2	5.2
9	0	3.6	36.6	6.6	44.8	3.0	8.8
10	0	1.4	38.0	3.2	48.0	1.8	10.0

A project is divided into two phases, a development phase lasting four years and a production phase lasting eight years but overlapping the development programme by three years. (This is a common situation where consideration is given to the production phase while development is proceeding but the cost accounts for the two activities are kept separate.) Table 10.1 shows the annual cost figures at current rates. Also shown is the expected revenue from sales (after tax). The total cost of the project over the ten years is £38 million made up of £4.7m. for development and £33.3m. for the production phase. The total revenue over the expected life of the project is £48m., there is thus a net benefit of £10m. on an expenditure of £38m. giving a benefit-to-cost ratio of 26.3% at current rates.

If, for example, a rate of return on investment of 10% could be expected over the life of the project, a discount rate of 10% can be applied to the cash-flow figures to determine the net worth of the project under these conditions; the resulting figure is termed the **net present value** (NPV). The formula for calculating the discounted value of any sum of money at some time in the future is:

$$D = \frac{1}{(1 + r)^n}$$ (10.1)

where: $D =$ the discount factor;
$r =$ the rate of interest as a decimal value;
$n =$ the number of years from start.

Thus, for a discount rate of 10% at the end of year 1 the factor is:

$$D = \frac{1}{(1 + 0.1)^1} = 0.9091$$

Discount factors can be calculated directly from the formula or it is sometimes more convenient to use a published table. Table 10.2 shows the calculation of the net present values for the whole project at the 10% rate. It will be seen that the £10m. profit figure that resulted from the undiscounted calculation is now reduced to £2.602m. It will also be realized that if a sufficiently high discount rate is chosen, the net worth of the project will be reduced to zero. The figure that produces this zero return is termed the **internal rate of return** (IRR) and the discounted cash flow method aims to find this figure. Figure 10.16 has been drawn showing the effect on this example of discounting at different rates. A discount rate of about 19.15% will produce a zero result, it is thus the internal rate of return in this case.

Table 10.2 Cash flow discounted at the rate of 10%

Year	Cash flow	Discount factor	Net present value	Cum. NPV
1	−0.5	0.9091	−0.455	−0.455
2	−1.6	0.8264	−1.322	−1.777
3	−2.2	0.7513	−1.653	−3.430
4	−3.2	0.6830	−2.186	−5.616
5	−1.4	0.6209	−0.869	−6.485
6	3.5	0.5645	1.976	−4.509
7	5.4	0.5132	2.771	−1.738
8	5.2	0.4565	2.374	0.636
9	3.0	0.4241	1.272	1.908
10	1.8	0.3855	0.694	2.602

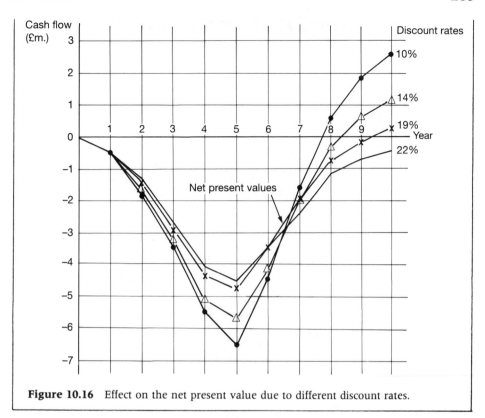

Figure 10.16 Effect on the net present value due to different discount rates.

The above example has been somewhat simplified when compared to many real situations where the additional effects of borrowed capital and investment grants, if available, and the effect of corporation tax including deferred payments, would have to be taken into account.

When evaluating the worth of projects, there are some arguments against using the internal rate of return as a suitable measure, in particular its difficulty of calculation and also the possibility, depending on the shape of the cash-flow curve, that two different IRRs can exist. The argument is therefore that projects should be evaluated by calculating the net present value using a predetermined hurdle rate as it is both simpler and avoids the problem of dual rates. Any project that yields a positive NPV at the set rate is potentially worth pursuing as, overall, it is wealth creating.

Although there is no fundamental flaw in the DCF or NPV methods, they have attracted some criticism as to their appropriateness. A statement sometimes heard is: 'any project can be DCF'ed to death', implying that setting the discount rate sufficiently high will make any project look unattractive. This is certainly true where projects with a return in the longer term are involved and, as Example 10.2 shows, a discount rate of 20% can reduce the benefit-to-cost ratio to zero. However, in applying high hurdle rates to DCF or NPV calculations firms must remember that investment in new products may ultimately be necessary for the firm's survival. To fail to invest could leave the company without anything to compete with against products developed by rivals who have taken a less cautious view.

The profit potential of new products

In the situation where all the development cost is to be recovered through sales of the production item, both the design and the production engineering must be aimed at generating a product that can be sold profitably and in a volume that makes the development programme worthwhile. However, the costs of production vary according to both the investment in capital equipment and the rate of output that is achieved. Unlike the amount spent on tooling where a decision can be made at the start, the rate of output will, in part, be governed by the the rate at which sales can be made. Attractiveness in the market will determine the amount of sales unless there are other influences such as a limit on output capacity or a desire to remain exclusive. Selling price will be a major factor in determining the level of sales but there are others such as changes in public taste, the amount spent on promotion, etc. To assess the profit potential of a new product it is necessary to determine the rate at which production costs change as the volume of output increases and set this against the projected volume of sales when related to selling price. The relationship between sales volume and selling price differs between products and the ultimate volume of sales will be set by the likely penetration into the market and the life of the product in terms of the time when its design becomes obsolete. For a product such as a personal computer the sales life may be no more than two or three years at most, but for an airliner it may, with continuous improvements, remain in production for more than 20 years. The general relationship between selling-price-to-volume and production-cost-to-volume is shown in Figure 10.17.

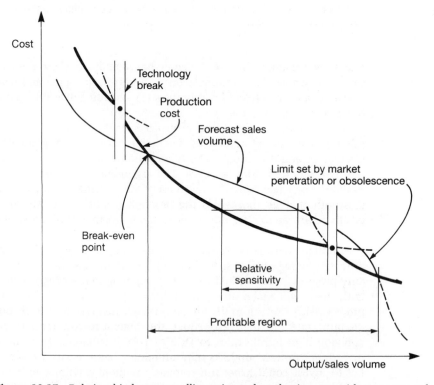

Figure 10.17 Relationship between selling price and production cost with respect to volume.

It will be seen that included in the production cost curves are breaks in production technology where a change in methods can produce a marked reduction in cost for a given level of output. For example, in an assembly process the first break of technology may come by changing from hand assembly with simple fixtures to operator controlled special-to-purpose machines, the second break may come with a fully automated assembly line with operator supervision. Each break represents a jump in output per operator but there is also a significant capital investment in the machinery and tooling.

As all sales forecasts are estimates, they are subject to error; hence a sensitivity analysis is necessary against both optimistic and pessimistic views of potential sales to assess the chances of making a loss. The technology breaks need careful consideration, particularly if they fall near the Marketing Department's limit of sales; if this turns out to be optimistic, then a product that was potentially profitable with simple tooling may become a loss-maker with an expensive, specially designed line.

The build up of production cost

Production costs can be considered to be made up in the way shown in Figure 10.18. In general, the longer the production run, the cheaper will be the product because (a) the amortization of initial tooling and capital cost is spread over a greater number, and (b) there will be reductions in operator times due to learning. A further reduction comes with increased output as the fixed overhead recovery per item can be reduced. From the factors shown in Figure 10.18 the unit production cost over a run of N items is given by the equation:

$$P = M \times \left(\frac{N}{2.718}\right)^a + L + (C_1 - L) \times \left(\frac{N}{2.718}\right)^b + \frac{J}{N} + \frac{F \times T_n}{N} \qquad (10.2)$$

where: P = the average production cost over N items;
M = the cost of materials and bought-out parts;
N = the number of items in the production run;
a = an exponent that describes the reduction in material price with quantity;
L = the fixed-cycle or irreducible minimum labour cost;
C_1 = the labour cost of the first item produced;
b = an exponent that describes the rate of learning;
J = the cost of tools, machinery and initial set-up;
F = the fixed overhead cost per month associated with the product;
T_n = the time in months over which N items are made.

This expression may not contain all the variations possible, but at the project evaluation stage many of the variables will be estimates and it is adequate for most analyses. The material cost expression:

$$M \times \left(\frac{N}{2.718}\right)^a$$

takes the same general form as the learning curve.

This is done here for convenience rather than as a definitive expression that describes all variations in material cost with quantity. In general, quantity discounts

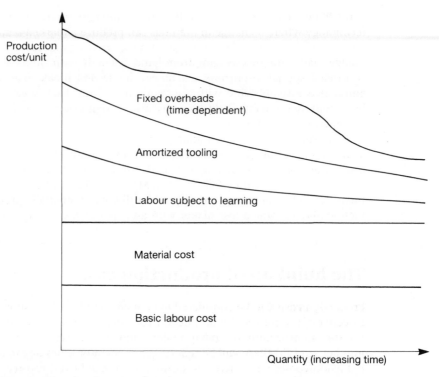

Figure 10.18 The elements of production cost.

do apply and, ignoring the effects of inflation, many material and bought-out items do show reductions in price (relative to inflation if not in real terms) as time proceeds (note the cost reductions in electronic components over the past few decades). Whereas elapsed time and production quantity are not strictly interchangeable, they are related to the extent that, as time proceeds, the quantity produced gets larger. Additionally, as production continues and operators learn to do the work with increasing efficiency, there may be a noticeable reduction in scrapped items leading to a reduced material demand per unit. Taken together, this reasoning forms the basis of the material cost expression; in practice, however, considerable research into the history of past products or industry forecasts of price variations may be needed to establish a suitable value for the exponent a. If this is not possible, then the material cost can simply be taken as the constant M.

The production cost for the nth item in a run of N items is given by:

$$P_n = Mn^a + L + (C_1 - L)n^b + \frac{J}{N} + \frac{F \times T_n}{N} \tag{10.3}$$

In some cases, all of the terms may not be required. The fixed overheads may not be easily attributable to the product in question as several products may draw on the same facility. However, if the product draws on a significant part of the company's capital resources, it is worthwhile establishing the proportion for the extra sensitivity it can impart to the result. The fixed overhead, besides covering capital costs associated with the plant, can also include regular running costs, such as heating and power, and a proportion of the general overheads, including such things as management charges. Where large promotional costs are expected at the time the product is launched, they can be added into the charge for initial set-up (J). Operator learning may not be considered necessary if job times are very short and the planned production run very long: however, learning is a real effect and the contribution it makes to cost reduction should not be overlooked if it can be established. In the case of large items with a high labour content, learning will have a marked effect on cost. The cost of the development programme is not included in the expression as this is normally paid for out of the fixed overhead burden at the time the work is done. Thus, when assessing the fixed overhead, an estimate of future R & D expenditure may be necessary.

Example 10.3: Profitable sales figures for a new product

A new product is to be launched with an assembly line and special tooling costing £2 million and designed to produce 35 000 units per year at normal working or 60 000 per year with two shifts. The product is estimated to have a sales life of six years and the market will be at its peak during the second and third years from launch. The sales forecasts at different pricing levels are given in Table 10.3.

The breakdown of the product costs are estimated as below:

- Cost of materials and bought-out parts: £42 per unit for the first batch but with discounts for bulk orders a 98% improvement curve is expected.
- Cost of labour excluding fixed overheads: £14 for fixed-cycle working and £7.20 for labour subject to learning. From previous experience a 90% learning curve is expected and the job will be considered fully learned at the 20 000th item.
- Fixed overheads are estimated at £30 000 per month irrespective of output.

To establish the profitable region of sales it is first necessary to assess the total market at the rates predicted above and this is given in Table 10.4.

For the six-year programme envisaged, the three cases of 212 500, 169 000 and 108 500 can be evaluated for the cumulative average unit cost.

The terms a and b in expression 10.2 are:

$$a = \frac{\log_e 0.98}{0.693145} = -0.0291$$

$$b = \frac{\log_e 0.90}{0.693145} = -0.152$$

The cost of labour subject to learning is given by:

$$C_1 = \frac{C_n}{N_a}$$

and

$$C_1 = \frac{7.20}{20\,000^{-0.152}} = £32.45$$

Table 10.3 Annual sales forecasts and market percentage at different selling prices

Year Case no.	Total market sales/year	1 100 000	2 200 000	3 250 000	4 150 000	5 150 000	6 100 000?
1	% at £65/unit	35	30	25	20	10	10
2	% at £80/unit	30	25	20	15	7	6
3	% at £85/unit	22	15	12	10	5	4

Table 10.4 Annual sales figures at different selling prices

Case	Year	1	2	3	4	5	6
1	Annual sales, £65	35 000	60 000	62 500	30 000	15 000	10 000
	Cumulative	35 000	95 000	157 500	187 000	202 500	212 500
2	Annual sales, £80	30 000	50 000	50 000	22 500	10 500	6 000
	Cumulative	30 000	80 000	130 000	152 500	163 000	169 000
3	Annual sales, £85	22 000	30 000	30 000	15 000	7 500	4 000
	Cumulative	22 000	52 000	82 000	97 000	104 500	108 500

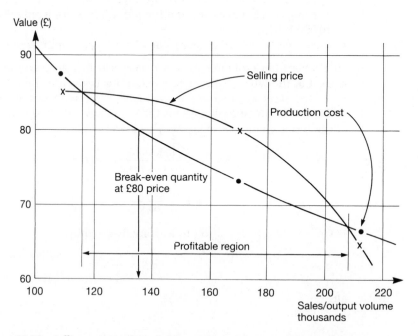

Figure 10.19 Selling price and production cost at various total output values.

Table 10.5 Unit production costs at different total sales figures

Case	Material cost	Fixed labour	Learning	Tool cost	Fixed overhead	Total
	$42\left(\dfrac{N}{2.718}\right)^{-0.0291}$	L	$32.45\left(\dfrac{N}{2.718}\right)^{-0.152}$	$\dfrac{2\,000\,000}{N}$	$\dfrac{72 \times 30\,000}{N}$	
1	$42\left(\dfrac{212\,500}{2.718}\right)^{-0.0291} = £30.25$	£12	$32.45\left(\dfrac{212\,500}{2.718}\right)^{-0.152} = £5.85$	$\dfrac{2\,000\,000}{212\,500} = £9.41$	$\dfrac{2\,160\,000}{212\,500} = £10.16$	£67.67
2	$42\left(\dfrac{169\,000}{2.718}\right)^{-0.0291} = £30.46$	£12	$32.45\left(\dfrac{169\,000}{2.718}\right)^{-0.152} = £6.06$	$\dfrac{2\,000\,000}{169\,000} = £11.43$	$\dfrac{2\,160\,000}{169\,000} = £12.78$	£73.13
3	$42\left(\dfrac{108\,500}{2.718}\right)^{-0.0291} = £30.85$	£12	$32.45\left(\dfrac{108\,500}{2.718}\right)^{-0.152} = £6.48$	$\dfrac{2\,000\,000}{108\,500} = £18.43$	$\dfrac{2\,160\,000}{108\,500} = £19.90$	£87.66

The terms in the expression are calculated in Table 10.5.

Figure 10.19 shows the selling price-to-volume and production cost-to-volume curves generated from these results. A profitable region of sales exists between sales of 121 000 and 206 000 units. For the latter figure, the selling price would have to be £68 and the project would only break even at the end of the run, a highly risky strategy. A selling price of £80 would be a good figure to choose as it is close to the maximum difference between price and cost at the expected sales figure and it also has a margin of 30 000 units over the break-even quantity of approx. 139 000 units. The margin at a selling price of £80 is £6.87 averaged over the whole run, but this figure rises rapidly if sales exceed the expected figure; it will be almost £9 per unit if sales reach 180 000. Provided prices can be maintained, sales above the expected figure are very profitable; alternatively, there will be scope for price cutting to increase sales and maintain production if that is considered desirable.

In this example, only 16 500 units are expected to be sold in the fifth and sixth years which is less than half the annual capacity; the question of whether to continue production in these years needs careful consideration. The final decision will have to wait until the third or fourth year when actual trading results have been obtained, the market strategy operating at the time is known and whether or not a new product is ready for launch.

Every analysis may not necessarily produce such a convenient result as the previous example; the profitability may, for example, be marginal over much of the sales volume. In cases such as this, the viability of the project is questionable and further study will be necessary. Areas to be investigated could include.

(a) a value engineering exercise to establish if further cost savings are possible;
(b) investigation into company overheads to establish if reduction or re-apportionment is possible;
(c) reduction in the performance specification if value engineering reveals that certain aspects of the performance requirement generate the need for high-cost parts (this exercise should be accompanied by reappraisal of the market for a product with reduced performance);
(d) substitution of parts made in house with items acquired more cheaply from subcontractors or overseas suppliers. (In this case, the loss of fixed overhead recovery due to not using company owned plant should be carefully investigated. Some firms have found this to be false economy when they find that, although parts may be coming in cheaper, they are left with idle capacity that is still consuming overheads.)

How much is spent on innovative projects?

Before leaving the subject of investment in innovative projects, it is worth considering what industry actually spends on innovation. The Confederation of British Industry has for some years carried out a survey of trends in innovation across the range of British industrial companies. The results of the 1991– survey (CBI/NatWest, 1992) are instructive as to the levels of expenditure and the attitudes to innovation

Table 10.6   Expenditure on innovation, by industry sector

Spend on innovation as percentage of sales revenue	Chemical industry	Metal goods industry	Mechanical engineering	Electrical/ electronic engineering	Food, drink, tobacco
0–2	22.9	60.0	27.3	17.1	41.2
2–5	54.3	32.0	60.6	45.7	29.4
5–9	11.4	4.0	6.1	28.6	23.5
9–14	5.7	0	6.1	5.7	0
14–20	2.9	0	0	0	0
20–30	2.9	4.0	0	0	0
>30	0	0	0	2.9	5.9

Table 10.7   Factors that customers consider to be most important, by industry sector

Factors of most importance to customers	Chemical industry (%)	Metal goods industry (%)	Mechanical engineering (%)	Electrical/ Electronic engineering (%)	Food, drink, tobacco (%)
Price	48	19	31	41	47
Quality	34	59	64	44	53
Delivery	9	10	3	4	4
After sales	0	0	0	0	0

that are current. Table 10.6 gives a summary of the amounts spent on innovation by industry sector.

It will be seen that the majority of manufacturers in all sectors spend up to 5% of the total sales revenue on product innovation and in some sectors notably Electrical and Food, approximately a quarter spend up to 9%. It is also in these industries that figures above 30% have been recorded. Mechanical Engineering is notable for the fact that 88% spend 5% or less and none in the survey sample spent above 14%.

Also recorded in the survey was the attitude to the amount spent on innovation; overall, 34% of the companies thought that the amount spent was inadequate – this tended to be concentrated in the smaller companies as the level of dissatisfaction fell to 16% in companies of over 5000 employees. It emphasizes the fact that for a given percentage of sales revenue, larger companies have a greater amount of risk money available for speculative research and development. The greatest dissatisfaction was in the electrical sector (at 38%) which is also the sector where the expenditure is highest. This may tend to indicate that over the long term, in the electrical sector, the large corporations will have a competitive advantage through innovation that some smaller firms will find difficult to combat.

Several factors emerge as being the prime motivators for innovative development:

- Rising levels of customer expectation, particularly quality and price
- Competition, particularly from within the home country
- Introduction of new standards and regulations

The CBI survey looked at what customers viewed as the most important attributes of the products they purchased; this is summarized in Table 10.7.

With the exception of the chemical industry, quality is currently considered more important than price and it represents, no doubt, a reaction to the demonstrably superior quality of imported goods over the past decade. Customers know from experience that good quality can be obtained at reasonable prices and now expect it of everything they purchase.

Although there is a wide spread of activity across the sectors covered, product development times are surprisingly consistent; over half the product development cycle times were in the one- to two-year range, although in the Electrical sector over half were of two to three years' duration. In the Mechanical Engineering sector nearly a quarter of all products took five to ten years to develop.

Product life cycles vary to a much greater extent, products with the longest life being in the Mechanical Engineering sector, nearly 50% being expected to remain in production for more than ten years; in the electrical sector this falls to 13% with well over half not lasting more than five years.

Summary

The question of project cost and the decision to invest in a project is a complex one. Nevertheless, investment in new products is vital for the survival of the organization and surveys have shown that industrial companies tend to spend about 5% of their total sales revenue on innovation. Formalized techniques, both manual and computer based, exist for the generation of estimates and for the evaluation of the worth of projects. The worth of these techniques is, however, somewhat diminished by the subjective nature of some of the initial estimating and the inaccuracy that, historically, has been shown to accompany it. In tackling anything new there is always an element of uncertainty regarding timescales, costs and market performance but a greater understanding of the nature of the project and the sums involved will result from a formalized assessment. In this respect, novel techniques such as parametric estimating may prove useful, particularly at the initial concept stage. The risks associated with investment in projects cannot be overlooked and the methods for assessing and controlling them are covered in Chapter 11.

11

Managing the risks

- Areas of Risk
- Risk Analysis Techniques
- Management Responses to Risk Situations
- Reducing Project Risks

However much we may choose to put the subject of risk out of our mind (and most of us do), risks surround us in our daily lives. In general, we accept these risks; we may choose to act in such a way as to minimize some of them but for the majority we forget about them and get on with living. It would be a very restricted and unrewarding existence indeed if we chose to assess all the risks that we encounter and sought to minimize them all. Businesses face risks in the same way that we as individuals face them, in that they are accepted as a part of life; to try to eliminate them all would be impractical and, ultimately, result in the demise of the organization. Risks cannot be avoided, for the world is in a state of constant change and to survive a business must adapt to the changing world around it. There must always be a chance that by choosing to make an adaptive change to something that is outside its control, that choice might turn out to be the wrong one.

The creation of a project is a visible expression of the desire for change; it is a response to a perceived need for something new and thus an opportunity to be exploited. But meeting the challenge does not assure success, the need may disappear or the opportunity may go to a competitor. A profitable outcome is the reward for taking risks in an uncertain world; it is not guaranteed and it may be negative. As businesses exist to make a satisfactory return for their investors, minimizing the risks to a satisfactory return must be a business objective.

A project is a response to a stimulus to create something where nothing existed before. Some projects have little in them that is new: they may involve something that is well known and understood, only the unique nature of the undertaking makes it worthy of the title 'project'; at the other extreme, a project may be an attempt to create something that has never been attempted before. The differences in the levels of risk between the two extremes will be obvious but it is also true to say that with projects that are largely based on proven experience, the techniques soon become well known and the effect of competition drives down the profit potential. With highly innovative projects, the chance of failure is much greater but the opportunity for profit is also greater until competitors acquire the knowledge. The potential for profit and the associated risk of failure has become a subject for study over the past two decades; industry has demanded it as both the pace of technological change and the associated costs have accelerated. It finds expression in the subject of **risk management**, and is one more field with which the contemporary Project Manager should become familiar.

The nature of risks

We shall define **risk** as: *exposure to adverse consequences, financial or physical, as a result of either the decisions made and pursued in the course of a project or the environment in which a project exists.*

This definition indicates that risks emanate from two main sources:

1. Those that are essentially in the domain of the project and result from the choices that present themselves and the decisions that are made: they could be right or wrong. The choices can be technical, financial, schedule, organizational or cultural; all are open to the project organization.
2. Those that are outside the domain of the project, but which result from changes in the nature of the environment in which the project is conducted: they could be beneficial or adverse.

Risks that stem from the external environment result in risks associated with internal decisions as choices have to be made in response to the changed circumstances. In general, decisions within the control of the project are less prone to risk on the assumption that the Project Manager acts in a rational manner – i.e. in a way that appears at the time of decision-making to reduce the chance of an adverse outcome. External changes can have a much more dramatic impact and are thus a much greater risk. Consider firms that may have decided to make private investments in developing 'Star-Wars' technology. This may have looked an attractive proposition (a technical edge over competitors, huge government orders, etc.) in the era before the break-up of Soviet Russia but the improving relationships between East and West may render this investment worthless if the threat is seen to diminish to the extent that the cost of the system does not justify the security it brings.

Definitions

Risk analysis is: *a methodology for studying the factors that make up the risks to which a project is exposed. It attempts to rationalize them in such a way that management can see the relative magnitudes and likelihoods of each factor and the risk to the project overall. The methods may be qualitative or quantitative.*

Risk Management is: *the practice of reacting to a perceived risk (through risk analysis or other observations) in such a way as to minimize the adverse consequences that may arise,* *should the risk materialize. It can form part of a plan; it can be a purely reactive procedure; or it can be a combination of both.*

Where are the risks?

Four basic areas can be identified into which risks can be seen to fall:

Risk area 1: Insurable risks. These are risks associated with misfortunes that have a known statistical history, they are the common but unfortunate things that happen: accidents, fires, losses, etc. The whole insurance industry is built around these risks and financial protection against them can be bought. For some risks insurance cover is a legal requirement, but for others it is not mandatory, here the risk is in choosing how much cover to purchase. Where risks can be minimized through preventive measures, these can be demanded by the insurers before cover is granted.

Risk area 2: Investment risks. These are risks associated with capital decisions – i.e. should a firm invest either money or employees' time and effort in pursuing a particular project? The principal determinant will be the expected benefit from the project against the expected cost. There are risks, however, in whatever investment decisions are made: failure to invest in new projects could lead to a loss of market share, but investing in the wrong projects could lead to unprofitable ventures.

Risk Area 3: Strategy risks. These are risks associated with choices about the way that projects are undertaken – i.e. the strategy employed. There are usually several ways that any project can be executed and an examination of the risks associated with each strategy should lead to the optimum choice. This type of analysis could include technical risk analysis and the construction of a plan to reduce risks of performance failures.

Risk Area 4: Conditional risks. These are risks associated with the conditions that actually arise during the course of the project: they could be different from that contained in the plan. As the future always contains uncertainties, the chain of events and the eventual outcome of the project cannot be stated with certainty. In these circumstances, what may happen can only be predicted in a statistical sense – i.e. how likely it is that something might happen.

If we put aside the area of insurable risks, the other three categories of risk each demand a different analytical approach and specific mathematical techniques have been developed to cope with them. Although the risk areas apply to progressive changes in the nature of the risk as the project proceeds, it should not be construed that each type of analysis should only be carried out at, or just before, the risk is expected to arise. During the feasibility study stage, prior to project start, the risks associated with all areas can be assessed and the results considered when deciding about starting the project or the plan that will be employed to see it through.

Analysis is all very well but someone has to look at the results and interpret them. Attitudes to perceived risk and the courses of action that one organization may take can be very different from that found in another. Culturally inspired attitudes can be deeply rooted but a well-researched analysis of where the risks lay and what can be done about them can overcome prejudices and, hopefully, result in a rational if not risk-free approach to decision-making.

Risk analysis

The creation of new products on a speculative basis with the expectation of profits from future sales is one of the most risky of all ventures. Despite the risks, companies do it all the time as they see opportunities created by new markets or new technologies. For this to be the case, the collective experience of companies must be that the risks associated with not investing in new products (loss of sales and market share) is greater than that associated with new development.

Initial project selection

The first big decision, which some may feel carries the greatest of all risks, is whether or not to start the project in the first place. To start means to commit resources, both financial and physical, but with no guarantee of a return, while not to start could imply a loss of eventual profitability. In assessing a new product two basic strategies can be considered:

1. Sell what you can make.
2. Make what you can sell.

Selling what you can make implies relatively little risk in the design and manufacturing technology, the risk lies in the market. The area for consideration lies in the acceptance by the market of the new product: will the market reject the product in favour of cheaper or newer technology alternatives, how much will have to be spent on promotion in order to achieve a satisfactory level of penetration, etc.? Making what you can sell implies an understanding of the market, the emerging trends, changing tastes and the likely effects of new technology. Deciding to enter the market with an apparently attractive new product has risks both in the areas of design if the trends and tastes are not interpreted correctly, and technology if the development proves to be difficult and expensive. Of the two strategies, making what you can sell has the lower overall risk as the market, being an external source of risk and one over which the producer may have only limited influence, is given the greater priority in terms of product specification. In this case, the major risks stem from decisions about the product, the technology, the development budget, etc. that are internal to the project and they can be taken in a way that attempts to reduce chances of failure.

To be a success a new product must satisfy three criteria:

1. It must be attractive to customers, i.e. it must satisfy a market need.
2. It must be technically feasible – i.e. it must be capable of being made to work satisfactorily.
3. It must be capable of being made for a cost that will allow a satisfactory profit when offered at an acceptable selling price – i.e. it must be cheap enough to produce to be competitive.

Each of these represents an area of risk; a product that fails in any of these areas fails overall. A careful examination of each of these criteria is necessary if a realistic assessment of the risks are to be made. Herein lies the first difficulty; it is one that will bedevil the concept of risk analysis throughout the remainder of this discussion and it is that of subjectivity. Although risk analysis can adopt strictly logical mathematical disciplines, the factors to which the maths are applied are, in many cases, subjective assessments. Any assessment of the outcome of events that will take place in the future contains an element of guesswork and that element can never be removed. However, the more detailed the study of the above criteria and the more evidence of past performance that can be taken into account, the more likely it is that the subjective assessments will be of the right order of magnitude. The term 'order of magnitude' is used here to indicate that precision is not expected; too much evidence exists to indicate that forecasts of the outcome of novel projects are often wildly inaccurate and almost always optimistic. Given that inaccuracy is a built-in feature of project assessment, senior management still demand, and rightly so, that it be done as the expenditure on product development must be justified on some grounds. Normally this is done on the basis of benefit-to-cost but that alone does not allow for the risk element. One way of identifying those projects that are worth pursuing is to set some boundary criteria which any new project must meet in order for it to gain approval.

A simple formula that can be used is:

$$M = \left(\frac{G}{C_d + C_p}\right) \times P_t \times P_m \tag{11.1}$$

where: M = an index-of-merit;
G = the gross profit from sales over the life of the project;
C_d = the total cost of development;
C_p = the total cost of the assumed production run;
P_t = the probability of a technical success (functionality and cost);
P_m = the probability of achieving the anticipated sales at the assumed prices.

It will be realized that this formula takes into account the three basic criteria for a successful product. It generates a dimensionless number (M) of value less than one and a minimum value such as 0.125 can be set as the boundary condition; any project that falls below this value is automatically rejected. There are, however, a number of obvious criticisms:

1. The magnitude of the costs relative to the organization as a whole is not taken into account; the same answer would arise if the costs and profits are in the same ratio for a £100 000 project as for a £100m. one.
2. The disparity in time between the expenditure and the accrual of profit is not included.
3. The eventual effect on the business of not having the new product in the market when there is a reasonable expectation that a competitor will have one is not taken into account.

When these three additional considerations are assessed, the boundary condition may become an issue that is far from simple. In the end, corporate culture (risk averse or the opposite) or long-term corporate strategy may become the final arbiter in the decision to go ahead.

Various formulae have been suggested that take into account the additional factors and they are of the general form:

$$M = \left(\frac{G}{C_d + C_p}\right) \times P_t \times P_m \times (M_t + M_b) \times S \times T \tag{11.2}$$

where: M_t = technological merit;
$\quad\quad\quad M_b$ = business merit;
$\quad\quad\quad S$ = strategic fit with other projects, products and markets;
$\quad\quad\quad T$ = timing or discounting factor based on the time at which profits accrue.

Formulae such as these have their place but they should also be treated with caution. Factors such as technological merit or business merit are complex issues, yet this formula demands that each is reduced to just a single number between 1 and 0. With so many factors that are gross simplifications or probabalistic estimates, the single figure that results from such a formula cannot be considered as definitive. It would be better to assume that it is merely a guide – and subject to wide error – as to how the project is viewed at one point in time. If formulae have a real merit, it may be at the extremities where they can clearly demonstrate either very desirable or undesirable projects. However, one would expect normal business acumen within the organization to identify these possibilities without much formal analysis. There is one other danger, and it is that formulae which contain so many subjective elements can be used to justify anything. All Project Managers associated with development know that the greatest obstacle to be overcome is that of initial selection. There may be a natural temptation to use formulae to justify the starting of projects in a wholly undeserved way, as part of the in-fighting that goes on in companies when it comes to development expenditure.

The question of deciding whether a new product is worth developing has already been discussed in Chapter 2. Figure 2.9 shows a new-product evaluation sheet and the methodology contained within it can be considered as an extension of the **index-of-merit concept**. It attempts to generate a numerical score by which proposals for projects can be judged and it does so by a two-stage process. Techniques of this type have become known as **multiple-criteria decision-making methods**. A series of attributes, either good or bad, that can apply to any project are identified and a weighting factor reflecting its importance to the decision-maker is attached to each. The weightings can either be assessed simply or by more complex techniques which involve making comparisons between each pair of attributes and scoring each in terms of how much more or less favourable it is than the other. By calculating the mean scores for each attribute when compared to all others and normalizing them, a weighting can be derived that reflects the relative importance of each. Once a system of weightings is established, the characteristics of the particular project are examined against each attribute and a score is given according to how well the project matches it. These scores are then multiplied by the weightings to give a weighted score. The sum of weighted scores provides an overall score for the project as a whole. Again, a hurdle value can be established; any project that falls below it is rejected.

Before leaving this subject, the question of risk trade-off should be considered. It is sometimes said that there is a balance between low risk and low-profit projects and high risk and high-profit projects. While it is clear that low-risk and low-profit projects do exist, the question is whether or not there really are high-risk, high-profit projects? The answer depends on how risk is defined and where the risks lay. A truly high-risk project is one in which there is both a high technical risk and a high risk of it failing in the market. If both these factors are known, it would be difficult to conceive of how its chances of making a high return could be seen as good because the odds are all against it. A project that has a high technical risk but a low market risk is far more likely to achieve a high return but such a project could not be said to be a high-risk project overall. Using the weightings of Figure 2.9 and

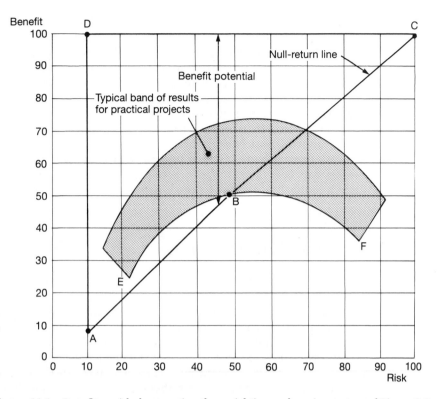

Figure 11.1 Benefit vs risk drawn using the weighting and scoring system of Figure 2.9.

considering the positive factors to represent the benefits and the negative factors to represent the risks, Figure 11.1 can be drawn. The null-return line, A,B,C, which joins points of equal high, medium and low scores represents the line above which any project must score in order to show a benefit that outweighs the risk. The boundary of this area is given by the figure A,B,C,D and it is clear from this that the greater the risk, the lower is the potential for high profits as the gap between the null-return line and the upper benefit boundary decreases with increasing risk.

In practical cases, the actual profit from low-risk projects tends to be well below the upper boundary because of the effects of competition; however, the ideal project is one that combines low risks with high earnings. High risks do not automatically carry the potential for high profits, it is far more likely that they will result in low or negative rewards, particularly if there is a large market risk. The Sinclair C-5 tricycle exemplifies a product with low technical risk but very high market risk; predictably it was a financial disaster. However, attempts to reduce market risk can also backfire; the Ford Edsel car of the 1950s was a product closely tailored to the perceived market requirement but it resulted in failure, the whole design approach lacked character and with that went customer appeal. The band E,F represents a far more typical characteristic for practical projects and it indicates that the best profit potential lies in the low-to-medium-risk category. Projects with potentially high risks may still have an appeal in certain circumstances; for example, where a failure to instigate a new-product project in the knowledge that a competitor is working on one would signal to the world a withdrawal from an important market sector; some recent aerospace projects have been undertaken on that basis. Where risks are seen to be high but there is a belief in the potential for high earnings, the approach should be one of moving the project into the medium-risk category either through further technical evaluation and market testing or the adoption of a defensive market strategy, letting competitors take the initial risks.

One suggestion that is sometimes put forward to counter this problem is a portfolio approach to projects in which a balanced mix of low-risk, low-profit and high-risk, high-profit projects is maintained. As has been pointed out, few high-risk, high-profit projects exist; thus, where high risks are concerned, it might be better to contain them to pure research projects, expecting most of them to be failures, but when one does look to be a potential success, the research will have already removed much of the risk before it goes to the development stage.

Alternative strategies

All projects at the outset are subject to a simple 'go/no-go' decision. However, a 'go' decision may not be straightforward as there may be alternative paths that can be followed. The paths that are open are termed **strategies** and the decision-maker has the choice of which one he pursues. Choices that can exist concern: the product specification – simple or sophisticated; the development timescale – extended or compressed; and the size of the development budget – extensive or shoe-string. These choices are not necessarily independent, it is difficult to develop a sophisticated product in a short timescale on a shoe-string budget, although some firms persist in thinking that this can be done. There are always choices to be made but some may be dictated by practical considerations such as the availability of staff, facilities and cash flow. It is important to note that whichever strategy is chosen it will have a bearing on the eventual profitability of the project. A choice thus represents a risk that the selected strategy may turn out to be the wrong one for the conditions that arise in the future.

Case example 11.1: Product and market strategy options

The choice of technology can have a dramatic effect on market prospects as shown by the rivalry between Sony and Philips for the next generation of recorded music. Sony started with Digital Audio Tape (DAT) in which video tape recording technology is used to encode the signal – this, however, involves the use of an angled, rotating recording head and a special cassette in order to record the large amount of digitized data; it is an expensive system. Philips' response is Digital Compact Cassette (DCC) using a cassette similar in style to existing ones and a simpler fixed head; it can do this because of a clever piece of technology developed by Philips. The human ear can only detect certain of the sounds that are emitted in music, Philips' system records only those sounds that are noticeable thus allowing better quality sound to be recorded on ordinary tape without the need for the angled head. The reasoning behind this approach lies in a study of market acceptability; here Philips took a clear view that, as cassettes are the most popular medium for recorded music, the new product will gain greater acceptance if:

- it uses cassettes that resemble the existing ones;
- the players can play normal analogue cassettes as well as the digital ones;
- the price of prerecorded tapes is similar to current cassettes.

This indicates choosing a 'make what you can sell' product strategy and directing technical development into those areas that will make the new product functional without departing from the basic concept. Sony appear to have gone the other way with a 'sell what you can make' strategy using existing, proven technology and relying on the technical appeal of the new product to overcome market resistance. In fact, DAT does not look likely to be a serious challenger to DCC and Sony have now replied with a new system: the MiniDisc. It is a derivative of compact disc technology that can be played on personal, Walkman-type players but featuring the capability for recording your own music. Again, this is a 'sell what you can make' response. Sales, in the end, will almost certainly be determined by the quantity of prerecorded music that becomes available in either format; electronics hardware makers have been engaged in a round of acquiring music and film companies for the rights to their material.

Techniques that can help in choosing between alternative strategies include qualitative methods (problem formulation, identification of objectives, etc.) and quantitative methods (games theory, simulation, etc.). The American mathematician J. von Neumann published his classic work on decision strategy during the Second World War, *The Theory of Games*. All competitive decision-makers can be viewed as analogous to players in a game, each has a choice of strategies with different outcomes but none can be sure what strategy the other will choose. Von Neumann showed that in a game there is always a best strategy that a player can adopt but the analogy with a business situation cannot be taken too far as the rules may not be defined with the precision of a game and each player may have different objectives. However, the concept of a best strategy is valuable to the decision-maker.

In any project there are always variable factors that are either controllable as they are internal to the project or external and outside of control; it is this interaction between the controllable and the uncontrollable factors that combine to determine the eventual outcome of any decision. The best strategy is the one which gives the best result over the range of possible outcomes. In the digital cassette situation, from either company's point of view the uncontrollable factors are market reaction to the rival new products and the response that each company makes to the other's marketing initiatives. The combination of these factors, together with the chosen price, available recordings, etc., will result in an outcome that can be defined in terms of market share, annual sales figures and revenue obtained, termed **outcome descriptors**. To evaluate the strategies that are open it is necessary to define outcome descriptors that are meaningful and can be used to gauge the success or failure of each decision. In formulating the choices the Project Manager must be able to select those factors which are relevant to the outcome while rejecting those which ultimately have no bearing on the issue.

Example 11.1: Choice of a development strategy

After a successful prototype testing phase of a new product, a company decides to start a full-scale development and production programme but there are three alternative approaches to the way the development programme is undertaken. Once a course of action has been adopted, it will be difficult and expensive to change to an alternative; the problem is which course to choose. The alternative approaches are:

1. Perform a minimum change development and productionizing programme based on the existing prototype and launch the product on the market in one year.
2. Perform further market research, refine the product definition, value engineer the design and launch the product in two years.
3. Invest more in development technology and launch a more sophisticated product in two and a half to three years.

The Marketing department have assessed the potential for future sales but find their estimates to be subject to wide margins; the best that they can do is to classify demand as 'high', 'medium' or 'low'. Six factors are deemed to be relevant to the sales potential and the eventual profitability:

(a) The cost of development including production tooling.
(b) The unit production cost.
(c) The unit selling price.
(d) The cost of promotion.
(e) The effect of competition.
(f) The shape of the market.

Factors (a)–(d) can be expressed in purely numerical terms but (e) and (f) are qualitative judgements that have a bearing on the size of the market. For each of the alternatives the assessments are as follows:

Strategy 1, Existing technology
(a) Cost of development   £2.5m.
(b) Unit production cost   £125
(c) Unit selling price   £150
(d) Cost of promotion   £0.7m.
(e) Effect of competition   Relatively little over the first year of sales
(f) Shape of market   Peak demand at end of first two years

Strategy 2, Further product refinement
(a) Cost of development   £3.0m.
(b) Unit production cost   £110
(c) Unit selling price   £135
(d) Cost of promotion   £1.0m.
(e) Effect of competition   Competition fierce after first year of sales
(f) Shape of market   Peak demand at end of first year

Strategy 3, More advanced product
(a) Cost of development   £4.0m.

(b) Unit production cost   £130
(c) Unit selling price   £150
(d) Cost of promotion   £1.5m.
(e) Effect of competition   Competition fierce at product launch
(f) Shape of market   Anticipated high demand for the advanced product

Table 11.1 Alternative sales estimates for various options

Option	Total sales		
	High	Medium	Low
1	500 000	400 000	200 000
2	600 000	500 000	200 000
3	750 000	550 000	150 000

The market forecasts, based on the above assessments, are as given in Table 11.1. For each case, the outcome, in terms of eventual profits, can be calculated (ignoring the effects of discounting): Taking Option 1 for high total sales, the total cost of the programme is made up from the development cost plus the promotion cost plus the cost of making 500 000 units:

$$£2.5m. + £0.7m. + £125 \times 500\,000 = £65\,700\,000$$

The total revenue from option 1 with high sales is:

$$£150 \times 500\,000 = £75\,000\,000$$

The total profit in this situation is thus.

$$£75\,000\,000 - £65\,700\,000 = £9\,300\,000$$

The outcomes in terms of profit for all the options and levels of sales are given in Table 11.2. The table is termed an **outcome array** and the alternative circumstances that may arise, in this case 'high', 'medium' or 'low' sales, are termed **states of nature**. Here 'nature' means the world in which the project exists; it contains uncontrollable and uncertain elements but it does not necessarily act in the same way as a competitive player in a game. Examination of the outcome array shows that there is no single option that is superior to the others in all cases, although Option 2 is always superior to Option 3. If one option exhibits superiority over the others in all cases, it is said to exhibit '**dominance**' and would be the best course to choose. As this example does not show a dominant option, it is necessary to consider other ways of making a choice. A cautious view would be to assume that things always turn out for the

Table 11.2 Profit forecasts for alternative options

Option	Profit from sales		
	High	Medium	Low
1	9 300 000	6 800 000	1 800 000
2	11 000 000	8 500 000	1 000 000
3	9 500 000	5 500 000	−2 500 000

worst and therefore only the worst possible outcomes (i.e. those associated with low sales) should be considered. Under these conditions, the option to choose is that which gives the best outcome from the worst conditions; in this case, it is Option 1 as this has an expected profit of £1.8m., whereas Option 2 has a profit of £1.0m. and Option 3 shows a loss. The advantage of this strategy is that the lowest level of profit is guaranteed; with any other state of nature, higher profits can be expected. This decision rule is termed a **maximin strategy** as is aims to maximize the minimum return. The weakness of this approach is that it ignores the chances of much higher profits that may be returned with the other strategies if things turn out better than the worst case. In this case, Option 2 shows a better profit of £1.7m. if high or medium sales arise. One could choose Option 2 on the grounds that it offers the chance of the best profit of all, a **maximax** strategy, but for all sales of nature other than the best, for the return will be lower.

A further course of action is to ask for more information, in particular: how likely are any of these forecast sales to be attained? The Marketing Departments of all companies should be able, with sufficient research, to attach some level of probability to any sales figure they derive. Suppose that the Marketing Department argue that because Option 1 gets the product to the market quickly and it has already established its appeal, a probability of 0.7 should be attached to medium sales and a probability of 0.2 should be given to high sales, while low sales should only be given a 0.1 probability. Option 2 involves better tailoring of the product to market needs and a more competitively priced item but it arrives later in the market and may face more intense competition. In this case, Marketing attach a probability of 0.7 to medium sales but high sales now get a probability of 0.1 and low sales go up to 0.2. Option 3 is much less clear as it involves new technology and is even further away in terms of product launch into a market which will be well supplied; in this case, Marketing attach equal probabilities of 0.333 to high, medium and low sales. Given this additional view of the likely state of nature, one can make a choice between options on the basis of the one that should give the best result in the long run. By multiplying the probability figures by the outcome values and adding the results the **expected value** from each option can be derived.

Option 1

Expected profit = £9.3m. × 0.2 + £6.8m. × 0.7 + £1.8m. × 0.1 = £6.8m.

Option 2

Expected profit = £11.0m. × 0.1 + £8.5m. × 0.7 + £1.0m. × 0.2
              = £7.25m.

Option 3

Expected profit = £9.5m. × 0.33 + £5.5m. × 0.33 − £2.5m. × 0.33
              = £2.78m.

On the basis of this calculation, one could conclude that Option 2 is superior and thus the best course of action. However, had the Marketing Department taken a slightly more cautious view by saying that the probability of medium sales is 0.6 and that of low sales is 0.3, the expected gain is reduced to £6.5m.

and Option 1 now looks more attractive. Calculations of this type are termed **sensitivity analyses**, they serve to show if small changes in assumptions can cause significant changes in the indicated outcomes. Sensitivity tests should always be carried out; where uncertainty is concerned, it is unwise to rely on a single-figure estimate. Looking again at the example, it is clear that there is little to choose between Options 1 and 2 but Option 3, being late into the market and with heavy development expenditure, comes out the worst in this analysis by any of the criteria. It tends to emphasize the point, made previously, that formalized analyses tend to point out the obviously best or worst extremes. In the middle region, choices are not so clear-cut and the risks of making the wrong decision still remain. In a case such as this, the choice between options would be made using additional considerations that have not been included in this analysis such as:

(a) The timing and need to fill the production shops with new work: if work is needed earlier rather than later, Option 1 is preferable.
(b) The cash position in respect of development funding.
(c) Longer-term corporate objectives.

Once the project has started, choices between courses of action will present themselves and decisions will be required on a regular basis. Some will be so trivial as to need little more than cursory consideration, but from time to time situations will arise where decisions could, if they are wrong, have serious consequences for the project. They may not be quite as momentous as the initial decision to go ahead, but the momentum of the project may mean that they have to be made in a relatively short timeframe and with less-than-perfect information. A similar procedure to that already described can be used as an aid to finding the best way forward. The following case shows one such decision situation and the course that was adopted.

Case example 11.2: Stabilizer fin decision

With air-launched weapons designed to fall freely it is common practice to use folding stabilizer fins to ensure the weapon strikes the target at the appropriate speed and attitude. During the development of an air-launched device, a problem arose with a stabilizer used on a weapon that was part of a larger system being managed by a prime contractor. The stabilizer fins were released by a timing device operating on a spring that opened the fins; a large number of these weapons were needed in the test programme. Due to the quantities involved, the weapon contractor had built a special assembly line and staffed it to meet the delivery rate demanded by the prime contractor's programme. Just when assembly work was due to start, some wind-tunnel work using models revealed that, under certain circumstances, the stabilizer might not open because the spring had insufficient energy; however, the amount of energy needed was difficult to establish. Furthermore, there was very little space for the spring and any increase in space could involve significant changes to the rear of the weapon. Concern grew and eventually a spring was designed with double the energy of the existing one that would still fit in the available space without extensive changes. Doubts, however, still remained; what was needed was a flight test.

Considerable urgency was attached to the test as the weapon manufacturer was aware of the problems that would follow if the new design proved unsatisfactory but, at the same time, he had a labour force ready to start production. One trials aircraft fitted with the special weapon release unit was available and preparation for a test with a prototype modified unit was put in hand. Shortly before the test was due, a sister aircraft to the trials plane suffered a fatal accident; investigation revealed a serious problem with the whole fleet and all were grounded including the trials machine. Repairs were expected to take between four and nine months and a suitably modified alternative aircraft was not available. The weapon contractor asked the prime contractor for a decision on how to proceed given that the labour force was in place; to stop would involve a lay-off of staff and a lengthy period of run-up once production resumed. However, if the spring did not work, a major redesign would be necessary.

This is the classic Project Manager's dilemma: is it better to go ahead knowing that if hardware is produced and the system has a problem it will result in expensive scrap, or would it be preferable to wait for a test knowing that a delay will affect the overall project cost significantly? With either decision, there is a risk that if fate is unkind both the cost and timescale of the project will be adversely affected. Before this problem can be analysed, some basic facts need to be assembled, they are:

- Availability of other aircraft: none that were not of the same type and affected by the same problem.
- Ongoing cost of the project: $0.75m. per month.
- Existing committed cost of weapons: $0.5m.
- Cost of 5000 test weapons to be supplied over six months: $1.5m.
- Salvage value of committed items: $0.25m.
- Slip if the new spring fails: 12 months.

Table 11.4 Stabilizer decision, outcome array

Decision \ Outcome	Stabilizer works		Stabilizer does not work	
Stop for 6 months Wait for trial	Hardware commitment	0.5m.	Hardware commitment	0.5m.
	Slip 6 months at $0.75m./month	4.5m.	Slip 12 months at $0.75/month	9.0m.
		$5.0m.	Salvage	−0.25m.
			Re-manufacture	0.5m.
				$9.75m.
Go ahead with 5000	Project on course Hardware cost	0	Hardware cost	1.5m.
		1.5m.	Slip 12 months	9.0m.
			Salvage	−0.25m.
		$1.5m.	Re-manufacture	1.5m.
				$11.75m.

Two strategies are open to the Project Manager: wait for possibly six months and conduct the flight test, then give the go ahead for weapon output or go ahead immediately with the batch of 5000 units and maintain the programme. Only two outcomes are possible: either the new spring works properly, or it does not. An array can be constructed of possible outcomes in terms of the position at the time when it becomes known if the retarder works (Table 11.4).

Using a maximin or maximax decision rule would not be the most appropriate decision strategy as a decision-maker in this circumstance would be expected to have some idea of the chance of success. The concept of 'expected value' has already been introduced and it can be used to determine the best decision on the basis that the manager would adopt the route of the lowest expected loss. In this case, the outcome array can be evaluated to find out what level of probability of the new spring working is necessary for the expected costs from both strategies to be equally likely. If the actual probability of it working is greater than this value, then going ahead will be the better strategy, if it is less it will pay to wait:

Let x = the probability that the new spring works.

Then the minimum probability for success occurs when the outcomes of both strategies have equal expected costs:

The expected cost of waiting for 6 months is: $5x + 9.75(1 - x)$

and the expected cost of going ahead is: $1.5x + 11.75(1 - x)$

$$5x + 9.75(1 - x) = 1.5x + 11.75(1 - x)$$

Therefore: $x = \dfrac{2}{5.5} = 0.36$

With any probability of the spring working that is higher than 0.36 there would be a benefit in going ahead with production of the weapons. In this case, it was judged that the likelihood of the stabilizer fins working with the new spring was above 0.9, the most sensible decision was to instruct the weapon maker to go ahead with production in the absence of the flight test.

What happened when this recommendation was put to the prime contractor's program manager? The reaction was not as one might have expected, or was it? He said, 'I don't think that we'll tell them anything; give them enough time and they'll decide to do something on their own accord. If they go ahead and it works: that's fine. If it turns out the other way and they're wrong, we can blame them.' This decision could be viewed as avoiding the issue, but the progress of the project is not the only issue involved. Clearly there is a risk but, in this instance, the manager viewed the greatest risk as a personal one, that of being seen to make a wrong decision. Such a perception of risk may lie in the corporate culture if it is one that tends to penalize wrong decisions, even if they are taken in the most rational of ways, this is the kind of decision-making that may result. Under these circumstances, the Project Manager may not act in a way that is rational in minimizing risk to the project.

As to what happened, the weapon contractor decided, unilaterally, to go ahead with production in the absence of a test. After about two months of further investigation, the prime contractor found that an alternative rig fitted to an aircraft of a different type could be modified to test the weapon. The rig was duly modified and the test carried out about a month later; it showed that the new system worked perfectly.

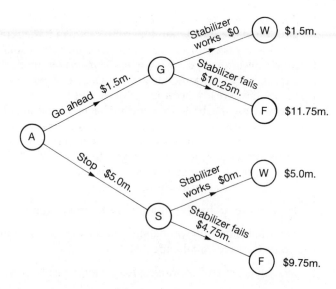

Figure 11.2   The manager's tree of decision options and outcomes.

The problem faced by the Project Manager in the case study is simply that of a more general formulation of the decision-making problem, namely the **decision tree**. They can be constructed as an aid to decision-making when there are conditions of uncertainty about the possible outcomes. Decision trees are a structured way of breaking down any decision problem and then evaluating the outcomes such that the best choice of strategy can be made.

The construction and evaluation of decision trees is a four-stage process:

1. The manager must set down the options that are open to him when a decision has to be made.
2. The outcome from each option must be evaluated in quantitative terms.
3. The probabilities of each outcome arising must be established.
4. The decision tree must be evaluated to find the expected values of the outcomes resulting from a decision.

If we consider the Project Manager's options in the stabilizer case, a simple decision tree can be drawn, as shown in Figure 11.2.

It will be seen that there are the four possible outcomes that were evaluated in Table 11.4; if instead of being given a 90% probability of the stabilizer working, as was the real case, suppose that he was given a figure of only 50% – i.e. the odds against passing or failing are even. This is the state of nature, it is the factor that is out of the manager's control but nature's decision tree can be drawn, and it is shown in Figure 11.3. When the manager's tree and nature's tree are combined, a decision tree is formed that can be evaluated for the expected outcome; this has been done in Figure 11.4.

The expected values of each decision are written in the rectangular boxes at the appropriate nodes. As would be expected, with equal probabilities of success or failure the route A,G (i.e. go ahead) shows the lower expected cost and would be the preferred decision. Suppose, however, that the Project Manager is still uncertain as to what to do and asks if there are any other alternatives that might be open; he

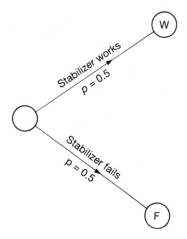

Figure 11.3 The decision tree according to the state of nature.

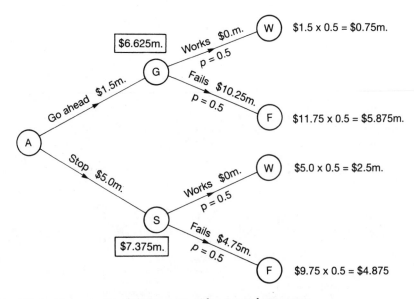

Figure 11.4 The complete decision tree with expected outcomes.

receives a suggestion that a full-scale wind-tunnel test is possible. Investigation shows that a test could be completed within two months but at a cost of $100 000; the test will not be conclusive, but he is assured that there will be a 90% chance that whatever is discovered in the wind tunnel will reflect what is found in flight. If the manager decides he would prefer to conduct the wind tunnel test before committing to a decision to go ahead with production, we can assess if this is advantageous by constructing an outcome array for this new course of action; it is given in Table 11.5.

The decision tree introducing the additional possibility of the wind-tunnel test is shown in Figure 11.5. The paths from node T are each given the probability of 0.5 as it is no more or less likely that the stabilizer will pass or fail the wind-tunnel test. The costs from the outcome array are shown at the end-nodes; on the basis of the confidence in the wind-tunnel test, a probability of 0.9 is attached to the outcome

Table 11.5   Stabilizer decision, outcome array after wind-tunel test

Decision \ Outcome	Stabilizer passes air test		Stabilizer fails air test	
Stabilizer passes tunnel test	H/ware commitment	$0.5m	H/ware commitment	$0.5m
	Slip 2 months	$1.5m	Slip 12 months	$9.0m
	At $0.75m/month		At $0.75/month	
	Test cost	$0.1m	H/W made	$0.666m
	H/W made	$0.666m	Salvage	−$0.25m
		‾‾‾‾‾‾‾	Re-manufacture	$1.166m
		$2.766m	W/T test	$0.1m
				‾‾‾‾‾‾‾
				$11.182m
Stabilizer fails tunnel test	H/W committed	$0.5m	H/ware commitment	$0.5m
	Slip 6 months	$4.5m	Slip 12 months	$9.0m
	Test cost	$0.1m	Salvage	−$0.25m
		‾‾‾‾‾	Re-manufacture	$0.5m
		$5.1m	Test cost	$0.1m
				‾‾‾‾‾
				$9.85m

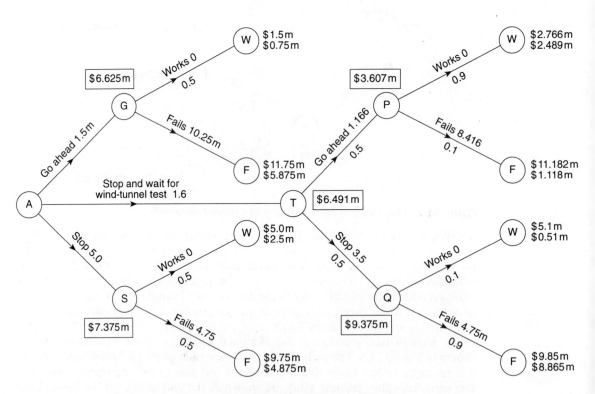

Figure 11.5   The complete decision tree including the wind-tunnel option.

that assumes a correct decision. Thus a decision to go ahead on the basis of a satisfactory wind-tunnel test leads to a 90% chance of a satisfactory flight test. The expected values at nodes P and Q are calculated as before and, given equal probabilities, the expected value at node T is found to be $6.491m. This is somewhat less than the expected value from an immediate decision to go ahead, hence waiting for the wind tunnel test results would be the better decision. An even better expected outcome would result if the manager decides to go ahead with production immediately and stop only if the wind tunnel test shows a failure. The reader is left to draw the decision tree for this option and evaluate it for himself.

The decision tree method is thus a formalized way of assessing complex decision problems and it can aid the decision-maker by:

(a) showing clearly good or bad options;
(b) showing marginal differences between options that can help in deciding how much it is worth paying for more information (e.g. through research or testing) in order to improve the decision.

Decision trees need care in their construction and evaluation, a logical and disciplined train of thought is essential. After the evaluation has been done, one thing should be noted: a manager who follows a logical and reasoned decision-making process can be said to be making good decisions and that is all that can be expected of him; there is, however, a difference between a good decision and a good outcome. The outcome is in the hands of nature and if fate chooses to be perverse a good decision can still lead to a bad outcome.

Conditional risks

So far, we have considered choices between alternatives where we wish to select the route that will give the least risky or most favourable result. There are other situations where the course of action is already determined but the risks lie in the project not going according to plan. Activities that are planned may take longer than estimated, failures may occur on test, resources may not be available when needed, etc. Such effects can and will combine to cause the outcome of the project to be different from that in the plan and, for the most part, they will make the position of the project worse. If it is known that some of these effects are likely to happen, they can be allowed for in the plan by adding suitable time and cost contingencies. The question becomes one of how much contingency to add and what faith can be had in the result?

The PERT concept, which deals with project durations, recognized that uncertainty is a feature of all estimating and it sought to quantify this, in part, by allowing three estimates of the task duration to be made and entered into the analysis. The estimates required are shortest, longest and most likely durations. The PERT technique seems to have fallen into disuse for reasons discussed in Chapter 4 but a revival of the idea has come about in some of the most recent software systems which are now being marketed with a 'risk analysis' module. One such system is 'Opera', a risk analysis package that accompanies the 'Open Plan' project management system. It uses the three-estimate method but this can be applied to both the estimated task durations and the estimated task costs. Whereas PERT used the statistical relationship between the three figures to calculate an average duration

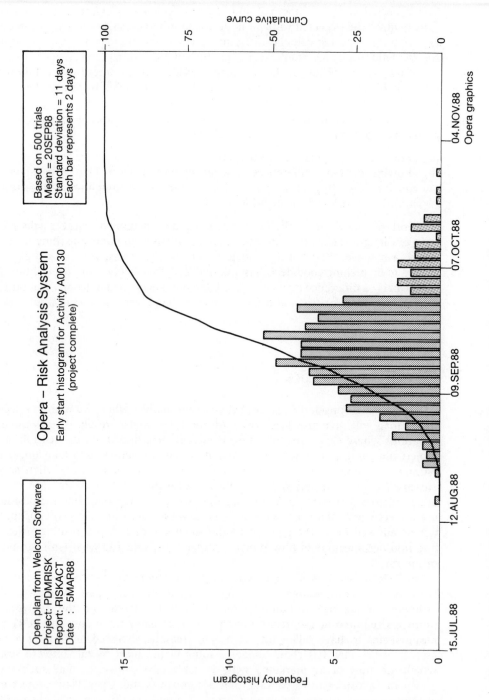

Figure 11.6 Histogram and cumulative probability for project completion using 'OPERA'.

and total variance, the new software uses a Monte Carlo simulation method. This involves choosing values of the duration or cost on a random basis but from a selected distribution and calculating the end-condition of the project by working through the network. When this is done many times, the distribution of probable outcomes can be seen. The calculation can be done for both durations and costs, these two variables may be treated as independent or totally linked, or some degree of linking can be specified on a percentage basis. Outputs are of two basic forms: (a) criticality indices for each activity, and (b) relative probabilities for various durations and costs. Based on the number of simulation runs that are done, an index is calculated for each activity that indicates its likelihood of becoming a critical activity. Presentation of this result is in the form of a shaded bar chart, where the denser the shading, the more critical is the activity. The probability figures for costs and durations are shown both as a histogram of individual frequencies and a cumulative probability curve. The cumulative curve shows the probability that a particular value of cost or duration will be achieved or bettered; Figure 11.6 shows an example of the 'Opera' output. Confidence limits can be placed on the probability calculations to show the spread of values associated with a given probability level. It should be noted, however, that the confidence levels are based on an assumption that the input information is perfect – i.e. that the plan is adhered to and that no costs or durations go outside the maximum and minimum limits specified. In real projects neither of these assumptions may hold good; the confidence limits may thus give an apparent sense of security that is not really justified. In essence, this type of package allows some risk analysis to be done within well-defined limitations; it does not allow for alternative strategies that may be adopted at various stages in the project, nor can it deal with such uncertainties as the chance of technical failures. For projects of the less innovative and more routine kind such as construction work, it can be a useful tool, but even here risks such as prolonged bad weather, trade union disputes and strikes cannot be taken into account.

Where software is not available, assessments can still be made of the spread of durations and cost under conditions of uncertainty using the rules of probability; in this case, more sophisticated models can be devised that allow the chance of alternative outcomes and different strategies at significant points in the project.

Example 11.2: Variability in durations of a development project

A company wishes to bid for a contract to design, develop and test a new item of military hardware. The project has a feasibility study phase followed by a full-scale development and pre-production phase. A fixed-price bid is required to cover both phases. At the end of the full-scale development programme, a production order will be placed but not until a pre-production example has been built and all environmental testing has been satisfactorily completed. The customer also wishes to be in a position to place a production order no later than 45 months from the start of the project. The bidding company notes that an existing item of equipment that it already manufactures can form the basis of the new unit but a significant amount of new design and testing will be needed to meet the customer's requirements. An examination of the programme shows that uncertainties exist in both the areas of pricing and duration, but for the purposes of this example only the durations will be considered. The programme can be divided into six major activities:

1. Feasibility study.
2. Detail design.
3. Acquisition of a prototype for testing.
4. Performance testing.
5. Environmental testing.
6. Construction of a pre-production example.

The activities are to be carried out in the order listed, with the exception that sufficient confidence in the design will exist at the end of the performance test for construction of the pre-production prototype to proceed in parallel with the environmental tests. Regarding the durations, uncertainties exist over the exact length of time that each activity will take and there are further doubts about success at the performance testing phase. Beyond the performance test, the exact amount of environmental testing is also difficult to establish. It is hoped that some environmental test results from the existing design will be capable of direct translation to the new design and thus shorten the test programme but this cannot be guaranteed; if changes turn out to be significant, then a full environmental programme will be needed. If a significant shortfall reveals itself during performance testing, then it is likely that further design alterations will be needed which, in turn, raises the chances of having to complete a full environmental test.

The first step in assessing the outcome is to express the problem as a logic diagram, showing the alternative paths that may be taken. The next step is to estimate the range of alternatives and then to assign probabilities to each. Figure 11.7 shows the logic diagram with the assessed durations and probabilities. In this example, all durations are given in months and the spread of durations has been kept deliberately small. A simple rule has been used for assessing the probabilities; either they are equal: 50/50, 33/33/33, or one outcome is more likely than the other: 70/30. In this case, it was felt that a satisfactory performance on initial test was more likely than a shortfall; however, if a shortfall does occur, it is likely to delay the end of testing by seven months. It was also felt that in the event of a satisfactory performance test, a short environmental test would be the more likely route, conversely, if a performance shortfall is revealed, then a full environmental test is more likely to be needed. The question becomes one of what confidence can be had in meeting the 45-month target; if the Board further decides that it is unwilling to bid with any duration which it has less than an 80% chance of meeting, what duration should be quoted?

In this example, a common time interval of one month has been chosen throughout to describe the spread of durations; this makes computation relatively simple and suitable for a pocket calculator, with differing time intervals computer software becomes essential. All the distributions are treated as independent. The method of calculation involves working through the whole project from the beginning and generating the distribution of durations at each stage. Here it is felt that the Feasibility Study (F) can have durations of six or seven months with equal probability and that the next stage, Detail Design (D), can take either 12 or 13 months, with the latter being more likely. By com-

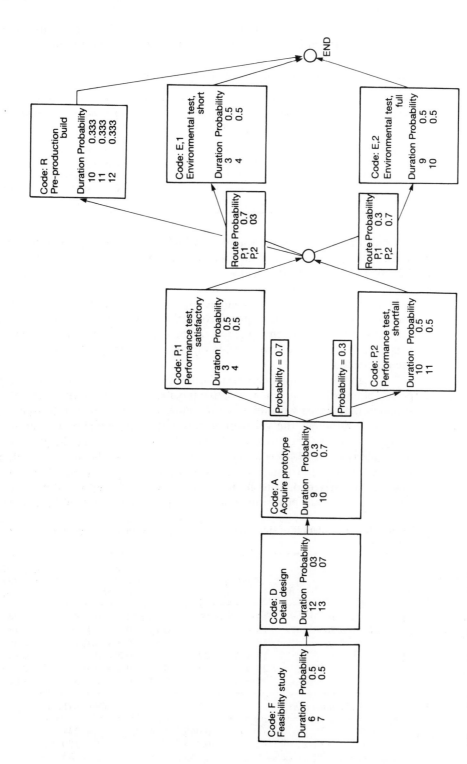

Figure 11.7 Project logic with alternatives and probabilities.

bining the distributions, a new distribution can be obtained for the time to complete the Detail Design phase. Table 11.6 shows the procedure.

Table 11.6 Calculation of durations and probabilities for the completion of detail design

Duration F	D	Probability F	D	Combined duration FD	Combined probability p (FD)	Cumulative probability Cum. p (FD)
6	12	0.5	0.3	6 + 12 = 18	0.5 × 0.3 = 0.15	0.15
7	13	0.5	0.7	6 + 13 = 19	0.5 × 0.7 = 0.35	0.50
				7 + 12 = 19	0.5 × 0.3 = 0.15	0.65
				7 + 13 = 20	0.5 × 0.7 = 0.35	1.00

Notice that there are two routes by which a duration of 19 months can be obtained, and the combined probability of 19 months is thus 0.35 plus 0.15 = 0.5. By a similar method, the duration at the end of the prototype acquisition phase can be established (Table 11.7).

At the next stage, two possibilities exist: either a satisfactory performance test, or a shortfall which requires correction. Each possibility must be considered separately; the same method can be used but the additional probability regarding which of the two possible outcomes will arise has to be inserted in the calculation (Table 11.8).

The shape of the probability distribution has now changed to one with two peaks (bimodal) due to the alternative possibilities for different durations. The situation that occurs with the environmental test can be treated in exactly the same way although the calculation becomes more complex as four sets of conditions have to be considered, they result from the fact that the performance test could result in either a pass or a failure. If there is a failure, it is likely that there will be design changes which will introduce a programme delay, and by making the design deviate more from the original concept, the chance of having to do a full environmental test is increased. This will be familiar to

Table 11.7 Calculation of durations and probabilities for the completion of prototype acquisition

Duration FD	A	Probability FD	A	Combined duration FDA	Combined probability p (FDA)	Cumulative probability Cum. p (FDA)
18	9	0.15	0.3	18 + 9 = 27	0.15 × 0.3 = 0.045	0.045
19	10	0.50	0.7	18 + 10 = 28	0.15 × 0.7 = 0.105	0.15
20		0.35		19 + 9 = 28	0.5 × 0.3 = 0.15	0.30
				19 + 10 = 29	0.5 × 0.7 = 0.35	0.65
				20 + 9 = 29	0.35 × 0.3 = 0.105	0.755
				20 + 10 = 30	0.35 × 0.7 = 0.245	1.00

Duration FDA	p (FDA)	Cum. p (FDA)
27	0.045	0.045
28	0.255	0.300
29	0.455	0.755
30	0.245	1.000

Table 11.8 Calculation of durations and probabilities for the completion of the performance test

Case 1, Satisfactory performance test (P1), $p = 0.7$

Duration FDA	P1	Probability FDA	P1	Combined duration FDAP1	Combined probability p (FDAP1)	Cumulative probability Cum. p (FDAP1)
27	3	0.045	0.5	27 + 3 = 30	0.7 × 0.045 × 0.5 = 0.01575	0.01575
28	4	0.255	0.5	27 + 4 = 31	0.7 × 0.045 × 0.5 = 0.01575	0.0315
29		0.455		28 + 3 = 31	0.7 × 0.255 × 0.5 = 0.08925	0.12075
					etc.	

Duration FDAP1	p (FDAP1)	Cum. p (FDAP1)
30	0.01575	0.01575
31	0.105	0.12075
32	0.2485	0.36925
33	0.2450	0.61425
34	0.08575	0.70000

Case 2, Shortfall on performance test (P2), $p = 0.3$

Duration FDAP2	p (FDAP2)	Cum. p (FDAP2)	Cum. p (FDAP1 + P2)
37	0.00675	0.00675	0.70675
38	0.045	0.05175	0.75175
39	0.1065	0.15825	0.85825
40	0.105	0.26327	0.96327
41	0.03675	0.30000	1.00000

many as the **knock-on effect of changes** – i.e. changes, once introduced, produce even more changes further on. The results are summarized in Table 11.9, which is not set out in full as the spread of duration runs between 33 and 49 weeks.

The pre-production build is dependent on the completion of the performance test and, again, can be treated in the same way as the environmental test. The results for the completion of the pre-production build are given in Table 11.10.

The end of the programme will occur when both the environmental testing and the pre-production item are complete. However, it should be noted that the pre-production build phase will always either equal or exceed the duration of the environmental test. In this case it is only necessary to consider the durations of the pre-production build as given in Table 11.10.

The most convenient way of expressing the result is in a cumulative probability diagram. Plotting the results, directly, yields a step function but it is more easily read if the mid-points of each step are joined to form a smooth curve; this has been done as shown in Figure 11.8. It will be seen that the chance of completing the project in 45 months or less is 50%, not good enough for a Board that normally demands an 80% chance of success. For this to be the case, the quoted duration would have to be 50 months. It is not difficult to see that an answer of this sort would be likely as it is easy to sum all the shortest durations and see that the shortest overall duration is 40 months and then to sum the longest durations and see that the longest time is 53 months;

Table 11.9 Calculation of durations and probabilities for the completion of the environmental test

---

Case 1 Short environmental test (E1) following a satisfactory performance test (P1), $p = 0.7$

Duration FDAP	Probability E1 FDAP	E1	Combined duration FDAP1	Combined probability p (FDAP1E1)	Cumulative probability Cp (FDAP1E1)
30	3 0.01575	0.5	$30 + 3 = 33$	$0.7 \times 0.01575 \times 0.5 = 0.005513$	0.005513
31	4 0.105	0.5	$30 + 4 = 34$	$0.7 \times 0.01575 \times 0.5 = 0.005513$	0.011026
32	0.2485		$31 + 3 = 34$	$0.7 \times 0.105 \quad \times 0.5 = 0.03675$	0.047776
				etc.	
34	0.08575		$34 + 4 = 38$	$0.7 \times 0.08575 \times 0.5 = 0.030013$	0.49

Case 2 Full environmental test (E2) following a satisfactory performance test (P1), $p = 0.3$

Duration FDAP	Probability E2 FDAP	E2	Combined duration FDAP1	Combined probability p (FDAP1E2)	Cumulative probability Cp (FDAP1E2)
30	9 0.01575	0.5	$30 + 9 = 39$	$0.3 \times 0.01575 \times 0.5 = 0.00236$	0.00236
31	10 0.105	0.5	$30 + 10 = 40$	$0.3 \times 0.01575 \times 0.5 = 0.00236$	0.00472
32	0.2485		$31 + 9 = 40$	$0.3 \times 0.105 \quad \times 0.5 = 0.01575$	0.01947
				etc.	
34	0.08575		$34 + 10 = 44$	$0.3 \times 0.08575 \times 0.5 = 0.012863$	0.21

The calculation must be repeated for cases P2 with E1 and P2 with E2 and the results combined.

Duration FDAPE	p (FDAPE)	Cum. p (FDAPE)
33	0.005513	0.005513
34	0.042263	0.047775
35	0.123725	0.1715
36	0.172725	0.344225
37	0.115763	0.459988
38	0.030013	0.49
39	0.002363	0.492363
40	0.019125	0.511488
41	0.060788	0.572275
	etc.	
51	0.012863	1.000000

joining these two points with a smooth S-curve will give a similar result. Of course what use is made of this information is a matter for the Board to decide, the important point is that the information is available and an appropriate strategy can be developed to contain the identified risks. Programme costs can be dealt with in exactly the same way, with cost substituted for duration and a resulting spread of probabilities obtained. Contingency values, over and above the basic estimate, can then be established to give an expected level of confidence in the estimate.

Table 11.10 Calculation of durations and probabilities for the completion of the pre-production build

Duration FDAPR	p (FDAPR)	Cum. p (FDAPR)
40	0.00525	0.00525
41	0.04025	0.0455
42	0.123083	0.168583
43	0.1995	0.368083
44	0.193083	0.561168
45	0.11025	0.671416
46	0.028583	0.7
47	0.00225	0.70225
48	0.01725	0.7195
49	0.05275	0.77225
50	0.0855	0.857558
51	0.08275	0.9405
52	0.04725	0.98775
53	0.01225	1.0

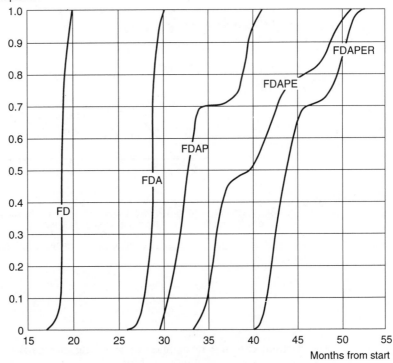

Figure 11.8 Cumulative probability curves for the completion of various events.

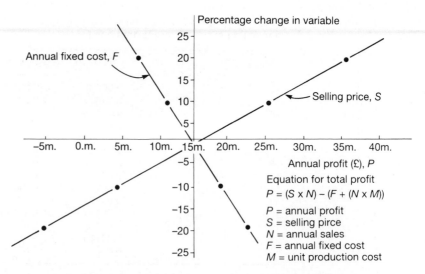

Sensitivity diagram for effect on total profit, variables altered independently

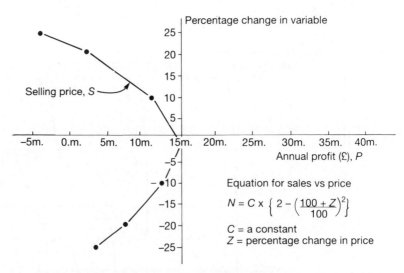

Sensitivity diagram for the effect of selling price on annual profit taking into account the effect of selling price on annual sales

Figure 11.9 Examples of sensitivity diagrams showing both independent and dependent variables.

The method can also be applied to assessing alternative project approaches, each with different identified risks. Selection of the most appropriate route will be the objective and the assessed chances of success with each approach will form a major part in that decision. Models of this type have to be specially constructed for each problem, although some generalized software has been produced and is mentioned in Chapter 13.

Sensitivity analysis is an important aspect of risk assessment; it highlights those factors or variables that have the greatest effect on the predicted outcome. Because of the tedious nature of the calculations, computer software is necessary as the model has to be run many times. Each variable is changed independently by a small amount and the effect on the overall outcome is measured. The results of the analysis are usually presented in a sensitivity diagram; they show the magnitude of the effect of each variable on the measured outcome. Care should be taken in interpreting sensitivity diagrams, they can be very misleading if they do not take into account the interrelationships between variables. Where significant variables do interrelate, a sensitivity diagram exploring this relationship should be drawn as it can provide an insight that is not apparent from the simple unrelated diagram. Examples of both types of diagram are shown in Figure 11.9; it can be seen that the effect on total profits due to altering the selling price looks very different from the simple, independent case when the effect that the selling price has on annual sales is taken into account.

New developments

The strict mathematical formulation used in the methods so far described presents obvious limitations in terms of the description of the problem and the variables that can be included. It is in the nature of future events that we cannot specify them with absolute precision as the future abounds with changes and surprises and never exactly resembles the past. Informed decision-makers or experts in a particular field, when asked to quantify a view of the future, may find that they can only express their opinion in such terms as: 'in the circumstances, I think X is more likely to happen than Y but don't forget Z.' Although this statement lacks the precision that mathematicians look for, it contains valuable information that should not be overlooked when assessing risks. The fact that such views are qualitative implies that they contain an element of 'feeling' about a proposition and they may give a greater insight into where risks lie than attempts at purely abstract estimates of the effects of various risks on time and cost.

If the value of such information can easily be lost in the more formalized treatments, then what is needed is a method of expressing and analysing problems that retains it. Several developments have come about recently that go some way towards capturing this insight and putting it into a framework where it can be subject to analysis and predictive methods. In particular, Knowledge Based Systems, Fuzzy Set Theory and Influence Diagrams have all been evolved with a view to exploiting the richness of experience that exists, and they are set to make an impact on the way in which risks are assessed and managed in the coming decade.

Knowledge-based systems are an attempt to contain within a computer programme a range of quantitative and qualitative knowledge that is held by an expert in a particular subject. The knowledge is structured in such a way that the interrelationships and inferences contained within it can be used to draw conclusions about a new proposition. One field in which knowledge-based systems have shown themselves to be effective is diagnostics. Symptoms of a problem can be put to the system and using its knowledge base it can suggest a diagnosis or several possible diagnoses

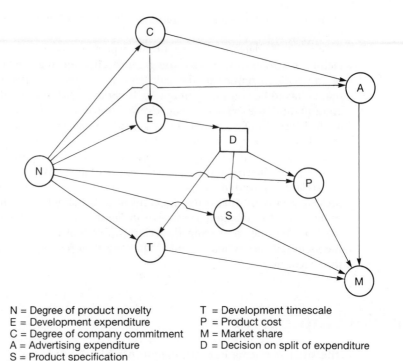

N = Degree of product novelty   T = Development timescale
E = Development expenditure   P = Product cost
C = Degree of company commitment   M = Market share
A = Advertising expenditure   D = Decision on split of expenditure
S = Product specification

Figure 11.10 Influence diagram for the effect of product novelty on market share.

with their respective likelihoods. Furthermore, using the knowledge base, remedial courses of action can be identified.

Fuzzy set theory can be considered as part of a knowledge-based system and is an attempt at defining the qualitative and quantitative nature of relationships from the way in which we express our views about things. For example, we may choose to describe the temperature in a room as 'warm', by which we may mean that is neither hot nor cold but tending towards hot. A fuzzy scale of temperature might go from 'freezing' to 'scorching' with other adjectives in between. Temperature limits can be placed against each of the adjectives in the scale; this may appear to give greater precision, but in fact something is lost. When we use the term 'warm', we are not just indicating the temperature but also implying our reaction to it. 'Warm' may imply a degree of pleasantness, but 'freezing' or 'scorching' indicates a degree of discomfort.

Business situations can show similar shades of feeling. It may be the only way in which we feel comfortable about expressing a view about a situation, and here fuzzy sets can help in drawing logical inferences from pure opinion.

The third technique, **influence diagrams**, allows the formulation of the logic that governs the factors that influence any situation. To take an example, if we look at the fuzzy scale of temperature we can say that, if asked to describe the temperature in a room, the home climate of the respondent (e.g. European or African) will have an influence on the description given of any temperature.

The influence diagram method is, perhaps, the most important new development in the treatment and understanding of business risks. It was devised in the USA in the late 1970s and early 1980s, and the methodology was formalized by R. A. Howard and J. E. Matheson in 1981 as a method for decision analysis. The influence diagram is similar in construction to a project network, in that it consists of arcs and nodes; nodes represent variables or decisions and arcs (or arrows) indicate the path and direction by which one node influences another. Variables are represented by a circular node and decisions by squares or rectangles. The full theory of influence diagrams is complex and beyond the scope of this text; readers wishing to know more about it are referred to the original work by Howard and Matheson (1984). Figure 11.10 shows an Influence Diagram that, in this case, has been drawn for assessing the influence of product novelty on market share.

The diagram features nine nodes in all, one of which is an input node (i.e. it has no predecessor nodes) and one is an output node (i.e. it has no successor nodes). There are also seven intermediate nodes that are both influenced by and have an influence on other nodes, one of these nodes is a decision node. The diagram shows that besides product novelty, seven other factors have been identified as having an influence on the resulting market share. The diagram may be interpreted by looking at each node and observing the variables that influence it. If node M, market share, is considered it will be seen that it is influenced directly by product cost, development timescale, advertising expenditure and product specification. It is affected in an indirect way by company commitment, development expenditure, the decision on how the expenditure is apportioned and product novelty. The path from one node to any other is a **causal chain**, and the diagram as a whole is the set of all causal chains.

When drawing the diagram, care needs to be taken to establish the correct cause-and-effect relationships. In the example, variable C, degree of company commitment, is shown as affecting two variables: advertising expenditure and development expenditure, this is because management policies tend to have their most direct effect in budgetary changes, increased budget allocation implying increased commitment. The development expenditure budget can be spent in three ways: through the amount spent on developing a high-specification product; the amount spent in an effort to reduce the development timescale; and the amount applied to developing a product with a lower production cost – the choice between the emphasis given to each of these routes is indicated by the influence arrows from D to P, S and T. Development budgets may increase above that planned without any implied increase in commitment; when that happens, it is normally due to technical failures or product specification changes but these tend to stem from the degree of product novelty; highly novel products tend to cost more to develop and are more likely to encounter development expenditure over-runs. This is shown by the influence arrow from N to E.

It will be seen from this example that the relationships and influences at work are not necessarily simple and can be both complex and subtle. In order to analyse the influence diagram and draw some conclusions about the relationship between novelty and market share, it will be necessary to define the nature of the influences. If, for example, we look at node M and, for the moment, ignore the effects of advertising, we could make the logical statement that if the timescale is short, the product cost is low and the product specification is high, the market share potential will be at its highest. A matrix of influences and effects can be drawn to reflect this logic and is shown in Table 11.11; for simplicity, only the extreme (short or long, high or low) conditions are considered, although it is obvious that an intermediate, medium, condition can exist.

Table 11.11 Influence of three direct variables on the market share outcome

		Timescale				
		Short		Long		
Product cost		High	Low	High	Low	
Product specification	High Low	Medium Low	Highest Medium	Low Lowest	High Low	Market share

Table 11.12 Influence of degree of novelty on project expenditure with assessed probabilities of occurrence

		Expenditure			
		High	Medium	Low	
Degree of novelty	High	0.7	0.2	0.1	Probability of occurrence
	Medium	0.2	0.6	0.2	
	Low	0.1	0.2	0.7	

The effect of advertising expenditure can now be assessed and added to the effects already tabulated. To further analyse the influence diagram it will be necessary to give some numerical dimension, both to the likelihood of any influence occurring and its size. These can be stated as conditional probabilities or fuzzy logic rules. For example, if we consider the influence of degree of novelty on development expenditure, we may decide on the probabilities given in Table 11.12.

Before the influence diagram can be solved, all the nodes have to be considered in this way and tables of outcomes established. If there are many inputs to a node, the analysis of influences and probable outcomes can become complex. Research by J. E. Diekmann (1992) has indicated that if a variable has more than four binary predecessors (i.e. showing two possible output states), assessment of conditional probabilities becomes too complex. If a predecessor can take on more than two states, then less than four predecessors is indicated.

The influence diagram can be solved by Monte Carlo simulation methods and, as such, is only suitable for computerized analysis. The method starts by inserting values into the initial node variables, then using either conditional probabilities or fuzzy logic rules, computing a value for the influence outcome using a random number. This value is transferred to the successor node where it and all other influences seen by that node are combined according to defined rules to compute another outcome which is, in turn, transferred to the next successor. This process is repeated throughout the diagram until the effect on the output node is established. The whole process is then repeated many times using different random numbers until an acceptably accurate distribution of the output condition is obtained. Because the influences are allowed to propagate throughout the diagram with appropriate reactions at each node, the technique of solving influence diagrams has become known as **dynamic risk analysis**.

The influence diagram, in this example, could be used for studying the effects on market share of different policies regarding the degree of novelty to be expected in new products and the degree of commitment required for each project. The input variables could be altered to reflect different levels of product novelty and the output could be in the form of a scatter plot, as shown in Figure 11.11.

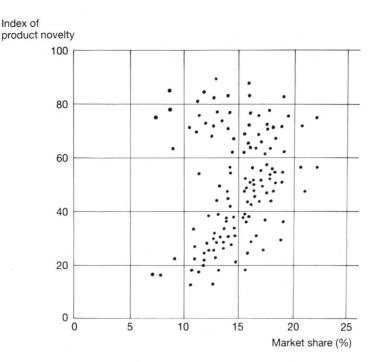

Figure 11.11   Example of a scatter plot output from a dynamic risk analysis.

The influence diagram can be used for assessing risks at any stage in the project; it may be considered as a universal tool for formulating risk problems and assessing possible outcomes. For example, the development timescale shown as a single node in the example could itself be the subject of an influence diagram where all the factors that have a bearing on timescale: work content, staff availability, chance of technical failure, etc., can be considered.

Several advantages come from the use of influence diagrams, chief among them being the intuitive nature of the approach. The diagram starts from a description of the problem that is a purely qualitative view, no numerical values need be considered. This makes it easier to formulate the problem and capture the opinion of experts than any other method. The diagram also provides a convenient way of expressing the nature of a problem to others and thus aids the general understanding of the factors that influence its outcome. Because of their intuitive nature, it is easy to learn how to construct them; experts in risk analysis are not needed once the basic method is understood. Relatively complex relationships can be simply formulated, thus allowing the behaviour of these relationships to be studied in a way that would be impossible by pure reasoning.

However, to obtain a useful result quantification is necessary and this can give rise to problems. In the example, there is a causal link between degree of commitment, development expenditure and product cost – the problem is one of quantifying how this relationship works. If it is assumed that reducing product cost increases market share, then a high degree of commitment would imply, among other things, a high level of spending on ways to reduce product cost; the difficulty is that it may not be known what reduction in cost is achieved for each extra pound spent on that activity. Because of the way that problems are formulated, the use of influence diagrams may require research into aspects of the company's workings that have not previously been examined and thus new insights may be gained.

The technique of drawing and solving influence diagrams is a very new one and suitable software has only recently become available. One system that has been launched is 'DynRisk', from TerraMar of Norway, and it uses a modified influence diagram as the sole means of problem formulation. Figure 11.12 shows an influence diagram as described in 'DynRisk', it also shows, in the upper part of the figure, 'folders' that can be used for structuring the model, so that specific aspects such as schedule, investment, income, etc. can be studied more easily.

With 'DynRisk', all relationships have to be expressed in probability distribution form and there are seven distributions to choose from. A risk variable can have two sets of properties, global and local. Global properties refer to the way in which any variable reacts to the external influences it receives, while local properties refer to the uncertainty that exists within each variable irrespective of any outside influences. Monte Carlo simulation methods are used to solve the diagram and output can be presented in a number of formats, typically cumulative probability curves, histograms or scatter plots.

Although relatively little software is currently on the market for influence diagram work, the power of the method for problem formulation and risk analysis is such that more can be expected to emerge in the near future. Prototype software that incorporates both Monte Carlo methods and fuzzy set theory has been run in a university environment in the USA.

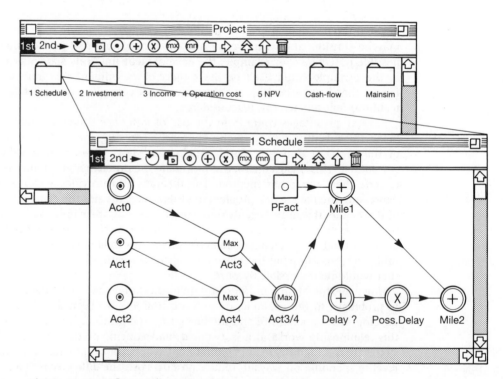

Figure 11.12   Influence diagram problem as described in 'DynRisk'.

In perspective

Risk analysis has been the subject of increasing interest and study over the past two decades and is finding its way into many of the project management courses as a topic that is essential knowledge for Project Managers. Despite the growing interest, the approach has been branded by some as a technique of dubious value or as 'pseudo-science'. The chief criticism is that any formalized analysis can only deal with identifiable risks, and in so doing demands perfect knowledge of the variables and how they will perform. Some would argue that the greatest risks lie in the unknown and unforeseen and these factors must lie outside the analysis. For example, in the case of Example 11.2, it was assumed that the durations never went outside those specified, that ultimately the product would complete its performance test satisfactorily and pass its environmental test. No allowance was made for the possibility, however remote, that the product's performance on test might be so inadequate that there can be no hope of it working without starting the design process again. Yet this kind of misfortune has overtaken many projects from the small to the prestigious; the failure of the airborne early warning Nimrod aircraft is a pertinent example.

Sometimes the causes of difficulty can be so unlikely as to be inconceivable at the outset. In the early 1950s the US Air Force carried out a development programme on supersonic propellers; however, the project had to be abandoned when it was discovered that the high-frequency noise from the propeller, when running at operational speed, induced extreme nausea in ground crew near the machine.

With examples such as those quoted, one can argue that project failures are going to continue to occur with or without risk analysis and it is in the nature of all innovative work that it contains the element of a leap in the dark. What can be said is that all knowledge is valuable and a properly conducted risk analysis can generate a greater insight into where the causes of failure may lie. If we look at Example 11.2, the true appreciation of risk lies at the point when it is realized that there is a real possibility of a performance shortfall and that a full environmental test might prove necessary. The mathematical processing of the durations and probabilities adds a little more insight. One could argue that the true worth of such processing can never be validated as, by their nature, innovative projects are singular events. In order to obtain distributions of probability that are statistically valid, one needs to repeat the process many times, yet for the most part this never happens. It is a criticism of the method that it brings with it a false sense of security; the apparent rigour of the mathematics cannot compensate for the subjective nature of the input or the unknown that is not included.

Risk analysis can never point out a route that can eliminate risk entirely, but the understanding it brings can help in the construction of a project programme where the possibility of adverse events is recognized and their effects can be held to a minimum.

Risk management

Attitudes to risk

How we choose to manage the risks that present themselves will be influenced by our own attitudes to risk and the attitudes adopted by the company. Entrepreneurial companies may tend to focus on the benefits of any project rather than the potential for losses and may adopt a 'go for broke' approach on the basis that some of the projects will be winners and highly profitable. Institutionalized organizations may adopt a more cautious approach expecting each area of identified risk to be thoroughly examined before any decision is taken. At the most extreme, a totally risk-averse culture may lead to management inaction; when important decisions have to be taken, a 'wait and see' approach may be adopted allowing events to proceed in their way until only one course of action is left open, management then agreeing to go down that route. Behaviour of this sort stems from the desire not to be seen to make a wrong decision; it can result in the kind of action that was taken by the program manager, in the stabilizer case study: to have made a wrong decision involving large sums of money might have called into question his competence as a manager. The risk-averse culture of the organization finds expression in high risks for the individual; it may also lead to high risks for the organization, although these may not be recognized at the time.

Corporate attitudes to risk and individual perception of where risks lie will lead to appropriate responses. Individual decision-makers may be astute enough to appreciate the culture and act accordingly. Others may choose to adopt a different strategy and run the personal risk of failure or loss of status. For those who can demonstrate success through a different approach, the rewards may be significant through pay and promotion, but it may also produce adverse results for the individual through jealousy or hurt pride in others. Organizations that undertake innovative projects should examine their own culture and decide on the stand that they take on issues of risks and assess how appropriate it is: too 'gung-ho' and money can be easily lost on ill-considered schemes, too restrictive and opportunities may not be grasped when they present themselves as initiative is stifled.

Risks within the task structure

Whatever culture exists, risks in the development phase can be reduced by a structured approach to the task. H. Mikkelsen (1990) divided risk into various elements, four of which the organization has control over, namely:

- *The project goal*: in determining the goal a risk may be incurred, the goal may be too ambitious in terms of expectation of the market and the technology; alternatively, the converse may prove true. The project goal can, however, be clarified and refined through feasibility studies, market research, checklists and selective tests, either in the market or on prototype samples. Screening methods can be employed to select only those projects that have a good chance of being successful.
- *The project plan*: planning is essentially the conceptualizing of a future reality, but the future may be poorly perceived and the reality different from expectation. The project plan can be made more robust by structuring it in such a way that:
  (a) difficult areas are subject to early evaluation and testing;
  (b) decisions are based on knowledge gained as the project progresses;
  (c) contingencies and allowances for failures are built in.
- *The project organization*: the strength or weakness of the organization stems directly from the management's perception of the task, the organization may be poorly staffed, lack knowledge or resources and thus be managed incorrectly. However,

staff can be trained, consultants and specialists hired and an organization structure set up that:

(a) focuses energies and skills on the project goal;

(b) demands responsibility for achievement;

(c) functions as a committed team.

- *The methods and procedures*: procedures may be poorly designed and fail to give signals of pending difficulties, risks may increase by reactive management and guesswork rather than evaluation and test. However, design and testing guidelines can be established, quality assurance methods can be implemented and reporting procedures can be instituted that measure both progress and performance and provide early warning signals.

- *The external environment*: this contains factors which can influence the project but over which it has little or no control. Awareness of the environment can be improved by such activities as market research, keeping open channels of communication to clients and customers, participating in trade associations, etc.

Risk-reducing measures

By addressing the various points, listed above, management can create conditions at the start which are favourable to a satisfactory outcome. Risk management goes well beyond creating a suitable start, for it is an ongoing process that needs to be carried out throughout the life of the project. Different responses to the risks and opportunities that present themselves will have to be adopted according to the stage of the project and the state of development of the product. Figure 11.13 shows a schematic process for risk management, together with the techniques appropriate to each stage. At the start it is important to identify the sources of risk, this may be a rather subjective process but a structured and analytical approach, while not eliminating the subjective element, can at least ensure completeness. Specific techniques can include the formulation of checklists based on experience of earlier projects; the new project can then be examined against the list and an opinion formed about each point raised. Structured interviews with responsible staff, perhaps using the checklist as a basis, can further refine the perception of where difficulties may be.

The external environment is always a source of risk and the one over which there may be no control; it is important to be able to see this very clearly and such techniques as market surveys and technological forecasts may be employed. They can serve to direct attention towards changing or emerging trends and these pointers must be borne in mind in formulating the project plan.

Having identified the principal sources of risk, they need to be quantified and ranked. This is, perhaps, the most difficult task as it involves both analytical thinking and making subjective judgements about the future. The best starting-point is the analysis of historical data, particularly if similar projects have been undertaken in the past. The best guide to a company's future lies in its past; unless some very major organizational change has taken place, things tend to proceed in the way they have done previously. An examination of previous projects including an assessment of similarities, differences, timescales, costs, failures and successes can lead to a more realistic view of each new proposal.

Modelling techniques, as shown in the previous examples, can be used to assess specific types of project risk, particularly those relating to cost and timescale. They

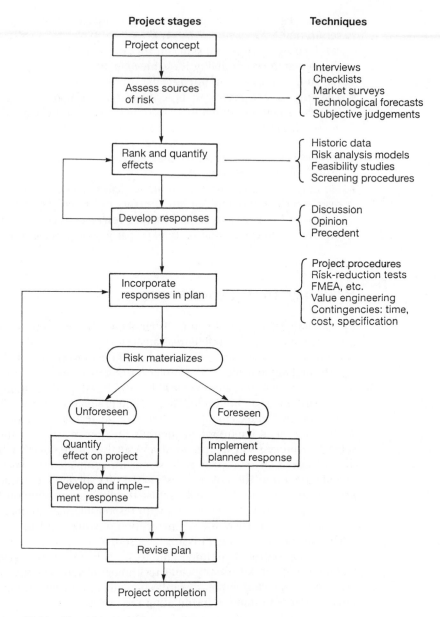

Figure 11.13 The risk management process.

can throw light on the range of probable outcomes but they must be treated with caution inasmuch as some of the input variables may be both subjective and untested. Analyses can be carried out on both the project itself and on the business as a whole – there could be risks both in going ahead with a project and having a failure and not going ahead and losing a market to the competition.

Feasibility studies have as their objective the testing of specific assumptions. Often they are applied to the engineering aspects of a project but they may not go as far as prototype construction and physical tests. Increasingly sophisticated computer modelling techniques can be used to simulate the function of new products. These models may not be generally applicable and thus may have to be constructed individually to the requirements of each new scheme. Functional and operational characteristics may be tested theoretically and much basic understanding of the design may be obtained. However, they are abstractions of the real item; they cannot hope to discover all that may be necessary to translate an idea that works on paper into a profitable product. Besides engineering feasibility, cost and timescale may be assessed by direct reference to the product description through the technique of parametric estimating. This does not contain the probabalistic methods that are contained in the project simulation models, but it can be very useful for assessing costs quickly and rejecting those ideas that have little chance of success for commercial reasons.

Having assessed the perceived risks, suitable responses need to be developed. Reasoned discussion and reference to preceding projects will be necessary; some of the ideas that emerge may be tested as alternative strategies using both the functional and programme modelling techniques. Most important, the responses to risks and the possibility of alternative strategies must be incorporated in the project plan.

Figure 11.14 shows a schematic project comprising three major phases. This is a common arrangement that starts with a prototype phase aimed at testing the basic functions of the product although without much engineering refinement. This is followed by a full development phase in which items that are much more refined and representative of the production unit are built and tested. Testing will normally cover three basic areas:

1. Structural tests: is the item strong enough to perform its duties?
2. Functional tests: does it work as intended and to specification?
3. Environmental tests: will it work properly under the conditions it is likely to meet when in use?

The final phase is full production and delivery to the customer.

Although some of the risks of technical failure are reduced and even eliminated by the two-stage approach to development and testing, the project programme can be made more robust by a recognition of specific technical risks and inserting into the plan responses to each risk at the appropriate point. Figure 11.14 lists some of the principal areas of technical risk, together with methods that can help in overcoming them.

Structural and systems failures that are discovered on test can have some of the most damaging effects on the project. Sometimes major redesigns are necessary, as well as repeat testing; it can lead to both cost and time over-runs and, possibly, liquidated damages payments. The technique of **failure modes and effects analysis** (FMEA) has been devised to investigate the effects that failures in one area have on the design as a whole. Where structural aspects are important, such as in aerospace products, the technique of finite element analysis can be used to evaluate stresses in structures at the design stage. The technique is a computer based one and involves constructing an abstract model of the proposed structure comprised of many small interlinked elements. When drawn, the abstract has the appearance of a wire model and is often referred to as a 'mesh'. Theoretical loads can then be applied and the most highly stressed members discovered. By using FMEA models, failures in highly stressed members can be simulated and any resultant failures that may occur can be studied. Structural failures are not the only aspect that can benefit from FMEA; failures in major systems can also lead to catastrophic results. For example,

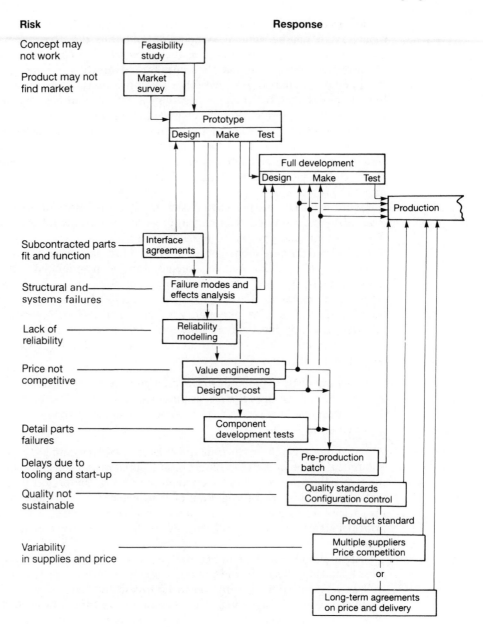

Figure 11.14 Technical risks and appropriate responses.

the failure of a fire suppression system in an oil refinery could lead to the loss of the whole plant if the failure occurred when a fire broke out. Primary control systems or safety-related systems are particularly important in this respect and failure modelling can lead to the discovery of latent faults in the design. Many modern control systems feature computers, and such systems can be doubly vulnerable as they can exhibit failures both in the hardware and software. In some industries, good design practice has insisted that critical systems are made in triplicate and are capable of functioning normally with one system either out of action or behaving abnormally. The software may also be triplicated with each suite of programmes being written independently by different teams.

Besides significant structural or systems failures, general reliability may be an area of risk. Much of the success of Japanese products in the consumer market has been due to the demonstrably superior reliability that their products have shown when compared with the home-produced article. In part, this is due to quality control procedures at the production stage, but proper evaluation of the inherent reliability of the product at the design stage is another reason. Reliability modelling techniques that make use of statistical methods have been devised; they are particularly useful in the design of electronic circuits where the life characteristics of standard components are well known. Mechanical parts may be less easy to deal with and statistical data, if it is available, may have to be based on earlier and similar products. Reliability figures are usually expressed in terms of 'mean time between failures' (MTBF), the time element is normally given in operational hours. MTBF values for the various elements are combined to give an overall value for the product.

Reliability can be kept to high levels by good design practice such as:

- Choosing high-quality, high-reliability components.
- Designing fail-safe systems and structures.
- Incorporating redundancy and robustness in critical features.
- De-rating electrical components according to the stress and environment they experience.
- Providing environmental protection for critical items through seals, covers, filters, finishes, etc.
- Selecting compatible materials.
- Avoiding dust and water traps.

Some of the features listed above will have cost implications for the end-product, while others can be obtained through careful design at no extra cost. Obviously, cost is a major factor in the commercial attractiveness and particularly at the initial purchase stage, but poor reliability can lead to excessive warranty claims and if it becomes generally recognized, loss of market share or a premature end to the product's sales life. Clearly there are risks in whatever design approach is taken and reliability is one area where the technical response to the risks associated with low reliability can lead to a commercial risk in terms of product acceptability.

Basic product cost must represent one of the largest factors that determines the overall profitability and success of any project that aims to generate goods for sale on the open market. A substantial risk must exist that the product, when it emerges, will be too expensive to compete effectively. The greatest savings in product cost are made on the drawing-board, not at the tooling-up or purchasing stage. Elaborate designs will always remain more expensive to produce than more simple items. The techniques of design-to-cost and value engineering have been developed as an effective way of forcing design activities along a route that ensures that, in formulating the product, cost is considered alongside all other parameters. There is an optimum point at which these methods should be applied and it is at the time when the full-scale development item is being designed. Both design-to-cost and value engineering are explained in Chapter 6.

It is a simple fact that in most products it is the detail of the design that determines whether of not it will work satisfactorily under all circumstances, and if failures do occur, what form they will take. Significant risk can be taken out of the design process by a properly constructed programme of tests on detail parts. This can be particularly useful where parts are subject to high stresses or harsh environments. In general, at the design stage stress-related problems are easier to discover than environmentally related difficulties. Items can be subjected to formalized stressing methods but a detailed study of a set of drawings may not discover problems that relate to the conditions under which an item is used. These problems only come to light when tests are carried out and sometimes the effects are both insidious and subtle. Vibration or extremes of temperature and humidity can cause failures through such effects as migration of lubricants, breakdown of surface finishes, change of friction characteristics, corrosion and any of a host of other effects. Testing components and assemblies in environments that are representative should be carried out as early as possible in the design process, ideally in the period between the construction of a prototype and the manufacture of a full development article. Environmental testing often takes place towards the end of a development programme, but if problems are discovered at this stage, it can have a serious effect on the production programme if changes have to be made.

Production start-up problems are traditionally dealt with by making a pre-production batch. This can be useful for proving tooling, checking assembly methods and assessing supplier's quality, it can also provide items for additional testing to ensure that any changes that have been made between the full development item and the production item are not detrimental to performance. The real value of a pre-production batch should, however, always be considered on its merits; if the items are a hybrid between the development unit and the full production item, they can sometimes be more trouble to produce than they are worth as they are not truly representative of anything.

Beyond the development stage, the technical risks in the production programme tend to lie more in the areas of quality control and supplier performance. As such, they tend to cross the boundary between the technical aspects and the purely commercial. Setting quality standards for suppliers to observe is one obvious safeguard against poorly made goods. Quality control personnel will require an input from the design staff when it comes to the identification of critical features and establishing the requirements for such things as workmanship standards, gauging and inspection sampling plans.

Changes of one sort or another are to be expected in the first few months of production as new problems, often associated with the production methods, come to light. Sometimes, however, correction of the problem can only be overcome by a design change. When this occurs, changes must be controlled rigidly; changes that are incorporated in an uncontrolled fashion can lead to the wrong standard of parts being ordered, with all the consequent disruption and costs that ensue. Configuration management procedures can be employed to combat this and the technique is explained in Chapter 5.

Once standards have been set for both design and quality requirements, competitive quoting and the use of several suppliers can serve both to ensure continuity of supply and favourable pricing. However, heavy investment in special tooling or the use of proprietary techniques may make using alternative suppliers difficult; in these circumstances, protection may be obtained through long-term agreements that cover price and delivery.

Exposure to technical risk can be limited by creating a project plan which includes risk-reducing measures. The decision to incorporate any or all of the techniques mentioned will depend on the perception of the likelihood of the risk materializing.

There is, however, a price to be paid; plans that include risk-reducing measures are more expensive as they contain additional work and they may also increase the project timescale. They tend to involve spending money early on investigative work, and if the project is subsequently cancelled, this money is lost. It is this cost and time penalty that must be judged against the possibility of a technical failure at the end of development or faulty products being released onto the market.

Where suppliers and subcontractors are used, risks that are both technical and commercial can arise; they can be reduced by appropriate actions such as:

(a) Obtaining early agreement on specifications to ensure that tasks and requirements are well understood at the start.
(b) Setting up interface control procedures to ensure that design changes that affect interfacing contractors can only come about in a controlled manner.
(c) Using fixed-price contracts to ensure price exposure is limited; however, caution should be applied if the true nature of risks is not appreciated by either party.
(d) Insistance on regular reporting of plans and progress to ensure visibility and thus awareness in both parties of the true state of affairs.

Risk management might therefore be seen as an extension of good management practice; although some of the formalized mathematical aspects of risk analysis may be new, the basic methods of handling risks in management situations remain.

Summary

Risks exist and will not go away, but by a reasoned assessment they can be discovered and appropriate responses can be developed that mitigate their effect, should they arise. Analytical techniques have been devised that can help Project Managers to evaluate the options that are open to them and aid in the process of decision-making at all stages in a project. The subject is still evolving and new analytical techniques are being devised that, in the future, may give new insights into risk situations. Analysis can help in identifying the areas in which risks lay and the process of risk management can reduce the adverse consequences through the inclusion of contingencies and taking specific actions in advance of a problem situation. Those organizations that practice risk analysis and management can comfort themselves by the knowledge that in tackling a new venture it is done with eyes wide open. For those that don't, the true nature of their undertaking may only become apparent at a point when it is too late to avoid failure.

12

Some commercial aspects

- Prime contractorship
- Forms of contract
- Liquidated damages
- Protection of intellectual property

In many cases, innovative development projects will be undertaken as in-house activities aimed at generating new products. In other instances, the development of new products will be done on behalf of a customer organization. Here a contractual arrangement will exist between the customer and the company carrying out the work. This situation is very common with government departments that let contracts with commercial organizations to develop and produce the material and facilities they need. The majority of defence equipment is generated in this way. It also occurs in the private sector where the supplier of a large and complex product may let contracts with specialist suppliers for the development of items of equipment that are to be installed in their product. This is common in products such as civil aircraft which contain many items of equipment specifically developed for new applications by firms that specialize in the particular technology.

Where contractual arrangements are in place, a greater degree of formality will exist in the conduct of the project than would necessarily be the case with in-house development. The organization that lets the contract will, in general, demand some visibility of progress from the contractor and this is often tied to the payment arrangement. Besides the financial aspects, a formalized arrangement must exist in respect of the product definition – i.e. the organization letting the contract must be able to define the characteristics of the product to the point where it can be understood and agreed to by the development contractor. Contracts are also let for research projects or for demonstrating the feasibility of a new technology; when this occurs, the formality in the product specification need not apply.

Prime contracts

When complex products were developed on behalf of the government, the department concerned used to let contracts with each contractor, individually, and managed the contractual and development matters itself. However, a change has come about in the past two decades with the introduction of the **prime contractor**. Here one contractor, usually the one with the most significant technical contribution, is appointed to lead the project team. Other contractors will be involved but they will act as subcontractors to the prime contractor. All contractual dealings between the customer and the project organization will be through the prime contractor, who will take ultimate responsibility for the performance of the project in terms of cost and timescale, as well as the performance aspects of the product. This relationship can become complex, particularly with military items, as it has become practice to designate companies with proven design expertise in particular fields as **design authorities**. The prime contractor organization is also likely to be a design authority in one or more areas of technology, though not for all the fields it will be required to manage. The prime contractor may also have an overall design authority role (although this has not always been the case for some large projects, AEW Nimrod being a well-publicized example of a project with two prime contractors, each with separate responsibilities), and here he will be required to manage subcontractors with design authority status in areas in which he does not have authority himself. Figure 12.1 shows the principal of the control arrangement.

From time to time, this organization can become fraught, particularly if subcon-

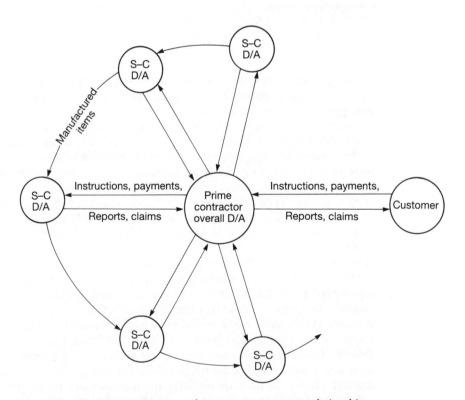

Figure 12.1 The prime contractor, subcontractor, customer relationship.

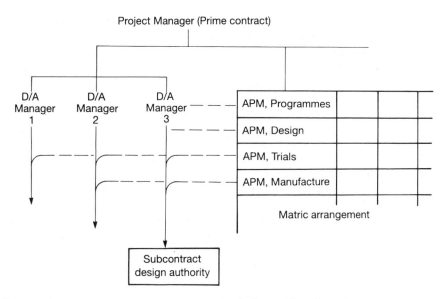

Figure 12.2   Project management structure for dealing with major subcontractors.

tract design authorities start to demand changes in other areas of the design to accommodate their wishes. When this arises, the prime contractor's Project Manager will need both diplomacy and technical judgement when resolving the issues involved.

Where a significant number of subcontract design authorities are involved, the usual project management structure may be altered to reflect the nature of the contract. A typical arrangement is shown in Figure 12.2; here the importance of managing the activities of each **Subcontract Design Authority** (S-CD/A) is recognized by the creation of an assistant manager reporting directly to the Prime Contract Project Manager but with responsibility for handling all aspects of the relationship between the prime contractor and the S-CD/A.

S-CD/A assistant managers cannot work in an autonomous fashion, reporting only to the Project Manager; they must liaise with the Assistant Project Managers (APMs), each with special responsibility for one aspect of the project. They will be required to interpret the plans and instructions of the APMs and convey them to the SCD/As. If required, they will tie up these requirements in a strictly formalized, contractual way. All communication between the subcontractor and the prime contractor should, in the first instance, be through their assistant manager.

Obtaining prime contractorships has been seen as a strategic objective by many leading companies. Besides the prestige associated with the position, it carries with it the opportunity for high profits as the whole of the project value passes through the prime contractor, even though the greater part of the work may be done elsewhere. Prime contractors are also able to lead the marketing effort for the production item and thus become the company whose name is primarily associated with it. However, there are proportionately greater risks associated with prime contractorships. In general, companies acting as prime contractors tend to reduce their contractual risks by letting contracts on their subcontractors that reflect the terms and conditions imposed upon them by their customer. This arrangement is often termed 'back to back' but all risks cannot be offset, in particular, consequential liability in respect of failures. Failures are to be expected in development programmes that involve testing and the plan should be robust enough to contain them. Where consequential liability can become a serious issue for prime contractors is in production programmes. Some products or systems may contain items that are low in cost in relation to the overall item but crucial to it functioning properly. Whereas the subcontractors responsible for these small items may be prepared to accept full liability for their performance, they may not be willing to accept any consequential liability. Thus a small subcontractor may be willing to repair or replace any item that he has supplied that is found to be faulty in service (within the terms of the guarantee). What he may not be prepared to accept is the cost of a return-to-works programme with a strip-down and rebuild if that is necessary to rectify the faulty items that have been supplied in the production systems. The prime contractor, as the ultimate guarantor of the total system performance, could find himself liable for the cost of the re-work programme unless he has been able to limit his liability to the customer for failures on the part of items supplied by subcontractors. He may be in a better position to do this if the subcontractors have been nominated by the customer rather than selected by himself.

Further problems can arise for prime contractors if liquidated damages (payments to cover losses) are applied for failure to deliver production items on time. This will be payable by the prime contractor to the customer and may be fixed at some value that is a small percentage of the total system price. However, the failure of one subcontractor to supply a low-cost but vital part that in turn holds up the whole delivery programme could leave the prime contractor exposed to paying the bulk of the damages, the amount recoverable from the errant supplier being small in respect to the amount payable.

Forms of contract

Contracts let for development projects fall into two basic categories:

1. Those in which the greater risk, in cost terms, lies with the customer.
2. Those in which the greater risk lies with the contractor.

Cost reimbursable contracts

Contracts in which the principal risk lies with the customer organization are of the **cost reimbursable** type; here the contractor can spend time, money and effort at the direction of the customer and whatever costs are incurred are repaid to the contractor with an additional fee. They are referred to as **cost plus fee**, **cost-plus** or sometimes as **limit of liability contracts** as it is usual for the customer to control spending on the part of the contractor by setting limits to the amount that he is currently willing to pay. When the limit of liability is reached, the customer can either: (a) increase it, in which case work can proceed, or (b) decide against doing so, giving the contractor the right to stop work.

Contracts of this type have been common in the public sector for development work until the early 1980s, since when there has been a move away from using them. The chief criticism has been that they contain little incentive for the contractor to complete the work as cheaply and quickly as possible; in fact the very reverse may prove to be the case as the more that is spent, the greater the profit (in real if not in percentage terms). Cost-plus contracts are still let for projects where the outcome is so uncertain or the chance of failure is so great that contractors are unwilling to undertake the work on any other basis. This can occur with feasibility studies, research projects or projects for the development or exploitation of new and untried technologies where the innovative nature of the work may mean that success is not guaranteed or excessive effort may be needed to generate a worthwhile result.

Several types of cost-reimbursable contracts have been devised, some with the specific intention of introducing a measure of incentive:

(a) *Cost plus fixed fee*

This is the simplest form of cost-plus contract and is used where it has been shown that making an accurate estimate of the work content is impossible, usually because of the exploratory nature of the work. Here a fixed, agreed fee is paid to the contractor on the basis of the costs incurred. The fee is often expressed as a fixed percentage of the costs submitted. From the point of view of the customer, this form of contract is the least preferable as there is no incentive for the contractor to hold down cost or maintain the schedule.

(b) *Cost plus award fee*

With this arrangement, the customer reimburses the contractor for all costs incurred but the fee is awarded on the basis of some agreed measure of project performance. To protect the contractor, a base fee is established and an overall maximum fee is also set. Between these limits an award can be made by the customer according to agreed criteria. However, some criteria may be subjective and this can lead to disputes over the size of the award. Some customers may insist on a clause that states that his decision on an award is final and not subject to a disputes procedure.

(c) *Cost plus incentive fee*

Where the project goals (in terms of cost, schedule and performance) can be specified with reasonable certainty, it may be possible to introduce an incentive based on achieving these parameters. For this to work, a target cost is agreed between the contractor and customer, together with a target fee that should be obtainable if the target performance is met. On either side of that figure, both a maximum and a minimum fee are set and are payable depending on the project outcome. Adjustment formulae must be agreed and they should include reference to project milestones, as well as demonstration of performance attainment. Considerable care must be taken in devising formulae, particularly where the three parameters of cost, schedule and performance all combine. For example, a customer might not find it acceptable if it was found that the formula awarded a high fee to a contractor that was running ahead of schedule and generating good product performance but at excessive cost. It is essential that whatever formula is chosen, it should be simple and straightforward. Complex formulae run the risk of being difficult to interpret and administer: they are also less predictable in their effects when a large number of variables is included.

For any of these contract types to operate successfully there are certain prerequisites:

1. A costed plan is lodged with and accepted by the customer.
2. A satisfactory project accounting system is in place.
3. A cost and progress reporting system is set up.

Prior to starting, the customer will expect to receive a fully costed and scheduled plan for the whole development programme. Enough detail should be shown for the customer to assess its feasibility and adequacy for meeting the project goals and it must also be sufficient for control and reporting. Plans such as these are sometimes referred to as **development cost plans** (DCPs); they form the basis of the agreement between the customer and contractor regarding the conduct of the project and its intended cost. As such, a DCP is a contractual document, and if sufficient changes occur in the course of the project, they will be reflected in revised issues of the DCP. A contract amendment will normally be raised to formally acknowledge the new issue of the DCP; it thus defines the revised budget for the project. Acceptance of the DCP by the customer will signify his agreement that the plan is reasonable and the sums of money shown appear adequate for the intended work. All performance measurements can then be made with reference to this agreed position.

Evidence of a satisfactory accounting system for project control may be demanded by the customer, particularly where government departments are involved. Accounting conventions differ between companies, and where public money is concerned, evidence may be required by government auditors that projects that are publicly financed are not attracting an undue allocation of overheads. In the UK, companies undertaking government-funded work are required to complete a Questionnaire on the Method of Allocation of Overheads (QMAC). Evidence will also have to be provided that costs attracted by a particular project are kept separate from all other projects. In the USA, contractors working on Departments of Defense and Energy projects will also be required to install cost reporting and control systems that conform to their respective specifications for cost/schedule reporting systems criteria, these are dealt with in Chapter 8. Where governments are not involved, customer organizations may still require proof that the costs claimed have actually been spent; this can raise issues of commercial confidentiality and contractors may be unwilling to divulge information directly that could be sensitive commercially. When this occurs, independent consultants may be used to verify the correctness of the claims.

Throughout the project, the customer will require regular progress reports and other information such as drawings, specifications, test results, etc., and it is usual to specify these items in an annexe to the contract, sometimes called a Contract Data Requirements List (CDRL). The DCP should contain either the frequency at which the data is required or the milestones for delivery for single items of data (e.g. a drawing package). Written reports covering cost, schedule and technical aspects may be demanded on a regular basis, together with face-to-face progress meetings. For ease of control and visibility of progress, milestones for achievement may be identified throughout the programme and progress against them will be monitored by the customer. They can be used as the basis of assessing performance where award or incentive fee contracts are in operation.

Payments, in general, under cost-reimbursable conditions are made on the basis of monthly invoices based on the actual costs incurred and generated through the company's accounting system. The basic part of the fee is added to this figure to give the invoice value. Awards or incentive payments are paid to the contractor at review points according to the agreed plan. A final adjustment to the award may be made at the end of the project based on overall performance.

Fixed-price contracts

In recent years, there has been a move away from cost-reimbursable contracts and customer organizations are attempting to procure development work for fixed prices. This is a response on their part to the growing financial risks associated with the development of innovative technology; it is placing those risks associated with development difficulties with the supplying contractor. There are, however, several preconditions for this type of contract to be applicable:

1. The basic feasibility of the project must have been established and be agreed by both parties.
2. The end-product of the development process must be capable of being defined in sufficient detail that no doubt exists with either party as to what is expected.
3. Competition exists among potential contractors.

In recognition of the first point, it is common to let feasibility study contracts before a full development contract. Both parties have the opportunity to assess the results before proceeding to the next stage; it is beneficial to both and should reduce the risks as greater realism should be contained within the specification and the plan. Feasibility studies typically include an analysis and sometimes a practical demonstration of the key technologies; this is fundamental to establishing the areas of potential risk. Promising feasibility studies usually conclude with an outline development plan, including provisional costs, together with a product specification. Analysis of the feasibility study reports and proposals by the customer often results in a re-think and refinement of the project goals. Before a full development programme is agreed, there is usually a period of negotiation between the customer and the potential contractor over both the development plan and the product. To obtain a range of possible solutions, customers sometimes let several feasibility study contracts with alternative suppliers but the product specification is likely to be based on the most-favoured concept to emerge, although that could be an amalgamation of ideas from different contractors. The term 'potential contractor' is used advisedly as it is practice with some customers to circulate a development plan and product specification among rival contractors, even if they have not participated in the feasibility study and some astute contractors may approach customers with a view to submitting an unsolicited proposal.

What is important is that all parties should feel that the final specification is complete, unambiguous and clear as to what is required. It then becomes a matter of judgement as to what contingencies should be allowed to cover the remaining development risks. This will be influenced by the severity of the competition and the attractiveness of the project.

Some contractors have taken the view that the lowest possible quotation should always be entered in a fixed-price situation as this is most likely to secure an order. Once the project has begun, the expectation is that the customer will begin to ask for changes to the programme or specification and these will provide opportunities to negotiate price increases which, if skilfully handled, can camouflage cost increases that may have arisen in the basic programme. Whatever one may think of this practice, it can be viewed as a response by the contractor to the attempt by the customer to off-load both the technical and cost risks and still obtain a low overall cost. If serious difficulties do arise, it is for the customer to consider his best interests; it may be far better to negotiate a new price than to see a supplier ruined as that could lead to far greater expense.

As with cost-reimbursable contracts, alternative forms of fixed-price contract have been devised for use in different circumstances.

(a) Fixed price, also called 'firm, fixed price'

This is the simplest form of contract. For the contract as a whole, or for each identified and separately priced element, a single-figure price is agreed, and unless there are specifically agreed changes to the programme or specification, no variations in the price are allowed. From the customer's point of view, this is the ideal form as the entire cost risk is borne by the contractor; it is also the simplest to administer. It does, however, place a burden on the customer to be very accurate in terms of design and performance specifications, as well as assuring himself that estimates submitted by the contractor are realistic and achievable. It is thus worthwhile assessing the technical and financial strength of a potential supplier when selection is based on the lowest price. The customer should satisfy himself that the true nature of the project, its technical and programme implications, are fully understood by the contractor. Estimates for innovative projects have been notorious for the degree by which they have turned out to be underestimates. If this happens, the contractor can come off badly and it can end in disputes; neither party benefits from this.

The fixed-price contract is a two-edged sword, useful in situations such as repetitive production programmes or projects with low levels of technology, but increasingly less applicable as the degree of innovation increases.

(b) Fixed price with escalation

Despite the fact that both governments and forecasting institutions have spent huge sums on developing economic models, forecasting inflation rates to a useful degree of accuracy has proved to be elusive. The effect of inflation on programme cost appears in two ways: (a) inflation above that allowed for in the estimate generates additional cost over which the contractor has no control, and (b) if the project is subject to slippage, not only is there more work than expected but also more is being done at a date later than planned, thus at a higher than expected cost. To remove this risk it has become common practice to include a clause in the contract that allows the sum of money paid at any point in the project to be varied according to the prevailing rate of inflation. Contracts of this type have much to recommend them; they remove a contentious element of risk by being seen to be 'fair' to both parties. The relative value of the contract in terms of purchasing power remains fixed, neither party being expected to shoulder the total burden of cost increases if inflation turns out to be higher than that expected or make an excess profit if it is lower. Price adjustments are made by the application of formulae which use published index number series as the impartial measure of price movements. The formulae are of the general form:

$$P_1 = \left\{ a \times L_0 + \left(\left(\frac{I_{lc}}{I_{l0}} \right) \times (1 - a) \times L_0 \right) \right\} + \left\{ b \times M_0 + \left(\left(\frac{I_{mc}}{I_{m0}} \right) \times (1 - b) \times M_0 \right) \right\}$$

$$L_0 + M_0 = P_0 \qquad\qquad (12.1)$$

where:
P_0 = the original contract price for the work under consideration at the economic date point (time zero);

P_1 = the price for the work under consideration at the date of raising the claim;

L_0 = the labour cost portion for the work at time zero;

M_0 = the material cost portion for the work at time zero;

I_{l0} = the labour cost index at time zero;

I_{lc} = the labour cost index at the current time;

I_{m0} = the material cost index at time zero;

I_{mc} = the material cost index at the current time;

a and b = factors of value less than one.

The formula is self-explanatory but the factors a and b which retain a portion of the contract price at the original level serve to reduce the calculated price slightly. This offsets a tendency for the formula to generate a figure higher than the actual costs to the contractor as it often happens that he can benefit from materials being paid for at a price agreed at the time of order placement, which may have been some months earlier. Typically a and b are set to 0.1, in which case the formula simplifies to:

$$P_1 = 0.1P_0 + 0.9L_0\left(\frac{I_{lc}}{I_{l0}}\right) + 0.9M_0\left(\frac{I_{mc}}{I_{m0}}\right) \qquad (12.2)$$

The constants a and b can be varied to reflect circumstances but this must be agreed before the start of the contract.

Index number series

The index number series can be taken from a number of sources but the principal one in the UK is that of the Central Statistical Office (CSO). Labour and material price indices are published regularly by HMSO in the *Monthly Digest of Statistics* and give comprehensive cover over a wide spectrum of industrial sectors. The CSO also issues to subscribers monthly labour and material cost index series for specific industry sectors under the title *Business Monitors*. Wage and salary statistics are generated by the Department of Employment and are published in the *Employment Gazette*. Other organizations such as the British Electrical and Allied Manufacturers Association (BEAMA) publish index series for use with the formulae in their standard contract. In the USA the Bureau of Labor Statistics is a prime source of data.

For the majority of people, the most familiar index series is the Retail Price Index (RPI); it is compiled from a 'basket of goods' that represent the consumption of goods and services for an average household. Each item is given a quantity or weighting representative of its use in relation to all the other items in the list. The total value of the 'basket of goods' is calculated on the 'base date' and the index set to 100. At later points in time, the value is recalculated using the same weightings but new prices, the total price is divided by the base date price and the result multiplied by 100 to give the new index figure. The advantage of index series is that they are a simple method of recording price movements that are easily used and understood and it is possible to combine index series to form new series with no loss of accuracy.

From time to time, index series are brought back to 100, usually when the pattern of consumption changes, so that the weightings no longer represent the world as it is. Advance warning of this is usually given by the publisher who may also continue to publish the old series alongside the new one for a time, to allow contracts begun under one series to be completed without re-basing the new series to reflect the old.

Methods of application of the formulae vary according to the format of the project plan and the contract. Payment may be linked to milestones, payment points or specific tasks with assumed durations. In each case, fixed sums of money, planned and agreed at the start, will be inserted into the formulae at the specified times. In the case of tasks with assumed durations, the index number inserted in the formula may be the average of all the index numbers published over the duration of the task or alternatively the index number that relates to the mid-point of the task. Using the latest published index figure to arrive at a price for a task that was performed over a six-month period will produce an artificially high result, hence the averaging or mid-point method. Things can get complicated when the project is subject to timescale slippages and careful wording needs to be applied as to what index values can be used: should it be those applicable to the durations in the original schedule or those relevant to the time at which the work was actually done? Such matters need to be resolved at the outset, innovative projects are notorious for slippage and the customer can be just as guilty of causing it as the contractor. The application of strict price provisions and rigid formulae implies a tightly structured relationship between the contracting parties and it should be reflected in a formalized approach to the control of the project plan; where slippage has occurred and it is recognized as a reality by both parties, the plan should be formally updated to reflect that fact.

Index numbers are usually published one month in arrears but it is often desirable to invoice the customer as soon as possible after completion of the work. To speed up the process of generating the price revisions and issuing invoices it is sometimes agreed that where the work packages are small (typically one month's work) and a single index number is used for calculation, it will be the one for the month prior to the date of the claim. Alternatively, initial invoicing may be allowed on the basis of the original sum to be followed by a supplementary invoice for the additional adjustment calculated from the applicable index published sometime later.

In some cases, a series of formulae may be derived, each relating to a particular aspect of the project work by using different factors and indices for the specific types of work or trades in use. Whatever formulae are devised and agreed between the parties, it is strongly recommended that the behaviour of the formulae and their associated wording is tested against an assumed set of future index numbers and schedule variations. This should ensure that the resulting price adjustments are as expected and that there are no arithmetic anomalies; these can sometimes occur if there is any ambiguity in the wording or the formulae and it can lead to protracted disputes over interpretation regarding what each party believed was intended.

(c) Fixed price, incentive

Occasionally situations arise where there is a possibility that cost savings can be made during the course of the project. This can happen where such uncertainties exist that it is impossible to agree a fixed price without including excessive contingencies. Customers will naturally want to avoid this and may therefore propose a contract that includes an inducement for the contractor to finish the project at a price lower than the fixed, maximum amount. The inducement is in the form of increased profit, even though the total contract value may be less. It means that the customer is sharing a proportion of the cost saving with the contractor. Inducements can be in the form of a price adjustment formula that relates to the final profit or a bonus payable if agreed cost thresholds are met.

It is normal to fix at the start both the maximum price (the 'ceiling price') and the assumed minimum level of profit. Below the ceiling price, a lower figure is agreed as the 'target price' which contains a higher level of profit and which the contractor feels he should be able to achieve. As the contract proceeds, claims are made in stages according to a payment plan and the observed progress. Profit at the low level can be included in the claims. At the end of the contract, a formula is applied to the value of the claims and if the total value is below the ceiling price an additional payment is made. Profits under the formula can exceed the target figure but it is usual to limit this by fixing the maximum profit whatever the final cost.

A simple price adjustment formula might be:

$$P_f = Pc + \frac{C - Pc}{K} \quad \text{for} \quad \frac{C - Pc}{K} < M \tag{12.3}$$

where: P_f = the final price payable;
Pc = the total value of submitted claims, including a minimum profit percentage;
C = the ceiling price;
K = a constant that determines the rate at which the incentive changes;
M = the maximum allowable price adjustment.

Example 12.1: Contract price adjustment using the above formula

A contract has a ceiling price of £1 million and contains a minimum profit of 5% (£0.05m.) on all claims below that. The profit may be allowed to rise to 10% if the final price payable is £0.8m. (profit £0.08m.) and a limit on the incentive adjustment is set at £0.06m. What is the maximum profit figure and at what total cost?

First, it will be necessary to evaluate the constant K:

At a final price of £0.8m. there is a profit of 10%, therefore the cost to the contractor must be: £0.8/1.1 = £0.727m.

On top of this a 5% profit can be added to give the submitted claim P_f of £0.727 × 1.05 = £0.7634m.

Substitution in the adjustment formula gives:

$$0.7634 + \frac{1.00 - 0.7634}{K} = 0.8$$

Evaluation yields: $K = \dfrac{0.2366}{0.0366} = 6.46$

The formula now becomes:

$$P_f = Pc + \frac{£1.0m. - Pc}{6.46} \quad \text{for} \quad \frac{£1.0m. - Pc}{6.46} < £0.06m.$$

The maximum profit is payable when $\dfrac{£1.0m. - Pc}{6.46} = £0.06m.$

This yields the maximum profit on a submitted claim of £0.612m. To this can be added a profit adjustment of £0.06m. giving a final price of £0.672m.; this contains a profit of £0.0891m. which is 13.2% of the final price. Below a claim of £0.612m., the total profit, in real terms, will begin to drop, although it will continue to rise as a percentage of the total cost.

Incentive contracts may be devised which also allow for price adjustments due to inflation. If a development programme were to last five years and it is wished to introduce an incentive element, putting in an escalation clause may be the only way it can be done. However, the situation can become complex and careful examination of the formulae, their method of application and the situations that may arise is essential.

Liquidated damages

Clauses are sometimes inserted into contracts that provide a financial remedy to the customer for a failure by the contractor regarding some aspect of the work, they are usually referred to as **liquidated damages**. These are often applied to situations where delivery of hardware, either prototype or production, is vital to the customer's ability to continue the project. It can also be applied to aspects of the specification where, if the product exhibits a performance shortfall, it has financial implications for the customer – e.g. excessive fuel consumption. In situations where delivery is concerned, the contractor may be required to pay a sum of money to the customer on a regular basis until the delivery situation is restored to that required. Liquidated damages clauses vary greatly according to the circumstances of the project and can range from the simple form where a set amount is paid for every day or week late to complex formulae based on total numbers delivered at any time and which also allow for recovery in deliveries after initial lateness. With performance shortfalls, the contractor may be required to make up the difference in operating cost above that guaranteed for a set period.

Because of the vast differences in the types of project to which liquidated damages can apply, these clauses are usually open to discussion; customer organizations may try to impose severe conditions but with good presentation of the risks involved and negotiating skill, mutually acceptable arrangements can be worked out that reflect the potential loss to the customer while not being unduly penal to the contractor. In general, the simpler the payment scheme the better – the more complex forms should be avoided unless no other agreement can be reached. As with the incentive contracts, the clauses should be carefully worked out and worded and it cannot be stated too strongly that an assessment of their behaviour under various circumstances is made; the greater the complexity, the more they run the risk of generating anomalous or apparently unfair results in some situations.

Intellectual property rights

Innovative projects by their nature lead to the generation of new products, designs and inventions. Ownership of novel creations and the rights to exploit them for commercial gain is a subject that may not be foremost in the Project Manager's mind, but it would certainly be remiss to fail to protect such intellectual assets from copying by competitors.

In the UK protection can exist in four forms:

1. Copyright
2. Design right
3. Design registration
4. Patents.

In addition to the protection given by the above, brand and company images can be protected by the registration of trade and service marks.

Copyright

Prior to 1988, both artistic works and industrial designs were protected by **copyright**, although the treatment was different. This changed with the Copyright, Designs and Patents Act 1988 which introduced a new scheme of design protection. Copyright now provides protection for designs that are essentially artistic, although capable of industrial exploitation. Copyright for artistic works not capable of industrial exploitation remains at 50 years plus life, but for designs that can be used industrially protection is limited to 25 years from first marketing. Copyright does not require registration and provides very limited protection against competitors exploiting a design as it covers only exact reproductions of the drawings; copyright cannot prevent a competitor making and selling articles that function according to the drawings. Copyright has its greatest use in publications and the media generally as reproduction, distribution and broadcasting are features of those industries. Where copyright can be useful in industrial designs is in the protection of distinctive features that mark out one product as being different to its rivals or associated with a particular maker. Direct copying of such features would be deemed an infringement of copyright.

Design right

The 1988 Act in the UK abolished copyright protection for design documents and models, although not for surface decoration incorporated in the design. The new Act, however, replaced the old protection by creating the new property called **design right**. This new right does not require registration and is similar to copyright, although it is a statutory right that is quite separate from artistic copyright. Design right subsists in a design that is original and non-commonplace where 'design' is defined as 'any aspect of the shape or configuration (whether internal or external) of the whole or part of the article'. There is no requirement for the design to have 'eye appeal' and protection is not given to features that are ornamentation. Also excluded are methods and principles of construction, interconnecting components or parts whose appearance is dictated by a larger item of which they are a part. Ownership of design right, in the first instance, resides with the designer unless it is: (a) a commissioned work, in which case it rests with the commissioner, or (b) the designer is an employee engaged for design work, in which case it rests with the employer.

Design right protection lasts for the shorter period of either:

(a) 15 years from the year in which the design was first recorded in a design document or model.
(b) 10 years from the year in which the item was first put on sale.

Design right gives the owner the exclusive right to reproduce the design commercially either in: (a) the form of the articles that can be made from it, or (b) the design drawings that allow another to reproduce it. Design rights may be assigned by the owner to another party, provided that it is recorded in writing. Reproduction of articles that are exact copies or substantially follow the design will be an infringement of design right and the owner has the right to sue to stop further reproduction. There is an exception, however, in that the Crown has immunity from action through infringement of design right if it copies the design for national defence, foreign defence or health services purposes. In the event that the Crown makes use of a protected design, the owner is entitled to receive compensation for loss of profit.

Registration of designs

In some cases, a design may evolve where it is felt that copyright or design right protection will be insufficient, particularly if other designers could generate the same ideas independently. In this case, protection from competition can be obtained through registration of the design. In the UK, the 1988 Act defines 'design' as referring to the appearance or features of a finished article. It gives particular emphasis to the visual aspect of a design as it excludes from registration methods or principles of construction or 'features dictated solely by the function which the article has to perform'. It forbids from registration both designs whose appearance is immaterial to persons that acquire or use them and designs whose features are dictated by the appearance of another article of which it is intended to form an integral part. It thus tends to restrict protection to items of a more artistic nature, purely functional items being covered by the protection of design right and patents. For a design to be capable of registration, it must show, in a visual sense, a degree of novelty that makes it substantially different from existing designs.

Registration must be obtained before the product is put on the market and the design must not be revealed to outside sources, it thus prevents any pre-sales marketing. If the design was generated in conjunction with other parties, then a confidentiality agreement should exist between them in respect of the design. Ownership of the registered design rests, in the first instance, with its creator but with similar exceptions to that for design right. Registration is made through application to the Designs Registry (part of the Patents Office) and takes about six months; fees are payable.

Protection is given for an initial period of five years but it can be extended by applying to the Registrar for further coverage in periods of five years up to a maximum period of 25 years. It gives protection against competition from designs that are essentially the same but which have been developed independently. However, where the public interest is concerned, through the evidence of the Monopolies and Mergers Commission, the Registrar can insist that licences are available for the design as of right. Crown immunity exists in the event of Crown use but with a provision for compensation for loss of profit. Compared to the use of patents, registration is a much less favoured process due to the drawbacks of the cost, timescale and the secrecy involved; court actions over design registration are comparatively rare.

Patents

If it is wished to exploit new inventions commercially without competition, then patent protection may be applied for. Unlike design right or registration, which refer to a specific and reproducible design, patents can be applied to an idea, provided that the idea meets four criteria; it must:

1. exhibit novelty;
2. not be obvious;
3. be capable of being defined in such detail that a skilled person could put the invention into effect;
4. be capable of industrial exploitation.

There are certain exceptions as some inventions cannot be patented, they include:

- Plant and animal varieties and 'biological processes for the production of animals and plants'.
- Intellectual creations such as mathematical models, computer programs and works of art.
- Medical treatments but excluding specific drugs.

Despite the exclusion of biological processes, microbiological processes are patentable and they are used in the production of drugs. It is also possible to patent an industrial process that makes use of one of the excluded areas, even if it is the only novelty. Thus a computer program may not in itself be patentable but a device or process that performs some novel function by way of that program could be patentable.

Applications for patents and the granting of patents

In the UK, patents are granted by the Patent Office after a two-stage examination process. Applications for patents can be made directly to the Patent Office by the inventor but most companies make use of patent agents to make the application for them. The patent agent will draw up the 'specification' for the invention, present it to the Patent Office and, if need be, negotiate its passage. Although not essential, using patent agents, with their knowledge of the relevant Acts, makes the whole process much simpler. Provided that the fees are acceptable, it is the preferred approach.

Application, individually or through an agent, is normally made by the inventor or the owner of the invention if the inventor is an employee; alternatively, it may be made jointly by both the inventor and his employer. The basis of the application is a specification that sets out a complete description of the invention. This must describe the new article or process in sufficient detail that a person skilled in the trade could put the invention into practice. An idea that can only be described in general terms without the detail to put it into effect is not patentable. The application must also contain a section that sets out the 'claims' for the invention, these define the novel features and describe them in precise terms that, in turn, define the scope of protection that the patent is intended to give. Wording of the claims is vital to both the success of the application and the eventual protection that is obtained, hence the need for the specialist help of the patent agent. Over the years, patent agents have developed a wording and terminology of their own which makes understanding patents difficult for the layman. In general, the less definitive the wording of the specification, the greater the scope of protection. This is because the more closely defined an invention is, the easier it is to circumvent the patent by making a basically similar item with only detail changes. If a challenge is made, it will be the wording in the claims that determines if the challenge is successful.

In a world where others may be working along similar lines, it is worthwhile submitting a patent application as soon as possible. This can be done by making an 'informal application'. A period of one year is allowed between an informal application and the final one. Sufficient detail of the invention must be shown in the informal application that the final application will support and amplify it. Providing this is so, the date of application will be taken as the date of the informal one.

The agent will submit the application for a preliminary examination, a search of earlier patents in the same field and publication of the application. The preliminary examination will also assess the correctness of the application. The question of patentability will not arise until the full examination is requested. When this occurs, the specification and its claims will be assessed for completeness, sufficient detail and comparison with the claims of earlier patents to establish the novelty of the application. The examiner must also consider obviousness, a somewhat arbitrary concept that must be looked at in the light of already published specifications. When considering novelty, the examiner must assess the specification in the light of applications filed but not yet published, hence the advantage of early application through the informal process.

The examiner may raise objections to the specification or its claims and it may come down to agreement on specific wording between the examiner and the agent before patents are granted. In the event that agreement cannot be reached, there is a further procedure that can go as far as the Patents Court.

Once granted, patents allow the owner to proceed through the High Court against parties that have infringed it since the date of publication. However, patents can be revoked if anyone can show that they ought not to have been granted in the first place. Provided renewal fees are paid, annually after the first four years, the period of protection lasts for 20 years from the date of filing. Patent rights have a commercial value, they can be sold by the registered owners and ownership transfers upon the transaction being registered by the Patent Office.

The discussion has so far dealt with patents in respect of UK law but there are more opportunities, as scope exists for the granting of European Patents through the European Patents Convention which brought into existence the European Patents Office (EPO) in Munich. Granting of patents by the EPO will allow identical patents to be enforced in all designated European countries. A further change will come about with the creation of the Community Patents Convention, which will mean that a single patent will be effective throughout the European Community.

There is a thus a choice depending on whether or not protection is required outside the UK; if it is only in the UK, then UK patents will suffice, but if protection is sought in several European countries, either European patents can be taken out or individual applications can be made to each country. Unlike a UK patent which conforms only to national requirements, a European patent can be applied in identical form in the member countries, provided a separate fee is paid to each country concerned. Initially, European patents are more expensive to obtain, but if protection is needed in more than three or four countries, it is probably cheaper than making individual applications. Outside Europe, individual applications have to be made in each country where protection is sought.

Other countries have patent systems similar to the UK, although the UK itself and some Commonwealth states are the only ones to allow the preliminary specification stage. Operation of patent protection in foreign countries is governed by an International Convention for the Protection of Industrial Property which dates from 1883. It states that the laws of a country that is a signatory to the convention will apply equally to citizens of all the convention countries; in this respect, the EPC is considered to be a convention country.

The benefit of a patent to the owner can be somewhat arbitrary, it can depend both on circumstances and the way in which the specification and claims were drawn up. Challenges can come many years after the patent was published when both technology and the market-place may have altered from that originally envisaged. No patent holder can stop a determined attack on his patent by a competitor and there are a number of ways of doing it. One way is to challenge its validity, but the most obvious way is to design something close to the invention but sufficiently different that it appears not to infringe the claims; the differences can be trivial. It is then for the patent holder to decide on whether or not he wishes to bear the costs of the uncertain outcome of a court action. Another method of creating a rival to a patented product is by making use of earlier expired patents. This arises from the fact that many patents are improvements to earlier ideas; where a product gets a foothold in a new market, competitors may enter the market by designing rival products based on old patents but making their own distinctive changes. Patents may thus be most successful in protecting a monopoly when the invention is not too important as the existence of a patent is sufficient deterrent. Competitors may simply not find it worthwhile putting in a lot of design effort to evade it or risking an unfavourable decision in the court if challenged. Some organizations have found a way of protecting their inventions, to the extent that they do not wish to become the object of an action for infringement from a competitor, but without obtaining patents. This is done by publishing articles that describe the invention without revealing the more relevant secrets; it prevents rival companies that may be developing a similar technique from patenting it as a patent will be held invalid if it can be shown that 'prior publication' of the idea exists.

Summary

The Project Manager engaged in work with an external customer will inevitably become involved in the commercial and contractual aspects of the task. This aspect is a growing feature of project management work as there is a trend towards more definitive and demanding product specifications and more stringent forms of contract. This is a response on the part of customer organizations to the growing risks associated with innovative projects. It has led to an increased use of fixed-price contracts but in the future this may come to be seen as inappropriate where high levels of development risk are involved.

Various forms of contract have been devised and each has its place; it is for the Project Manager to ensure, as far as he is able, that the type of contract reflects the nature of the work. Where payment arrangements are designed to provide some form of incentive, the formulae used should be kept as simple and unambiguous as possible and should always be tested against an assumed set of future circumstances.

Protection of the intellectual assets that derive from the project is an important issue. Protection exists in four forms, each giving a different level of protection: Copyright and Design Right exist as of right, but Design Registration and Patents have to be purchased. Patents give the most comprehensive cover but they are not a complete remedy against attack by a determined competitor. It is for the inventor or the company that made the invention to decide on what degree of protection it requires.

13

Software for the Project Manager

- Features of project management software
- Developments in computing technology
- Software products to suit different needs
- Choosing suitable software
- Listing of contemporary software products

Today's Project Manager has never been so well served for computer systems to suit his needs. New packages or improved versions of established software are coming onto the market each month. System configurations are as various as the companies that use them, ranging from large-scale, company-wide, integrated systems operating through local area networks to small personal computer (PC) based systems.

Computers made their way into business life in the mid-1950s, and by the early 1960s the majority of large companies had introduced computerized techniques in the accounting and record-keeping fields and for some specialist engineering calculations. Network analysis methods were the first systems that could be recognized as specific to project management; the computer was essential to their operation and they were well established as a management tool by the late 1960s. Large, centrally located mainframe computers were needed; processing was normally done in a batch mode with output in tabular form. Throughout the 1970s and 1980s the most striking feature of computing was the huge reduction in the size and cost of computers and the increases in processing speed. First, minicomputers were introduced, then in the 1980s the PC made its début and it has revolutionized the workplace. The old central mainframe systems are being replaced with distributed arrangements that allow computing to be more personalized, faster and with better communications and transmission of data. Cheap and available computing has generated an industry based on the creation of software products and project management is a field that it has not been slow to exploit. Although much of the project management

355

software is still based on the critical path methodology, contemporary systems offer more than just time analysis: project costing, performance measurement, risk analysis and graphics are some of the features that now come built-in or are available as add-ons to current packages.

Contemporary software

It will be realized from the previous chapters that project management is an amalgam of many disciplines, each of which has its own techniques. However, the systems that have become specifically known as 'project management software' have centred on the management of tasks; that is, they are designed for the purpose of planning, scheduling and monitoring the progress of tasks or activities. Other functions, such as risk assessment, configuration management, estimating, etc., which also form part of the work of the Project Manager may need software which is quite separate from that contained in the normal context of project management software.

'Project management software'

It is beyond the scope of this text to look deeply into the wide range of software that is available, and many readers will already be familiar with the systems in use in their own firms. However, in surveying what is currently marketed it is clear that all the leading systems bear a certain similarity and this is not surprising as they all set out to solve the same problem. Currently, the core of all software packages is a network analysis routine, and this is the vehicle for holding the time and event relationship. Additionally, they all have the ability to carry extra information about each activity, in particular, the resources employed, the hours required and the charge rates.

The basic facilities that the better-quality systems offer are:

1. Network analysis: the ability to store a project plan defined in the form of a set of activities with known durations and fixed logical relationships, together with the ability to analyse the plan to determine critical activities, start and finish dates and floats.
2. Resource scheduling: the ability to allocate resources to activities with or without reference to the available resource levels. Where resource levels are specified, the activities can be scheduled in such a way that the levels are not exceeded and the effect on the project plan can be calculated.
3. Project costing: the ability to calculate project costs where resources and charge rates are defined.
4. Project monitoring: the ability to carry information on actual progress and costs and use this in calculating new criticalities, costs, etc.
5. Report production: the ability to generate reports in a predetermined format, both tabular and graphical, of the principal data of interest to the Project Manager.

Although the basic features are similar throughout the range of software, the input screens and the report formats can vary between systems. With most current systems data is input in an interactive way with the planner working at the computer which displays the input demand in a pre-determined screen layout. Plans may be drawn directly on the screen using 'mouse' with a series of 'point', 'drag' and 'click' operations; criticalities may be displayed through the use of colour as the plan is being created. Prompts and pull-down menus help the planner to find his way around the system. Context-sensitive help screens are usually provided; these are accessed through one of the function keys or the mouse and give a certain amount of information to aid the planner in using the program. Data displays in the form of tabulations and charts are available on the screen and greatly help the user to visualize the programme.

A comprehensive set of ready formated reports is available which covers the main requirements that most projects are likely to need. Reports can be in tabular or chart form and generally mirror the reports seen on the screen. The more advanced systems contain a database, this is extremely useful as it allows the compilation of reports which are specifically tailored to the user's requirements. Those reports which are primarily graphical; Gantt charts, networks, resource histograms, etc., are usually more restricted in terms of the variation that can be applied. However, the more refined packages do allow some measure of report design in choosing symbology, scale factors, insertion of markers, etc., while the most advanced systems have sophisticated graphics packages allied to them that allow almost unlimited report and chart creation involving shading, inserts, annotation and superimposition on the screen.

While all the packages contain network analysis features, the way that they handle the logic differs. Some systems are more restricted than others in terms of the logic that can be defined; in particular, some do not allow a start-to-finish relationship between activities. Hammock activities are another difficult area, the software may define them as summary activities rather than adhere to the original definition which is an activity of indeterminate duration but controlled by the start and end of other activities. The task of managing the project is a good example of a hammock activity in the original sense; where such activities exist, the logic can only be maintained by manual intervention – i.e. these activities have to be treated as fixed-duration activities but their duration has to be determined after the initial scheduling has been done and further revised after each subsequent change.

Resource scheduling is a feature that is particularly useful to the Project Manager; the generation of labour demand curves is one of the principal uses of project management software as labour is normally finite and in demand by several areas at once. The systems offer the option of generating a schedule assuming either infinite resources or finite resources if the capacity is specified. Where finite resources are specified, the activities are allowed to move in such a way that the logic is not violated and the resource levels are not exceeded. Although networks can be time-analysed to generate a unique solution (all the software packages will give the same answers regarding critical activities, durations, etc.), the same is not true if resource scheduling is applied. In practice, there may be many feasible schedules for any set of circumstances. Each system has its own scheduling algorithm and there is no guarantee that any two systems will produce the same schedule for the same conditions. It follows that there can be no guarantee that the schedule generated will be an optimum one in any sense; in fact the schedule may be far from optimum. It is also worth noting that there is a considerable variation between systems in respect of the degree of sophistication with which (a) resources can be defined and (b) the scheduling rules can be specified; inevitably, this affects the schedule that results.

The scheduling difficulty stems from the fact that many systems make use of a serial approach to fitting demands into available resource levels – i.e. activities are taken in the order in which they start, and once an activity is scheduled against a resource, it cannot be moved when later activities are scheduled, even though that may be highly desirable. This method does not reflect real life as activities actually take place in parallel and in an interactive way; it is also the reason for the difficulty with the hammock activity. When pure network analysis is done, there is no problem in coping with activities of unknown duration as they are not a constraint on the logic because they take on the duration determined by their end-activities. When it comes to scheduling, things are different as both durations and dates will alter as the demands are fitted into the available resources. The 'once and for all' serial approach cannot deal with activities whose duration is not known at the time they start as it has no way of making a change to the duration of an activity that has been scheduled before the scheduling of a subsequent activity that indicates a new end-date. This will remain a problem unless a satisfactory parallel scheduling algorithm is used that simulates the project in a way that reflects how things actually happen. Nevertheless, all the systems allow manual intervention in the logic by imposing start and finish dates on activities, so it is usually possible to generate a better or more practical schedule after the initial work has been done by the software.

Besides the basic logic and duration data for analysis and scheduling, general information about the company, such as the working day calendar, hours in a day, holiday periods, overtime, charge rates for labour grades, departmental numbers, etc., can be specified. When the charge rates are used, a cost can be produced for each activity or the project as a whole.

Developments in technology

The technology of computing is changing as rapidly as the advances being made in software. Gone are the days when piles of input forms had to be taken to the central computer office to be punched and run overnight. With the PC, everybody has instant access to a computer. Although the advantages of affordable and personalized computing have made the PC popular, it has created new problems, in particular, how to get all the PCs to communicate. Problems of this type have far-reaching consequences as they imply standardization at every level in terms of the hardware and software interfaces and the data structures that are used. **Local area networks** (LANs) provide a way in which PCs can communicate with each other and with a central computer. They can be considered to be a data transmission system that can link a variety of computing devices together within a restricted geographical area. Large organizations may not wish to be restricted to relatively small geographical areas and **wider area networks** (WANs) can be constructed to allow LANs to communicate, these normally require data to be transmitted via a public telecommunications company. Despite the distributed way in which data is generated and used, many organizations have found that the most efficient way of working is one in which information is held in large central databases and shared with many different users in various parts of the company. File/server and client/server systems have been devised for this purpose. They allow the PCs that form the user interfaces to talk to the host machine on which the data is held, and connection is established between user and host via a LAN.

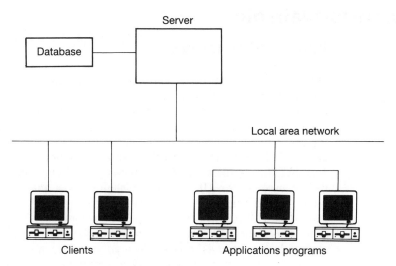

Figure 13.1   Schematic client/server architecture.

With the older file/server environment, when the database is queried the entire dataset has to be down-loaded and sent via the LAN to the PC. As the number of users increases the danger of overloads and bottlenecks also rises. To overcome this the latest development is the **client/server arrangement**; it is a major improvement, in that when requests are made, only the data that is needed is accessed, transmitted or updated rather than the whole dataset. This processing is done at the server end, allowing the client to get on with something more useful while the server does its job. Application programmes that are specific to client needs can be run on their own PCs or exported to the server for processing, depending on whichever is seen as the more efficient at the time. The net result is in a much faster, flexible and more reliable set-up. Figure 13.1 shows a schematic view of one possible configuration for a client/server system.

Central to the client/server concept is the language by which instructions between client and server are sent and interpreted; **structured query language** (SQL, pronounced 'Sequel') has evolved for this function and is now embodied in ANSI and ISO standards. However, it is more than just a query language, in that it allows updating, data definition, control, consistency and dictionary functions.

Two important advantages are seen from the client/server approach:

1. Better control, updating and access to corporate data is obtained as multiple sources of data are no longer needed and both human and computer effort is reduced.
2. Traditional mini- and mainframe computer architectures can be replaced with lower cost but equally powerful PC–LAN hardware, this process is currently referred to as 'downsizing'.

At the time of writing (1992), the first project management systems specifically aimed at the client/server environment are coming onto the market.

Products available

Principal features

PERT or CPM systems have been available as computer packages since the 1960s and they were the first 'project management systems'. They were, however, limited to the network analysis function and produced little else besides. In the late 1970s Metier Management Systems introduced into the UK a database system that allowed the user to generate his own management reports, the system was called 'Artemis' and could be used in conjunction with a network analysis system called 'Apollo'. Together they formed the first integrated project management system to become widely used in the UK and the system is now marketed in a variety of forms under such names as 'Artemis Team', 'Artemis 7000', 'Artemis 9000', etc. Since it started with Metier, its parent company has changed hands several times and now has other project management products, unconnected with the original Artemis, but now sold with the 'Artemis' prefix. Throughout the 1980s many other software houses brought out project management packages; popular ones are sold under such names as 'Artemis ProjectView', 'Plantrac', 'Micro Planner', 'CA-SuperProject V2', 'Open Plan', 'Project Manager Workbench', 'Primavera Project Planner', etc., and the range is continuing to grow. The majority of these packages originated in the USA and are still supported from there but are sold through outlets in the UK; there are about 50 packages to choose from, not all offer the full range of features. At the time of writing, prices for the PC versions can range from a few hundred pounds to £5500+ but mini-, mainframe and LAN versions can be significantly more expensive; prices could reach £50 000 or more depending upon the configuration, number of remote terminals, etc.

A point to note is that some systems come with a database built in, while others need a proprietary database to be bought in order to run; one such example is 'Open Plan' which requires dBASE IV. Many of the systems are available in versions that suit the range of hardware and operating systems from the smallest to the largest; typically, PC systems will use PCDOS or MSDOS, minicomputers will need DEC VAX or UNIX compatible versions and LAN capability is needed where multiple work-stations and data sharing is required. Although the software vendors do provide their products in versions to suit the more common environments, some systems are restricted in terms of their application environment and this is an important consideration when it comes to choosing software.

Additional features

The features described earlier form the core of a typical project management software package but they do not constitute all the facilities that the Project Manager requires; some systems are now marketed with additional packages that will integrate with them to enhance their usefulness.

Reports and graphics

Graphics and report-writing is an area where improved capability is beneficial, Primavera Systems provide 'Executive Summary Presentation' (ESP) as an additional system to 'Primavera Project Planner'. 'Artemis Presents!' is a very sophisticated report and graphics system available in its own right or in conjunction with 'Artemis ProjectView'.

Cost/schedule performance measurement

In the past few years most of the major systems have undergone considerable upgrading due to the growing adoption of cost/schedule performance measurement (earned value) techniques. Some systems have performance measurement features built in, while in others a separate module needs to be acquired. 'CORoNET', from Computerline, accompanies 'PLANTRAC'; 'Cobra', from Welcom Software Technology, can be used with their 'Open Plan' system; and 'Parade' accompanies 'Primavera Project Planner'. They can also be used as stand-alone systems. The principal users of cost–performance measurement have been contractors to the US Energy and Defense departments, and these systems have been configured to meet the very precise reporting formats that these organizations lay down. They may not suit exactly the requirements of UK companies, but 'Cobra' comes with its own facility for generating customized reports. 'Parade' conforms precisely to the requirements of US DoD 7000.2 and DoD 7000.10 but also has additional features which make it even more useful.

A comprehensive system designed specifically for the cost management problem using performance measurement techniques is 'Artemis CostView'. It contains on-screen Work Breakdown Structure creation, pricing and costing features and an estimating facility that includes both the use of learning curves and the ability to import cost histories from previous projects. All the performance measurement features are covered including the recording of all changes to estimates from the baseline position and the generation of best, worst and most likely Estimates at Completion based on actual performance.

'Cascade', from Mantix Systems, is a large-scale, fully integrated system that uses cost–performance measurement as the central concept. Unlike the others, it is not an add-on package but a complete project management system with all the expected features. However, its emphasis on cost management as the principal aspect of project control is a break with tradition; it is the first system of its type and it can be expected that more will follow. It is designed for the larger corporate user and follows the principles laid down in the US DoD specifications; however, application is not confined to projects in the aerospace and defence sectors as the merits in its concept are being recognized by civil and commercial organizations. Examples of the output reports from some of these systems are given in Chapter 8.

Risk analysis

The ability to assess both the probabilities of project completion within a given time-frame and the expectation of completion within a set budget is something that many

Project Managers will find useful. Examples of add-on systems that integrate with a standard project management system include 'Opera' which accompanies 'Open Plan'; 'Plantrac-Marshall' which goes with 'Plantrac'; and 'Monte Carlo™' which goes with 'Primavera Project Planner' and other project management packages. All make use of the random number simulation method for assessing the distribution of possible outcomes. 'Monte Carlo™' is particularly sophisticated, in that it allows probabalistic branching (i.e. alternative paths can be followed according to fixed probability rules) and branching when specific conditions arise. There is an extensive range of probability distribution types that can be applied to durations, costs, escalation rates, resources, etc. Factors such as the influence of weather, procurement, delivery and the effects of availability, reliability and maintainability can also be modelled.

Systems not specifically 'project management software'

Besides the systems mentioned above, there are a range of software packages that do not contain the features that apply to 'project management systems' in the sense that it has come to be known, but are of use to the Project Manager for specific aspects of his work. The range is very broad and it would be impossible to mention anything but a few of the products on offer.

Estimate generation systems

All the project management systems that contain a costing facility can be used to generate an estimate of the project cost but this has to be built up from a detailed assessment of all the tasks in the project. Sometimes this is not known at the time the estimate is required and other methods are necessary. The principal method is parametric estimating and is described in Chapter 10. The most well-known package for parametric methods is 'PRICE' which originated with the RCA Corporation. 'PRICE' is a generic name for a variety of sophisticated systems, each designed to model various aspects of cost relating to different types of project. Particular models deal with electrical/mechanical hardware development and production, microcircuit development and production, software development and the life-cycle costs of owning and operating equipment. In 1992, PC-based versions of 'PRICE' models were launched. Also available as a PC-based product is 'Match' from Highbrook Services Ltd; this is specifically tailored to hardware cost estimating. Examples of 'Match' outputs are shown in Chapter 10.

Highbrook Services also supply 'Marshall' which allows the compilation of bids and estimates in the more traditional manner. It features database of cost, price, escalation, scope of work, schedule factors, etc. which allows the easy manipulation of data to build up cost estimates and record changes. Software projects have special requirements, one estimating package that has been developed specifically for software development is 'GECOMO Plus', from GEC-Marconi. It employs a complex modelling system that allows the project to be described in some detail, together with its cost drivers; it generates estimates of cost and timescale that take into account the practical constraints of staff availability and skill levels. Input is via pull-down menu screens and output is in both report and graphical form. Parametric estimation techniques are used in 'Estimacs', a software estimating package from Computer Associates. Data on 13 000 projects gathered over a 10-year period is supplied with the product; 25 key predictors must be defined by the user and a series of equations is used to derive the output.

Resource management

Utilizing resources to the best effect is an issue that will concern many Project Managers; for the most part, resources are either in short supply or expensive. Resource-levelled plans and histograms of staff requirements can be produced by the better-quality project management packages but it is sometimes necessary to implement a system specifically to deal with staff management in cases where a range of projects is involved. A suitable system is 'Planview': a Windows based planning system that runs in a Client/server mode, importing task information from standard project planning systems while scheduling resources on the basis of such factors as skill, location, grade etc. Resource utilization can be optimised across multiple projects and time reporting and progress information can be entered to give an instant picture of current staff deployment. In addition, with labour rates added, manpower cost schedules can be generated.

Risk analysis

Mention has already been made of risk analysis packages that can be run as an addition to a project management system but there are also systems that are designed to be used as stand-alone modules. A relatively inexpensive PC-based system is '@RISK' (pronounced, 'at risk'); it makes use of a Lotus 1–2–3 or Microsoft Exel spreadsheet format and must be used in conjunction with that software. The logic of the project (i.e. the interaction between one activity and another) is defined by the relationship of one cell in the spreadsheet to another. Each cell contains a risk variable and there is a choice of distributions to define its characteristics. Risk analysis is done by simulation using Monte Carlo and Latin Hypercube techniques, and output is in the form of S-curves, histograms and summary graphs. Another spreadsheet-based product that uses the Monte Carlo approach is 'PREDICT!'.

The Controlled Interval Method of calculation was used in Example 2 in Chapter 11; this method is less popular than the Monte Carlo simulation technique, but one system that does use it is 'PERK'. It is a file-based spreadsheet program that performs the analysis using the standard probability theory calculus. A variety of input distributions including user defined ones are available.

Possibly the most advanced system is 'DynRisk' from TerraMar; currently it is unique as a commercially available package as it makes use of the influence diagram for problem formulation and is described in Chapter 11. In terms of its problem formulation capability, it is potentially more adaptable than any other system on the market at present.

Configuration management

Despite the importance of this subject, there is little package software that is commercially available. Where companies do use computerized systems, they tend to be ones that they have specifically developed to their own requirements. One of the undoubted problems of configuration management is that it a subject that spans the design, quality control and manufacturing organizations of a company and traditionally these have used their own systems without necessarily integrating them. Elements of configuration management can thus be found in drawing office graphics systems which include recording drawing issues and updates and in MRP production control systems; it is in these areas that the reader should look for suitable software. 'Configuration Management Facility', from GEC-Marconi, has been created for control of software development. Some of its features could also make it suitable for hardware-based programmes but specific advice from the vendor will be necessary on this point.

Knowledge-based systems

Knowledge-based systems that are applicable to the project management task are a very new subject but one which has potentially great scope for the future. One system that has recently come onto the market is 'ProjectGuide', from Deepak Sareen; this uses a new and interactive planning approach in which the user enters requirements and the system proposes tasks. Projects of similar types have to be defined in advance; this information is called a 'Guide' and is contained in an interactive script which forms the knowledge base. 'ProjectGuide' comes without any knowledge built in, other than that for the demonstration example, hence the user must first construct the knowledge base. This can be done through the Professional Edition of 'ProjectGuide' which includes a Guide Programming Language in which the guide scripts are written. Once compiled, the guide scripts can be used by planners to construct their programmes and for this the simpler Runtime Edition can be used. 'ProjectGuide' is a rule-based system rather than a true artificial intelligence program but, for projects that tend to be variations on a familiar theme, it could prove a speedier and more thorough way of planning than the more conventional approach.

Some factors in choosing project software

Developing and installing software has often proved to be among the most disappointing of all types of project; this has been particularly true of those requiring custom-designed programs as over-runs in both software cost and delivery date, together with less than satisfactory performance of the end-product are common occurrences. Some of the risks associated with software can be removed by using package systems that have been proven in use and here the Project Manager is fortunate as there is a wide range to choose from. With package software, the potential user has the benefit of being able to see it operating before any decision to purchase is made. The question of choice still remains and the array of products can make this seem bewildering. Whereas all the products exhibit a minimum level of functionality in terms of the basic operations of project planning, scheduling and reporting, they can differ widely in their suitability for any particular application.

If it is decided to introduce a computerized project management system or change to a new one, the first questions must be: from whom did the request come;

what did he have in mind and how will a choice be made? Requests for improvement can come from anywhere in a company; for example, it could come from a Project Manager dissatisfied with the systems he has at his disposal, from the Data Processing Head who is looking to rationalize the systems in use across the company or from the Chief Executive who is not satisfied with the performance or the information on the projects undertaken. No matter whence the instigation comes, there will be more parties interested in the choice than the person whose idea it originally was. All three persons mentioned will have an interest: the Project Manager will have to use it, the data processing staff may have to install and maintain it and the Chief Executive, as well as looking at its output, may have to authorize the expenditure. In the case of small, stand-alone projects, the Project Manager may have complete discretion for the software he buys, provided that it stays within a given budget, but where integration with other systems within the company is involved the views of others will have to be taken into account.

Where large-scale systems or company-wide procedures and operations are concerned, it is common practice to form a working group to study the options, recommend a course of action and steer the acquisition and implementation through to a conclusion. There is much to be said for this approach as it does ensure that the views of all interested parties are taken into account; but it also has dangers, and the worst is that the leader of the working party does not really understand the problems of successfully operating a project management system in a project environment. It might seem strange that this can happen, but it can quite easily; for example, as a project management system is primarily software, a data processing person could be appointed to lead the working group – he may know much about computing but mention earned-value performance measurement and he may have no idea what it means or how to implement it. Similarly, if projects are primarily about the development of technology, the Technical Director may be put in charge – he may be good at engineering design but have little real interest in, or understanding of, the project management process and its requirements for data.

Whoever is appointed to lead the working group must have a thorough understanding of all the issues involved; he must be able to draw out the opinions of the group members and organize them into coherent and viable whole that can meet a properly defined set of objectives in a practical way. Clear and logical thinking from the leader is of paramount importance; the more permissive leader who likes to take decisions on the basis of a show of hands is not suitable as there is no guarantee that decisions taken in that way will fit together in a coherent fashion. Computer systems are all about logical procedures and precise data definitions, it is essential that somebody has in his head, at all times, the logic of how all aspects will fit together and that he can convince others of its rightness – it is easier if that person is the leader. Sometimes such a person may not exist within the company; in such a case, some firms find it useful to employ a specialist consultant either to lead the team or to be part of it, so that an experienced outside view can be obtained at each stage.

The first task that a working group should set itself is to define the objectives for the system – i.e. what is it expected to do and how is it proposed to work? These are fundamental questions and they deserve careful thought; there is a very great difference between buying a PC system for a Project Manager to run one or two small projects that are a sideline to the company's mainstream activities and choosing a total project control system that will affect the company at every level.

Some objectives that might be sighted for installing a new project management system are:

1. To install project management procedures where none currently exist.
2. To introduce a common system of management across all projects in a company and establish a common pool of data on all projects.
3. To reduce the amount of data handling and input effort.
4. To provide better and more timely reporting.
5. To provide forecasts of future trends in project progress.
6. To provide better planning and utilization of company-wide resources.
7. To perform 'what if' analyses of future scenarios.
8. To integrate automatically with the accounting and production management systems.

Besides these objectives there may also be some constraints that can be identified; typically, these could be:

(a) The system must be capable of running on existing hardware, or must not involve the purchase of significant new hardware.
(b) The system costs must be less than x thousand pounds.
(c) It must be compatible with the company's LAN system.

The above basic objectives and associated constraints form the overall framework for the system, and it is important that they are established and understood at the start; changing them later on could result in much wasted effort. What they do not state, however, is how anything will actually be done, yet this will be necessary to make a definitive choice. What is needed is a more detailed assessment of how the system is expected to work and the output required. This goes much deeper than the framework of objectives as it details the precise functions that the system will perform. A considerable amount of research and discussion with all parties that interface with the system will be needed before a full description of the necessary functions can be compiled. The proposed functions, together with any constraints, are the basis of a 'requirements specification' against which potentially suitable products can be tested.

Some typical features of a requirements specification might be:

1. Operational environment
   (a) Must be VAX compatible
   (b) The system costs must be less than x thousand pounds.
   (c) Must service up to eight remote terminals at once
   (d) Must have secure but instant access to all live projects
   (e) Etc.
2. System functional features
   (a) Must have full earned-value cost reporting
   (b) Tasks must be able to be related to the work breakdown structure and the organizational breakdown structure simultaneously
   (c) Must be able to handle networks of up to 5000 activities
   (d) Must have multi-project scheduling capability for up to 5 major and 20 minor projects
   (e) Must have customized report facilities
   (f) Etc.
3. Vendor support and services
   (a) On-site training required

    (b) 8 am to 7 pm help-line required

    (c) Vendor to be responsible for on-site installation and testing

    (d) Vendor commitment to continuous product improvement

    (e) Etc.

4. System costs

    (a) Total acquisition costs to be less than £X

    (b) Annual operating costs (support, updates, etc.) to be less than £Y

    (c) Etc.

Once the requirements specification is complete, input and output formats can be defined and together they can be issued to software vendors who are invited to tender proposals. Obviously, the kind of response that one will get is different for a £500 PC product and a £50 000 complete system. In the former case, one can expect a general letter of response plus brochures, a visit from a representative and an invitation to visit the vendor for a system demonstration if the representative is not able to give one on site. With the full-scale system, however, a detailed response answering every point in the requirement specification can be demanded, particularly if the vendor knows that he is in a competition. When the responses have been received, they must be assessed against a set of scoring criteria; these will need to be devised by the working group and should address (a) the required attributes and characteristics, and (b) the relative importance attached to each. Figure 13.2 shows a typical software evaluation sheet.

When the responses have been received from the suppliers, they can be scored and several packages can be selected for detailed assessment. How that assessment is done can vary but the best way is to put the onus on the vendor to prove that his

AW	SOFTWARE EVALUATION SHEET			
Product Title	Vendor:		Ref:	
			Date:	
Attribute	Weighting	Score out of 10	Weighted score	
Overall Functionality	78			
Cost of Acquisition	8			
On-going Costs	10			
Documentation	4			
Methodological Approach	4			
Development Capability	8			
Vendor Credibility	5			
Training Facilities	5			
Other (Specify)				
Other (Specify)				
Overall Score				

Figure 13.2 Project software evaluation sheet.

software is the right one. One should remember that it is a buyer's market, and if suppliers want to sell their software, they will have to demonstrate that it meets all the requirements. The simplest way to do this is to devise a series of tests that replicate the functions that the system will have to perform in service, then demand that the vendor sets up the tests with all the relevant inputs and outputs on his own equipment and demonstrates the system in operation. He should then be required to perform further tests with unfamiliar data and situations contrived to test the limits of its capability; scores should be awarded for each test result. By this process, a selection can be made with reasonable confidence that the chosen software will perform as intended. This process may demand a great deal more work from the suppliers than they may be used to with other customers – but that is a problem for them, what the Project Manager wants is something in which he can be confident from the outset and a practical demonstration is the best way. As a final step, the supplier should be required to 'present' his solution to all interested parties in the company, so that their reaction can be gauged and any suggestions that they may have can also be incorporated in the final specification for the package as it is to be supplied.

The Working Group should not disband once the selection has been made, but continue to work with the vendor to ensure a satisfactory installation and also devise the training programme. Their work will be complete when the system is fully integrated into the company operations.

Summary

No Project Manager should be without some form of computerized aids for his daily work. Versatile and efficient software is available to cover a range of the management techniques and at prices that make them accessible to all. Much of this is due to the advent of the PC and one can expect to see greater and more rapid developments in the future. Most contemporary project management systems use a network as the principal data model and this does not seem likely to be displaced in the near future. However, the development of predictive techniques, such as parametric estimating and knowledge-based systems, may eventually take computerized methods in a new direction.

Appendix:
Products and vendors

All the software mentioned in the text is here listed with the vendor's name and address in the UK; in some cases, US outlets are also quoted.

Product name	Vendor
'Artemis'	Artemis International
'Artemis Presents!'	Artemis House
'Artemis ProjectView'	219 Bath Road
'Artemis CostView'	Slough
	Berkshire
	Tel: 081 848 3400
	Fax: 081 573 3884
'@RISK'	4-5-6 World Ltd
	Wellington House
	Butt Road
	Colchester
	Essex CO3 3DA
	Tel: 0206 44456
	Fax: 0206 763313
	Palisade Corporation
	31 Decker Road
	Newfield
	NY 14867
	USA
	Tel: (607) 277 8000
'CA-SuperProject V2'	C.A. Computer Associates Ltd
'Estimac'	Computer Associates House
	183–7 Bath Road
	Slough
	Berkshire SL1 4AA

Tel: 0753 577733
Fax: 0753 5825464

Computer Associates International Inc.
711 Stewart Avenue
Garden City
NY 11530-4787
USA

'Cascade'   Mantix Systems Ltd
                                    Mantix House
                                    London Road
                                    Bracknell
                                    Berkshire RG12 2XH

                                    Tel: 0344 301515
                                    Fax: 0344 301083

'CMF' ('Configuration   GEC-Marconi Software Systems
   Management Facility')   Elstree Way
'GECOMO Plus'   Borehamwood
                                    Hertfordshire WD6 1RX

                                    Tel: 081 906 6238
                                    Fax: 081 906 6362

                                    Marconi Systems Technology
                                    4115 Pleasant Valley Road
                                    Suite 100
                                    Chantilly VA 22021

                                    Tel: (703) 263 1260
                                    Fax: (703) 263 1533

'DynRisk'   TerraMar
                                    Sandviksveien 26
                                    1322 Hovik
                                    Norway

                                    Tel: (02) 12 54 54
                                    Fax: (02) 12 54 57

'Match   Highbrook Systems Ltd
Marshall'   PO Box 65
                                    Ghyll Road
                                    Crowborough
                                    East Sussex TN6 1YT

                                    Tel: 0892 667880

'Micro Planner'   Micro Planning International
                                    34 High Street
                                    Westbury-on-Trym
                                    Bristol BS9 3DZ

Tel: 0272 509417
Fax: 0272 508377

'Open Plan'   Welcom Software Technology
'Opera'   South Bank Technopark
'Cobra'   90 London Road
                               London SE1 6LN

                               Tel: 071 401 2626
                               Fax: 071 922 8865

                               Welcom Software Technology
                               15995 North Barkers Landing
                               Suite 275
                               Houston TX 77079
                               USA

                               Tel: (713) 558 0514
                               Fax: (713) 584 7828

'PERK'   K&H Project Systems Ltd
                               Felco House
                               72A Richmond Road
                               Kingston-upon-Thames
                               Surrey KT2 5EL

                               Tel: 081 549 0056
                               Fax: 081 546 2465

'Plantrac'   Computerline Ltd
'CORoNET'   Tavistock House
'Plantrac-Marshall'   319 Woodham Lane
                               Woodham
                               Weybridge
                               Surrey KT15 3PB

                               Tel: 09323 51022

                               Computerline Inc.
                               PO Box 308
                               52 School Street
                               Pembroke MA 12359
                               USA

                               Tel: (617) 294 1111

'PREDICT!'   Risk Decisions Ltd
                               27 Park End Street
                               Oxford OX1 1HU

                               Tel: 0865 727025
                               Fax: 0865 725720

'PRICE H'   PRICE Systems
'PRICE HL'   Price House
'PRICE M'   Meridian Office Park
'PRICE S'   Osborn Way
'PRICE SL'   Hook
'PRICE A'   Hampshire RG27 9HX
'PRICE D'
                                   Tel: 0256 760012
                                   Fax: 0256 762122

                                   GE PRICE Systems
                                   General Electric Company
                                   Suite 12, 101 Woodman Drive
                                   Dayton, OH 45431
                                   USA

                                   Tel: (513) 252 4226

'Primavera Project Planner'   Primavera Systems
'Parade'   27 Old Cross
'Monte Carlo™'   Hertford SG14 1RE
'Executive Summary Presentation'
                                   Tel: 0992 587059
                                   Fax: 0992 589495

                                   Primavera Systems Inc.
                                   Two Bala Plaza
                                   Bala Cynwyd
                                   PA 19004
                                   USA

                                   Fax: (215) 667 7894

'ProjectGuide'   Deepak Sareen Associates
                                   Bydell House
                                   Sudbury Hill
                                   Harrow-on-the-Hill
                                   Middlesex HA1 3BR

                                   Tel: 081 423 8855
                                   Fax: 081 423 8992

'Project Manager Workbench'   Hoskyns Group plc
                                   Hoskyns House
                                   130 Shaftsbury Avenue
                                   London W1V 7DN

                                   Tel: 071 434 2171
                                   Fax: 071 437 6223

'PlanView'   PlanView Inc
                                   7320 North Mopac
                                   Suite 312
                                   Austin
                                   Texas, USA

Tel: (512) 346 8600
Fax: (512) 346 9180

PlanView Europe
Molenstraat 60
6721 WP Bennekom
The Netherlands

Tel: 08389 15600
Fax: 08389 13625

Further reading

Battersby, A. (1970) *Network Analysis*, 3rd edn, St Martins Press, USA.

Benkowski, M., Walker, R. and Allen, K. *Government Support for British Business*, EPC/University of Strathclyde.

Berridge, T. (1977) *Product Innovation and Development*, Business Books, London.

Blanco White, T. and Jacob, R. (1986) *Patents, Trade Marks, Copyright and Industrial Designs*, Sweet and Maxwell, London.

CBI and NatWest (1992) *Innovations Trends Survey*, No. 3, CBI, London.

Chapman, C. B., Cooper, D. F. and Page, M. J. (1987) *Management for Engineers*, John Wiley Sans.

Cleland, D. I. and King, W. R. (1968) *Systems Analysis and Project Management*, McGraw-Hill, New York.

Clifton, P., Nguyen, H. and Nutt, S. (1985) *Marketing Analysis and Forecasting*, Chaucer Press.

Dean, E. and Unal, R. (1991) *Designing for Cost* AACE Transactions, Vol. D4, pp. D41–D46.

Department of Trade and Industry (DTI) (1991) *Simultaneous Engineering: An Executive Guide*, DTI, London.

Diekman, J. E. (1992) Risk analysis: lessons from artificial intelligence. *International Journal of Project Management*, **10**(2), May, pp. 75–80.

Dobbins, R. and Witt, S. F. (1988) *Practical Financial Management*, Basil Blackwell, Oxford.

Feller, M. (1969) Configuration management. *IEEE Transactions*, **EM16**(2), pp. 64–6.

Fleming, Q. W. (1988) *Cost/Schedule Control Systems Criteria: The Management Guide*, Probus Publishing, Chicago.

Flint, M., Thorne, C. and Williams, A. (1989) *Intellectual Property – the New Law: A Guide to the Copyright Designs and Patents Act 1988*, Butterworths, London.

Glover, J. H. (1966–7) Manufacturing progress functions: pts 1–3. *International Journal of Product Research*, pp. 15–24, 43–59, 279–300.

Hantz, F. and Lager, A. (1968) Configuration management: its role in the aerospace industry. Conference on Product Assurance. Hempstead, NY, USA, June, pp. 295–302.

Hendrix, C. D. (1991) Signal-to-Noise Ratios: A wasted effort. *Quality Progress* **24**(7) July, 75–6.

Howard, R. A. and Matheson, J. E. (1984) Influence diagrams, in: *The Principles and Applications of Decision Analysis. Vol. 2: Professional Collection*. Strategic Decision Group.

Learning curves – the simpler the better. (1982) *Production Engineer*, March.

Lin, P., Taguchi, G. and Sullivan, L. (1990) Using Taguchi methods in quality engineering. *Quality Progress*, September, pp. 55–9.

Lumby, S. (1991) *Investment Appraisal and Financing Decisions*, Chapman & Hall, London.

McDonough, E. F. and Leifer, R. P. (1986) Effective control of new product projects: the inter-action of organisation culture and project leadership. *Journal of Product Innovation Management*, **3**, pp. 149–57.

McLeod, T. (1988) *The Management of Research, Development and Design in Industry*, Gower, Aldershot.

Mikkelesen, H. (1990) Risk management in product development projects. *International Journal of Project Management*, **8**(4), November, 217–21.

Miles, L. D. (1961) *Techniques of Value Analysis and Engineering*, McGraw-Hill, New York.

Ministry of Technology (1960) *Report of the Steering Group on Development Cost Estimating*, HMSO, London.

National Economic Development Council (NEDC) (1985) *The Role of the Project Manager in a Manufacturing Company*, NEDC, London.

Noori, H. (1989) The Taguchi methods: achieving design and output quality. *Academy of Management Executive*, **3**(4).

Parsons, S. A. J. (1966) *Production Tooling Equipment*, Macmillan, London.

Samaris, T. T. and Czerwinski, F. L. (1971) *Fundamentals of Configuration Management*, Wiley Interscience, New York.

Taguchi, G. (1986) *Introduction to Quality Engineering*, Asian Productivity Organisation, Tokyo.

Taguchi, G. (1987) *System of Experimental Design*, Kraus International, White Plains, New York.

Taguchi, Elsayed and Hsiang (1989) *Quality Engineering in Production Systems*. McGraw-Hill, New York.

Tribus M. and Szonyl G. (1989) An Alternative View of the Taguchi Approach. *Quality Progress* **22**, May, 46–52.

Twiss, B. (1980) *Managing Technological Innovation*, Longman, London.

US Department of Defense (DoD) (1987) *Cost/Schedule Control Systems Criteria. Joint Implementation Guide*, US DoD, 1 October.

US DoD (1975) Directive No. 5000.28, Design to Cost, US DoD, 23 May.

US DoD (1977) Instruction No. 7000.2, Performance Measurement for Selected Applications, US DoD, 10 June.

US DoD (1979) Instruction No. 7000.10, C/SCSC Reports – CPR; CFSR; C/SSR, US DoD, 3 December.

US DoD (1984) Instruction No. 7000.11, Contractor Cost Data Reporting, US DoD, 27 March.

Withers, S. (1982) Value analysis – used and understood by too few engineers. *Production Engineer*, October.

Yeo, K. T. (1990) Risks, classification of estimates and contingency management. *Journal of Management in Engineering*, **6**(4), October, pp. 458–70.

Index